W9-BEO-142

SERGEI WITTE AND THE INDUSTRIALIZATION OF RUSSIA

SERGEI WITTE AND THE INDUSTRIALIZATION OF RUSSIA

by Theodore H. Von Laue

Atheneum 1969 New York

The transliteration used in this volume
is based on the Library of Congress system
with some modifications

Published by Atheneum
Reprinted by arrangement with Columbia University Press

Library of Congress Catalog Card Number 63-10520
Manufactured in the United States of America by
The Murray Printing Company
Forge Village, Massachusetts
Published in Canada by McClelland and Stewart Ltd.
First Atheneum Edition

To my family,
to whom the writing of this book
has brought a few delights
and many hardships

Acknowledgments

I WOULD LIKE to acknowledge at the outset all the good instruction, helpful advice, time-consuming assistance, and financial support which have gone into the preparation of this book. Whatever merit the book may have I want to ascribe to Raymond J. Sontag and Robert R. Palmer, my principal teachers at Princeton, and to Felix Gilbert. I am also deeply indebted to the staff of the Russian Institute of Columbia University for an excellent interdisciplinary introduction to Russian studies. Next I bow to the librarians, to Doctor Maria Widnäs of the Slavic Library of the University of Helsinki and to Maisteri Paul Kopperi of the Central Statistical Bureau in Helsinki, to Dr. Sasse of the German Foreign Office archives in Bonn, to the reference department of the Saltykov-Shchedrin Library in Leningrad, and to the indefatigable providers of interlibrary loans at the University of California at Riverside, Miss Berry and her staff. I also owe thanks to Henry L. Roberts for his generous criticism of the entire manuscript; to Michel de Enden, a fellow student of Witte's life and work, for his numerous suggestions and corrections; and to my colleagues Hugh Aitken, Arthur Mendel, and particularly Nicholas Riasanovsky (and his father), who have read parts of the manuscript. Professor John A. White has given me the benefit of his knowledge of Russian policy in the Far East, Holland Hunter of his knowledge of Russian railroads, and Gerhart Sinzheimer of his training in Russian economic history. I would also like to express my profound gratitude to Miss Louise Luke of the Russian Institute and William F. Bernhardt of the Columbia University Press for their painstaking and sympathetic editing of my manuscript.

All my Russian studies, I hasten to add, would have been impossible except for the generous financial assistance of the Social

Science Research Council, which has awarded me several grants; of Columbia University, which gave me a Senior Fellowship at the Russian Institute; of the U.S. Education Foundation in Finland, which made possible nine months' residence in Finland as a Fulbright scholar; of the Inter-University Committee on Travel Grants, which enabled me to visit the Soviet Union; and last, but not least, of the University of California, which supplied welcome research funds and time for writing.

I would like to point out that I consider the present volume a part of a larger study of the impact of industrialization on Imperial Russia in the Witte period. Other publications of mine on this subject (to 1962) are listed in the bibliography.

Two minor explanations in conclusion: (1) As for the spelling of Witte's name, I have chosen the prevailing Western version, although its customary English pronunciation will grate on the ears of those who know the Russian (which may be rendered as Viitte). (2) As for my translations from the Russian, I have tried to improve the frequently vexing clumsiness of the original only when necessary for conveying the meaning.

THEODORE H. VON LAUE

West Dover, Vermont
January 5, 1963

Contents

Illustrations

SERGEI WITTE AND THE INDUSTRIALIZATION OF RUSSIA

The more rapidly the genius of discovery and industrial improvement as well as of social and political progress advances, the more rapidly is the distance between stationary nations and those which are progressive increased, and the greater is the peril of remaining behind.

FRIEDRICH LIST

Abbreviations

ASEER	*American Slavic and East European Review*
Bonn	German Foreign Office archives, Bonn
Grosse Politik	*Die Grosse Politik der europäischen Kabinette, 1871–1914*
KA	*Krasnyi arkhiv*
NA	National Archives, Washington, D.C.
PRO	Public Records Office, London

Witte's *Memoirs* are cited as *Detstvo* and *Tsarstvovanie Nikolaia II.*

A glossary of Russian terms used in the text will be found on p. 309.

1. The Penalties of Backwardness

You cannot live in Europe without following the innovations and discoveries in physics, chemistry, mechanics, finance, administration, and society.

MIKHAIL POGODIN

The bourgeoisie, by the rapid improvement of all instruments of production, by the immensely facilitated means of communication, draws all, even the most barbarian nations into civilization. . . . It compels all nations, on pain of extinction, to adopt the bourgeois mode of production; it compels them to introduce what it calls civilization into their midst, that is, to become bourgeois themselves. In one word, it creates a world after its own image. KARL MARX

I

IN FEBRUARY, 1900, the Minister of Finance, Sergei Iulevich Witte, addressed a Most Respectful Report to Nicholas II "On the Condition of Our Industry." The Emperor, to his eventual sorrow, paid scant attention. Yet the report was an epoch-making state paper, for it laid down, in the uncouth but straightforward manner of its author, basic truths which have guided Russian industrial development ever since.[1]

The ambitions of economic and industrial nationalism set the tone of Witte's report. In the staccato of statistics with which it began, he demonstrated the increasing tempo of Russian industrial production, particularly in the heavy industries, and proudly announced: "In the speed and force of this expansion Russia stands ahead of all foreign countries that are economically developed. And there is no doubt that a country which showed itself able to increase its mining and manufacturing industry more than

[1] "Dokladnaia zapiska Vitte Nikolaiu II," *Istorik Marksist,* No. 2–3, 1935, pp. 130 ff.

threefold within two decades certainly contains in itself a rich store of internal resources for further development." But then the Minister of Finance sounded a warning which has persisted, with varying intensity, to more recent times. "No matter how great the results so far, in relation to the needs of the country and in comparison with foreign countries our industry is still very backward." As proof of Russian backwardness he referred to the per capita consumption of key items like coal, iron, and cotton in various western countries and in Russia, and to the fact that Russia was predominantly an agricultural country and one suffering greatly from the uncertainty of its climate.

After these preliminaries the Minister of Finance came to the fundamentals: Without industry, he argued, no country could consider itself independent. "The experience of all peoples clearly shows that only the economically independent countries are fully able to assert their political power." The success of Germany, England, and the United States, so Nicholas II read, testified to that fact as eloquently as the failure of China, India, Turkey, Persia, or the South American states. "At present the political strength of the great powers which are called to fulfill great historical tasks in the world is created not only by the spiritual valor of their peoples but also by their economic organization. Even the military preparedness of a country is determined not only by the perfection of its military machine but by the degree of its industrial development. Russia with her vast multinational population, her complex historical tasks in international relations, and her many-sided internal interests," so the Emperor was further instructed, "needs perhaps more than any other country a proper economic foundation for her national policy and her culture, so that Your Highness's empire will not only be a great power politically and agriculturally but also economically." Then followed the decisive thrust of the argument: To slow down the present industrial development of Russia would be a fatal error.

International competition does not wait. If we do not take energetic and decisive measures so that in the course of the next decades our industry will be able to satisfy the needs of Russia and of the Asiatic countries which are—or should be—under our influence, then the rapidly growing foreign industries will break through our tariff barriers and establish themselves in our fatherland and in the Asiatic countries mentioned above and drive their roots into the depths of our economy. This may gradually clear the way also for triumphant political penetration by foreign powers. . . . It is possible that the slow growth of our industries will endanger the fulfillment of the great political tasks of the monarchy. Our economic backwardness may lead to political and cultural backwardness as well.

By 1900, in short, Russia's Minister of Finance was keenly aware of the pressure of international competition both in foreign policy, where competition was taken for granted, and equally in regard to the economic and social factors of domestic life. Political power was now also measured in terms of industrial productivity.

In his report Witte was speaking from bitter experience. Russia's poverty and backwardness were forever reproaching him. On his desk lay the urgent requests of the minister of war and the minister of the navy for more funds for the modernization of Russia's armed forces. In the mind of the Tsar the military services naturally stood in the forefront of any comparison between Russia and the other great powers; Russian arms had to match those of Austria-Hungary and Germany or of Great Britain. The foreign minister likewise was hampered by Russian economic weakness in the world. The French entente of 1891 and the subsequent alliance could not fully compensate for the fact that Germans and Austrians had openly rejoiced over the great famine of 1891 and the seemingly permanent poverty of Russia, which some day might even eliminate her as a political rival.[2] Whenever the Tsar called for a decision on foreign policy, Witte was consulted as a matter of course. And he invariably advised caution.

[2] Cited by Langer, *Franco-Russian Alliance*, p. 228.

As with individuals, so with governments, nothing establishes so acutely the fact of poverty as constant demands for money that cannot be met. From all points of the administrative compass the indices of Russian poverty and backwardness were driven home to the minister of finance. Russia needed more railroads and better highways. Her rate of illiteracy was a scandal among civilized nations; she needed more schools. Public welfare and health also cried for attention. Wherever he turned, the minister of finance was besieged by requests for funds, most of them for the legitimate purposes of modernizing state and society. And at the same time there piled up on his desk the reports of tax arrears from many provinces, of local famine, rural distress, and the exhaustion of "the paying powers of the population."

Of all the ministers of the tsars the minister of finance bore the brunt of official invidious comparison between Russia and the other great powers of Europe. More than any other government servant he had to assume responsibility for Russian poverty and the search for an escape from it. His function in the government thus became by necessity ever more crucial. He was in charge of the purse and presumably he could call the tune, at least how funds were to be secured, and perhaps also how they were to be divided. How far his responsibilities would carry a minister of finance was a matter of circumstances and personality. Under the right conditions he might well become the real master of the government or even of Russian society. Yet whatever his personal powers, he had to rank very high among his colleagues in technical competence and modernity of views, qualities not easily recruited in Russia. It was no accident then that the great Russian finance ministers of the nineteenth century bore Western names: Egor Frantsevich Kankrin (1823–44), whose real name was Krebs; Mikhail Khristoforovich Reutern (1862–78); Nikolai Khristianovich Bunge (1882–86); or Sergei Iulevich Witte (1892–1903). If Ivan Alekseevich Vyshnegradskii (1887–92) was an exception by name, he still conformed to the type: He had

had a distinguished career as a professor of mechanical engineering before he became minister. All these men stood for modernization after the Western example; their natural bias was liberal, pro-Western. Although they were all loyal servants of their respective Imperial masters, public opinion (which was predominantly critical) respected their position. No minister of finance was ever assassinated. In a study of the impact of industrialization upon the Russian government the figure of the minister of finance must thus occupy the center.

And yet industrialization, it stands to reason, had only come gradually to its commanding position as the clue to modernization and power. Witte was the first Russian minister of finance to give it that priority. But he benefited from a long period of preparation.

II

Modern Russian history, whether considered from an economic or political point of view, did not begin, as is often assumed, with the emancipation of the serfs in 1861. It began with the Russian defeat in the Crimean War. Marxist writers in the early 1890s justly considered that war a decisive turning point in Russian history with results as revolutionary as the opening of China after the first Opium War.[3] Both defeats resulted in the admission of alien influence hitherto carefully contained. Not that Nicholas I had withdrawn Russia so completely from all contact with western Europe as the Manchus had done in China, but he had carefully and not unreasonably limited it. Russia, so he had assumed, could manage largely out of her own material and spiritual resources. The triumph of Western arms at Sevastopol had shattered that complacency, and under his heir, Alexander II, the

[3] See particularly F. Engels's letters to N. Daniel'son of June 18 and September 22, 1892, in *Perepiska K. Marksa i F. Engel'sa s russkimi politicheskimi deiateliami,* pp. 160 ff.; also his "Postscript 1894" to *Internationales aus dem Volksstaat,* p. 67. Also see Nikolai-on, p. 3.

domestic course was changed to a rapid absorption of Western accomplishments, so that Russia could catch up and hold her own again in the future.

Thus a new chapter in the Westernization of Russia began. Henceforth Russia, in the terminology of the intelligentsia, fell under the sway of "capitalism." The abolition of serfdom was the most spectacular step in the new course, and on it hinged the success of the many others. But all measures aimed (some, however, rather halfheartedly) at the liberation of individual initiative and the free economic and cultural creativity of the citizen so characteristic of the West. Only the peasants continued to live under the collective discipline of their households and the village communes. And even here the new mode of life soon made its destructive inroads.

In this timely revolution from above—forced in the last analysis at least as much from without, by the Russian defeat in 1856, as by the threat of peasant revolution within—the liberation of the serfs and the administrative and judicial reorganization of Russia have customarily received the most attention. But the economic, industrial, and cultural measures of the reform era were even more significant in the long run. The gates were opened to foreign penetration. The tariff was lowered, foreign capital and know-how invited. As Russians hurried again to western Europe, Western books, ideas, goods, experts, and standards of doing things flowed into Russia. For a time the new freedom of the press and the moderate atmosphere of the buoyant years of the reforms greatly accelerated the foreign influx.

One of the very first measures of the new course was the promotion of railway construction. The modernization of Russian transport, for military as well as economic reasons, was imperative. "In our untiring concern for the welfare of our fatherland which lies so close to Our heart," a ukase of Alexander II proclaimed as early as January 26, 1857,[4] "We have long recognized that our

[4] Printed in *Polnoe sobranie zakonov, sobranie vtoroe,* item No. 31448.

fatherland, equipped by nature with abundant gifts but divided by huge spaces, especially needs suitable communications. . . . Intensive study indicated that for convenience and speed it was best to turn, according to the example of all other countries, to private industry, our own as well as foreign, and to the latter so that we could utilize the considerable experience which has been gained in the construction of thousands of miles of railways in western Europe." Private enterprise and foreign example were the keynotes of the modernization of Russia, and railways were to be its first accomplishment. Railroad construction, however, like every other measure for catching up with western Europe, cost money. And money was the responsibility of the minister of finance.

As part of the modernization of Russia after 1856 the organization of the government finances was overhauled.[5] Two fiscal experts were sent to western Europe and the United States for a study of government finance and budget procedure. Subsequently, following the French and American examples, a unified budget was made mandatory under a law of May, 1862, which concentrated the bookkeeping of the government revenues and expenditures in the Ministry of Finance. The budget with all its detailed allocations was published annually; each ministry had to adhere to its provisions. Furthermore, no government agency was allowed to retain funds of its own (some did all the same); the minister of finance was supposed to administer them all. In this way, new powers devolved upon him. If he wanted, he could haggle with every one of his colleagues over every item in their departmental budgets. Yet he did not proceed unchecked (or unaided), for at the same time the office of State Control was instituted (raised to

[5] The main texts on Russian economic history for this period are V. Wittschewsky, *Russlands Handels-, Zoll-, und Industriepolitik von Peter dem Grossen bis auf die Gegenwart;* P. I. Liashchenko, *Istoriia narodnago khoziaistva SSSR,* Vol. II; P. A. Khromov, *Ekonomicheskoe razvitie Rossii v XIX-XX vekakh;* A. P. Pogrebinskii, *Ocherki istorii finansov dorevoliutsionnoi Rossii* (*XIX-XX vv.*).

the rank of a ministry in 1892). The state controller audited the accounts of all government agencies under the budget except the Court and the military authorities. Finally, out of the old government banks a central State Bank was established with branches scattered throughout Russia. The government, however, wisely kept the right of issuing paper money in its own hands. In this way the minister of finance was made master of Russian finances for the first time in Russian history.

Yet with his new powers he inherited a multitude of problems. Not only did he have to attend to the financing of the great reforms, which proved a relatively minor matter, but there was also the permanent and utterly recalcitrant set of five complex and interrelated problems: (1) stabilizing the Russian currency, (2) balancing the budget, (3) financing railroad construction, (4) attracting foreign capital to Russia, and, (5) as her bullion reserves remained inadequate and her foreign debt soared, promoting an active balance of payments. The poverty and backwardness of Russia were thus translated at once into a series of intricate and interlacing technical problems which often assumed an intense reality of their own. And yet, compared with the daily needs of the Russian people, these problems always appeared remote and abstract. This fact imposed upon the finance minister yet another task, less acute, even neglected, but in the long run crucial—the task of public relations. How could the Russian public be made to understand the complexities of high finance which baffled even the educated, and to perceive the connection between the dry and crabbed calculations of the Ministry of Finance and the live misery of the Russian masses? The tsarist empire fell, one might even maintain, because it could not teach its people the hard truth that the fruits of poverty are poverty, and that backwardness is both the result and the cause of backwardness.

A brief look at the work of Mikhail K. Reutern, the first minister of finance after the budget reform of 1861, may illustrate that bitter lesson. Reutern was a man well fitted for his task.[6] As one of the experts sent abroad, he had been in the thick of the legislative preparation of the new system; he had studied foreign fiscal technique, first in Prussia and later, for a longer period, in the United States. Before his travels he had served conspicuously in the financial departments of various ministries. He also possessed what may in part account for his successful career, a background of honesty and thoroughness in a German family which had gone into the Russian service during his father's time. And he was wide awake to the weakness of Russia in the European state system. He told Alexander II: "Without railways and mechanical industries Russia cannot be considered secure in her boundaries. Her influence in Europe will fall to a level inconsistent with her international power and her historic significance." [7]

His foremost task was the consolidation of the Russian currency, left in chaos by the Crimean War.[8] A large sum of paper money had been issued during the war; the result was inflation at home and a steady drop of the ruble in foreign money markets. Because of the new domestic policy which called for heavy foreign loans and foreign purchases, the government could ill afford the decline of the ruble's purchasing power abroad. It tried to uphold the value of the ruble by buying up its paper rubles in the chief financial centers of Europe, but with no results except a draining of its bullion reserves. And thus in 1858 the convertibility of the paper ruble, which had been in effect for several decades, had to be suspended. The Russian government, however, was fully aware that a nonconvertible paper currency was a poor medium for economic growth, if the country was to rely so largely on foreign capital and skill.

[6] See the biographical sketch in *Ministerstvo Finansov, 1802–1902,* I, 389 ff.

[7] Quoted by I. F. Gindin in a significant article, "K voprosu ob ekonomicheskoi politike tsarskogo pravitel'stva v 60–80 godakh XIX veka," *Voprosy istorii,* No. 5, 1959, p. 61.

[8] See Wittschewsky, p. 131, and Pogrebinskii, *Ocherki,* pp. 52 ff.

How then was Russia to acquire a sufficient bullion reserve enabling her to return to free convertibility? The orthodox prescription was that, as her own production of gold was as yet minimal, she must either buy bullion abroad from a surplus in government revenues (this had its complications) or, more effectively, show an active balance of trade by which the excess of her exports over her imports would result in an influx of bullion from abroad. Both methods are a matter of course in a prosperous country; in Russia, however, they were largely out of the question. The average government deficit ran to about 50 million rubles a year in the first six years of Reutern's administration; deficits, indeed, were notorious until the late 1880s.[9] And as to the balance of trade (and the balance of payments), it was persistently passive in Reutern's time because of the heavy imports attendant upon the new domestic policy. There remained a third, though dubious, solution, the influx of bullion through foreign loans negotiated, say, for the construction of Russian railroads. But the Russian government could hardly hope to obtain such loans on reasonable terms unless (to consider only the economic aspects) the Russian currency were both stable and convertible or the Russian government could give guarantees that the dividends would be paid in bullion. This, however, could not be done without the accumulation of a sufficient bullion reserve to start with.

Nonetheless, Reutern soon after his appointment reintroduced convertibility. Yet within a year and a half the experiment ended in a colossal failure.[10] As in 1858, convertibility led to a run on the government's bullion reserve, which fell to less than one half. Thus in November, 1863, during the uproar over the Polish rebellion, convertibility was again suspended (it remained so until 1897), and the Russian currency went back to a paper basis and to all its usual vicissitudes. Reutern and his successors, however, never gave up the hope of returning to convertibility. How else

[9] Liashchenko, *Istoriia,* p. 177.

[10] See Pogrebinskii, *Ocherki,* pp. 65 ff.

could foreign credit be obtained on reasonable terms and in large volume and the Russian economy grow strong?

Next, there was the annual agony of balancing the budget. Government expenditures could hardly be pared further without risk to the national interest. Take the main items in the budget of 1863 as an example.[11] The army obtained 36 percent (in round figures), the navy another 5 percent. Reutern's own ministry received 14 percent. The charges on the national debt amounted to another 13 percent. The Ministry of Communications was granted 6 percent, the Ministry of the Interior 3 percent. Justice, Education, and the Church each claimed less than 2 percent, as did the Court. Russian diplomacy accounted for not even 1 percent.

Since spending could hardly be further curtailed, balancing the budget meant mostly increasing the government revenues. Reutern devoted much effort to developing a system of indirect taxation, which henceforth became the basis of government revenue. But the most important form of direct taxation, the "soul tax" on the peasants, was also increased—by 80 percent over preemancipation days.[12] Yet even so—what with the costs of the reforms, the railroad construction, and the economic slump following upon the emancipation decree—Reutern could not make ends meet. In order to disguise Russian poverty and to take the heaviest burdens out of the budget, he followed the example of other governments and divided the budget into a regular and an extraordinary one. The latter contained the costly expenditures, such as new arms or railroad construction; these were paid out of extraordinary resources, mostly domestic and foreign loans. While this method helped to balance the ordinary budget and thus gave an impression of financial solidity, it could not prevent the over-all deficits over the years. And thus Reutern borrowed freely for ordinary and extraordinary purposes, accumulating in the years 1866–75 a total

[11] In percentages according to the figures given in Khromov, pp. 514 ff. The figures given there do not add up to the total listed on p. 516.

[12] Pogrebinskii, *Ocherki,* p. 64.

of one billion rubles in foreign loans at high rates and considerably more from domestic lenders.[13]

Thus he saddled himself and his successors with another intricate technical problem far removed from the daily needs of the Russian people: the management of a huge state debt held to a large extent abroad, under the highly adverse conditions of an unstable currency and uncertain foreign credit. The prompt payment of the interest charges abroad became an intrinsic feature of Russian prestige in Europe. Like their armaments, their foreign debt cost the Russian people a pretty penny. And it intensified the need for a stable, bullion-based currency.

If it is possible to establish priority among absolute necessities, railroad construction may be called the third most important task confronting the Minister of Finance. Railways were as important to Russia as a stable currency. Without them Russian economy (not to speak of Russian military power) could hardly develop. What Count Cavour had written in 1846 of the influence of railroads in underdeveloped countries such as contemporary Italy applied also to Russia.

> The railroad will not only be a means to greater wealth but also a powerful weapon, by the use of which these countries will eventually triumph over the reactionary forces that have held them back in a state of industrial and political infancy. . . . The locomotive has a mission to diminish, if not to obliterate completely, the humiliating inferiority to which several branches of the great Christian family are now reduced.[14]

The ukase of 1857 had already stressed the need for railways; Reutern now did his best to give free rein to the locomotive. In his time, and through his assistance, the Russian railway network grew from 2,195 miles in 1862 to 13,980 miles in the year of his resignation (1878).[15]

[13] Wittschewsky, p. 131.

[14] Quoted by Thomas C. Mendenhall *et al., The Quest for a Principle of Authority* (New York, 1953), p. 181.

[15] The figures from Khromov, p. 462 (3,516 km to 22,371 km).

And the locomotive fulfilled its mission. In connection with railroad construction industrial activities multiplied. In southern Russia the heavy industry of the Ukraine got a start, largely through the initiative of an Englishman named John James Hughes, who began exploiting the iron ore of Krivoi Rog and the coal of the Donets basin. The Nobel brothers developed the oil wells of Baku. Machine building expanded in St. Petersburg and the Moscow area with the help of Western and native firms; the textile industry became modernized through the efforts of Ludwig Knoop. The first private banks were founded. In short, a mild industrial boom (with a moderate case of *Gründerzeit* fever) took place in the second half of the 1860s when the dislocation of the emancipation had been overcome. Russian private enterprise was now established on a capitalist basis. It began to move forward, although far too slowly for Russian needs.

One reason for the slow growth of industry was the acute shortage of native and foreign capital; Russia was a poor country. The influx of foreign capital was impeded by many factors; the fluctuation of the Russian currency, the poverty of the Russian consumer, the obstacles put in the way of foreign initiative, the brutality and anti-Semitism of Russian officials, and the uncertainty of conditions in general. A few foreign banking houses, notably the Mendelssohns of Berlin, assisted in the establishment of private banks in Russia. And the ties between Russian and German—later French and Belgian—banks remained a characteristic feature of Russian economy. On the whole, however, foreign investors remained indifferent. If they invested in Russia, they preferred government bonds, for unlike the private citizens the Russian government scrupulously paid its debts and paid them in gold. Foreign loans, if obtained at all, were thus channeled through the government, which made them at once a pawn of power politics. Foreign governments would always try to influence Russian foreign policy by manipulating the sluices of foreign credit. This was a weapon against which the Russian government could not retaliate. It thus faced a heavy handicap in shouldering the financial responsibility for the most important private industry in Russia—railroad construction.

According to the ukase of 1857, this crucial job had been turned over very largely to private enterprise. As a result, the Main Company, the most famous of the private firms, absorbed even the oldest long-distance line, that from St. Petersburg to Moscow. At the end of Reutern's career, indeed, all Russian railways were in private hands. There sprang up then in this pioneer era an unscrupulous group of Russian financiers and railway kings analogous to the English or American type, men of no particular social background, Russians, Poles, Jews, or Germans, energetic and gifted, learning rapidly to manage affairs on a grand scale. They were assisted by a generation of corrupt but technically competent railway engineers, who worked for their own pockets rather than the public welfare. And it seemed as if the government in its eagerness to make the locomotives roll conspired with their greed. In order to persuade the private companies, and above all the foreign investors, to undertake the risks of constructing extensive lines through economically fallow regions, the government had guaranteed their debts. No matter how uneconomically or irrationally the railway companies operated, the government was obliged to make up their deficits out of its own treasury, that is, largely from more foreign loans, without being able in any way to exert adequate control over their operation. It could be milked indefinitely by an unscrupulous railroad management.

As the result of its railroad program the Russian government found itself saddled with an ever larger foreign debt. It was deplorable, of course, that Russian progress should depend so much on the goodwill of foreign investors. Yet such dependence could not be avoided except at the price of still greater economic and political weakness. The best the Russian Minister of Finance could do under the circumstances—this was a fourth responsibility of his office—was to keep a close watch on the international money market and learn how to manipulate it to the Russian advantage. Thus he became one of the most skillful international speculators, playing the market with subtle and sometimes undignified finesse through the means of propaganda, financial shrewdness, and large expense accounts. In order to do this successfully, he was forced to keep his ear close to the ground, maintaining his own intelligence network through agents in the financial centers of Europe—all in the hope of improving the credit of the Russian government. Alas for Russian credit! As Kankrin once remarked, the moment you begin to speak of credit, it already begins to vanish. What with the violent fluctuations of the ruble and the vagaries of "His Majesty the Harvest," who determined the size of Russian exports—not to speak of Russia's internal instability and the ups and downs of her international reputation—Russian credit abroad had a mercurial nature indeed.

As already stated, Russian credit, like her currency, depended to a large extent on the balance of trade, which thus became the fifth matter of concern to the Russian Minister of Finance. If there was a sizable export surplus, the government could expect better conditions for its loans, because the country was earning large sums of foreign currency, which reassured the foreign creditors. But how could the country obtain such a surplus? The volume of exports was an unpredictable quantity; nature rather than human effort determined its size. Furthermore, the new government policy after the Crimean War had greatly stimulated not exports but imports, for the quickest way of overcoming Russian backwardness seemed to be through importing European goods. Railroad construction demanded instruments and equipment; industry called for raw materials like cotton and for semifinished goods or machinery. And the Russian ego yearned for the culture and distinction which western Europe possessed. In order to facilitate this beneficial penetration, Reutern lowered considerably the traditional high tariff barrier. But in this way a favorable balance of trade could hardly be expected. Indeed, in half of the years between 1862 and 1878 it was adverse, as was the total balance for the entire span.[16]

Even more important than the balance of trade from the point of view of Russian credit was the balance of payments, that is, the relation between *all* foreign expenses and *all* income from foreign currencies. On this more elusive ledger certain "invisible" items like the expenses of Russian travelers abroad—estimated as high as one tenth of her total imports[17]—and the upkeep of her foreign missions had to be added to Russia's visible imports. And if the balance of trade was negative, the balance of payments was definitely more so.[18] In modern parlance, Russia suffered from a "bullion gap." A negative balance of payments over the years meant an outflow of bullion, the very thing which for the sake of the Russian currency the Minister of Finance wanted to prevent at all costs. How then could Reutern ever hope to close the drain on the Russian bullion reserves while facing a stubbornly negative balance of payments?

And yet he did manage to keep his bullion reserve, and even slowly to increase it, but by the same dubious expedient which he used to cover his deficits—he borrowed abroad in loans paid in bullion. This, however, did not stop the dismal chain reaction of impoverishment and indebtedness; it merely opened a short cut to its logical result, the increasing influence of foreign creditors over Russia's finances. All told, it was clear that in Reutern's time Russia was living beyond her means and that she was buying her present pittance of prosperity, industrial growth, and economic power at the expense of her future, and in growing dependence upon foreign bankers. Whether these expedients would turn the trick in the long run and increase the productivity of the Russian economy faster than her indebtedness was, of course, another question.

[16] *Ibid.*, pp. 468 ff.
[17] Pogrebinskii, *Ocherki*, p. 114.
[18] *Ibid.*, pp. 146–47.

Amazingly enough, after a dozen years of Reutern's skillful stewardship the state of Russian finances seemed to belie all pessimism. With the help of constant foreign loans he had managed to maintain a fairly stable currency, albeit on a paper basis. The ruble stood moderately high in the foreign money markets and was guarded by a bullion reserve at the command of the Minister of Finance sufficient to offset sudden foreign sales of the ruble although too small for conversion. Trade and industry had grown considerably, although their progress was temporarily interrupted by the depression of 1873. Above all, the railway network was constantly being enlarged, bringing Russian grains more cheaply to western markets and thus improving the balance of trade. Under Reutern's leadership, a modern tsarist economic policy was fashioned by a loose combination of traditional fiscal techniques and wider measures for the improvement of Russian prosperity as a whole.

And yet, within a short time, all of Reutern's work was undone and the basic poverty of Russia laid bare again. It was the political ambition of the Russian government, or rather of the vocal Pan-Slav minority forcing its hand, that was responsible for the new economic disaster. In 1876 the choice before Alexander II and his ministers was either to let Slav peasants in the Balkans be butchered by the infidel Turk and preserve the modicum of economic stability which Reutern had accomplished or to go to war against the Turk and accept financial chaos. Inevitably, and in spite of Reutern's bitter protests, power politics took precedence over financial soundness; the government moved toward war. The result was a sharp drop of exports, while imports increased. Foreign credit fell off; the Russian government-guaranteed railway bonds were not selling as usual. There followed a disastrous run on the government's bullion reserves, organized by a foreign syndicate with the help even of Russian bankers, and the ruble took a sharp dip on the European courses. Eventually, when the war with Turkey broke out in 1877, the government had to issue one billion new paper rubles.[19] At the end of the brief war, Reutern, who had continued in his office only because his resignation would have made matters still worse, retired in despair. Russian finances were back almost where they had been after the Crimean War. And the internal situation was even more unsettled. The war had brought scant glory and no profit; it did not restore the prestige of the government. Further, it was daily becoming more obvious that the emancipation had not improved the economic conditions of the peasants. Moreover, the industrial workers were beginning to organize. And worst of all, the conspirators of the Narodnaia Volia kept the government in continuous terror until they succeeded in assassinating the Tsar Liberator himself. In these years Russia's economic stability was indeed a hopeless cause.

It was not that Russia lacked the resources for a modern economy. The generation that grew up after the emancipation was daily becoming more aware of her latent riches in fuel and metals. Private initiative, both native and foreign, was just starting to bring them into production. But could the government guarantee profitable and uninterrupted industrial and commercial operations? After the Turkish War the prospects were gloomy. As for Russia's cereal exports, her chief guarantee of financial stability, it was becoming obvious now that their once privileged position in the world market was seriously challenged by the competition of American grains. The chances were that the value, though not necessarily the volume, of her exports would decline, while there was no prospect that her need for imports would lessen. And behind the pressing problems of Russian economy loomed the political uncertainty: Could autocracy maintain order and stability? On the surface, Alexander III, called to the throne by his father's assassination, quickly succeeded in breaking the revolutionary movement and even in assuaging the revolutionary temper of the late 1870s. But could he provide the proper setting for modern capitalist enterprise?

[19] *Ibid.*, p. 111.

III

In Reutern's time industrialization, except for railroad construction, had played only a minor part in Russian economy. It remained on the fringe of his policy, a welcome by-product. This could hardly have been otherwise, for the pressure for industrialization was as yet relatively small. England as the prototype of a predominantly industrial country still stood in a class by itself. On the continent French industry, to be sure, had made considerable progress under the Second Empire. In Germany, likewise, industries had grown conspicuously in the 1850s and 1860s; but then, after 1873, a depression had interrupted the boom. The great industrial upsurge in Europe and the United States, and with it the novel phenomenon of the competition of industrial empires, still lay ahead. When it came at last in the 1880s it reached also into Russia and became a problem to the ministers of finance, first to Bunge, more urgently to his successor Vyshnegradskii.

After the prolonged interregnum at the Ministry of Finance caused by Reutern's resignation and the aftereffects of the Turkish War, a firm economic policy was resumed at last when in 1881 Alexander III appointed N. K. Bunge minister of finance. Bunge had had an unusually successful academic career. From a professorship in economics and finance at the University of Kiev, topped by the deanship and rectorship, he had advanced into the city administration of Kiev and thence into government commissions on peasant affairs. In 1880 he had joined the Ministry of Finance. He was a learned, if somewhat ineffectual, man of liberal views, whose approach to government finance was kindled by a warm concern for the welfare of the Russian people. Decidedly he was not one of Alexander III's reactionary ministers, but he could hardly escape the old furies of poverty and indebtedness which had already hounded Reutern. In addition, he had to face the evil heritage of the Turkish War.

Like his predecessor, Bunge moved almost at once to put the

ruble on a gold basis.[20] He pleaded before the State Council for convertibility (now it was definitely the gold standard), but was refused. Thereafter he proceeded toward his goal indirectly by trying to improve the Russian balance of payments and thereby to increase the country's gold reserve. A new fiscal expedient, which Reutern had spurned and Bunge, under obvious necessity, now introduced, was the restriction of imports. In other words, he was trying to force the country to live somewhat more within its means. Thus after the cautious free trade policy of the reform era a new age of protectionism opened. (It was Reutern himself who, in the financial crisis of 1876, had started the process by demanding that import duties—then still low—had to be paid not in paper rubles but in gold. This not only brought new gold reserves into the country but also increased the tariff by the difference in value between the paper ruble and gold.) Bunge now deliberately raised the tariff on various items, including iron and steel, achieving by 1885 a 20 percent increase for most imported goods.[21] The new protectionism, it should be clear, thus arose out of the fiscal necessity of an active balance of payments and the government's eagerness to abandon the paper ruble. It also produced incidentally more government revenue. And finally, though this motive carried the least weight, it aided Russian industrialists by reducing foreign competition.

As regards the budget, Bunge seemed more concerned with improving the sources of revenue in the long run than with balancing the budget then and there. And improving those sources meant easing the lot of the taxpayers, above all of the peasants, whose growing economic misery had just been revealed by a government investigation. Bunge completed the recasting of the tax structure begun under Reutern by abolishing, except for the redemption

[20] On Bunge's economic policy see Wittschewsky; Pogrebinski, *Ocherki;* and Olga Crisp, "Russian Financial Policy and the Gold Standard at the End of the Nineteenth Century," *Economic History Review,* VI, No. 2, 157 ff.

[21] Wittschewsky, p. 140.

dues, all direct taxes for the peasants. Thus disappeared the notorious "soul tax" of Russian serfdom (except for Siberia, where it lasted until 1899). Hereafter the bulk of the indirect taxes was raised from the sale of matches, alcohol, tobacco, and other items of consumption. The tax on salt, however, was abolished. As a result, according to a critic of later ministers of finance, the tax burden of the peasants was reduced by as much as one quarter.[22] But the government revenues suffered correspondingly. As a further boon to the peasants Bunge established a Peasant Land Bank, through which peasants could acquire, singly or in groups, additional lands. A Nobles Bank, founded a little later, undertook a somewhat analogous relief measure on behalf of the Russian nobility, whose economic fortunes likewise were on the wane.

Next after rural welfare Bunge took up factory legislation. There had been as yet no effective government measures designed to mitigate the lot of the factory workers. He therefore introduced laws protecting, first, children and, somewhat later, women against the abuses of long hours in the factories. In 1886 a comprehensive law was promulgated which put the entire relationship between employer and employee in the factory under government supervision. In the years ahead the generous provisions of this law helped much to smooth the advance of industry in Russia, but its immediate benefit to the budget was nil.

And, finally, under Bunge the entire system of railroad construction and management was overhauled. As long as their profits were guaranteed by the government, the private railroad companies were under no compulsion to rationalize their methods. As a result, during the Turkish War the railway system had shown serious flaws. The military had complained of delays and accidents. The Ministry of Finance was even more concerned with the drain on its resources and the effects of high and chaotic freight rates upon the national economy. After a thorough investigation by a government commission headed by Count Baranov, appointed

[22] Cited by Shvanebakh, *Nashe podatnoe delo,* p. 9.

before the Turkish War, the government reversed its former policy and under Bunge began again to construct railways at its own expense. It also bought back some private roads for the creation of a state-owned system of railroads. Moreover, it strengthened its legal powers over the private companies and with its new controls established for the first time a common Russian railroad network composed of both state and private lines. Henceforth rolling stock could be interchanged and traffic coordinated. The new system added greatly to the efficiency of Russian railroads, because it permitted at last the drafting of a unified freight tariff, which could be tailored according to the needs of the entire Russian economy. And yet, as with Bunge's other reforms, the new system weighed heavily upon the budget.

By these measures Bunge applied himself to mending and patching the fabric of Russian national economy in those spots where he felt that it needed attention most immediately, in agriculture, labor legislation, and railway transportation. He thus gave the economy a more solid foundation for the years to come. But he labored, it seemed, for the benefit of his successors rather than his own, since he miserably failed to make ends meet. In his five years at the Ministry of Finance he never succeeded once in balancing the accounts. So he too fell back on the dubious expedient of borrowing, not least from abroad.

But whose fault was it if he could not balance the budget? The responsibility, he protested, lay with the military.[23] In the twenty years from 1866 to 1885 the Russian army and navy had accounted for 32 percent of the government expenditures. The service of the government debt claimed another 28 percent. And if the expenses of railroad construction by the government were added, 70 percent of the total outlay was reached. Only a little more than one quarter of the government's revenues thus became available for the productive expenditures (apart from railroad construction) which increase popular welfare. For the decade 1875–85,

[23] Crisp, *Economic History Review,* VI, 160.

which included the Turkish War, the figures were still more appalling, as nearly 33 percent went to the army and navy and 34 percent to the service of the government debt.[24] In short, the hands of the Minister of Finance were tied by his country's ambition to maintain an army worthy of a great power and by the extensive drafts on her future made by his predecessors. Here lay the tragedy of Russian welfare: the present need for maintaining her position in the world vitiated all efforts to build up the country's strength for the future. No straining at the bootstraps could raise Russia above her backwardness, particularly if her government became involved in costly military adventures. But in this respect Alexander III pursued a different policy from that of his father; while he too could not escape expensive crises in foreign policy, he at least avoided the financial catastrophe of war.

The last year of Bunge's tenure at the Ministry of Finance was, as usual in the careers of Russian ministers of finance, one of calamity. The government's financial condition, already strained by annual deficits, was further weakened by tension over Afghanistan, which endangered the Russian bonds in the London stock market, and next by the more formidable Bulgarian crisis. The danger of war with Austria-Hungary over the question whether Alexander of Battenberg or Ferdinand of Coburg should be king in Sofia called for an increase in Russian armaments, which Bunge's budgets could not sustain. The ruble fell to its lowest level in history,[25] and Bunge resigned with the somber warning that taxes could not possibly be increased. The noble experiment of improving the prosperity of the people while neglecting the fiscal necessities of the government had failed. But would the opposite experiment work more successfully?

The man whom Alexander III chose to apply this prescription was I. A. Vyshnegradskii. With him a new type of official entered the Ministry of Finance. His predecessors had been a *chinovnik*

[24] Pogrebinskii, *Ocherki,* p. 93.

[25] Crisp, *Economic History Review,* VI, 160.

and an economist with an academic background and close ties to the administration, men standing above economic interests and pressure groups, guided primarily by the state's impartial concern for public and social welfare. Vyshnegradskii, on the other hand, was a newcomer in the government service, steeped in the new field of rising industry and capitalism, in science, technology, business, and finance, a man who might not always know the dividing line between personal and public interest. The product of a seminary for the training of priests, he had risen to a professorship of mechanical engineering at the St. Petersburg Technological Institute and to considerable professional reputation as author of the book *The Theory of Governors.*[26] He was also an expert in military technology and, in his subsequent capacity as director of the St. Petersburg Technological Institute, an authority on technical education in Russia. His advice was frequently sought by the government. At the same time he made his way also in the new world of budding Russian capitalism, becoming a director of the great Southwestern Railway Company and several other enterprises. For his knowledge of modern business and technology he was made a member of the Council of the Ministry of Finance in Bunge's time, and after January 1, 1887, was appointed minister of finance, the first official with close ties to industry to hold that position.[27] Upon taking office, however, he did not relinquish his business associations nor change over to the code of disinterestedness traditional in the bureaucracy. He showed little sympathy for Bunge's factory laws, and he participated in speculation on the fall of the ruble when it was his duty as minister of finance to raise the value of the ruble. The story goes that when Alexander III was told of his minister's gains in this and other speculations, he laughed the matter off: "Let him make ten million, as long as he makes a hundred for the government." [28] Vyshnegradskii's succes-

[26] Stephen P. Timoshenko, "The Development of Engineering Education in Russia," *The Russian Review,* July, 1956.

[27] See the biographical chapter in *Ministerstvo Finansov, 1802–1902,* II, 7.

[28] Cited by Korostowetz, *Graf Witte,* p. 32.

sor, Sergei Witte, however, denied that as minister of finance Vyshnegradskii had ever acted improperly.[29]

Whatever the truth of the charges against him, Vyshnegradskii raised far more than a hundred million for the state, being the first Russian minister of finance since the Crimean War consistently to balance the budget and to produce a sizable annual surplus. He, for one, made ends meet by pursuing a rigid and somewhat unimaginative policy of fiscal orthodoxy aimed foremost at the introduction of the gold standard, whose value for Russian industry and business he knew from experience.[30] The reason for his ability to balance both the ordinary and extraordinary budgets was that he greatly increased the indirect taxes, contrary to Bunge's parting advice. He even talked of taxing the passports of Russian travelers abroad, for the sake of improving the balance of payments at the price of severely curtailing the volume of travel to western Europe, against which he had otherwise no prejudice. And he introduced new taxes for the urban population as well. While he thus considerably increased government revenues, he practiced, on the other side of the ledger, "a salutary thrift in government expenditures," [31] going so far even as to retard railroad construction. Hardly any state funds were plowed back into the national economy for an increased yield in the future.

Vyshnegradskii saved further millions for the state through his expert knowledge of international finance; he refunded part of the Russian foreign debt at a lower interest rate.[32] His success in this field was due partly to his skill and partly to political circumstances. In 1887 Bismarck had in effect banished the Russian government bonds from the German money market, in an attempt

[29] Witte, *Detstvo,* p. 249.

[30] On Vyshnegradskii's policy see Wittschewsky; Pogrebinskii, *Ocherki;* Crisp, *Economic History Review,* VI, 157 ff.; Schvanebakh, *Nashe podatnoe delo.*

[31] Cited by Shvanebakh, *Nashe podatnoe delo,* pp. 13–14.

[32] A. L. Sidorov, in "Konversii vneshnikh zaimov Rossii v 1888–1890 gg.," *Istoricheskii arkhiv,* 1959, No. 3, makes the point that the net savings from the lowering of the interest rate from 5 percent to 4 percent were minimal.

to coerce the Russian government into withdrawal from Bulgaria through economic pressure. For once, however, Bismarck had made an egregious miscalculation. The Russian bonds were bought with enthusiasm by French investors.

Hence sprang up the close ties between French *haute finance* and the Russian government which lasted to the end of the Imperial period. After Bismarck's fall the new financial bonds were consolidated by a firm political guarantee, the Franco-Russian entente and eventually the alliance of 1894. Vyshnegradskii quickly made the most of his advantage. In 1887 he sent a onetime professor of physiology named Tsion to Paris as his agent. While Tsion soon proved corrupt and even turned traitor, the tradition of intimacy was established. As for making friends and influencing the opinions of French newspapers, politicians, investors, and the public at large, the representative of the Russian minister of finance in Paris knew all the tricks of a modern publicity agent. He had to cover up the economic weakness of his country, but he could always stress the value of the Russian alliance. And almost always he found the French investors willing to believe that political advantage constituted also sound economy. Yet exchanging French for German creditors did not eliminate the basic fact of Russian dependence on foreign moneylenders (and their governments) or sweeten the humiliation of such bondage.

Hand in hand with the amelioration of Russian credit went a much improved balance of trade, for Vyshnegradskii forced Russian grain exports to the utmost. He was favored in his first years by exceptional harvests, which served to outweigh the calamity of falling grain prices in the world market. But he also increased the volume of grain available for export through artificial and often brutal means. He ordered that taxes be collected in the fall and thus compelled the peasants to dispose of their harvest when grain prices were at their seasonal low. The peasants had to sell at once, even if they had no grain left for the lean months of the spring. But, as Vyshnegradskii put it—it was a phrase heard again in the twentieth century and not in Russia alone—"We must export though we die." In order to facilitate the cheap transport of Russian grain from the interior to the ports, he reduced the freight rates for grain export. He was thus the first minister of finance to take advantage of the new unified freight tariff to promote the economic interests of the government. A bonus given to sugar exporters was another example of the government's export drive. Russian sugar was dumped on the London market at one third of the domestic price, which meant that the Russian peasant had to drink his tea unsweetened.

Such forceful expansion of exports was coupled with a far more drastic curtailment of imports than Bunge had ever contemplated. Under Vyshnegradskii's prompting, the protective tariff as the most effective means of import-throttling became a major instrument of Russian fiscal policy.[33] Its foremost justification lay in the fact that it helped to improve the balance of payments and thus the bullion reserve. After four years of careful consultation of all economic interest groups, a rather drastic customs tariff was imposed, the famous tariff of 1891, the cornerstone of Russian economic and financial policy to 1917.

While there can be no doubt about his fiscal purpose, the motives of the Minister of Finance were not entirely unmixed. The very fact that he had consulted so extensively the spokesmen of industry and agriculture was significant; he wanted the widest possible public support for a measure which certainly would harm the Russian consumer. And he had powerful allies. There had grown up by the end of the 1880s a strong protectionist sentiment in the country. The agitation for tariff protection was loudest in Moscow, the country's industrial center. In the last years of his life the well-known publicist M. N. Katkov had made himself the mouthpiece for the protectionist sentiment of the Moscow *kupechestvo*. The economic creed of industrial self-sufficiency which

[33] On the tariff of 1891 see M. N. Sobolev, *Ocherki tamozhennoi politiki Rossii.*

Katkov preached was a convenient weapon against the growing pressure of foreign competition; it harmonized well with the rising nationalism of the age. Vyshnegradskii, too, sympathized with its tenets.

There were good reasons then why Vyshnegradskii should characterize his tariff as a protectionist measure. He even denied outright that it had any fiscal motive[34] (and he was right to the extent that the new tariff was not designed primarily to procure revenue, although it accounted soon for up to one quarter of the regular government receipts). Liberal economists and other free traders in Russia, on the other hand, stoutly refused to be convinced by these assertions. They pointed out that in some cases the government had raised the tariff far above what had been suggested by the industries concerned. In other cases, the import duties were pegged at such excessive levels that industries relying on these imports were put at a disadvantage.[35] But no matter how justified these protests, the government clung to its interpretation. It obviously wished to anchor the new tariff firmly in the spirit of nationalism which linked the government and the public. It is doubtful whether Witte, who became minister of finance in 1892, ever clearly understood the fiscal character of the tariff. To him it appeared as the government's chief instrument for the promotion of a rapid industrial advance.

The core of the new tariff dealt with raw materials and semifinished goods, which constituted the bulk of Russian imports. At the time these duties aroused no loud protest. It was otherwise with the duties on agricultural equipment, which had also been raised. The agrarian interests argued that Russia should be able to buy as cheaply as possible the same farm machines which her foreign competitors used. How else could she hope to compete with them in the world market? But the only concession made to

[34] Wittschewsky, p. 151.

[35] *Ibid.*, p. 141.

the agrarian interests was the postponement of these duties until the current famine had passed.

Thus it was with only minor opposition that Russia enacted the highest tariff then in existence in the world. The general level was about one third of the value of the imports; some of its rates were almost prohibitive. As a result, so its opponents never tired of pointing out, the Russian people had to buy their manufactured goods at prices two or three times above the world market, and goods of much poorer quality.[36] And yet, to look at this measure also with modern eyes, in blaming the tariff were the critics not unreasonably refusing to pay the price of their country's backwardness? There was an obvious limit to the Russian ability to catch up with the increasingly rapid tempo of the West through the import of Western goods. Russia's growing foreign indebtedness demanded categorically that her government, and her subjects as well, reduce their foreign spending. Paradoxically, if they wanted to keep up with the pace of Western development, they had to forego imitating the Western standard of living and save up for the necessary industrial expansion. If they wanted to catch up, they had to fall behind.

How much the tariff of 1891 actually promoted the development of Russian industries was, however, another matter. Most likely it was not the import restrictions which made the subsequent decade stand out in the history of pre-Soviet industrialization; it was rather the new boom in government-sponsored railway construction. And as a fiscal device, the tariff failed to curtail imports. As a result of the subsequent boom, Russia's imports—even at the highly increased prices—rose considerably and the balance of payments was again thrown into question.

All told, Vyshnegradskii's "system," as his interlocking measures came to be called, seemed to work well. The revenue surplus looked impressive, at least to the uninitiated who did not know

[36] Liashchenko, *Istoriia,* p. 193.

that the Minister of Finance had deliberately underestimated the anticipated revenues so as to show a larger surplus. In regard to Russia's gold reserves, his efforts were likewise well rewarded; he increased them by nearly 300 million gold rubles, thus laying the ground for the conversion later achieved by Witte. He was not quite so successful in stabilizing the exchange value of the ruble. The stranglehold of the Berlin stock market, which by its speculations profoundly affected ruble prices, was too strong for the Russian treasury to break. At times the Russian Minister of Finance himself actually connived with exporters and bankers, perhaps for his personal profit, certainly in order to stimulate Russian exports, in engineering a fall in the ruble. As a result, the value of the ruble fluctuated as violently as ever. Yet despite these difficulties Russia's exports flourished and the balance of trade was positive.

These successes, however, could not break the tradition of failure. Unexpected and complete disaster overtook the Vyshnegradskii system in its fifth year. While he had succeeded in making ends meet at the orthodox junctures of state finance, the very fabric of Russian national economy gave out. In 1891 a sudden famine followed a crop failure in some twenty provinces of central Russia, and in the wake of the famine rode the cholera. Crop failures were not unusual in Russia. But what made the famine of 1891 so disastrous was the absence of any savings in money or provisions that the peasants could fall back on. The government had taken everything in the form of taxes. In the drive for exports the peasants had surrendered their crops, and now they were dying of hunger and disease. The government did not permit Russian journalists to dramatize the conditions in the afflicted regions. But even the colorless and measured official summary of the compounded misery conveyed a sense of the suffering:

> The crop failure of winter as well as spring grains in vast parts of practically all the black-soil area of Russia and in several [other] provinces as well; the complete absence of any kind of reserves or sur-

plus for sale; the consequent impossibility of meeting current expenses, various dues, and debts; the absence of any grain in the grain-exporting provinces not only for provisioning themselves but in several cases also for reseeding the fields; and the necessity of buying grain at prices almost prohibitive to the majority of the peasants—all this put a large part of the population of European Russia into an extremely difficult situation, and in some places, into a hopeless condition. Our peasant economy has come to a full collapse and ruin, from which it will not recover in several years even with good harvests.[37]

The charges were raised at once that the Russian peasant had been crucified on the cross of Vyshnegradskii's gold, that his policy of balancing the budget and accumulating a gold reserve at any price had left the peasant exhausted, and that he had done nothing to make the population prosperous; in short, that the state had grown fat and people had withered.

In several ways the famine of 1891 proved a turning point in Russian history. The government, to be sure, tried to minimize its effects. For the sake of its prestige at home and abroad, especially for its foreign credit, it could not do otherwise. The Russian public, however, was much aroused over the unexpected demonstration of Russian poverty and backwardness—a civilized country did not suffer from famine. It rushed to the rescue where it could, never appreciating the government's reasons for reticence and angrily suspecting that the bureaucrats were not pleased by such initiative. And there revived, in a growing revulsion against Russian backwardness, the latent energies of opposition and underground organization which had been crushed in the 1880s. This ominous mood culminated in the Revolution of 1905.

Faced with catastrophe, Vyshnegradskii took what measures he could to alleviate the suffering. He stopped exports at once and hurriedly negotiated for a foreign loan to tide Russia over the emergency. But in Paris the Rothschilds proved difficult. They were upset by the expulsion of the Jews from Moscow and St.

[37] Cited by Shvanebakh, *Denezhnoe preobrazovanie i narodnoe khoziaistvo*, p. 34.

Petersburg which the government had recently decreed. And the French government, which wanted to exert pressure on the Tsar in order to speed the Franco-Russian entente, did nothing to overcome their pique. Thus the loan failed.[38] The relief measures cost the government some 150 million rubles (not to speak of the more indirect costs to the balance of trade and the government's tax receipts). It might as well not have collected these millions from its subjects in the first place and possibly have spared them their misery. The Vyshnegradskii system ended in disgrace, as had the systems of all his predecessors.

IV

What made Vyshnegradskii's failure particularly galling to the government was the fact that it had just then pledged itself to the construction of the Siberian railroad. On March 17, 1891, the start of "a railway through Siberia" was announced by Imperial rescript.[39] Two months later, on May 19, the Tsarevich Nicholas, during his stay in Vladivostok, laid the first stone of the line linking that port with the small town of Grafskaia on the Ussuri River near the Manchurian border to the north. At last a beginning was made to a long-cherished plan.

The trans-Siberian railroad was an old and, in an age of continent-bridging railroad construction, an inevitable project.[40] The Siberian governors had long clamored for it, particularly the governor general of the Amur District, who cited Chinese plans for the development of Amur River transportation. It was also known in St. Petersburg that the other great powers were advancing their lines of communication in the Far East; the Japanese were pushing designs for the economic development of the mainland nearest to their islands. Russia, obviously, could not remain

[38] Crisp, *Economic History Review,* VI, 165; see also Langer, *Franco-Russian Alliance,* p. 179.

[39] *Putevoditel' po velikoi Sibirskoi zheleznodoroge,* ed. A. I. Dimitriev-Mamontov and A. F. Zdziarskii, p. 60.

[40] *Ibid.,* for the background of policy planning for the Siberian railroad.

behind. But the decision always had to be deferred, because the treasury could not afford the costs. The seeming successes of Vyshnegradskii's skilled administration, however, encouraged the plunge into the venture. With the budget balanced and an active balance of trade, the time seemed ripe for the big job of linking the center of Russia with its Pacific coast. But just as the decision was announced for the start of the project, the famine broke out.

In this quandary Alexander III turned to a man who was intimately associated with Vyshnegradskii, formerly as head of the Railway Department in the Ministry of Finance, where he had been the moving spirit behind the planning of the Siberian railway project, and now since February, 1892, as minister of communications in charge of its construction. Rumormongers later whispered that this man—it was Sergei Witte—had intrigued at court against his friend and superior, suggesting that the Minister of Finance was a sick man incapable of continuing his responsible position in these difficult times. But Witte was already well known to the Emperor for his conspicuous ability, energy, and robust health. He could boast of a remarkable record of achievements; and in the summer of 1892 he was performing wonders in organizing the campaign against cholera along the Volga. That summer Vyshnegradskii's policy was discredited; a new "system" had to be tried. Thus in the aftermath of the great famine Vyshnegradskii, who indeed had suffered a minor stroke, retired with the familiar warning that the "paying powers of the population" were exhausted. Witte was appointed in his stead, the first genuine industrialist to hold that position. The journalist Prince Meshcherskii, who with all his faults was an intelligent observer of men, remarked that it was one of the great appointments of Alexander III.[41]

What could be a more demanding challenge to the new minister? The Russian national economy had just suffered a profound

[41] Meshcherskii, pp. 356 ff.

calamity. The condition of the peasants, who constituted the majority of the taxpayers, was deplorable. In some areas the arrears in redemption dues amounted to two or even three times the yearly payments; everywhere they were considerable. Trade and industry, though expanding, were underdeveloped in comparison with the great powers of western Europe. The finances of the state were inadequate for such great tasks ahead as the Siberian railroad. Above all, every known expedient, every "system" of previous ministers designed to strengthen Russian finances, had failed. But it was not Witte's nature to be discouraged. His first Most Respectful Budget Report outlined, in his labored and clumsy style, a program more comprehensive and, in the light of modern Russian history, more basic than any yet undertaken:[42]

The Minister makes bold to say that as a result of the special historical conditions of its political structure and development, fiscal policy in our fatherland cannot be contained in the strictly limited framework of the financial needs of the government, as they are traditionally understood. In the understanding of the Russian people the sincere conviction prevails that it is within the power of government authority to be concerned with everything touching the welfare and the needs of the people. In all cases of public misery, whenever it assumes considerable proportions, the people turn to the authority of the Tsar with their hopes and their trust. Considering the weak development of the habits of self-help among the population, the whole burden of coping with public misfortune falls inevitably upon the government.

The government, in other words, was fully responsible for the entire economy of Russia.

After having made this claim—a familiar one in Russian history from Peter the Great to Stalin—Witte outlined the policy which he meant to pursue.

Government thrift [he wrote with pointed reference to the parsimony of his predecessor] has its limits. Refusing justified claims upon government expenditure can inflict serious difficulties upon the normal development of the civil and economic life of the country. Our father-

[42] Quoted from *Russkiia vedomosti,* No. 2, 1893.

land overflows with all kinds of natural riches, but it has not yet utilized those riches to any degree desirable for the increase of its wealth. Financial policy should not fail to pay attention to the undesirable effects of excessive thrift in meeting the growing demands, but, on the contrary, should give reasonable assistance to the development of the productive forces of the country. Such a policy should show better results also in regard to government finance and raise not only the welfare of the population but also its paying powers and increase the sources of government revenue. In order to attain these ends *one must above all aim at removing the unfavorable conditions which cramp the economic development of the country and at kindling a healthy spirit of enterprise* in accordance with the natural conditions and demands of our national industries.

By these words the new Minister of Finance promised a redoubled effort to develop the natural riches of the country. This could best be done, under the conditions of these years, by expanding the railroads and heavy industry, in short, through industrialization. By doing so, he further asserted, he would also promote private initiative. The new wealth developed by the active entrepreneurs of Russia, so the prediction ran, would then find its way back into the treasury and relieve it of its chronic embarrassment.

In the history of Russian economic policy since the Crimean War—or, in fact, since Peter the Great—Witte's plan was the boldest yet. As it turned out, no tsarist minister of finance could boast a more rapid pace of industrial advance during his tenure of office. Witte even claimed in his *Memoirs* that he had laid the foundation of Russian national industries.[43] And, as his colleagues at the Ministry of Finance said of him on his tenth anniversary as minister, he felt his position to be that of "the executive director of the great economic corporation of the Russian people." [44]

[43] Witte, *Tsarstvovanie Nikolaia II,* I, 226.

[44] *S. J. Witte, 30. August 1892—30. August 1902. Ein Gedenkblatt zum 10 jährigen Minister-Jubiläum des russischen Finanzministers.*

2. The Making of a Tsarist Minister of Finance

I have never been led by anybody's advice or direction, but always relied on my own judgment and especially my own character. WITTE, Memoirs

This man knows what he wants and he will make a great career for himself as a statesman. BISMARCK TO MAXIMILIAN HARDEN

I

IT MAY NEVER be possible to bring the image of this unusual statesman of Imperial Russia—one of the giants in the succession from Peter the Great to Lenin—into precise historical focus. His early accomplishments and his successes as minister of finance were overshadowed by his later failure as chairman of the Council of Ministers in the Revolution of 1905; his political career was caught up in the impending collapse of Imperial Russia. His life and his work as a whole, furthermore, were all too quickly thrust into "the garbage pail of history" by the fall of the Imperial government and the Bolshevik Revolution. Even his own *Memoirs* do him scant justice. When between 1907 and 1912 he surveyed his life, his mind was embittered by the recent events and by the misunderstanding which he had encountered ever since he had entered the government. And when the time came for a second and more objective look at his work and plans, the Revolution swept away his friends and foes alike and buried in oblivion all his pleas and projects. In Russian history as viewed by the Bolsheviks, Lenin and Stalin, not Witte, were the originators of industrialization. So the Western biographer of Witte must re-

SERGEI WITTE AS MINISTER OF FINANCE

construct his career and his personality from lean and fallible sources.

There is no question, however, of his physical appearance as Imperial minister of finance. He was what in Germany would be called a *Sitzriese,* a man with a massive head, a long and heavy torso, and weak, oddly short legs.[1] At closer range he appeared more harmonious and dignified. An official photograph,[2] taken sometime before 1900, shows him dressed in a simple dark broadcloth suit—not in court uniform—in the prime of his life. He wore a well-trimmed beard in the style fashionable during the reign of Alexander III, and his hair, smooth and still full, was combed back from a prominent, unruffled forehead. His face had the serious expression of a man used to handling hard facts and able to master them. It betrayed both the arrogance and the humility of greatness, and the determination of a man who never spared himself. By his own testimony,[3] he had worked sixteen hours a day ever since he was a student.

Witte's qualities as a government official, at least in the early years of his career, might be viewed through the sympathetic impressions of Prince Meshcherskii.[4] This journalist had met Witte first in Vyshnegradskii's office and was much taken by Witte's qualities. He found it a pleasure to talk to the newcomer and observe his lively, original mind in action, with its precision, depth, and searching agility. At the same time, Meshcherskii discovered, Witte knew how to listen. He grasped at once what was meant and responded in a quiet, unbiased manner, charming his partner by the unexpectedness and novelty of his thought. In short, he captured Meshcherskii's heart by his modesty and impressed him by his energy, his quick decision, and his human accessibility. Yet Meshcherskii was not blind to Witte's imperfections. He admitted

[1] This description of Witte in Korostowetz, *Graf Witte,* p. 20.

[2] According to the portrait accompanying the official biography in *Ministerstvo Finansov, 1802–1902,* II, 323.

[3] Witte, *Vorlesungen über Volks- und Staatswirtschaft,* I, xxi.

[4] Meshcherskii, pp. 356 ff.

that Witte was a rough diamond, untrained in all but railroad matters. His French was poor, German he knew not at all, and, as the American minister to Russia, Andrew D. White, reported in 1893, he neither read nor spoke English.[5] He had tasted Western European literature only in a few translations; the visual arts and indeed European culture were largely unknown experiences to him; Russia stood very much in the foreground. To be sure, Meshcherskii judged from the fastidious point of view of a St. Petersburg cosmopolite. But he had put his finger on what was generally considered Witte's weak spot: he lacked polish and style.[6] Although of aristocratic upbringing, by training and outlook he was a big businessman; the rival orientations never fused in his personality. As a result he suffered, it became more obvious later, from a secret snobbishness which made him deprecate himself as a "plebeian" and yet crave titles and decorations. These flaws constituted a handicap in the official world of the capital and at court.

He was also barred by his industrial and commercial career from making an impression on the intelligentsia. Not that he was inarticulate. On the contrary, he could express himself, in a rough and ready manner, with remarkable vividness. His sensibilities, however, differed profoundly from those of "the thinking public" which determined Russian opinion, for his contributions to Russia's destiny were based on railway construction and economic promotion. He was, one might almost say, a man of the coming Russia which subordinated poetry to the five-year plan.

The career of Sergei Witte up to the time of his appointment as minister of finance was an unusual one, not so much in terms of social advancement as in the variety of experiences upon which it drew and the unexpected turns which it took. It was, in some ways, a running commentary upon the changes occurring in Russia after the Crimean War.

[5] Andrew D. White to John W. Foster, May 12, 1893, NA.

[6] See, for instance, Bülow's characterization in 1897: "ein hervorragend bedeutender Mann, aber macht nicht einen besonders angenehmen Eindruck auf den ersten Blick." *Grosse Politik,* XIII, 82.

Sergei Witte was born in 1849 in Tiflis. His father, Julius Witte, was then head of the agricultural department in the office of the governor general of the Caucasus. What exactly Julius Witte's background was, the son, whom his enemies later accused of being a "German," never told. In his *Memoirs* he merely stated that he came of a Dutch family settled in the Baltic provinces when the Swedes were still masters there.[7] The official biography added that the Wittes had acquired hereditary nobility in the province of Pskov,[8] but the Soviet archives reveal that this had officially taken place only six years after Sergei's birth.[9] The archives also show that Christoph Heinrich Georg Julius Witte—Iulii Fëdorovich to the Russians—was the son of Friedrich Wilhelm Witte and his wife Luise (nee Kramer) and was raised as a Lutheran. Friedrich Wilhelm Witte, who ended his career as chief forester in Kurland with the rank of titular councilor,[10] sent his son to Dorpat, the university of the Baltic Germans;[11] thereafter he went to Prussia for further instruction.

After his return the foreign-trained expert entered government service. In the early 1840s he managed a model state farm in the province of Saratov and in 1844 married the eldest daughter of

[7] Witte, *Detstvo,* p. 8.

[8] *Ministerstvo Finansov, 1802–1902,* II, 323.

[9] I am indebted for the details on Witte's paternal ancestry to the reference department of the Leningrad Public Library. They have traced in the files of the Leningrad branch of the Central State Historical Archives (TsGIA) the report of the Pskov Assembly of Noblemen to the Heraldry Department of the Senate. It states that the children and grandchildren of the titular *sovetnik* (councilor) Friedrich Witte had been inscribed into the third part of the Registry of Noblemen of Pskov province on December 21, 1855. This was confirmed by the Senate on January 31, 1856.

[10] The parentage and birth of Julius Witte are recorded in the Church Register of Friedrichstadt for 1814. The data on the career of Friedrich Witte are taken from his service records and the testimony of the Kurland provincial administration in 1854 that he was a Russian subject. All this from the Leningrad TsGIA.

[11] Witte, *Detstvo,* p. 1.

According to E. Seraphim, "Zar Nikolaus II und Graf Witte: Eine historisch-politische Studie," *Historische Zeitschrift,* No. 161 (1940), p. 279, the name of Julius Witte has not been found in the student directory of Dorpat University.

his chief, Andrei Mikhailovich Fadeev, the governor of Saratov.[12] "God blessed this marriage with family happiness," the father of the bride reminisced many years later.[13] The governor was soon transferred to an important post in the government of the Caucasus, and in 1847 Julius Witte, who had given up his Lutheran creed, followed him and became entirely absorbed with his own growing family in his father-in-law's palatial and old-fashioned household in Tiflis. Professionally the two men worked closely together,[14] Julius Witte eventually even succeeding to Fadeev's position. Both were, in modern parlance, colonial administrators bringing the Caucasus with its many and often barely subdued nationalities under Russian rule and beginning to develop the resources of that area. It fell to Julius Witte, for instance, to open up the manganese deposits at Chiaturi.

Sergei Witte thus was not educated in the manner of the Baltic Germans but grew up under the influence of his mother's family (where French was spoken) in the best tradition of the Russian service nobility. It was his maternal grandmother Elena Pavlovna who made the deepest impression upon him. Born a princess Dolgorukaia, she came from one of the oldest families in Russia. Among scientists she made a reputation for herself as an explorer of the Caucasus flora. Her children, too, achieved distinction. Andrei Mikhailovich's beloved son General Rostislav Fadeev, Sergei Witte's uncle, was a famous military hero, a bold, if erratic, spokesman of "Russian" views, anti-German, and a protagonist of Russian expansion to the Adriatic. One of his sisters achieved modest fame as a writer (and one of *her* daughters in turn became a well-known author of children's books). The other sister, Sergei Witte's aunt—how the family must have been shocked!—emerged as the international adventuress and theosophist Madame Blavatsky.

[12] Fadeev, Part I, p. 182.
[13] *Ibid.*
[14] *Ibid.,* Part II, pp. 170, 203, 207.

But there was merit also on Julius Witte's side of the family. His brother was a member of the Senate, the chief judicial body of the Empire. In 1866 he occupied an important post as head of the Warsaw school district. On both sides of his family, in short, Sergei Witte came from a respectable segment of Russian society, although his mother's family outranked his father's. Julius Witte's own family, in turn, maintained that position of respectability. One son, Alexander, served as major in the army before his premature death. Another son, Boris ("who did not distinguish himself," in the opinion of Sergei),[15] eventually became president of the Odessa district court. The third, Sergei, became Real Privy State Councilor—to give his full title—and finally even a count. The two girls in the family remained single and lived modestly in Odessa, suffering in later years from consumption.

Among the Fadeevs, Sergei Witte spent a happy childhood. He grew up in an affectionate, if somewhat casual, household in which the bustle of public affairs, a sense of duty and professional integrity, and the amiability of the Russian character were happily combined. The family were united in their deep loyalty to the Tsar and to the Orthodox Church. His father's and grandfather's work was inspired by a belief in Russia's destiny.

A further element proved an advantage to the young Sergei, the frontier character of the Caucasus. Witte's personality was formed out of reach of the restraints and doctrinaire prejudices of the capital. To judge from his *Memoirs*,[16] in the Caucasus the frontier spirit was still strong. What mattered were not nationality, race, or cultural refinement, but character, vitality, and the innate force of personality. The bane of compulsory Russification had not yet been introduced; tolerance and friendly assimilation prevailed, symbolized by the appointment, after the end of the long wars with the Caucasus tribes, of their leader Shamil's son to the Tsar's suite. Witte always remembered his childhood in the Caucasus with

[15] Witte, *Detstvo,* p. 13.

[16] *Ibid.,* Chap. III.

pleasure. The freedom of the frontier suited his expansive personality. But by his own admission, his formal education in Tiflis left much to be desired.

When he reached the age of sixteen, Sergei Witte's life suddenly began in earnest. He and his older brother Boris were sent to Odessa to study at the Novorossiisk University. It turned out that their preparation was insufficient for admission. Now Sergei Witte had to show his mettle. Many years later he wrote in his *Memoirs*: "Then for the first time dawned on me the special character which has guided me all through my life, so that up to the present time I have never been led by anybody's advice or direction, but always relied on my own judgment and especially my own character."[17] His early self-reliance bore fruit. With his brother he withdrew for a year to the neighboring town of Kishinev, where they knew no one, and studied diligently at the local *gimnaziia.* It was there that Witte discovered his talent for mathematics, which was his chief subject when he finally entered the Novorossiisk University.

The years of study in Odessa were not easy ones for him. His father and grandfather died within a short time of each other, leaving the family deep in debt from the failure of the Chiaturi mines. His mother dissolved the Tiflis household and moved with her children to Odessa, living in rather reduced circumstances. But the turn of fortune did not diminish Sergei Witte's intellectual vigor. His dissertation on infinitesimal numbers—an odd topic for a future minister of finance who pushed the state budget into the billions—was translated into French and would have received, its author stated later,[18] a gold medal had he not just then pursued the charms of an actress. After his academic success he even contemplated a university career. But the Fadeevs told him that a professorship was unbecoming to a nobleman. Instead, on the advice of the minister of communications, Count Bobrinskii, who was

[17] *Ibid.,* p. 54.
[18] *Ibid.,* p. 59.

a friend of the family, he chose railway administration. The Minister's counsel was a wise one; the engineers, who held the chief positions during the period of railroad construction, were inept managers of the lines after they were built. Now men were needed with business experience, administrators familiar with finance and economic theory.

Thanks to his mother's connections, Witte started at a comfortable salary, first as titular councilor (the ninth *chin*) in the chancellery of the governor general of Odessa and Bessarabia (1871–74), and later in the Odessa office of the Ministry of Communications, studying railroad administration in the Odessa State Railway.[19] In 1877, when under Reutern's policy all state railroads were transferred to private ownership, he shifted entirely to private employment. Wherever he served, he went about his job with creditable thoroughness. From the start he was caught up in the bourgeois discipline of professional life. The sobering effect of his family's poverty left him no choice. Thus he escaped the romantic lures of the country estate or the social ambitions (and distractions) of the capital, which spoiled so many of his contemporaries in high stations.

He could truly claim that he knew railroading from the bottom up, for he had started in the ticket office and worked his way from there. Soon he was supervisor of the traffic office. During the Turkish War, he wrote later, he was practically the sole manager of the Odessa Railway, through which all the traffic to the front was passing. And he boasted that, in a transportation crisis, he had worked out a satisfactory train schedule, letting the locomotives be run by a double shift of engineers in order to keep the traffic moving. He succeeded, he wrote in his *Memoirs*, because he "was young, decisive, and of firm character." [20] But in his position he had also to take the blame for a frightful accident in which more than a hundred soldiers were killed. The jail term to which he was

[19] *Ibid.*, pp. 76 ff.
[20] *Ibid.*, p. 92.

sentenced, however, was suspended during the war, as his services proved indispensable, and was afterwards quashed by Alexander II. Alexander III, on the other hand, would not hear of such clemency and made Witte serve his term, in a mild yet irritating form, while he was in St. Petersburg on business.

It would be wrong, however, to consider Witte in these years merely an expert railway administrator. His personality called for involvement on the larger stage of public affairs, in the debate of public issues. In his tastes and convictions Witte was by no means a doctrinaire conservative, and under the influence of his environment he was becoming more broad-minded. Odessa, although not yet a hundred years old, was the third city of Russia and the fastest growing of all, with a population of over 200,000 (by 1894, 350,000). The chief export harbor for Russian grain, unencumbered by tradition, thoroughly capitalist in outlook, a melting pot of skills and races, it offered unusual opportunities despite the corruption in the city administration. In all of Russia no more receptive entrepôt for Western ideas and institutions could be found.[21] It also possessed a large Jewish community led by a cultured elite, some of whom had adopted the Russian Orthodox faith.

As a student Witte served as tutor in the house of the Raffaloviches, an influential banking family, whose close friend he remained in after years. Odessa also boasted what most other Russian cities lacked, a lively press and an active public life. Here an ambitious young official could be well apprenticed to the ways of modern capitalist society.

Witte prospered in this setting; after the Caucasus he called Odessa his second fatherland.[22] He owed much to the friendly give-and-take of able men from various fields and was not afraid to stand by those who were politically suspect. He had his friends at

[21] See the article on "Odessa" in Brockhaus-Efron, *Entsiklopedicheskii slovar'*, and the characterization by the sociologist Iuzhakov in his column "Khronika vnutrennei zhizni," *Russkoe bogatstvo,* September, 1894.

[22] A. E. Kaufman, "Cherty iz zhizni grafa S. Iu. Vitte," *Istoricheskii vestnik,* CXL (April, 1915), 222.

the university, in business, in the press. He particularly cultivated the company of newspapermen; on occasion he himself turned journalist and author.[23] Nature had given him an expansive curiosity about people and a good memory for personalities; he prided himself on being a perceptive judge of men. Eventually, in recognition of his popularity, he was elected an Honorary Justice of the Peace in his city.[24] As minister of finance two decades later he was even made an honorary citizen and had a street named after him.[25]

After the Turkish War, Witte's activities expanded with the growth of the Russian economy. In 1877 the state, in one of the last applications of Reutern's policy, had sold the Odessa Railway to one of the railroad kings of the age, Jan Bloch, who subsequently combined it with a number of others into the Southwestern Railway Company. This network served the western Ukraine and Poland from the Baltic to the Black Sea, with links into Germany and Austria-Hungary. Thus Witte advanced into big business, becoming associated with the railroad kings, those self-made men who since the ukase of 1857 had done so much for the development of Russian railroads (and their own fortunes). Through them he made the acquaintance of Russian bankers and their associates abroad. Witte was impressed by these men and for good reason.[26] His own boss, Jan Bloch, had started as a petty Jewish railroad official in Poland. With his first earnings he had gone to study at a German university, then married the daughter of a banker (a beauty, it was said), turned Catholic for respectability, and with his father-in-law's resources kept a lavish house and widened his banking contacts. From finance he advanced into railroads, buying up the stock of the three major lines which went into the Southwestern system. He picked able men to run the railway for him. Vyshnegradskii, already a high-ranking *chinovnik*, was his director

[23] *Ibid.*, p. 228.

[24] *Ministerstvo Finansov, 1802–1902,* II, 325.

[25] Kaufman, *Istoricheskii vestnik,* CXL, 222.

[26] Witte, *Detstvo,* pp. 98 ff.

in St. Petersburg; Witte became his business manager and eventually (in 1886) his executive director, with a large salary and an office in Kiev. In his later years Bloch turned to a still bigger task (where for once he proved unsuccessful)—the prevention of war.

Perhaps even more remarkable was Lazar Solomonovich Poliakov, who, after a start as a small postmaster in southern Russia, established a veritable dynasty of financiers and industrialists which played a role among the Moscow *kupechestvo*. A third railroad magnate, Von Derviz, was the schoolmate of Reutern and for that reason, it was whispered, received the concession for the profitable Moscow-Riazan-Koslov railroad. In later years he spent all his money in Italy, keeping a court and a large opera company for his own amusement. These and other great entrepreneurs of that time like Von Meck, Gubonin, and Kokorev—the last two were former peasants who had bought themselves out of serfdom—were fully conscious of their importance. But they hardly fitted into the hierarchy of Russian society. After a big court reception, according to an anecdote in Witte's *Memoirs* which illustrated the proud airs of the railroad kings,[27] the grand dukes, generals, and ministers waited for the special train which was to take them back to St. Petersburg. To their surprise, however, Mr. Polovtsov, the director of the Main Company, had his private train pulled in first and left triumphantly ahead of the assembled dignitaries. Alexander III was shocked. But, Witte conceded, these were big men, shrewd, with a touch of cunning. And in their company he acquired the ways of a magnate himself. Always the moving spirit in whatever he undertook, he sometimes succumbed to the tycoon's fallacy that everything that happened under his jurisdiction was due solely to himself. It was rather surprising that he preserved for so long an innate humility.

He had reason to be proud. While he was its manager, he put the Southwestern system on its feet and made it one of the most

[27] *Ibid.*, p. 352.

profitable railroads in Russia. He did so despite constant quarrels with the Ministry of Communications, which, until Vyshnegradskii was appointed minister of finance, consistently refused to confirm Witte's position. According to the Ministry of Communications, where the engineers had a monopoly, only engineers knew how to operate railroads and Witte was not an engineer. He was not depressed, however, by their contempt; the engineers obviously failed to make the railroads pay for themselves, while he was a master of railroad economy and a down-to-earth business executive.[82] He deliberately attracted freight by opening a commercial agency to solicit potential shippers and by granting loans on grain in transit. He learned that a railroad could not be prosperous without prosperous customers, and tried to increase the prosperity of the areas which his road served. Among railroad men he acquired the reputation of being a *praktik*, a man with a practical bent of mind, because of his unorthodox but effective measures. In search of sound information, he was the first to introduce accurate railway statistics, and it was said that through his secret intelligence system he knew more about other railroads than their own managers. His greatest contribution, however, a result of his combining mathematics with economic theory, was the design of an effective freight tariff. Here lay the crux of his success as a railroad manager. Because of this innovation he was able to lower the freight rates on his line and to increase its revenue, nearly doubling the value of its assets.[29]

For this work he assembled a group of able assistants, Jews, Poles, Russians, some of whom he even sent to Germany for further training. By all accounts he was an admirable boss who gave his subordinates a free hand regardless of their origin.[30] Like Odessa, the Ukraine was a melting pot of races, creeds, and nationalities. It offered much opportunity for ability, and in the economic ad-

[28] V. V. Maksimov, quoted in B. B. Glinskii, "Graf S. Iu. Vitte (Materialy dlia biografii)," *Istoricheskii vestnik,* CXL (April, 1915), 239.

[29] *Ibid.,* p. 237.

[30] V. I. Kovalevskii, *ibid.,* p. 256.

vance the benefits of toleration, expert knowledge, and good human relations were abundantly demonstrated. Thus through his many local ties Witte, in the happiest years of his life, became a man of the western Ukraine, even in the peculiarities of his speech.[31] It is not surprising that he was spoken of as a liberal influence in Kiev.

And yet, even in these years Witte was more than a successful director of a prosperous private railroad. Since childhood the government point of view was deeply ingrained in his personality. Considering his qualities and his career, it was inevitable that he should be invited to participate in the formulation of government policy on railroad affairs. As stated in the previous chapter, after the Turkish War the government changed its attitude in regard to railway ownership. When the Baranov Commission, of which Witte was a member, had made its investigation, the Ministry of Finance bought back some lines and began to construct others under its own management. And it took a further step toward government control over all railroads by the imposition of a unified freight schedule upon the many separate and mostly unprofitable lines. As Witte had already proved in his own road, the secret of profitable railway management lay in the structure of the freight tariffs. Through the Baranov Commission (and not through the Ministry of Communications, which had shown no aptitude for such matters) he now applied this principle to the entire rail network of Russia. Before this could be accomplished, however, the government had to acquire the proper legal powers. And so the Baranov Commission also drafted a model statute for Russian railways.[32]

From membership in the Baranov Commission, which was disbanded late in 1884, it was a logical advance for Witte to step into the Ministry of Finance. In 1889 Vyshnegradskii invited Witte to create a Railway Department in his ministry, which would supervise the application of the new unified tariff and manipulate it according to the needs of Russian economy as a whole. Reluctantly,

[31] *Ibid.*, p. 255.
[32] Witte, *Detstvo,* p. 164.

and only on the Emperor's special urging, Witte accepted the offer.

For a complete measure of Witte's stature at that time, however, one has still to consider two more dimensions of the man, first, his almost fanatical loyalty to autocracy (although not necessarily to the current policies of the government) and, second, his deep interest in the theories of political economy. The first took an almost ludicrous turn immediately after the assassination of Alexander II.[33] Under the impact of the news Witte wrote to his uncle Rostislav Fadeev in St. Petersburg proposing the organization of a secret society of counterrevolutionaries called, in a touch of romantic medievalism, the Holy Druzhina (Brotherhood). The idea caught on at Court, and Witte, according to his *Memoirs*, was sent to Paris to spy on an agent who had been ordered to kill one of the plotters against the Tsar's life. If this agent did not kill the would-be assassin, Witte was to kill the agent. At the last moment the government called off the fantastic plot, and Witte, disgusted with his assignment, resigned from the Holy Druzhina and returned to railroads. The adventure cured him of any sympathy with underground police work, but it showed his headstrong devotion to the autocrat. This zeal went to the core of the man, too deep to be dislodged or diminished by the force of reason.

Later, in his position as railroad manager at Kiev, he had occasion again to show his loyalty.[34] In his official capacity he accompanied the Imperial train whenever it passed through his network, as it frequently did, for the Southwestern Railway connected the capitals, St. Petersburg and Moscow, with the Imperial palace at Yalta. He himself has told how during these trips he sat up all night with Alexander III's valet, who mended the Imperial clothes, questioning him about his master. Once he even

[33] *Ibid.,* p. 112. See also Witte's account of the episode as he told it to the Countess Kleinmichel, *Memoirs of a Shipwrecked World* (New York, 1923), Chap. XX. For a modern analysis of the Holy Druzhina see S. Lukashevich, "The Holy Brotherhood: 1881–1883," *ASEER,* Vol. XVIII, No. 4.

[34] *Detstvo,* p. 172.

clashed with the Tsar, insisting, contrary to the regulations of the Ministry of Communications, that the Imperial train proceed slowly over the light roadbed of this "Jew road," as Alexander III was pleased to call the Southwestern system. But when in 1888 as a result of undue speed on this road the Emperor was involved in a serious wreck, he recalled Witte's blunt remark that it was better to sacrifice speed than the life of the Emperor.

II

It was in the other dimension, Witte's preoccupation with economic theory, that he gave the most convincing proof of his ambition and abilities, and of his advancing vision. Even more, he revealed the inner uncertainty with which he, one of Russia's leading railroad men, faced the penetration of industry and of "capitalism" in general into his fatherland.

His first book, *Principles of Railway Freight Tariffs,* published in 1883, was primarily a technical treatise dealing with his specialty. He was justly proud of its professional excellence; his knowledge of mathematics was bearing fruit. But his work also carried a broader message. In the second edition, printed the following year, he undertook, in the manner of the economic speculation current among the intelligentsia, a discursive but highly characteristic analysis of prevailing economic theories and their application to Russia.[35] He confessed here that he had based his tables of freight tariffs on the laws of supply and demand as evolved by English classical economy; they could not be disregarded in his world of efficiency and profit. But what should he make of the critics of classical economy who now led the contemporary discussion? He surveyed the views of the famous German scholars of the time, Rodbertus, Schmoller, Adolf Wagner, and Karl Marx, and could not conceal his sympathy. But all these schools of thought left him still dissatisfied. His chief motive in this consideration was patriotic. In the conflict of ideologies, which

[35] Witte, *Printsip zheleznodorozhnykh tarifov no perevozke gruzov,* pp. 107 ff.

school of thought should Russia follow? Russia under Alexander II had been in tow of the classical school and, Witte acknowledged, had derived some benefits from it. But there had also been "ulcers," because that school of thought was not sufficiently adapted to Russian conditions; foreign trade, the currency, industry, and the population as a whole had suffered. These ulcers then brought about a reaction against the Manchester doctrines. What was needed now was an adaptation of economic doctrines to Russian realities.

What was that proper Russian doctrine? According to Witte, the Russian critics of the Manchester school answered, oddly enough: imitation of Bismarck. But Witte himself was not so easily satisfied. Bismarck's solutions—Witte was thinking of the antisocialist law and the social insurance legislation—were applicable only under the historic conditions of Germany. The Russian doctrine—and here Witte's thinking was as erratic as the path of a housefly—must be based on the foundations of Russian life, upon Faith. As long as the Orthodox faith lasted, so Witte asserted, Western socialism, an evil doctrine, would gain no foothold in Russia. But there was, on the other hand, a legitimate Russian type of socialism, based on man's inner perfection and the imitation of Christ. It had no political, no outward, form. But—and Witte did not seem troubled by the obvious contradiction—spiritual rebirth was also reflected in economic institutions. Perhaps Christianity could, if not abolish, at least limit poverty. The teachings of Christ gave the power of love to the powerless and a heightened sense of social morality to the upper classes. The latter should set an example of simplicity, devotion to work, and justice; they should take the leadership in social improvement, teach thrift, self-reliance, and a puritan concern for the common good. Morals, in other words, must soften the harsh laws of economic life (which apparently were not superseded even by Russian socialism).

The Orthodox faith, Witte further proclaimed, encouraged public life far more than the new German doctrines of state interference, toward which he was rather cool. The remedy for the economic ills of Russia would lie above all, he concluded, in revitalizing the Church. But would this remedy be adopted?

If things are left as they now are, then the conditions which created Western socialism could indeed arise also in Russia. Thus a Bismarck who wanted to set Russia aright would arouse an active and live Russian Church, which would deal with all aspects of national life in the spirit of life and freedom, not of compulsion, in a spirit which in turn would influence the world and assure an equal distribution of the population of Russia upon her vast lands.[36]

Then, in a sudden inspiration of Jeffersonianism, Witte demanded that the land be made available to all, and all be made free through landownership: "A wide distribution of property is the best guarantee against militant socialism." What Russia needed, in short, was a democratic agricultural regime like Switzerland's or Norway's. With a still further lurch of his train of thought he concluded that Bismarck had a devoted and idealistic bureaucracy to carry out his work. But Russia, of course, had something still better than an admirable civil service—the abundant powers of nature. He did not say what he meant by that, but returned to his previous thought. A bureaucracy of the German type did not exist in Russia. The large population and the great distances, Witte argued, would make the creation of such an organization very difficult.

The subsequent discussion of state socialism seemed, by contrast, more down-to-earth, largely because it touched upon a concrete problem of Witte's profession. Should the Russian railways be nationalized, and did state management of the railroads constitute state socialism? Bismarck, after all, had nationalized the German railways and had toyed with socialist ideas; and even Gladstone had supported state interference in the insurance business. Thus state intervention was nothing new, Witte conceded; yet it might lead to economic absolutism. How far such interference would go

[36] *Ibid.*, p. 130.

was again a matter of national tradition. In the United States the spirit of enterprise and intellectual curiosity was part of the historic heritage; individual initiative, therefore, could be given free rein. In Russia, on the other hand, faith prevailed and the material welfare of the individual was neglected (this was at last a more realistic estimate of Russian conditions, although not easily reconciled with his previous call for a Russian socialism based on the Orthodox faith). But Witte did not wish a sudden conversion of all railways to state ownership; the transition had to come slowly.

What now, after this ramble through the lofty mansions of theory, were Witte's concrete suggestions? Indeed, he had none. Yet as to the need for a Russian theory of economic development he left no doubt:

> As long as Russian life does not evolve a national economic system of its own based upon the unique conditions of the Russian scene, we shall waver between the various economic theories of the day, and follow one today and another tomorrow; we shall hear from the same mouths logically incompatible economic theories and projects. What we created yesterday will be useless tomorrow, and today we recreate what was destroyed yesterday. It is understandable, therefore, why we have no orderly economic life but follow in the tow of foreign ideas and of various speculative notions at the expense of the national welfare.[37]

What is one to make of all these vapid and often pointless ideas, coming from a man trained in mathematics and the concrete world of business? The bizarre zigzag of his inconclusive and vague assertions may be ascribed to a businessman's clumsiness with abstract questions of basic policy or even philosophy. But may it not equally well have stemmed from the fact that Witte and his generation were not thoroughly at home in the new industrial and capitalist era? The confusion of ideas was not entirely their fault. It was inherent in the Russian situation. The country was adrift in the new world of Western capitalism; it was desperately search-

[37] *Ibid.*, p. 132.

ing for a firm mooring of meaning and purpose in its new economic activities. It needed an ideological link between its tradition and the new technology. Men like Bloch, Vyshnegradskii, and Witte were trying to hitch Russia to the Western pattern of economic growth, but inwardly no one in that generation had yet made his peace with the new forces. Witte himself had not found the vital link between his job as a railroad manager on the one hand and, on the other, the basic requirements of Russian national economy and what he felt, however vaguely, to be his country's destiny.

An article which Witte contributed to the Slavophile periodical *Russ* (Rus') in 1885 gave a further glimpse of his ideas as they were gradually sobering and hardening into workable shape.[38] It was entitled "Manufacturing Serfdom" and dealt more specifically with the controversy between free traders and protectionists, which had moved into the foreground as Bunge raised the tariff and developed Russian factory legislation. Protectionism was on the rise, Witte asserted; imports were declining and Russian production expanding. Thus Russia was facing a stage of development which had already been passed by the Western countries. Under the rising tariff protection she was being transformed from a purely agrarian state into one which combined industry and agriculture. In these circumstances it was the government's responsibility to avoid, or at least to tone down, the frightful miseries which had accompanied that transition in the West.

But unfortunately, Witte thought, in their desire to increase their wealth even the Russian people did not pay sufficient attention to those maladies. As a warning he described how under the sway of Adam Smith's doctrines labor had been viewed as an abstraction and the individual worker forgotten. To be sure, he added, freedom of competition had resulted in an advance of industry far beyond all expectations. But it had also created a

[38] Reprinted as a reproach by *Russkii trud* under the heading "Fourteen Years Ago" (No. 42 [1899], pp. 10 ff.) at a time when Witte held very different views.

proletariat torn from the land, living from day to day, thoughtless automatons. The destructive mentality of these robots had already been turned against the very foundations of Europe. Now Russia was facing the same gloomy prospects. "Will not the necessity of increasing the abstract 'wealth of the country' through the development of Russian industry lead up to the breakup of our immemorial social order and the transformation of at least part of the Russian people into factory automatons, unhappy slaves of capital and the machine?" [39] The question showed that Witte was fully aware of the contrast between the new industrial order and the mentality of the Russian peasants. The Russian people, he asserted, were above all agrarian; they loved the land and despised work in the mills. Their spiritual essence was intimately tied to the "beautiful, exalted, and ennobling work on the soil."

The railroad promoter turned Slavophile thus accepted the common assumption of the Russian intelligentsia that Western capitalism degraded human beings. He cited—in good Marxist fashion—a Dr. Aiken on the evils of Lancaster child labor in order to drive home his point. Russian industry, by contrast, was to take a different line of development. It was to center around the production of consumer goods, processing agricultural products, and helping Russian agriculture. The orientation was thus toward economic autonomy. Dependence on foreign raw materials was evil, export was uncertain, and foreign trade did not sufficiently stimulate the exploitation of Russia's natural wealth. It was in just these tremendous natural resources that Russia's superiority over other countries lay. The workers, therefore, were to stay close to the soil. The *kustar'* industries, which combined agriculture with the crafts, were to be strengthened, and the opportunity for work on the land was always to be reserved for the children of workers. Labor legislation was to protect the health of women and children and provide security against accidents. But, above all, the spiritual needs of the workers demanded attention. Church holidays were to

[39] *Ibid.,* p. 11.

be duly observed. Thus a barrier was to be raised against the materialism of Western socialism. And in order to buttress his conclusions for this thoroughly Russian path of development Witte quoted from a novel by Eugène Sue, the Frenchman!

One can see from this article how closely at this stage his thought (except perhaps for the conservative emphasis upon the Church) paralleled that of the Russian intelligentsia. Unquestionably the moral approach to the questions of economic development (which also endeared Marx to the Russians) was a spontaneous one in Russia. The deep moral undercurrents of Russian life springing from the medieval mold of Muscovy flowed through Witte's mind. But how could he relate them to the surface of Russian life, to the new world of railroads and profits?

Inevitably the lure lay in the new order. Witte's next work, a lengthy pamphlet on Friedrich List, published in 1889, the year in which he entered the government, showed the direction in which he and Russia were traveling. In the writings of the German economist Witte at last found a basis for a Russian system of economic development; it remained the foundation for his thought and action thereafter.

Friedrich List, who had died in 1846, had contributed to Russian economic development more than a generation later the most significant ideology of Russian modernization prior to Leninism. Whether in the light of modern analysis List was right or not does not matter. What counts was that in the 1880s he offered the only suitable prescription for solving Russia's economic and financial problems, and in formulations highly convenient to the Ministry of Finance. At the same time he held out a long-range perspective of economic development tailored to Russian political ambition. In his book *The National System of Political Economy*, published in 1841,[40] List set forth a vision of European, and indirectly of global, economic development which gave hope to Rus-

[40] Here cited from the American translation by G. A. Matile (Philadelphia, 1856).

sia that, with proper policy, she could eventually equal the most civilized countries of western Europe. For List was far more than the spokesman for German liberalism and nationalism; he was a prophet of the ambitions of all underdeveloped countries. His views, therefore, are basic for an understanding of Witte and even of Soviet industrialization.

List was a prophet because he himself had keenly felt the sense of inferiority compounded of admiration and jealousy which is the natural reaction of the "backward" countries toward those nations that stand out as the leaders of their age. All his life he had worked under the shadow of Great Britain. England to him, indeed, was the model nation par excellence.

> Far from having been stopped in its progress by England [so List wrote], the world has received from her its strongest impulse. She has served as a model to all nations in her internal and external policy; in her great inventions and grand enterprises of every kind; in the advancement of the useful arts; in the construction of roads, railways and canals; in the discovery and cultivation of lands in a state of nature, particularly in displaying and developing the natural wealth of tropical countries, and in the civilization of tribes, savage or subsiding into barbarism. Who can tell how far behind the world would have been if there had been no England? [41]

He was particularly impressed by the triumphs of British industry, "a study of which should precede the construction of systems, or the giving of advice to statesmen who hold in their hands the destiny of nations." [42]

List, like other spokesmen of backward countries after him, was obsessed by the fear that his people might fall back in the race for progress. "The more rapidly the genius of discovery and industrial improvement as well as of social and political progress advances, the more rapidly is the distance between stationary nations and those which are progressive increased, and the greater is the

[41] *Ibid.*, p. 437.
[42] *Ibid.*, p. 114.

peril of remaining behind."[43] "The peril of remaining behind," the fear of political defeat through economic backwardness—here lay the driving power for an intense national effort to catch up. *The National System of Political Economy*, a refutation of the cosmopolitan system of the English classical economists and the substitution of a national system for it, was a plea for an accelerated pace of economic development for the backward countries.

It is only fair to add that in List's ideal the economy remained balanced between agriculture, trade, and industry. Yet it was industry that set the pace. There never was a more inspired paean to urban-industrial civilization than Chapter Seven, Book II, of the *National System*: "Of Manufacturing Industry and of the Personal, Social, and Political Productive Forces or Powers of a Country." A rural society shows, one reads there, "slowness of apprehension, bodily inactivity, adherence to old ideas, old processes, old usages, old habits, a defective education, with lack of comfort and personal liberty." Trade and industry, on the other hand, stimulate "the desire for a continual increase of moral and material wealth, emulation, and a love of liberty." Here indeed was first spelled out what Marx a few years later in the *Communist Manifesto* called "the idiocy of rural life." Urban man, on the other hand, "is incessantly buying and selling, exchanging and negotiating. He is everywhere in collision with men, with laws and institutions; and he is kept at all times on the alert by changing circumstances; he has a hundred-fold more occasion to exert his mind than the peasant." Further on one reads: "The well-known fact, that among manufacturers time has an incomparably greater value than among farmers, testifies to a higher estimation of labor. The degree of civilization of a people and the estimate they fix upon labor cannot be better measured than by the value they set upon time." In the city, List continued, "the law of the division of labor and the association of productive power brings manufacturers together with an irresistible influence. The collision

[43] *Ibid.*, p. 61.

of minds emits sparks of intelligence, as the smitten flint emits fire. There is no intellectual friction but where men are brought together."

But enough of these panegyrics. According to List, liberty, civilization, national power, in short, the highest goals of contemporary mankind, flowed from urban-industrial life as exemplified by England. In other words, through industrialization the backward could catch up with England. Thus List fused nationalism and industrialization in an ironbound combination more fitting to the twentieth than to the nineteenth century.

But there was even more for Witte in List's book, for it dealt also with the special problems arising out of the economic relations between a predominantly agricultural country and a highly industrialized one. During his residence in Pennsylvania, List had gained some insight into the penalties of economic inferiority. The prosperity of the United States, he and his American fellow protectionists had felt, was at the mercy of the British. From Witte's perspective, List's account of his American experience applied to Russia as well, a Russia heavily indebted to Germany and France, depending for her well-being on her exports of grain to a highly competitive market with disastrously falling prices, and her credit triply undermined by her debts, her uncertain exports, and her paper money. List's categorical remedy for all these problems was more national industry. Industry would restore the balance of trade, which he, in contrast to the free traders, again justified as a government concern. It would reduce the country's dependence on foreign markets and on foreign producers, strengthen her agriculture, stabilize the currency, and civilize the country as a whole. Industrialization, in short, was the panacea for all the economic ills of Russia with which the ministers of finance had so vainly tried to cope.

In 1889 the *National System* was of particular relevance in Russia, for it supplied the Russian protectionists with an ample supply of arguments proving that agriculture would prosper as a result of industrial expansion. The growing urban population would supply a more reliable domestic market, land values would rise, farming methods would be perfected, crops would increase—even the rural population stood to gain from tariff protection. In the face of the growing opposition of the agrarian interests to the tariff, Friedrich List was an invaluable ally.

Finally, it was significant that embedded in List's pleas was a rudimentary theory of economic development for underdeveloped countries.

> Production renders consumption possible, and the desire of consuming excites production. A purely agricultural country depends for its consumption on the condition of foreign countries, and when that is not favorable to it, the production excited by the desire of consuming ceases. But in a nation uniting in its territory both manufacturing and agricultural industry, their reciprocal existing influence does not cease and the increase of production proceeds on both sides, and so also of capital.[44]

In others words, industrialization (or "capitalism," as the Russian intelligentsia called it) created its own markets. As for the order of priority among industries that were to be promoted, List placed "the industries of luxury" last and machine-building industries, the "manufactures of manufacturies," first. The latter indeed had "very special claims upon the direct favor of the State."[45] He also warned that the effort to promote industrial expansion would entail sacrifice and privation of material riches; present advantages had to be exchanged for future benefits.[46] Yet while these blueprints of economic development were rather blurred, the driving ambition which prompted their subsequent elaboration was clear enough:

> Poor, weak, and uncivilized countries have not infrequently attained power and wealth by a judicious commercial system, whilst others have

[44] *Ibid.*, p. 314.
[45] *Ibid.*, p. 392.
[46] *Ibid.*, p. 223.

sunk from a high rank for want of such a system; nations have even lost their independence and their political existence because their commercial policy had not aided the development and the consolidation of their nationality."

Yet there was one profound catch to the application of Friedrich List's theory to Russian realities, as will appear from List's specific advice to Russia:

The want of civilization and proper political institutions may prove a great obstacle to the advance of Russia in industry and commerce, unless the Imperial government should succeed in advancing general civilization in accordance with the claims of industry by establishing good municipal and provincial organizations, by first regulating and then completely abolishing all servitude, by improving the methods of interior communication, and finally by facilitating the means of transportation to Asia. Such are the measures which Russia has to accomplish within this century, such is the condition of her further progress in agriculture, manufacturing, industry, as well as in commerce, mercantile navigation, and naval power. But that such reforms may be possible, that they may be accomplished, it is necessary that the Russian nobility comprehend that their material government interests are closely connected with them.[47]

By 1889 serfdom had been abolished, new municipal and provincial organizations established; the government was improving the methods of interior communication. But these reforms hardly sufficed. The burden of List's thinking was that "nations in the enjoyment of a good constitutional government succeed better than others in industry, commerce and navigation." [48] According to the English model, liberty was a prerequisite of industrial progress. In Russia on the other hand, liberty was signally absent. Nor did the Russian ruling class wholeheartedly embrace industrialization and modernization. Friedrich List, as a liberal, took over the English model in its totality. Empire, parliamentary constitution, industrialization, religious toleration—these qualities

[47] *Ibid.*, p. 163.
[48] *Ibid.*, p. 374.

constituted civilization itself. All this was far more than Witte could offer.

His pamphlet *A Propos of Nationalism: National Economy and Friedrich List*,[49] published before the first Russian translation of List's book, was little more than a string of suitable quotations from *The National System of Political Economy* adjusted, with the help of a few comments, to fit Russian conditions. In his preface Witte praised List as the prophet of Germany's present greatness, saying that his book was read in all German universities, that it lay on Bismarck's table. It ought also to lie, he preached, on the table of every Russian statesman and be read in Russian universities so that in future Russia could follow a consistent commercial system. In introducing the author he stressed List's activities as a railway promoter and industrialist and a man of practical affairs, but also the fact that as a prophet in his own country he had won little honor in his lifetime. From List, Witte moved on to Bismarck, who again was cited as a paragon of enlightened statecraft. Bismarck had followed up his Sedan, Witte wrote, by an industrial Sedan; after unification Germany had become a powerful industrial nation. In Russia, unfortunately, Witte mused, nothing of that sort was ever done; no political victory was followed up by an industrial advance.[50]

In all Witte's comments one will not find a word of List's liberalism nor of the larger social and political implications to Russia of his advice. All the reader would gather from Witte's brochure was that industrial development fostered by a protective tariff would advance civilization in Russia also. But he was warmly directed to consult List himself. One wonders whether List's Russian readers realized that the ideal of industrialization carried with it, in tiny seeds, the ideals of constitutional government and liberty. With Witte these seeds seemingly fell on barren ground. He

[49] Witte, *Po povodu natsionalizma: Natsional'naia ekonomiia i Fridrikh List*. According to a footnote on p. 16, the first Russian translation of List's work, by K. V. Trubnikov, did not appear until 1891.

[50] *Ibid.*, p. 18.

never ceased to assume that the economic factors of industrial growth could be lifted unharmed from the surrounding social and political tissues and be made to succor autocracy.

After 1889 Witte was won over to List's doctrines. In his search for the proper theory of Russian national economy he had at last found a suitable ideological bridge linking Western and native conditions; it did not bother him that the theory had been devised by a German. In contrast to his earlier opinions, it was specific, practicable as well as comprehensive, a fitting creed for a future minister of finance. Such a discovery was no mean accomplishment for a man with an eminently practical bent of mind. Though tragically inadequate for a country so backward as Russia, it provided answers for the most pressing problems of the Ministry of Finance and gave Witte's own activities as a railroad promoter (and later as minister of finance) a crucial significance in Russian life. He now hitched his own ambition to a modern conception of Russian greatness in the world; the very survival of Russia as a great power seemed to depend on his work. If Russia was ever going to have a chance of organically developing her native endowment, as England had done, she had to hold her own in the world. This meant, paradoxically, taking over the Western pattern of industrialization. While the Western creative genius rushed ahead at such incredible speed, top priority in Russia had to be given to avoiding "the peril of remaining behind."

It was Witte's personal tragedy—as it was List's before him—that so few contemporaries would appreciate the logic of this view. List's book, despite its intrinsic merits and Witte's plea for it, never attained any popularity in Russia. For the ruling circles it was too liberal, for the intelligentsia too "capitalist." It failed to express those deeper antipathies to industrialization which even Witte had voiced earlier. It was Karl Marx rather than Friedrich List who appealed to these sentiments. Through Marx one could accept industrialization and yet loathe it, hoping for the socialist revolution to make it acceptable to the moral humanitarianism of

Russia's medieval mentality. Witte, however, was determined to weld industrialism onto the existing system of autocracy.

III

In 1889, when Witte came to St. Petersburg to stay, he was barely forty years old. But he was one of the best-qualified men in Russia to assume high office. Of all the *sanovniki* he had the most intimate knowledge of capitalist Russia, of her merchants and industrialists, journalists and professors, city councilors, lawyers, and engineers. He had observed the necessity and benefits of efficient cooperation, of religious and political tolerance, and of the scientific temperament. Public opinion was a reality to him, and the press a power to be reckoned with. In his personal life he subscribed to bourgeois ethics, submitting to the relentless discipline of his work without the reckless escapades only too common even among the dignitaries in the government. What might seem Russian about him was his ambition to create things in a grand way. But did he not share this with some of the American tycoons in his generation? Like most self-made men he was perhaps opinionated in lesser things; here he betrayed his Russian heritage. But in his work, in his ideas of social action, he was modern in the manner of Western urban-industrial civilization; here his father's heritage prevailed. The basic problem which from now on overhung Witte's career was this: How would official Russia, the Court and the bureaucracy, take to the spirit of the new age which Witte tried to infuse into the government?

The start of his career (and indeed his first five years while Alexander III was master of Russia) was auspicious enough. Alexander was constantly being told by Pobedonostsev: "Cherchez des capables." In Witte he had at last found an exceedingly able, honest, and energetic executive, and he was willing to smooth his path and listen to his advice.[51] Promoted seven *chiny* above his

[51] R. F. Byrnes, "Pobedonostsev on the Instruments of Russian Government," in *Continuity and Change in Russian and Soviet Thought,* p. 120.

former rank in the Odessa office of the Ministry of Communications, Witte found himself, at a rank which conferred hereditary nobility, near the very top of the Imperial bureaucracy. The only disappointment in his promotion was the inevitable and considerable financial loss which the transfer from private business entailed. Although the Tsar increased his salary above the statutory limit, it was less than one third of his former earnings.[52]

He fully deserved the Tsar's encouragement, for as head of the Railway Department of the Ministry of Finance he was a conspicuous success. The railway deficits which had burdened the state budget soon disappeared. Moreover, Witte made his department the center of Russian railway management. He reduced the Council on Railroad Affairs, established by the Baranov Commission under the Ministry of Communications, to a secondary position and transferred its most important functions to his own office.[53] Hereafter only the technical aspects of railroad construction remained in the hands of the Ministry of Communications. Financing and planning were now handled by the Ministry of Finance. Having transferred many of his closest advisers from his Kiev office to St. Petersburg, he had as usual an excellent staff for his projects. The greatest of these projects, of course, was the Siberian trunk line. Witte vigorously pleaded for its construction, but Vyshnegradskii resisted on the grounds that the launching of such a costly undertaking might lower Russian credit abroad.[54]

It was inevitable that among the *chinovniki* Witte's rapid promotion and his extensive powers created some envy. The petty courtiers were apt to snub the *kupets* with the Ukrainian accent. His fellow railroad managers disliked the concentration of responsibility in his hands, until they were won over by the profits they made under the new regime.[55] On the whole, however, as Prince Meshcherskii's recollections showed, Witte made a favorable im-

[52] Witte, *Detstvo,* p. 186.

[53] See the pamphlet *K dvatsatipiatiletiiu soveta po zheleznodorozhnym delam.*

[54] *Ibid.,* p. 256.

[55] *Ibid.,* p. 220.

pression. He was consulted in all matters affecting Russian industrial interests. Bunge was said to have remarked of him: "What we get out of books he gets out of his own head." [56] Within a year he was made his ministry's representative in the Ministry of Communications. He also sat on the commission which drafted the tariff of 1891, and on another dealing with the enlargement of the Russian merchant fleet, to mention only his more important assignments.[57]

In February, 1892, he was appointed minister of communications with the construction of the Siberian railroad as his chief task. When he received the news he bowed, deeply moved, before the icon in his office.[58] But his gratitude did not go very deep. He who had suffered in his railroad days from the arrogance and jealousy of the engineers would still have his revenge. He challenged his predecessor to a duel (which never took place) and so humiliated one of his senior officials in the presence of a newspaper editor that he immediately resigned.[59] His first task in his new office was untying a railway traffic snarl which had aggravated the great famine and which his predecessor had proved incapable of solving.[60] At the same time he breathed some of his sense of efficiency into this notoriously inept ministry, laying down, incidentally, the rules governing the movements of the Imperial train. But before he could reorganize the highway and river transport departments of his ministry, another assignment intervened.

In the summer of 1892 the Tsar sent him as the government's trouble shooter into the cholera-ridden Volga provinces, and he traveled fearlessly among the suffering population.[61] Realizing the desperate shortage of physicians, he called on the medical students for help. They responded eagerly, although they were considered

[56] V. V. Maksimov, *Istoricheskii vestnik,* CXL, 252.

[57] *Ministerstvo Finansov, 1802–1902,* II, 324.

[58] Propper, p. 158.

[59] *Ibid.,* pp. 161–62.

[60] Witte, *Detstvo,* pp. 225 ff.

[61] *Ibid.,* pp. 236 ff.

politically unreliable. He also mobilized the Jewish grain dealers for the provisioning of the stricken areas. These unconventional acts showed the character of Witte's initiative. "Let us forget our suspicions and prejudices," he seemed to proclaim. "There is a big job ahead. Let us join hands and get it done. In this way we will grow together and create a strong and proud country." In August, 1892, when his job in the provinces was done, Witte was appointed minister of finance. Characteristically, after receiving his appointment he held a divine service in the ministry's chapel with Father John of Kronstadt officiating.[62]

As the new minister of finance Witte was in a very strong position because he had the full support of the Emperor.[63] Witte always spoke with sincere admiration of the man who had raised him so high. He and Alexander III understood each other in their forthright and unpolished manner that contrasted so strongly with the official tone. Witte felt that he could speak freely in the Emperor's presence. On occasion he even opposed the Emperor on his anti-Semitism, knowing that in essentials Alexander agreed with him. Witte never harbored any illusions about his master's mental abilities. He considered him below average in intellect and education, in contrast to his son Nicholas II. But he always emphasized the Emperor's great "wisdom of heart," the purity of his motives, and his firmness of character. Witte always knew where he stood in Alexander's innermost thoughts. At the same time he also felt a deep mysterious reverence for the "Imperial personage." The Tsar, he stated in his *Memoirs,* stood above "all selfish interests which prevail among ordinary mortals, above all the egotistical and material interests which so often corrupt the human heart." [64]

As minister of finance Witte especially appreciated the parsimony of the Emperor. Throughout his reign the budget allocations for the Imperial court remained constant while all other govern-

[62] Witte, *Tsarstvovani Nikolaia II,* II, 450.
[63] Witte, *Detstvo,* pp. 169, 187 ff., 365 ff.
[64] *Ibid.,* p. 368.

ment expenditures rose. And he could not but admire the peaceful nature of Alexander's reign, for the Russian finances could not stand the strain of war. On railway matters both men were of one mind. Alexander was determined to begin the construction of the Siberian trunk line at the earliest moment. As regards the over-all direction of the government's economic policy they also thought alike. "Alexander III recognized," Witte wrote in his *Memoirs*, "that Russia could be made great only when it ceased being an exclusively agricultural country. A country without strongly developed industry could not be great."[65] On the basis of that premise Witte could even urge the Emperor toward a more liberal political course, convinced that the Emperor was turning spontaneously in that direction.[66] He had been frightened, Witte reflected, by the assassination of his father, but the panic had worn off. In his last year, Witte recalled, Alexander III even warned him of Pobedonostsev: "An excellent critic, but not a creative man. He had had his use in 1881, but now it was necessary to go forward and to create. He had long ceased to pay any attention to the counsels of Pobedonostsev and his like."[67]

But what perhaps endeared autocracy most to Witte—at least in the reign of Alexander III—was the fact that under its firm protection a man could do a good job. Witte was an autocrat in his own right. Autocracy both as a symbol of government and as a concomitant of the industrial opportunities of the day favored men of his type. What he wanted was a secure position from which to direct the affairs entrusted to him. Under Alexander III, the last Romanov who made his will felt throughout the government, he could do his job with the efficiency that comes from the possession of a delegated share of absolute power.

Witte also had private reasons for his praise of Alexander III. Soon after his appointment as minister of finance he deeply tried the Emperor's prejudices by marrying a divorced woman of shady

[65] *Ibid.*, p. 372.
[66] *Ibid.*, p. 375.
[67] *Ibid.*, p. 334.

reputation. The circumstances of this marriage were characteristic of the man. His first wife, the daughter of a marshal of the nobility in the Chernigov Province, had died soon after their arrival in St. Petersburg; their marriage does not seem to have been a happy one. Soon his eye fell on Matilda Ivanovna Lissanevich, the wife of an inconsequential physician, whom Witte met at one of the *salons* which Mme Lissanevich held on the edge of official society and which were frequented by guard officers and young *chinovniki.* Her relations with some of her guests were whispered by Witte's enemies to have been more intimate than official morals permitted. Whatever the truth, Witte was determined to wed her and arranged for her divorce at the price, it was rumored, of 30,000 rubles.[68] So the Imperial Minister of Finance was married to the daughter of an obscure postmaster from Lithuania, "eine kluge, sehr intrigante Jüdin," as Count Münster, the German ambassador, reported to Caprivi.[69] According to all accounts Witte was devoted to his second wife, although their marriage may have had its stormy moments.[70] There is no question of Witte's affection for his stepdaughter. Whatever may be said of his marriage, in his relations with women he was far more correct than many of his colleagues in the government.

Yet what could have been more impolitic than this marriage? He was aware, of course, that a divorced woman with a dubious past could not be admitted at Court and that his marriage would be an insuperable obstacle to social success in the capital. Knowing the strict moral code of the Emperor, Witte offered his resignation. But Alexander cherished the economic development of Russia above his moral convictions. Here, too, he took a liberal view. During the next reign, however, in the eyes of Nicholas II and still more of his prudish wife, the offense was bound to appear

[68] *Ibid.,* p. 245, for an oddly indirect account; also Propper, p. 165, and the reminiscences of Witte's stepdaughter, Vera Naryshkina-Witte, *Zapiski devochki.*

[69] In his dispatch of October 13, 1892, in *Grosse Politik,* Vol. VII, No. 1522.

[70] Radolin's report of February 9, 1898; Bonn, Series 82, No. 2.

in a more serious light. Among his enemies, of course, there was no end to the tattling about Matilda Ivanovna's numerous lovers.

But while Witte had nothing to fear from his first master, he had isolated himself from St. Petersburg's society. The difficulties before him were great; his position was one in which he could not help antagonizing important dignitaries. And what he may have gained in domestic happiness he lost in public sympathy among those circles whose cooperation was necessary for the modernization of the Empire. He craved the social recognition that befitted a grandson of the Dolgorukii family. But now more than ever he faced an uphill struggle, and inevitably the social barriers increased the bitterness which was growing out of his battle against Russian backwardness.

Thus he was trapped in the "contradictions" (to use a Marxist term so appropriate to Russian conditions in this age) which stemmed from the disparate combination of Western and native elements in his parentage, in his career, and in the Russia in which he rose to power. He was trapped by circumstances that lay beyond his control, and he fought back with weapons both Western and native, good and bad. He could be as brusque as a Bolshevik and yet melt in ready pity for human suffering. He could flatter, cajole, be mean, devious, secretive, and vindictive. Yet he also was good-natured and expansive. He could play up his Western sense of efficiency and be critical of his less disciplined colleagues or relax in the Russian manner and act like a good friend. He shared the common Russian trait of shifting his moods and even his opinions in lesser matters with unexpected suddenness, of violently alternating between extremes.[71] He could affect, in short, a great variety of roles. But in all his engagements during the early years of his power there was an element of largesse, of vision and generosity, of rectitude, and even of a charm that was peculiarly Russian. At the start success favored his best qualities.

[71] For the best characterization of Witte's personality see E. J. Dillon, "Two Russian Statesmen," *The Quarterly Review,* CCXXXVI (1921), 402 ff.; see also his book *The Eclipse of Russia,* p. 112.

3. The Witte System

The term "system" characterizes a complete course of action, which is as coherent as a well-integrated and strong-willed personality can make it. Personality is expanded into an economic system. V. WITTSCHEWSKY, *describing the policies of Bunge, Vyshnegradskii, and Witte in* Russlands Handels-, Zoll-, und Industriepolitik

In a country like Russia the task of economic policy at present lies in an energetic and resolute protectionism. The effectiveness of such a policy is guaranteed by the gifts and the industry of the people and the inexhaustible riches of the country, which offer the fullest possibility of producing almost all consumer goods under the most advantageous conditions.

SERGEI WITTE, Lectures on National and State Economy

I

THE MINISTRY OF FINANCE (or at least its main departments) occupied a large building, which it shared with the Ministry of Foreign Affairs, across the Palace Square from the Winter Palace in St. Petersburg. Its back lay against the Moika Canal, which in a carelessly drawn semicircle guarded the rear of the chief monuments of tsarist government, the Admiralty, the Winter Palace and the Hermitage, the Cathedral of St. Isaac, the barracks of the Horse Guards, and other landmarks. The section of the building belonging to the Ministry of Foreign Affairs bordered on the little bridge which led to the Imperial Choir School just across the Moika, whence the Imperial Foreign Office was occasionally referred to as the "Choristers' Bridge." Beyond, to the north, lay the Imperial Archives. In the opposite direction, the Ministry of Finance adjoined the offices of the General Staff by way of a magnificent arch. Was it by chance or design that of all the government agencies the General Staff and the ministries of Foreign Affairs and Finance should be located nearest the autocrat, and that the Ministry of Finance should hold the center between the other two? After 1892, thanks to Witte, it became indeed the foremost ministry.

Witte's advent at the Ministry of Finance amounted to a minor revolution.[1] He replaced the stiff bureaucratic tone with the informality of modern business. The uniforms of the *chinovniki* gave way to frock coats, the written communications to staff conferences. Vyshnegradskii had kept his officials in constant turmoil, working more at night than by day; Witte restored the normal routine, although he himself spent longer hours at his desk than his subordinates. As at the Ministry of Communications, he introduced new blood into the staff, drawing from among the men with whom he had worked at the Southwestern Railway, as well as among friends, professors, and bankers from Odessa and Kiev. He also made a drastic effort to raise the level of technical and scientific competence among his subordinates, even contravening civil service regulations by appointing personnel with sufficient training to positions for which they did not possess the required rank.[2] His influence radiated even further. His anteroom was always crowded with visitors, St. Petersburg journalists like Propper of the *Stockmarket News* (Birzhevyia Vedomosti) or Suvorin of the *New Times* (Novoe Vremia) mingling with "public men," industrialists, professors, some of them even politically suspect. In contrast to his colleagues, Witte relaxed the official reserve of an Imperial minister and went out among the public in search of talent and allies. Let fashionable society snicker that he looked and acted like a *kupets*.[3] Everybody conceded that he ran the most efficient ministry.

Efficiency was certainly needed to administer so large an establishment as the Ministry of Finance. Its head, assisted at

[1] See the reminiscences of Maksimov in *Istoricheskii vestnik,* CXL (April, 1915), 252; also Propper, p. 155, and Lutokhin, Chap. III.

[2] *Obzor deiatel'nosti Ministerstva Finansov v tsarstvovanii Imperatora Aleksandra III, 1881–1894 gg.,* pp. 2–3.

[3] Romanov, *Rossiia v Mandzhurii,* p. 13.

the outset by only one assistant minister (but ending up with four in 1902), was not only boss of the seven departments, the Treasury, the three revenue collecting agencies, the Border Guards, the Department of Trade and Industry, and the Department of Railway Affairs. He was also responsible for the State Bank, the Nobles Land Bank and the Peasant Land Bank, the Mint, the Government Publishing House, a Special Chancellery for Credit Matters, and some other important commissions, committees, and councils. His housekeeping office for this welter of specialized branches was the General Chancellery, to which a Scientific Committee was attached as a research agency. The Chancellery was Witte's personal headquarters. Enlarged to cope with the various problems arising from the construction of the Siberian railroad, it eventually became the center for his diplomatic ventures in the Far East. The personnel of these central offices amounted to well over a thousand *chinovniki.* The local agents of the Ministry of Finance, its host of tax collectors and factory inspectors, the Border Guards, the employees of the Vodka Monopoly, and the clerks of the Treasury's local branch offices added many thousands more to its payroll.[4]

By contrast to the efficiency in Witte's own house, the organization of the economic activities of the Russian government as a whole was rather chaotic. It was a corollary of autocracy that the government possessed extensive economic powers and derived no mean income from its holdings.[5] It was the largest landowner in Russia, claiming over 38 percent of her territory. Much of this land, to be sure, was of little value, consisting mostly of forests (the government owned 60 percent of all forest lands) located in northern or eastern Russia, where exploitation was difficult, yet yielding some revenue. Its arable lands, leased to peasants, likewise brought a small, but slowly growing, profit. More will be said

[4] *Ministerstvo Finansov, 1802–1902,* II, 326 ff. Unfortunately this account does not give absolute figures for the total staff.

[5] Liashchenko, *Istoriia,* p. 184.

subsequently of the government railways, which by the mid-nineties constituted the larger part of the Russian network. In mining and metallurgy the government was the biggest entrepreneur. It owned valuable deposits, particularly of precious metals, in the Urals, Siberia, the Altai region, the Caucasus, and southern Russia, and operated large armament factories. The government thus exercised considerable influence over the economic development of these regions, although the revenue from these sources again was small. The postal and telegraph systems likewise produced a surplus. Finally, through the State Bank and its affiliates the government controlled the flow of credit either to agriculture, or to trade and industry. Altogether, the government sector of Russian economy was considerable, even larger than in Prussia.

The administration of these far-flung economic resources, however, was divided among a number of authorities. The Ministry of State Domains, which in 1894 was expanded into the Ministry of State Domains and Agriculture, had charge of government lands and mines. The arms factories, naturally, were in the hands of the Army or Navy. The mail and telegraph service belonged to the Ministry of Communications, the State Bank to the Ministry of Finance. The railways operated under the divided control of the ministries of Communications and Finance. The financial transactions of most government agencies, the armed forces and the Court excepted, were audited by the Ministry of State Control. Finally, to mention an important body without administrative responsibility, the Finance Committee determined the government's credit policy, particularly as regarded foreign loans. Eight major agencies in one way or another looked after the government's economic holdings.

Supervision of private enterprise was likewise distributed among several authorities. Trade and industry were overseen by the Ministry of Finance and mining by the Ministry of State Domains and Agriculture, which also had charge of the peasant crafts. The craft guilds of the towns, on the other hand, were assigned to the

Ministry of the Interior. The latter also exercised jurisdiction over peasant affairs in general and thus a measure of influence over Russian agriculture. The permission for the establishment of new industries, particularly foreign ones, lay in the hands of the Committee of Ministers, but it required also the approval of the local administrative organs of the Ministry of the Interior. Jurisdictional complications were aggravated by the vagaries of official nomenclature. Agriculture and mining were lumped together as branches of "extractive industry." By contrast, "processing industry" was concerned with the manufacture of articles from the raw materials supplied by the former. The first was the province of the Minister of State Domains and Agriculture, the second of the Minister of Finance. Inevitably, the latter ranked above the former, for his authority was more inclusive. So it happened at the end of Witte's career as minister of finance that he was made chairman of a Special Conference on the Needs of Agricultural Industry, to the chagrin of his colleague.

It is easy to see that under these conditions the progress of any comprehensive economic legislation would be difficult. Even limited projects of the Minister of Finance had to pass first through the Department of State Economy in the State Council and finally through the State Council sitting in plenary session. Here the divergent views of the different ministries had to be reconciled. Special projects might be put before an *ad hoc* conference of the ministers most directly involved, before being introduced to the State Council. Occasionally the State Council could be bypassed altogether. If there was to emerge a forceful and unified economic policy from this administrative pluralism, it could be formulated and carried out only under the leadership of a strong personality backed to the hilt by the Tsar. It was not an auspicious arrangement for a minister of finance with strong convictions and a powerful ambition, both running counter to rooted tradition.

When Witte was made minister of finance, his chief task was to repeat his success with the Southwestern Railway on a larger scale. He had to put Russia's economy on a sound basis and make it prosperous. As he set to work, his personality, experience, and convictions, faced with the hard facts of Russian poverty, combined in the manner made familiar by his predecessors to create a new "system," the "Witte system." Its main features, as they were announced, modestly enough in his first budget report, have already been stated. By a policy of public works, above all by means of railroad construction, the government was to stimulate individual enterprise in the exploitation of the vast but idle resources of Russia. (Witte never ceased to advertise the fabulous potential of Russian economy. "In the tremendous variety of climate and soil conditions, in its inexhaustible wealth, Russia contains all the factors necessary for full economic independence," he stated in his second budget report.) The increased exploitation of these riches would make the Russian people prosperous. Their prosperity, in turn, would fill the treasury and, repaying many times the initial outlays, would solve the government's difficulties. For the moment, however, the emphasis lay upon increased government spending. The economic misery of the great famine had been caused in part by the niggardliness of his predecessor. Witte was to follow the opposite course: "For the progress and successful development of industry we have to take measures which must inevitably lead to government expenditures, both in single grants and constant subsidies." [6]

How Witte arrived at this early version of deficit financing does not appear in the available records. He himself never attached any theoretical significance to his departure from his predecessor's policy. He merely called his course of action a protectionist policy, because the chief agent in the promotion of economic activity was the state, and state interest always came first, if necessary with the full ruthlessness of autocracy. Yet by design, it

[6] Budget report for 1893.

should be added, it was an experiment in state capitalism, not socialism. The government was to set going the wheels of Russian economy in the vital field of transportation. But the main energies sustaining and advancing Russian prosperity were to come, so Witte hoped, not from the government but from the people. Eventually the machine was to run by itself, as in the West. How this experiment premised on Western experience was to work in the predominantly agrarian, almost medieval mold of Russian tradition, remained to be seen.

Considering the fact that Witte's policy was one of state capitalism, one would look in vain for a complex and detailed modern "plan" of industrialization. The basic pattern remained a simple one. Extensive railroad construction would stimulate the growth of the metallurgical and fuel industries supplying rails and other equipment. In turn, the expansion of the heavy industries would create favorable conditions for the growth of the light industries. In the end the new vigor of the industrial and urban segment of the population would raise rural production and prosperity as well. Railroad construction thus served as the flywheel for the entire economy.

In some ways, the Witte system constituted an improvement over List's prescription. It placed greater emphasis on public works (like railway construction). Yet Witte, too, relied on the spontaneous effects of economic incentives for the better part of the job. Where government railway construction left off, private enterprise had to take over. Even in the sphere of private enterprise, however, much had to be done by the government in order to clear away obstacles and to provide the right climate. On closer analysis, then, the Witte system reduces to an uneven flow of interrelated projects and policies, all aiming at the promotion of rapid industrial growth, but none embodied in a comprehensive and integrated timetable of accomplishments. Some of these projects were spectacular, like the construction of the Siberian railroad, some more commonplace, like the manifold small favors to trade and industry or the promotion of technical and commercial education, and others seemingly unrelated, like the introduction of the gold standard. The novel features of industrial promotion and the traditional concerns of the Russian Ministry of Finance were interlaced in the Witte system.

Let us now analyze each of the chief aspects of this system in turn.

II

It was natural for a railroad-man-made-minister-of-finance to think first of the economic opportunities inherent in railroad transportation. Witte frankly proclaimed in his second budget report that the Russian government, through its control of the Russian railroad network, possessed "a very powerful weapon . . . for the direction of the economic development of the country." [7] The railroads constituted the largest single industry of the country, employing 400,000 workers in 1900.[8] They increasingly determined the flow of goods and thereby the prosperity of every region and of every branch of the national economy. Furthermore, they were a prime agent of cultural progress. Witte once boasted: "The railroad is like a leaven, which creates a cultural fermentation among the population. Even if it passed through an absolutely wild people along its way, it would raise them in a short time to the level prerequisite for its operation." [9]

The minister of finance, who sat at the controls of railroad development in Russia, was, however, no tyrant. For the coordination of all railroad affairs the Baranov Commission had originally established, under the Ministry of Communications, an advisory Railroad Council which represented both government agencies and private companies. This council, to be sure, like the ministry under which it operated, had lost much of its power in 1889 when Witte

[7] Budget report for 1894.

[8] Witte, *Konspekt lektsii o narodnom i gosudarstvennom khoziaistve,* p. 343.

[9] *Ibid.,* p. 345.

established the Railway Department in the Ministry of Finance.[10] But that department, too, proceeded collectively through a special Tariff Committee which regulated the rates for the entire Russian network. As railway tariffs were a vital concern to the economic community in general, an additional advisory body, the Council on Railroad Tariffs representing all interested groups, was created directly under the minister of finance himself. It was to Witte's interest not to proceed arbitrarily in these matters.

In railway affairs the minister of finance was also the superior of the minister of communications. Prince Khilkov, who occupied the latter position for most of Witte's career as finance minister, had learned railroading in the United States during the 1860s and proved himself, as Witte put it, a good "chief mechanic," but no more.[11] He loyally left the statesmanship of railroad expansion to his more brilliant colleague. One agency, however, stood above the minister of finance in railway affairs, the Committee of Ministers. It decided not only disputes between government lines and the private companies but also important questions of railroad policy which touched the interests of the government as a whole. Here, as in economic policy in general, the minister of finance could prevail only by force of his personality or, in the last instance, by the favor of the Tsar.

Under Witte's guidance railroad construction advanced by leaps and bounds. His largest and most impressive project, of course, was the trans-Siberian line.[12] Witte's first major accomplishment as minister of finance was to get the huge job started at last. The prospects of building a railway of 5,400 miles through

[10] See *K dvadtsatipiatiletiiu soveta po zheleznodorozhnym delam;* also *Obzor deiatel'nosti Ministerstva Finansov,* pp. 88 ff. Incidentally, each private railroad had on its board of directors a representative of the Ministry of Finance and the Ministry of Communications.

[11] Witte, *Tsarstvovanie Nikolaia II,* I, 23.

[12] On the Siberian railroad see *Sibir' i velikaia sibirskaia zheleznaia doroga*; *Putevoditel' po velikoi sibirskoi zheleznodoroge;* Migulin, *Nasha noveishaia;* Glinskii, ed., *Prolog russko-iaponskoi voiny*; and Romanov, *Rossiia v Mandzhurii.*

unexplored and undeveloped territory, a railway longer by two thousand miles than the Canadian transcontinental link from St. John on the Atlantic to Vancouver on the Pacific (not to mention the shorter American lines), had for many years frightened the Russian finance ministers into inaction. The estimated costs were enormous. In the steppes neither stone nor wood could be procured, gigantic steel bridges had to be thrust over the Siberian streams, swamps crossed, mountains tunneled. Local reservoirs of skilled—or even unskilled—labor hardly existed; the economic conditions of the areas traversed by the projected line were primitive. It would be decades before the venture could begin to pay for itself. But while economics tended to delay construction, politics hurried it forward. The increasing foreign penetration in the Far East and Russian weakness in Siberia demanded that the government link its Pacific and Far Eastern borders with the centers of European Russia.

Since the Crimean War schemes for a Siberian railway had not been wanting, but the question of its exact location had aroused considerable controversy. Should it take a northern route, from St. Petersburg eastward, to Viatka, Perm, and the industrial regions of the Urals around Ekaterinburg and thence to the Siberian rivers in the Ob basin? Should it perhaps go along the Volga to Nizhni-Novgorod and Kazan, then swing east to Krasnoufimsk and thence out into Siberia? Or should it follow a southerly course from the easternmost point of the Volga at Samara, then along the old caravan route to Ufa, Cheliabinsk, and southern Siberia? And which of the two capitals should be the terminus of the new railroad, St. Petersburg or Moscow? Some progress was made in the late 1870s and early 1880s along both the northern and southern alternatives.[13] By 1882 the waterways of the Kama, a tributary of the Volga, and of the Irtysh, a tributary of the Ob, were connected by a railroad that ran from Perm to Tiumen through the northern Urals; it had no rail outlet, how-

[13] *Putevoditel' po velikoi sibirskoi zheleznodoroge,* p. 58.

ever, from Perm to the west. Along the southern route the Volga had been bridged at several points, and a railroad constructed to Orenburg, and from Samara to Ufa. By 1888 the latter line was being pushed across the steppe to Zlatousk, with the intention of linking it eventually to the Ural railroad. Meanwhile, in the first year of Vyshnegradskii's regime a special conference of leading officials was called to consider still further construction, and Alexander III sent instructions that the trans-Siberian trunk line be built quickly and cheaply. The Imperial will could not prevail, however, over the parsimony of his minister of finance and no progress was made.

When news came that the Chinese government had engaged an English engineer for the construction of a railroad into Manchuria, another special conference was called in December, 1890. Then at last one of the basic preliminary decisions was made. On the recommendation of the Ministry of Communications it was agreed that the Siberian line should start from the easternmost point of the present network, at Zlatousk, or rather a hamlet named Miass still further east, to which that line was currently being extended.[14] The government thus chose the old trade route, which was the wisest course from an economic point of view, as it passed through the most populated areas of Siberia. It also had the advantage of a ready connection with the European network, which the northern route did not possess; Moscow thus won out over St. Petersburg.

In the spring of 1891, as related earlier, the decision to build the trans-Siberian railroad was formally announced and construction was begun from the two terminals, from Vladivostok westward and from Miass eastward toward Cheliabinsk, a small settlement on the Siberian boundary. The famine, however, cut short all further work. Only when it had abated could the project be resumed. Meanwhile Witte had been made minister of finance. Now he was fully master of the undertaking.

[14] *Ibid.*, p. 62.

With Witte's arrival the project was placed in a new light. The strategic and political motives which had stood so much in the foreground of the original planning—and which never ceased to surround the project—now were supplemented by economic considerations as well.[15] As Witte saw it, the chief purpose of the new railway was to promote the prosperity of the country. In addition to developing the dormant resources of Siberia with the help of the industries of European Russia and in turn providing new markets for the latter, it was, more significantly, to link Europe and the Far East in an intensified exchange of goods. Russia was to become the chief carrier of the East-West trade, shortening the long steamer voyage by almost three weeks. From the start, so Witte hoped, the road would thus be able to produce revenue and quickly repay the appalling costs of construction. Always putting his projects into the largest perspective, he announced that the construction of the Siberian railroad was "one of those events" that "usher in new epochs in the history of nations and not infrequently bring about a radical change in the established economic relations between states."[16] Russia would capture the Chinese markets from the English, friendly relations with the Chinese would result, and eventually even a new solidarity of political interests with the North American states would emerge.

With such prospect of early profits, the administrative preparation for the construction of the Siberian road quickly got under way. Three months after Witte took office, in November, 1892, the Emperor called a special conference attended by the ministers of war, the navy, the interior, communications, agriculture, the former Ministers of Finance Bunge and Vyshnegradskii, the State Controller, the governor general of Irkutsk, and leading members of the State Council. Before that conference, each member of

[15] For the following see *Prolog russko-iaponskoi voiny*; Romanov, *Rossiia v Mandzhurii*; and the budget reports for 1893 and 1894.

[16] Quoted by Romanov, *Rossiia v Mandzhurii*, p. 2.

which had a special stake in the project, Witte outlined his plans.

As for the crucial matter of finance, he proposed, to the consternation of his two predecessors, resorting to the printing press. He had already been forced into that dubious expedient when he assumed his office. There was no money on hand with which to pay even the salaries of the *chinovniki.*[17] Now he suggested issuing more than 90 million rubles for the start of construction.[18] Currency problems, admittedly, were not Witte's specialty, and his adviser Professor Antonovich, whom he had brought from Kiev, had persuaded him of the advantages of an inconvertible paper currency. At the news of this plan, Bunge rushed to Witte in dismay, warning him of the consequences, and quickly won him over to the gold standard. The change of plans, however, hardly improved the financial prospects, although the closer relationship with the French government just then emerging strengthened the Russian position in the French money market. The Siberian railroad remained a poverty project. Thrift determined its character above everything else. All decisions concerning the details of construction and routing must be understood in this light.

Witte was again on firm ground when he outlined his construction schedule.[19] The road was to be built in three stages. The first, most extensive in mileage but easiest in construction, was (*a*) to advance the present line from Cheliabinsk to the Ob River under the care of a West Siberian branch office, (*b*) to construct a mid-Siberian line from the Ob to Irkutsk, (*c*) to connect the northern Ural line with the Siberian trunk line, and (*d*) to finish the Far Eastern branch from Vladivostok to Grafskaia. In the second stage the Far Eastern line was to push westward from Grafskaia to Khabarovsk on the Amur River, while the Siberian road advanced from the opposite direction linking Lake Baikal with

[17] Witte, *Detstvo,* p. 328.

[18] Migulin, *Nasha noveishaia,* pp. 285 ff. Witte, incidentally, later ordered all copies of this report to be destroyed. See Maksimov's reminiscences, *Istoricheskii vestnik,* CXL, 252.

[19] *Putevoditel',* pp. 60 ff.

Sretensk, a town on a western tributary of the Amur. In the third and final stage water transport over Lake Baikal and along the Amur River was to be replaced by rail transport. This last phase, traversing as yet entirely unsurveyed territory, was to be finished at the end of 1902, exactly a decade after the beginning of the project. Thus prepared, construction at last began.

Needless to say, the Siberian railroad could flourish only if Siberia flourished. Thus Witte proposed a variety of auxiliary enterprises, such as the organization of peasant migration into the Siberian frontier and the surveying and exploiting of Siberia's mineral wealth. Coal in particular was important for the road itself, likewise iron ore. As a result of his recommendations a careful inventory was drawn up of industrial enterprises along the proposed road which could be utilized in the construction. The geological survey of Siberia was pushed feverishly, and much hope was expressed for the expansion of the Ural industries. Silver, copper, lead, and gold were discovered, the last of great value to a government which had long aimed at conversion to the gold standard. The gold mines, incidentally, were turned over to foreign enterprise, which promised the speediest results.

Among the subsidiary policies which Witte pushed, the resettlement of the peasants encountered considerable difficulty. The departure of Russian peasants to Siberia threatened to drain manpower from the central and most overpopulated provinces of Russia. This diminished the supply of cheap local labor, reduced the inflation of rents and land values, and lowered the income of the landlords. Witte observed in his *Memoirs* that what he called "serfdom Russia" bitterly opposed his resettlement policy.[20] Fortunately the minister of the interior, Durnovo, who was the spokesman for the landowners of central Russia, was outvoted by his colleagues. Thus under the energetic supervision of the secretary of the Siberian Committee, A. N. Kulomzin, an ever-growing wave of migrants moved into Siberia. In 1892 the population was al-

[20] *Detstvo,* p. 399.

THE CONSTRUCTION OF THE TRANS-SIBERIAN RAILROAD

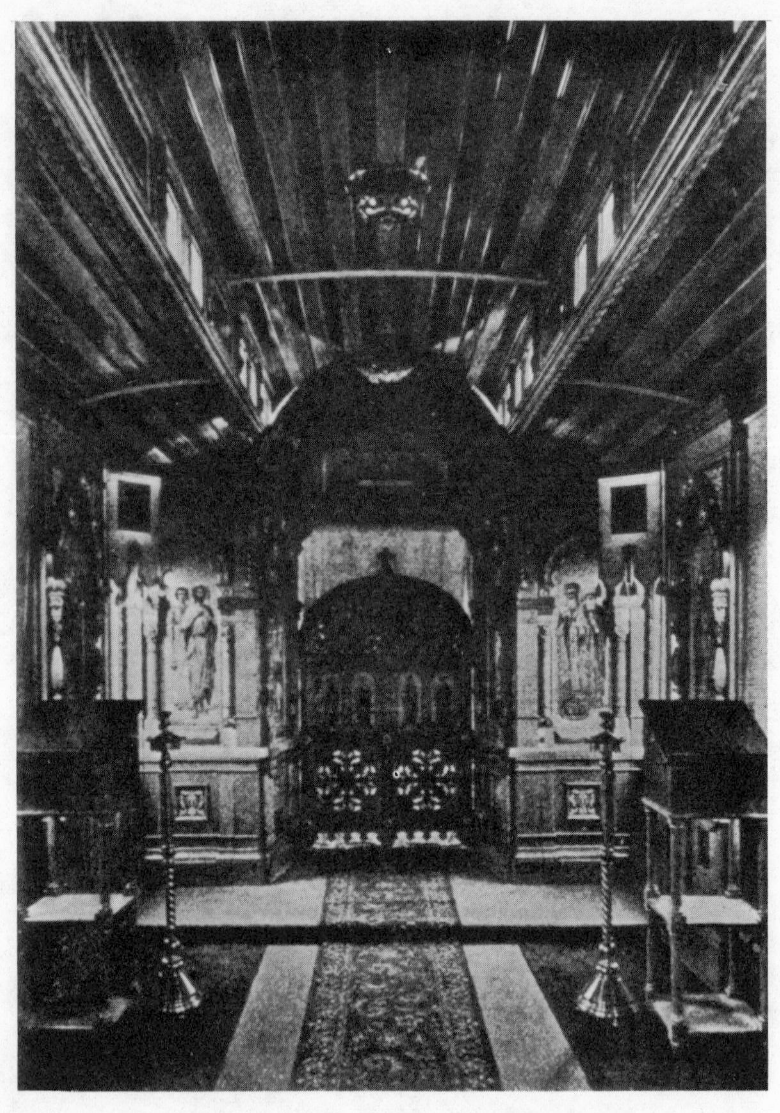

THE INTERIOR OF THE CHURCH-CAR
OF THE TRANS-SIBERIAN RAILROAD

ready twice as numerous as that along the Canadian Pacific Railroad. By 1902, when through traffic commenced, at least 900,000 more settlers had been added.[21]

Another phase in the opening up of Siberia was the exploration of the northern sea route around Siberia.[22] In 1893 Witte financed a naval expedition to the mouths of the Siberian rivers, hoping that the construction crews might be supplied with rails and other bulk goods by sea. Typically enough, the leader of this expedition was an Englishman named James Wiggins, who searched for markets for English goods on ships manned by non-Russians.[23] (To 1914 shipping in the White Sea and the Bering Sea remained in foreign hands.) But rails and other equipment were delivered as planned, and Russian explorers gained vital experience. In connection with the development of the northern sea route, incidentally, Witte won out (over the protest of the Russian navy) in the commissioning of a powerful icebreaker, the *Ermak* of Soviet fame, built by the English firm of Armstrong at Newcastle. It was he too who encouraged the pioneer of Russian arctic navigation, Admiral Makarov.[24] For the quick development of Siberian shipping as well as of Siberian economy in general, the Ministry of Finance also granted a number of tariff privileges to imports coming into Siberia in order to offset the high transportation costs and obtain high-quality equipment. Thus, in many different ways, "the planned development of Siberia," as Witte later called this phase of his work,[25] got a start. If it showed no spectacular results in his time, the reasons lay in the vastness of the territory, the adverse climate, and the poverty of the state.

The final point in Witte's program at the special conference of November, 1892, was the formation of a permanent Siberian Committee, which could bypass the cumbersome machinery of the State

[21] Krypton, p. 103. Also Treadgold, pp. 107 ff.
[22] For the following see Krypton.
[23] *Ibid.*, p. 67.
[24] See Ostrovskii, pp. 194 ff.
[25] *Detstvo,* p. 399.

Council.[26] Witte had the sagacity to suggest that the Tsarevich, who had taken a special interest in the Far East, be appointed chairman; Bunge was made vice-chairman, and all ministers and Siberian governors were members. The committee established a special interministerial subcommittee on colonization, while the Ministry of the Interior created a department for resettlement, and the Ministry of Communications one for the technical work on the railroad. The Committee of Ministers acted as the executive for the Siberian Committee, of which it formed the nucleus. Thus, under Witte's guidance, administrative power was sufficiently coordinated for speedy and extensive results.

And yet, while admiring the scope of the enterprise, one cannot overlook its background of hurry and parsimony. The Siberian railroad was built on a shoestring, under precautions considerably less strict than those regulating the roads of European Russia.[27] The rails were of an unusually light type, the roadbed narrow, the curves sharp, and the gradients steep. Such flimsy construction permitted only three trains a day in either direction, and at low speeds. Thrift explained other anomalies—Cheliabinsk and Omsk, for instance, were separated by several *versts* from their railway stations; another large town, Tomsk, was completely bypassed; and Irkutsk remained separated from its station by a river. Any deviation from the straight line was ruled out, as the road was planned for the quick profits of the anticipated through traffic. Within a few years, however, this proved false economy and delayed the economic development of Siberia. But in 1892 the government had no choice except to accommodate itself to Russian poverty. The Russian public, unfortunately, failed to appreciate this point and complained bitterly of the seeming idiocy of its officials.

[26] *Ibid.*, p. 392; also Migulin, *Nasha noveishaia*, p. 282.

[27] Migulin, *Nasha noveishaia*, p. 283. A leading American expert of the time, Arthur M. Wellington, justified light initial construction, with later improvements when traffic justified them. See his book *The Economic Theory of the Location of Railways.*

Witte, however, was undaunted in his expectations. The Siberian railroad, he announced in his first budget report, was "one of the greatest enterprises of the century in the entire world." Eager to make his mark in the government and brought up to believe in Russia's mission, he let himself be carried away by the expansive visions of contemporary Russian imperialism. Thus a host of impure political motives were mixed with the economic necessities. An adventurer of Buriat extraction and Slavophile sentiments named Badmaev sent him in February, 1893, a memorandum which contained the most tempting prospects.[28] A spur of the Siberian road might be built to Lanchowfu, in the Kansu province of China. From that center Russian agents (like Badmaev) would stir up Mongols, Tibetans, and Chinese to overthrow the Manchu dynasty. The nobility in these regions would then ask the Tsar to be their sovereign. Witte was pleased at the prospect of branch lines funneling Chinese trade to the Siberian railway. And if Badmaev's schemes succeeded, Russia's geopolitical position would become impregnable. "In possession of the lands between the shores of the Pacific and the heights of the Himalayas, Russia would dominate not only the affairs of Asia but those of Europe as well," [29] Witte explained to Alexander III, to whom he forwarded Badmaev's report; Russia would become a truly Eurasian power.

Sharing the intelligentsia's penchant for ideological constructions, Witte even added some significant reflections of his own on the global position of Russia:

Standing on the confines of two such different worlds, in close contact with each of them, Russia none the less represents a world apart. Her independent place in the family of peoples and her special role in world history are determined both by her geographical position and, in particular, by the original character of her political and cultural development, a development which has been achieved through the living interaction and harmonious combination of three elements that have

[28] For the following see *Za kulisami tsarizma,* pp. 77 ff., and Malozemoff, pp. 47 ff.

[29] *Za kulisami tsarizma,* p. 80.

manifested their full creative power only in Russia. These elements are: first, Orthodoxy, preserving in purity the true spirit of Christianity, as the basis of education and upbringing; secondly, autocracy as the basis of state life; thirdly, the Russian national spirit, as the basis of the internal cohesiveness of the state, a national spirit that creates a strong inward center, closely united yet free from nationalistic exclusiveness, possessed of a vast capacity for friendly companionship and cooperation with the most diverse races and peoples. It is on these bases that the whole edifice of Russian power has been built up, and it is therefore impossible for Russia to be fused with the West. At the same time she has long since appeared among Asiatic peoples as the bearer of the Christian ideal, striving to spread among them the principles of Christian enlightenment, not under the standard of Europeanization, but under her own special standard. In a word, in the Asiatic East Russia has long since taken upon herself the mission of cultural enlightenment in the spirit of those principles which have given a special character to her own development.[30]

This was Witte's version of Russia's imperialist mission. But it was no more grandiloquent than the contemporary creeds of a Cecil Rhodes or a Lord Curzon.

The Emperor's comment on Witte's report was laconic and frigid: "This is so new, unusual, and fantastic that it is difficult to believe in its success." His common sense prevailed, and Witte henceforth turned a deaf ear to Badmaev's pleas for financial support, although for years the ambition continued to linger in his mind. How, one wonders, could the Minister of Finance entertain such grandiose dreams when his purse was so lean? Did he not, in the Siberian Committee and his budget reports, always give first place to the role of the Siberian railway as a peaceful instrument of international trade? [31] However we resolve the contradiction in Witte's behavior, we must admit that even at the moment of his greatest temptation by imperialist ambition he preferred peaceful economic infiltration to military annexation.

[30] *Ibid.*, p. 78. The translation is adapted from B. H. Sumner, "Russia and Europe," *Oxford Slavonic Papers*, No. 1.

[31] Even in the report just quoted, the voices of caution and economic calculation can be heard.

After the Siberian railway, Russian railroads in general claimed his attention. By 1892 the basic pattern of the Russian network had been completed. The grain-producing areas had been linked with both the ports and the grain-consuming regions, the capitals and chief administrative centers had been connected, and the strategic north-south arteries had been completed. In the 1880s, to the tune of Anglo-Russian diplomatic crises, a railway had been laid into Central Asia east of the Caspian Sea. In the 1890s, apart from the Siberian road, the main job consisted of improving and increasing the rail network in European Russia, double-tracking existing lines, shortening connections, laying new lines to areas hitherto unserved, for example, Archangel, the border regions of the Caucasus, Tashkent in Central Asia, and southern ports like Kerch or Mariupol. While no other single project could rival the Siberian railroad in magnitude, the same feverish pitch of activity prevailed everywhere. Almost three times as many new miles of railway line were laid west and south of the Urals as in Siberia. After 1896, when the construction boom had been under way only three years, more than 1,250 miles were opened to traffic every year until 1902; in 1899 it was more than 3,125 miles.[32] The private railroads and the government lines vied with each other in the rapid tempo of new construction. The government, for the most part, built the less economical lines which the private companies could not afford. But at the same time government ownership of railroads increased, because Witte bought up one road after another, and at boom prices, as an aid to private enterprise. In the end the state roads comprised two thirds of the network and carried even more of the total traffic.[33] Thus the civilizing stimulus of railway transport penetrated ever more deeply into Russia.

[32] These figures from Khromov, p. 464, here cited in miles instead of kilometers.

[33] In 1901 the government network amounted to 68.3 percent of the total; it carried 69 percent of the freight and 71.8 percent of the passengers. Neopikhonov, pp. 76 ff.

Meanwhile, the government carefully directed that stimulus through its control of the freight rates. Where transport costs are large in relation to production costs, as in Russia, the manipulation of freight rates represents a particularly effective form of economic power. Witte had taught the government the uses of that power when he was head of the Railway Department in the Ministry of Finance; after 1892 only a few changes were made.[34] In 1893 he introduced a double tariff, one for agricultural exports, which was kept low, and the other for internal consumption, which was higher. The railroads were thus made to aid the export drive, which Witte carried on as determinedly as Vyshnegradskii, with the costs falling, in the last analysis, on the Russian taxpayer. Another crucial feature of the new tariff was the encouragement of long hauls over short ones; this not only helped Russian exports but also aided the economic consolidation of the far-flung empire. Furthermore, Witte promoted the processing of agricultural goods, which would make Russian exports more valuable. Milled grain, for instance, traveled at a particularly low charge. Conversely, goods brought inland from the ports were charged high rates, which acted as a further deterrent to imports.

Naturally the government's policy did not always meet with public approval. The chief complaint in these years came from the grain growers in the central black-soil provinces, whose meager profits were threatened by the cheap Siberian grains now appearing on their markets. For their protection the government instituted the "Cheliabinsk basing point." Freight from beyond Cheliabinsk was charged a higher rate, thus preventing the Siberian grains from competing in Moscow. These grains were designated for export instead, and a new railroad was built to carry them from Perm to Kotlas on the Northern Dvina, whence they were shipped by river to Archangel. Yet the dissatisfaction over the

[34] See Zagorskii; also Migulin, *Nasha noveishaia,* p. 330, and *Ministerstvo Finansov, 1802–1902,* II, 569 ff.

discrimination between short and long hauls persisted. The outlying areas received a larger subsidy than the central ones.

Industrial freight was treated differently from agricultural freight. Oil or manganese ore, which fetched a high price on the foreign market, had to pay high rates, which amounted, so their shippers charged, to an export duty. As for passenger rates, Witte took a bold step in reducing them considerably in 1894, also instituting cheap fourth-class accommodations for peasants and workers. The largest reductions, again, were effected in long-distance travel, but in 1896 local fares were also cut. It was to Russia's advantage in the industrial age to improve the mobility of her population. Inevitably, the Minister of Finance was subject to criticism in these sensitive issues. Yet it was much to his credit that he created a country-wide rate system and, with the help of periodic reviews before the Tariff Committee, maintained it as a flexible instrument of national economic planning.

Russia, however, not only needed railroads; she wanted a commercial fleet of her own as well, and ports to give it employment. In 1893 Witte wrote a report to Alexander III on the development of the Russian merchant marine.[35] Almost 90 percent of all shipping in Russian ports, his figures proved, carried non-Russian flags. Such reliance on foreign ships cost the country heavily in foreign exchange and adversely affected the balance of payments. As a result of his initiative, a special commission was formed within the government and later, in 1898, a special council with representatives of all interested groups. But the chief obstacle, the high cost of shipbuilding in Russian yards, could not be overcome in a hurry. Thus an exception was made in the customs tariff, permitting the import of foreign seagoing ships duty free. Still the merchant marine showed little progress.

Meanwhile (after 1897) Witte granted new privileges to Russian vessels engaged in coastwise shipping and in the trade be-

[35] For the following see *Ministerstvo Finansov, 1802–1902*, II, 550.

tween Russian ports on different oceans; since 1889 the Ministry of Finance had already been paying the Suez Canal dues on Russian ships. It subsidized various steamship companies plying the Black Sea or White Sea and encouraged active trading with the Danubian ports. In connection with the Siberian railroad, it chartered a special steamship company for its subsidiary, the Chinese Eastern Railroad; this was to feed freight from the eastern ports to the railheads. Witte also took a special interest in the possibility of an ice-free port on the White Sea and personally inspected the harbor of Murmansk, favoring the development of that port rather than of Libava on the Baltic. In 1901, impatient with the many delays, the Minister of Finance formed a Council on Maritime Commerce and a Committee on Port Affairs, and in the following year a Maritime School for the training of captains and mates. Many of these measures stemmed from the later years of Witte's career as minister of finance, but they were part of the grand design which directed his energies from the start.

III

At this point the question arises: How could the Minister of Finance influence and accelerate the course of industrial development set in motion by his railroad projects? In the first place, what links existed between his ministry and Russian industry which he could employ for his purposes?

The branch of the Ministry of Finance especially concerned with industrial affairs was the Department of Trade and Industry.[36] Its growth after its establishment in 1881 constitutes an index of Russian economic modernization. Entrusted with supervision of all commercial and industrial affairs of the Empire, it had its hands full in dealing with patents, joint stock companies, trademarks, Russia's merchant fleet, factory inspection, the stock exchanges, and weights and measures. In 1881 it employed twenty-

[36] *Obzor deiatel'nosti Ministerstva Finansov,* pp. 80 ff.; for the period after 1894 see *Ministerstvo Finansov, 1802–1902,* II, 328 ff.

eight officials distributed in its divisions of commerce, industry, and foreign trade relations, and its chancellery and accounting office. Four years later two more divisions were added for statistics and commercial taxes, and in 1892 a third for expediting the grain trade. In 1893 the department listed fifty-eight *chinovniki.* In the following year it was reorganized altogether and its staffs enlarged. It also took over the new technical schools set up on the initiative of the Ministry of Finance. In 1899 its personnel had increased 75 percent since 1894.

In the following year it was revamped again; four main divisions then emerged. The Division of Commerce was in charge of internal trade, the fairs, stock exchanges, and other commercial institutions, the affairs of the merchant guilds, the laws of incorporation, weights and measures, commercial taxes, and foreign trade relations (except customs). The Division of Industry was concerned with technical matters relating to the construction and maintenance of factories, the ever-growing task of factory inspection, the customs tariff, patents, exhibits of industry, and the industrial arts. A third division looked after the growing number of technical schools, and the fourth, the Division of Maritime Commerce, supervised the development of the Russian merchant marine. At the same time the entire Department of Trade and Industry was entrusted to a third assistant minister of finance, who kept his own secretariat. Clearly it had become the most important department in the ministry.

This department, like the entire ministry, could discharge its functions best if it worked closely with Russian industry.[37] From the outset it was Witte's wish to establish good relations between the government and the Russian business community. The *kuptsy* could hardly complain of being disregarded. Their opinions—to take but the formal links between government and business—were heard in the special Council on Railroad Tariffs mentioned earlier.

[37] See Karpov, ed., *Ob otkrytii i soderzhanii zavedenii obrabatyvaiushchei promyshlennosti.*

Within the Department of Trade and Industry they expressed their views in the Council on Factory Construction. In addition, the Minister of Finance could convene the Council on Trade and Manufacturies, which set the regulations for the construction of new factories, as well as for health and safety. At the same time the Russian businessmen could also state their needs in their own local organizations. Committees of Trade and Industry could be founded, for instance, with the permission of the Ministry of Finance, in any town of commercial significance. These bodies were closely allied with the elected town dumas—in which the merchant guilds predominated—and could make recommendations to the government (which was careful to insist, however, that under the laws of autocracy it was not bound by them). A further focus of commercial and industrial opinion was the Stock Exchange Committees, which handled the local stock markets. Here again the merchant guilds played the leading part. These committees were useful agencies because they introduced uniform trading practices throughout the country, and Witte fully encouraged their extension throughout Russia. Both the Committees of Trade and Industry and the Stock Exchange Committees could be considered semi-official bodies. The Tsar bestowed upon many of their members the title Commercial Councilor after the manner of the German *Kommerzienrat* and made them members, however superficially, of the bureaucracy.

In addition the most important Russian industries had formed associations which acted as lobbies in St. Petersburg.[38] The southern mines and metallurgical industries were affiliated in a congress which met yearly for the discussion of common interests and petitions to the government. The Ural industries, the oil producers, the private railroads, and the Polish mineowners were likewise organized. The ironmasters in turn had established a Permanent Advisory Office of the Ironmongers. And the common interests

[38] This survey from Lur'e, pp. 66 ff.; also A. Ermanskii, "Krupnaia burzhuaziia do 1905 goda," *Obshchestvennoe dvizhenie,* I, 313 ff.

of all Russian industries could be aired before the Society for Assistance to the Improvement and Development of Manufacturing Industry, with views as conservative as its name was long, or the Russian Technical Society. Finally, at rare intervals, an All-Russian Congress of Trade and Industry convened. Under Witte's guidance, as will appear in the next chapter, the third of these congresses met at Nizhni-Novgorod in the year of the coronation of Nicholas II.

In short, whether through official arrangement or informal contact, the Russian government did not lack opportunities of hearing and influencing the views of Russian trade and industry. All depended on its willingness to make use of them. As for Witte himself, there could be no doubt of his intention to do so. One might even say that the Ministry of Finance was the bourgeois ministry, in contrast to the Ministry of the Interior, which stood for the landed aristocracy and rural Russia.

What then could Witte do for this industrial class? It was his task to advance them from their local or specialized interests and old-fashioned habits to a perception of the larger needs of the Russian economy. He had to reeducate them by providing them with new, more comprehensive opportunities. As usual autocracy had to lead, to prod. He could not adopt their suggestions unless he considered them to be in the national interest. (Thus there was ample opportunity for disagreement and misunderstanding.)

Reorienting the business community meant, in the first place, making sufficient capital available for industrial expansion, a large job in itself. In order to facilitate the financing of Russian industrial expansion Witte in 1894 reorganized the State Bank; thereafter it was also permitted to issue industrial loans.[39] He also encouraged public saving and emphasized the importance of savings banks for the accumulation of native capital. Every railroad station and school was empowered to install a savings bank

[39] Migulin, *Nasha bankovaia politika*, pp. 240 ff.; on the savings banks, *ibid.*, pp. 214 ff.

branch. The savings banks themselves were reorganized in 1895 under a new model statute, which very much improved their solidity.

But Witte did more than hoard kopeks. By the conversion of domestic loans to cheaper foreign loans in 1894, he freed in one staggering credit operation over one billion rubles for reinvestment, creating a sudden and somewhat unsettling boom on the Russian stock market.[40] Here was a fair purse for use in rapid industrial expansion. There were still other forms of assistance to industry, such as the heavy orders of railroad equipment at prices considerably above market level, which amounted to special subsidies to favored recipients.[41] In all his financial transactions with private firms, the Minister of Finance showed an unusual largesse. He never skimped when it came to passing financial benefits to private enterprises whose expansion he considered vital. Most important, however, he provided the conditions for sound credit and stable finance through the establishment of the gold standard.

Besides capital, Russian industry needed a suitable legal framework. In his budget report for 1893 Witte had spoken of "the unfavorable conditions which cramp the economic development of the country." He had in mind, at least in part, the fact that Russian legislation had not kept pace with the requirements of modern economy. Russian patent laws, for instance, required revision so as to stimulate technical inventions. Thus in 1896 a new patent statute was issued and, in the same year, a law protecting trademarks.[42]

For similar reasons Witte reorganized, in 1893, the Bureau of Weights and Measures, a Russian version of the United States Bureau of Standards.[43] Its head was Russia's most famous scientist,

[40] S. Prokopowitsch, "Über die Bedingungen der industriellen Entwicklung Russlands," *Archiv für Sozialwissenschaft und Sozialpolitik,* Ergänzungsheft 10, 1912, p. 60.

[41] Liashchenko, *Istoriia,* p. 195.

[42] *Ministerstvo Finansov, 1802–1902,* II, 561.

[43] *Ibid.,* p. 557.

Dmitrii Ivanovich Mendeleev. In 1890 this eminent chemist had presented a student petition to the minister of education and in consequence had been dismissed from his professorship at the University of St. Petersburg. Vyshnegradskii had then appointed him to the Ministry of Finance, but it was Witte who made the most extensive use of his talents. Mendeleev soon made vigorous efforts to introduce the metric system into Russian usage. Standardization of weights and measures, as well as of other trade practices, was necessary for the economic unity of Russia, and also for greater profits in foreign trade. It was applied with special diligence in the grain export.

Witte was less successful in his efforts to facilitate the formation of new joint stock companies under a model statute. A commission under Professor Tsitovich investigating this subject made little headway.[44] The advocates of the Western type of corporation law could not prevail against the Russian system of administrative review of each separate case. While no definite evidence on this matter has come to light, it seems that the Russian government, as well as Witte too toward the end, was afraid of the superior power of foreign syndicates and trusts that would have made their way in Russia more easily under Western than under Russian practice. At any rate, through his efforts the usual delays in the opening of new enterprises and factories were somewhat shortened, although the complaints on this score never ceased.

The new encouragement of private enterprise penetrated also into factory inspection. Under Bunge the task of the factory inspectors had been to protect the workers against their employers. Under Witte the emphasis changed.[45] The factory inspectors were now to work also for the dissemination of useful technical information to the management. They became agents of industrial promotion more than of the workers' welfare. Not that Witte was unaware of the needs of the workers. In 1894 he tried to introduce

[44] Migulin, *Russkii gosudarstvennyi kredit,* Vol. III, Part II, p. 395.

[45] See the author's article, "Factory Inspection under the 'Witte System': 1892–1903," *ASEER,* Vol. XIX, No. 3.

an act making employers liable for death or disability as a result of industrial accidents. Running into strong opposition in the State Council, headed by Pobedonostsev, he dropped the matter, but in 1897 he introduced and carried a bill limiting the hours of labor. In the same year he obtained the consent of the State Council for a law simplifying the issuance of passports, the indispensable identification needed by peasants working away from home, and extending their term. This again helped to increase the mobility of the Russian people and thereby aided industrial expansion.

But what did the new opportunities avail, if the Russian people were not qualified to take advantage of them? Thus Witte, already an advocate of universal elementary education, became the patron of technical education.[46] In 1894 the Ministry of Finance was given charge of all new commercial schools. At that time only eight such schools existed in Russia—in contrast to the Western countries which, Witte stated, boasted many hundreds. He invited the cooperation of the merchant community, and with their assistance over a hundred new such schools were opened during the next decade. Societies for the promotion of commercial education were formed in Kiev, Kozlov, Simbirsk, Moscow, and St. Petersburg. The Moscow society was particularly active; its school was soon attended by four thousand pupils. More specialized institutions were created in various fields, such as a distillery school, another for opticians and watchmakers, and a number of textile schools. On the university level, polytechnical institutes rose in Kiev, Warsaw, and St. Petersburg. The last, established toward the end of Witte's career as minister of finance, was one of his proudest creations.

One additional service which the Ministry of Finance could, and increasingly did, render for the Russian business community was the collection and dissemination of vital information. It was Witte who made the census of 1897 possible by allocating (in 1894) the

[46] *Ministerstvo Finansov, 1802–1902,* II, 603 ff.

necessary funds. He also improved the distribution of commercial and financial news.[47] When he took over the ministry, he decided that the weekly issues of the *Financial Messenger* (Vestnik Finansov) (started in 1885) were inadequate. They were supplemented, beginning in January, 1893, by the daily *Trade and Industry News* (Torgovo-promyshlennaia Gazeta). By 1897 this house organ of the Ministry of Finance took its place as one of the big St. Petersburg dailies. In 1899 and 1900 it even boasted a literary supplement. For the promotion of economic studies the Ministry of Finance undertook the publication of the *Russian Economic Review* (Russkoe ekonomicheskoe obozrenie), for several years the only learned journal in the field. In 1899, to round off this phase of its work, it issued a *Statistical Yearbook* for Russia (thus encroaching upon the prerogatives of the Central Statistical Bureau of the Ministry of the Interior), and in 1903 a directory of all factories and mills in European Russia. Finally, the Ministry of Finance maintained a telegraph office for commercial information, which in 1903 became Russia's official news agency.

These examples of Witte's aims and actions concerning the promotion of industrial expansion, some dating from his first years in office, others from later years, sufficiently characterize his basic orientation. He sought to liberate private initiative from all obstacles and thus clear the way for industrialization through private enterprise. Stated in a formula his prescription read: Railroad construction plus capitalism equals industrialization. His aim was capitalist industrialization after the Western model. And no fitter conclusion can be found for a description of this phase of his work than his praise of the virtues of capitalist speculation embodied in his budget report for 1896.

> That kind of speculation arouses and sustains the keen intellectual force which guides and leads labor, capital, credit, and exchange; invents better techniques of production; develops demand; finds and

[47] The various publications of the *Ministry of Finance* are listed in *Periodicheskiia izdaniia Ministerstva Finansov, 1865–1915.*

opens up new sources of profit; broadens the field for national enterprise; shows ever new possibilities to entrepreneurs; introduces into production unexplored techniques; provides capital for existing enterprises—in a word that kind of speculation appears as the most energetic promoter of industrial progress, taking upon itself all those tasks which are connected with every forward step in the field of economics.

Now that Witte was showing the way, it was up to the Russian people to prove their talents. Those who rose above the general lethargy and took advantage of the new opportunities were his allies. He was building their Russia.

IV

While the way was being cleared for the initiative of private enterprise, the Ministry of Finance was still charged with the all-important, if unspectacular, fiscal staff work for industrialization. Witte had to find the assets for the "judicious expenditure" of state funds which he had promised. He had to balance the budget, safeguard the currency, increase the gold reserve, and provide for all the other needs of the Russian government. The fiscal base of industrialization never captured the imagination of the public, yet in it lay the key to success.

How much the Russian government spent for its various economic activities in these years may come as a surprise. Roughly totaled, the appropriations for all economic ministries (Finance, Agriculture, Communications) and the service on the government debt (contracted largely for railroad construction) amounted to over 52 percent of the combined ordinary and extraordinary budgets in 1894 and 55 percent in the following year.[48] The army and navy combined claimed about half as much, nearly 29 percent in 1894, but only 22.5 percent in 1895. What was left went to the administrative agencies, the Ministry of the Interior with its extensive organization and the police, the diplomatic service, schools and universities, the Church, the courts of law, the Ministry of Justice, and the Imperial household. Obvi-

[48] The figures are taken from Khromov, pp. 518 ff.

ously the economy rather than defense was the beneficiary of Witte's financial management.

What a struggle it was to raise the revenues necessary for all the needs of the government! Almost one half of the government's income was derived from indirect taxes on consumer goods.[49] Witte always preferred these over direct taxes. He argued, perhaps with some justice under Russian conditions, that they were paid by those who could afford them. The rural masses in a natural economy tended to be self-sufficient; they would not buy the taxed goods. Unfortunately, he ignored the fact that even among the peasants a money economy was rapidly spreading (as a result of his own policy). Nor did he adhere to his principle. Soon after his appointment he proposed to revive the tax on salt, an item which everybody had to purchase.[50] This particular tax, abolished by Bunge, was wisely denied him by the State Council. But other items like tobacco, matches, kerosene, and sugar, which in capitalist Russia were becoming part of the peasant household, were taxed more and more steeply. In the fall of 1892 Witte needed money desperately, and, despite Vyshnegradskii's warning about the exhaustion of the paying powers of the population, he proposed an 11½ percent over-all increase in indirect taxes.[51]

Not all his requests were approved, but the trend toward higher taxes remained constant during his time. The total increase in the yield of indirect taxes between 1880 and 1901 has been estimated at 108 percent, which greatly exceeded the rate of population growth.[52] To be sure, Witte began to shift some of the burden from the peasants to the town dwellers. But as he hoped for the accumulation of native capital in the hands of those most likely to employ it productively, he was very loath to touch industrial and commercial profits. The peasants and the common folk in town and city thus continued to bear the growing tax load.

[49] Liashchenko, *Istoriia,* p. 190.
[50] Shvanebakh, *Nashe podatnoe delo,* p. 17.
[51] Shvanebakh, *Denezhnoe preobrazhenie i narodnoe khoziaistvo,* p. 29.
[52] *Ibid.,* p. 30.

In addition to indirect taxes the peasants had to pay their redemption dues, not to speak of local imposts to the zemstvos and their own peasant institutions. Nearly everywhere redemption dues were sadly in arrears, occasionally running three times their yearly amount in some regions of central Russia.[53] At the coronation of Nicholas II and in after years, some relief was offered to the most heavily indebted peasants. But the total picture of peasant poverty remained as grim as ever. The state took every spare kopek which might have helped the peasant to improve his lot. Some of the outlying regions of Russia in the southwest or southeast fared slightly better than the central provinces, but the difference hardly mattered.

A special form of indirect taxation developed by Witte in his early years at the Ministry of Finance, and one of his proud accomplishments, was the liquor monopoly, which he introduced at the request of Alexander III.[54] It was, for those days, a new venture for the state to enter big business. It meant no less than creating and operating a network of government liquor stores throughout Russia. Capitalist Europe, Witte's opponents reminded him, offered no model. But the Tsar considered it the only effective antidote to drunkenness. Not that intoxication was a unique feature of Russia; the per capita alcohol consumption (so far as it could be officially measured) was low. But when the peasants or workers drank, at Easter or family celebrations, imbibing was apt to be extreme. In the new factory towns it was often a menace. Thus, Witte explained in his *Memoirs,* Alexander III in his patriarchal, if aloof, benevolence had urged a state monopoly upon Bunge and Vyshnegradskii. But only Witte, so he himself wrote, had the energy and experience to undertake the assignment.

Whatever the moral impulse behind the new institution, the Minister of Finance was quick to appreciate its fiscal possibilities.

[53] In the budget report for 1893.

[54] *Ministerstvo Finansov, 1802–1902,* II, 506 ff.; also Witte, *Tsarstvovanie Nikolaia II,* Vol. I, Chapter IV, and Shvanebakh, *Nashe podatnoe delo,* pp. 51 ff.

He could tax liquor consumption more effectively than ever and, in the long run, more than make up for the heavy outlays required for the organization of so large an enterprise (which in the end counted about 40,000 employees). Witte set about his task with his usual dispatch. In 1895 the new agency was tried out in a few eastern provinces of European Russia and then gradually extended over the entire Empire; by 1901 it was complete. He supervised the work personally during several inspection trips and met with no serious criticism. What opposition he encountered came from the tavern keepers and their influential friends, particularly in St. Petersburg. On the other hand, he gained the support of the big landowners who ran distilleries on their estates and found in their production quota a steady source of income.[55] The government distilleries earned universal praise as model factories.

The only doubt in the public mind concerned the motives of the government. Had Witte aimed primarily at controlling drunkenness or at raising government revenue? His enemies insisted, against his vehement protests, that he had favored the latter, and he could not deny that revenue from the sale of vodka increased by almost one quarter as a result of the monopoly.[56] As in the tariff question, he gave no explanation of the government's mixed motives.

That the government in its campaign against drunkenness was not entirely insincere may be seen from the organization of semiofficial temperance societies, the Wardens of Popular Soberness, which followed the establishment of the liquor monopoly.[57] The chief dignitaries of a town or city, the archbishops or bishops, governors, generals, and school directors, gave luster to these societies. The appointment of the head of the St. Petersburg branch was confirmed by the Emperor himself. The good work, paid for by the state or by private donations, consisted of spreading tem-

[55] According to Benckendorff, p. 108.

[56] Shvanebakh, *Nashe podatnoe delo,* p. 51.

[57] See the article "Popechitel'stvo o narodnoi trezvosti," in Vol. XLVIII of Brockhaus-Efron, *Entsiklopedicheskii slovar'*.

perance information and, more effectively, of providing amusement and recreation outside the taverns. Tea rooms and reading rooms, popular lectures and theatricals were offered in competition with vodka. For the incurable addicts special sanatoria were set up. These steps were enlightened and well meaning, and in St. Petersburg and some other cities the Wardens of Popular Soberness made a genuine if small contribution to Russian life.

On the whole, however, the heavy weight of official patronage, the presence of the governor's wife or the police chief, for instance, caused the moral inspiration to wither. The government failed to arouse crusading instincts similar to those of American temperance societies, which were contemporaries of the Wardens. Thus the fiscal greed of the liquor monopoly stood out ever more nakedly. Yet there was at least one gain to industrialization: The sale of vodka on holidays could be strictly controlled in factory towns, thus preventing much hooliganism and loss of work on the day after, particularly in the new industrial centers of the south.

Besides the liquor monopoly, the customs tariff was a profitable source of income, particularly as imports increased. The direct taxes and the income from state properties, relatively small items, completed the ordinary revenue of the government.

Witte, like Vyshnegradskii, tried his best to make it appear that all these taxes and imposts, pressed with such severity from a desperately poor population, were sufficient for the needs of the government. The ordinary budget was easily balanced. By underestimating the expected revenue he produced a confidence-inspiring annual surplus of well over 100 million rubles in 1895 and after.[58] The more discerning observers, however, looked past these figures at the extraordinary budget, which listed, on the debit side, the expenditures for loan conversions, railway construction, and special military purposes, and, on the credit side as the chief item of income, the government loans both domestic and foreign. Anyone going to the trouble of adding the ordinary and extraordinary

[58] Liashchenko, *Istoriia,* p. 188.

budgets would find out that, year after year, the total budget balanced only with the help of these loans. In other words, despite the impressive show of balanced budgets, which Witte knew how to stage to advantage, the Russian government could not make ends meet. In its heavy outlays for railroad construction it was forced into perpetual deficit financing.

Attention thus shifts from the budget to the extraordinary sources of income. In order to balance the combined budgets Witte borrowed heavily in both the foreign and the domestic money market, but more extensively in the latter. He did so to the tune of two and a half billion rubles of the total three and a half billion by which he increased the Russian state debt.[59] The yield of the domestic market, however, was limited, for it also had to supply much of the capital for private enterprise. Moreover, it netted the government only paper rubles, while for a number of reasons gold was needed. As before, therefore, the foreign money market was of greater significance.

Witte's chief sources of supply for foreign loans, or of gold (which meant the same thing), were the big French banking houses and the small French investor.[60] It was a paradox that the Russian drive for industrialization should be financed so largely out of the French rejection of industrialization. Under the Third Republic, France was overflowing with savings that wanted investment. It is only fair to add, however, that Russia would never have obtained French capital so readily if money had not been equally abundant in the other money markets of the world. The 1890s were a good era for debtors; credit was cheap. No wonder that part of Europe's wealth flowed down into the cultural hinterland on remarkably easy terms.

It was Vyshnegradskii, it will be remembered, who had first succeeded in orienting the French money market toward Russian opportunities. The French response, however, was prompted more

[59] *Ibid.*, p. 189.

[60] Feis, Chapters II, V, IX.

by political than economic motives. In its search for an escape from the diplomatic isolation in which Bismarck had kept France, the French government was eager, on the whole, to extend financial support to Russia and to convert the incipient financial ties into a political and military alliance. After the conclusion of such an alliance it was patently to French advantage to help promote the Witte system. By 1900 one quarter of French foreign investment was held in Russia.[61]

Under these conditions, the French banking houses gladly availed themselves of the fat commissions which the Russian government paid. The Rothschilds, though in decline as a financial empire, were still very influential. Witte won the confidence of the head of the house, Baron Alphonse Rothschild, and obtained many loans for Russia with his assistance. Russian anti-Semitism normally did not prevent the conclusion of such loans. Of all Paris banking houses, however, it was the Credit Lyonnais which was the chief broker of the Russian government. In view of Russia's new dependence on the Paris banks, the manipulation of the French bourse became an ever more pressing concern of the Russian Minister of Finance. Through his agent in Paris, Arthur Raffalovich, Witte kept abreast of affairs and learned to manipulate them to Russia's advantage. As the disciple of Jan Bloch and the railway kings Witte proved an extremely expert speculator. When, for instance, he intended to float a new loan, he created, by the skillful use of Russian gold holdings abroad, a temporary glut on the European market and thus secured unusually favorable terms.[62]

Witte was also keenly aware of the value of a favorable press and proceeded to buy pro-Russian sentiment on a large scale among the French newspapers. So successful was he that next to the French state *rente* nothing was so gilt-edged in the esteem of the French *rentier* as the Russian state bonds. How matters had

[61] *Ibid.*, p. 51.

[62] Olga Crisp, "Russian Financial Policy and the Gold Standard at the End of the Nineteenth Century," *Economic History Review*, VI, No. 2, 171.

changed since Kankrin or Reutern! Witte needed only to ask for credit, and the French investors came rushing. In 1897, when the Russian pressure for French loans had become so frequent that the French government refused the listing of Russian securities on the bourse, the Credit Lyonnais disposed of them by private sale. Needless to say, there was another side to the extensive loans which Witte obtained from France. Financial dependence constituted political dependence as well, particularly as, in 1899, 37 percent of the Russian national debt was held abroad. But of that in another chapter.

It is one thing to borrow abroad, however, and another to maintain one's credit while continuing to borrow, as Russia did. It was absolutely necessary that Russia pay her dividends punctually, and pay them in gold. Thus the balance of trade required Witte's attention as it had that of his predecessors. In the last analysis Russia had to earn her gold by her exports. Witte followed tradition by forcing exports to the utmost. He also improved the marketability of Russian exports. He tried to increase the value of Russia's cereal exports, for instance, by favoring the processed goods over the bare raw materials.[63] In the grain trade he encouraged new ways of improving the quality and uniformity of the various grades.

Yet during his first years in office the situation was more desperate than ever. In 1894 the world prices for grain hit bottom. At a time when Russia increased its industrial imports for the sake of rapid industrial expansion, its agricultural exports fetched about one half of what they had brought in the 1870s. This meant that despite the recent famine Russia had to export still more. Under Witte 15 percent of the grain crop was exported, as compared with 5 percent under Reutern.[64] Fortunately the weather proved propitious and supplied good crops for the first years.

Other agricultural exports, however, came to Witte's aid and

[63] Wittschewsky, p. 191.

[64] Khromov, p. 253, and Liashchenko, *Istoriia,* p. 138.

took up the slack. Siberian eggs and butter of good quality now entered the foreign market in ever larger quantities. Sugar from the Ukraine was another indispensable export and, for that reason, was much supervised. In 1895 Witte established a sugar cartel, allocating the production quotas through his own ministry. In 1902 he proved utterly intractable when it came to the international regulation of sugar marketing; Russia could not surrender a strong gold earner. Besides sugar, timber and flax played their part. Next to agricultural exports, which constituted more than three quarters of the total, oil and manganese found good markets abroad. In the case of oil (as of sugar) the Ministry of Finance had a special interest in maximizing the profits of the producers and for that reason favored marketing agreements among them. As early as 1893 a syndicate of Baku oil producers had been formed under its supervision. In order to strengthen the syndicate in its competition with Rockefeller's Standard Oil Company the government also granted it preferential rates on the trans-Caucasus railroad, over which it shipped its oil to the Black Sea.[65] But, everything considered, it was still humiliating that Russia exported mostly cheap, unprocessed raw materials. And it was too early to expect any earnings of foreign currencies from the Trans-Siberian Railroad.

Thanks to the various efforts of the Minister of Finance, however, the balance of trade remained favorable despite all difficulties. The official figures on imports and exports showed, like the budget, a respectable balance. Although no longer as high as under Vyshnegradskii, the surplus still ran well above a hundred million rubles a year, at least until 1899.[66] These figures, incidentally, were considered too conservative at the time. As in his fore-

[65] M. Ia. Gefter, "Tsarizm i zakonodatel'stvoe 'regulirovanie' deiatel'nosti sindikatov i trestov v Rossii," *Istoricheskie zapiski,* No. 54 (1955). See also A. A. Fursenko and L. E. Shepelev, "Neftianye monopolii Rossii i ikh uchastie v bor'be za razdel mirovogo rynka v 90-kh godakh XIV v.," *Materialy po istorii SSSR,* VI, 47 ff.

[66] See Khromov, p. 469.

cast of revenues, the Minister of Finance deliberately underestimated Russian exports in order to present, when the actual figures had become available, a more favorable balance of trade.[67]

The concomitant of export stimulation was import restriction. In this matter Witte was the chief beneficiary of the tariff of 1891, which he left largely untouched. Further raises in the tariff rates were not feasible, for they would seriously hamper the industrial expansion on which Witte had staked so much. Even the existing rates, it could be argued, already had that effect. Russia had reached the limits of tariff protection for still other reasons. As it happened, Germany, the chief consumer of Russian exports, was also the chief supplier of Russia's imports. Was it not fair that she should refuse to absorb Russian grains unless she were given an equal opportunity for her industrial exports? As might be expected, the tariff of 1891 aroused serious repercussions in Germany, and soon after Witte took office he was forced into a tariff war with the German government.[68]

Tension over tariff policy was an old story between the neighbors. After 1879 Bismarck, under the pressure of the Prussian agrarians, had gradually raised the duties on Russian imports. In 1891, Caprivi, embarking upon his New Course, granted some European countries (and likewise the United States) rather large concessions on agricultural imports. Russia, however, was barred from similar privileges because her tariff of that year had seriously curtailed German industrial exports to Russia. As a matter of fact the German government had tried to forestall the application of the Russian tariff of 1891 to German goods, but the Russian government had insisted upon full tariff sovereignty; the tariff was too crucial a factor in Russia's road to economic independence to be easily revised.

As neither side was willing to make concessions, a tariff war broke out between German manufactured goods and Russian food-

[67] Crisp, *Economic History Review,* VI, 160, note 5.
[68] Wittschewsky, pp. 160 ff.

stuffs. Witte soon took the offensive. As Germany had rejected Russian conciliatory moves in 1892, he began to retaliate by imposing a 20–30 percent increase over the regular tariff rates on goods from all countries discriminating against Russia. In addition he raised the rates for German shipping and finally slapped a punitive 50 percent tax on all German goods. The German government, giving tit for tat, then charged an additional 50 percent tax on all Russian goods. There the matter rested. Meanwhile Witte took measures to dispose of the export grain without an appreciable price drop and granted especially low rail fares to grains exported through Austria-Hungary and Rumania. On their part, German and Austrian diplomats gloatingly predicted the inevitable economic collapse of Russia and her decline as a great power.[69]

To end the stalemate, Witte finally threatened to stop the seasonal migration of farmhands from Russia into the Junker estates of eastern Germany, which would have meant ruin to the latter.[70] Eager for a settlement himself, he thus brought the German government to heel. Under the Russo-German trade treaty of March, 1894, Russia did reduce her tariff in regard to certain industrial items but regained her competitive position in the German grain market. Yet harmony between the partners was never fully restored. In subsequent years the Germans never ceased to complain that Russian authorities, while not violating the letter of the agreement, interpreted it in a rigorously pro-Russian spirit. While German commercial travelers and salesmen steadily strengthened their position in Russia, the Russian government fought desperately for every kopek's worth of Russian economic sovereignty. The lesson of the tariff war was clear. Russia was still too dependent upon her foreign customers to achieve the full autonomy necessary for the rapid development of her internal

[69] Langer, *Franco-Russian Alliance,* p. 228, note 60.

[70] See Kovalevskii's reminiscences in *Istoricheskii vestnik,* CXL, 256.

resources. But that was no reason to accept such dependence forever.

Whether complete freedom in tariff affairs would have improved the foreign trade balance of Russia was another question. For out of her export surplus she had to pay not only her imports but also the charges for foreign loans contracted by both the government and private enterprise, the maintenance of her foreign missions, shipping and insurance fees, and the expenses of Russian travelers abroad. Behind the balance of trade loomed the balance of payments. Here, too, Witte made progress. One improvement in the balance of payments resulted from his continuous efforts to convert the old state loans to new ones on better terms. The interest rate for international loans was slowly falling, which provided Witte with an opportunity to refund the government's debt at slightly less than 4 percent.[71] He also tried his utmost to transfer the shipping of Russian imports and exports from foreign to native bottoms and thus again save foreign exchange. In addition, he tried to increase the output of Russia's gold mines.

Yet, for once, Witte's efforts proved insufficient. If the foreign currencies earned by Russian exports were balanced against the payments due in foreign currencies, a significant, though undetermined, deficit resulted, with all the evil consequences which Russian ministers of finance had come to know only too well.[72] Thus it was imperative that Witte conclude foreign loans with which to balance the accounts. In effect, he paid for the old loans by contracting new ones, and part of the gold never left the French vaults at all.

Some of the foreign gold, however, did enter Russian ownership and increased the gold reserves necessary for the conversion of the ruble to the gold standard. All Russian ministers of finance

[71] This figure is from the budget report for 1902.

[72] The deficit was estimated by the economist Taburno at 895 mill rubles between 1892 and 1896, at 1,222 mill rubles between 1897 and 1901. Wittschewsky, p. 175.

since Reutern had aimed at this step. Witte had originally given no thought to the matter until persuaded by Bunge. Afterward he applied himself seriously to the Herculean task of providing Russia with a stable currency. And in this field too he quickly showed a masterly touch. One big preliminary step toward conversion was the stabilization of the paper ruble, which required first that all foreign speculation with the ruble cease. This, in turn, meant an attack upon the stronghold of such speculation, the Berlin ruble market.[73]

It was another indication of Russian backwardness, and more specifically of the weakness of the Russian banking system, that most foreign exchange transactions took place in Berlin. A large part of Russian foreign trade, both import and export, centered in Germany. It was therefore natural that, for lack of suitable facilities in Russia, exporters and importers of both countries should bank on the German side of the border. From Königsberg or Breslau the rubles then drifted to Berlin. It was equally natural that so large an accumulation of rubles should incite speculation. The Berlin speculators would take bonds and stocks to Russia, use them as collateral for loans of paper rubles, and then return to Germany. Having exchanged their rubles for marks, they would buy up more securities and repeat the process. After several such transactions large quantities of rubles would accumulate in Berlin and their price would fall, whereupon the speculators redeemed their securities in Russian banks at a reduced price. Such speculation played havoc with the stability of the ruble; more than once it had brought the Russian treasury to the brink of bankruptcy. Witte was resolved to end it for good. Now that France had replaced Germany as a source of loans and the new trade agreement had been concluded with Germany, he could do so with impunity.

Witte had already prepared the ground in 1893 when he secured, over the protests of the Russian banks (which had too

[73] For the following see Schulze-Gävernitz, *Volkswirtschaftliche Studien aus Russland,* pp. 502 ff.

often connived at ruble speculation), the right to control the outflow of money. He had also intermittently engaged in the buying and selling of ruble drafts, so as to offset the fluctuation in the ruble. His opportunity came in the fall of 1894, when rumors about the fatal sickness of Alexander III began to circulate. Anticipating domestic disturbances, the Berlin speculators then began to speculate *à la baisse*. They sold large quantities of rubles cheaply and spread rumors inducing others to do likewise. Witte meanwhile instructed his agents to buy up all the rubles offered. Suddenly, in October, there were not enough rubles left in Berlin to fill the contracts which the bankers, expecting further supplies of cheap rubles, had made with the Russian government. As the Russian banks were not allowed to export rubles without permission, the German speculators were at Witte's mercy. They had to buy back from him the required rubles, at a gain, it was guessed, of 20 million to the Russian treasury.[74] In the end he let them off relatively lightly, having taught them a lesson they would not forget, until the introduction of the gold standard made further tampering with the ruble impossible.

Thus the stage was being set for the introduction of the gold standard. Vyshnegradskii had already laid the foundation. With the help of foreign loans, the export drive, import restrictions, and domestic gold production netting the government about 50 million rubles a year, Witte increased the gold reserves within three years to a point at which conversion could be attempted. What the Russian ministers of finance since Reutern had vainly attempted, Witte was on the point of achieving. The economic scene, and the prospects of industrial expansion, brightened considerably. Once the ruble was converted to the gold standard, Witte expected, foreign capital would flow freely into Russian private enterprise; industrialization would rapidly get under way, repay the government for its outlays, and enable it to reduce its foreign debt. After conversion the formula of the Witte system

[74] Oldenburg, I, 83.

would be amended to read: Railroad construction plus capitalism plus the gold standard equals rapid industrialization.

V

This survey of the Witte system as it unfolded during his early years at the Ministry of Finance would be incomplete without at least a brief mention of its relation to agriculture. Agriculture was the one phase of Russian economy which, despite its pre-eminence in Russian life, was most foreign to the Minister of Finance. As a railroad executive and government official he had thus far worked only with the most flexible and modern segments of Russian society; they continued to be his special care. How would he look at rural Russia?

He would look at it, once he became seriously interested, through the eyes of Friedrich List. Agriculture, so List's argument ran, would be stimulated through the industrial expansion, which would increase the consumption of food, provide better transportation and technical equipment, and, by the outflow of intelligence from the cities, gradually civilize the countryside. According to this view no special efforts on behalf of agriculture were necessary.

For a Russian minister of finance, however, List's condescending indifference toward rural life was not quite enough. The urgent need for increased and improved exports brought agriculture more directly to his attention. Rural welfare and efficiency strengthened Russia's economy as a whole. The great famine had already dramatized, among other things, the primitive method of cultivation prevailing among the peasants. One result of both famine and Witte's new economic policy was, as related earlier, the creation (in 1894) of a ministry of State Domains and Agriculture, which for the first time raised agriculture to a state concern. Its head was E. A. Ermolov, an expert on agrarian problems, although no match for Witte's ebullient energy.

Undaunted by departmental boundaries, the Minister of Finance reached directly into Ermolov's domain, at least in regard to one major crop, Turkestan cotton. Foreign cotton constituted the largest single item in Russia's imports. If it could be reduced, her trade balance would be substantially improved. Thus it was logical that the Ministry of Finance should encourage native cotton production. After again raising the tariff on cotton in 1894, it also granted its own growers considerable tax relief in 1900.[75]

Witte's interest, however, was not limited to a single crop. A Russian minister of finance determined to direct Russia's national economy as a whole could not but come to grips sooner or later with the basic problems of Russian agriculture. It was not surprising that Witte's experiences as minister of finance produced a gradual but profound evolution in his views of agrarian affairs. At the outset he was too preoccupied with the Siberian railroad and other responsibilities to pay more than passing attention to agriculture, but it was never far from his mind. In his budget report for 1894 he used the obvious facts of peasant poverty and falling grain prices as a further justification of his policy of industrialization; Russia had to become economically autonomous in order to escape the unprofitable and humiliating dependence on foreign markets. A few months later he pleaded in the State Council for an exploratory study of the legal organization of peasant life.

In the following year's report (1895), he created a stir by denying that the declining grain prices—they had reached bottom in 1894—were universally harmful to Russian economy. No question but what the private producers were suffering. But the consumers were actually gaining, as long as there was no over-all shortage of grain. Among the consumers the peasants themselves formed a large group. To bolster up his argument Witte, always eager for professorial endorsement, set a group of Russian econo-

[75] J. Whitman, "Turkestan Cotton in Imperial Russia," *ASEER,* XV, No. 2 (April, 1956), 199.

mists headed by the Moscow professor A. I. Chuprov to work.[76] When their book appeared it contained the assertion that, since 70 percent of the peasants in European Russia did not raise enough food for themselves and had to buy some, the cheaper it was the better. Cheap and abundant foodstuffs would greatly accelerate industrialization. This argument, however, aroused much protest when it was published.

In his budget report of 1895 Witte, under pressure from the agrarians, also stated that Russian agriculture called for improved techniques and better economic conditions in general. As for the low grain prices, he wrote, he was trying to offset the trend through the new trade agreements with Germany and Austria-Hungary, which gave Russian grains more advantageous terms in their chief markets. In his report of 1896 Witte suddenly stopped offering conventional remedies and struck out in a new direction. After a passage that amounted to an endorsement of the kulaks as the element most helpful in liberating the masses of Russia from their inertia, he announced: "Our agriculture is moving along the road of capitalist development." He did not spell out the revolutionary implications of his observation and declare the peasant commune obsolete, but his remark indicated his opposition to the collective mode of peasant farming and thus to the entire legal and social order under which the peasantry lived. A few years later Witte did indeed step forward as the champion of agrarian reform even more drastic than Stolypin's later legislation.

The budget report for 1896 showed where Witte stood in the discussion of the agrarian question. Instinct and economic considerations placed him on the side of the kulaks. By the same token he was a bitter enemy of the Russian landed nobility; he viewed their decline with an icy objectivity. They had been spoiled by easy credit and "exaggerated hopes for government assistance," he declared in a speech before the State Council in 1895.[77] Since

[76] Chuprov and Posnikov, Vol. I, p. ii.

[77] Cited by Baturinskii, p. 55.

emancipation the government had wasted two billion rubles on that class. "Whatever the reasons, there can hardly be any doubt that only a tiny part of this money was spent for the improvement of agriculture or other productive purposes. As far as credit is concerned, the government has done on its part all that can be done to enable the landowners to hold their own." Witte therefore refused to pamper these wastrels any longer. For the same reason he distrusted the zemstvos, which acted as their spokesmen. But in 1895, when he tried to facilitate the transfer of land from the nobility to the peasants through adding to the powers of the Peasant Land Bank, he was stopped short; he failed to carry the consent of his fellow ministers.[78] It was no easy task to override the resentment of the victims of the new order and of their allies in the bureaucracy.

Obviously, the task Witte had set himself required the support of the Russian public, and propaganda efforts to win it. From the beginning of his career he had been unusually alert to the value of publicity. Of all ministers of the Tsar, he alone possessed a sense of modern public relations.[79] Under his management the annual budget reports became instruments of public enlightenment. Through them Witte took issue with the criticism of his opponents, offering thereby an invaluable commentary on his policies, the economic conditions of Russia, and the problems of the national future. Written in a layman's language, they appealed to the intelligence of the Russian reader in trying to enlist his enthusiasm for a great common effort. Occasionally the ring of passion would break through the calm arguments and dry statistics. To judge by the comments in the contemporary press, his reports were closely read; some magazines reprinted them in their entirety.

The extent of Witte's publicity effort was impressive for its time. He not only saw to it that he enjoyed a good press in Russia; he arranged for Russian participation in all the great world's

[78] *Ibid.*, p. 54.

[79] See A. E. Kaufman's reminiscences in *Istoricheskii vestnik,* CXL, 224, 229.

fairs of the time as a demonstration of Russian aims and accomplishments.[80] For each he supplied a splendid volume on Russian trade and industry, written by the foremost experts. He also maintained a network of agents abroad, whose tasks included influencing the local press, refuting all attacks on his system, and advertising the economic and cultural progress of Russia in general.[81] Finally, he enlisted the support of the professors, who supplied scientific data for his arguments and conclusions. Russian credit abroad and his own success as minister of finance at home depended on persistent dissemination of the official optimism. He had to advertise economic victories. He also served notice thereby that henceforth Russia wished to be considered economically and industrially a great power.

Looking back over the wide range of Witte's activities as minister of finance one cannot but admire his determination and foresight. He was truly "the executive director of the great economic corporation of the Russian people." Thus his ministry throbbed with energy while he was at work in his calm, efficient, and (everything considered) amazingly selfless way.[82]

Being mortal, he had his foibles which made his subordinates smile in astonishment. It was small matter that he made grammatical mistakes[83] and showed his lack of general education in his speeches before the State Council.[84] More eyebrows were raised in his ministry over the fact that he played up to titled courtiers or others with close relations to the Court. Why should he be so

[80] *Ministerstvo Finansov, 1802–1902,* II, 567.

[81] A good example is Anspach, *La Russie économique et l'oeuvre de M. de Witte.* Witte had his agents in Paris, London, Berlin, and Genoa.

[82] This was the considered opinion of his closest associates. See, for instance, *S. J. Witte, 30. August 1892—30. August 1902: Ein Gedenkblatt zum 10 jährigen Ministerjubiläum des russischen Finanzministers.* The authors of this pamphlet need not have written, unless they really meant it, that Sergei Iulevich was a modest man who never liked to advertise his actions.

[83] Propper, p. 155.

[84] According to A. A. Polovtsev. See "Iz dnevnika A. A. Polovtseva," *KA,* Vol. XLVI, entry for April 4, 1900.

obsequious?[85] Most of all one wonders what his subordinates thought of their head in his role as chief of the Russian Border Guards.[86] In 1893 these guards, whose task was the collection of customs and the prevention of smuggling along Russia's boundaries and who in 1902 numbered 62,000 men, were placed under the Minister of Finance. As a result the Emperor granted Witte a special uniform, and occasionally, in the grandest pose which the Minister of Finance could strike, he would review his troops on horseback. Thus he tried to fit himself, somewhat incongruously, into the military pageantry of the Empire.

But whatever his shortcomings, it was to his lasting credit that he designed the first modern experiment in speeding up the economic development of a backward country.

[85] Maksimov's reminiscences in *Istoricheskii vestnik,* CXL, 253.
[86] *Detstvo,* pp. 318–21.

4. Mid-Passage

[Witte] was eager to produce a set of conditions economically and politically, in which the newly qualified elements of the community could grow and equip themselves morally and intellectually for the leading part they would one day be called upon to play in Russia and perhaps in Europe.

E. J. DILLON, The Eclipse of Russia

All revolutions proceed from the fact that the government does not satisfy in time the demands of the people as they arise. They proceed from the fact that the government remains deaf to the needs of the people. WITTE, Memoirs

I

WHEN WITTE set out on his career as minister of finance, the political atmosphere of St. Petersburg, as observed by foreigners, was dense with suspicion of the West. The American minister to Russia, Andrew D. White, was obviously upset by the sentiments which he encountered: "There has never been a time probably," he reported home in July, 1893, "when such a feeling of isolation from the rest of the world and aversion to foreign influence of any sort have prevailed in Russia as at present. It is shared by the great majority from the highest to the lowest, and it is echoed in the press." [1] He was particularly aroused over the process of Russification just then culminating, so he wrote, in Poland, the Baltic provinces, Finland, and elsewhere.

It was not only the American who was shocked. The German Ambassador, Prince Radolin, gave a similar description of official opinion two years later:

Western Europe is rotten and, so the Russians think, must be purified before Russia could pay attention to it. For the time being, it is still a moral danger to Russia, and therefore she must prevent close contact

[1] Andrew D. White to John W. Foster, July 6, 1893, NA.

with the West as much as possible. Nihilism and all revolutionary ideas are, according to opinion here, the product of European civilization. I would not have believed it possible that such an intense fanaticism could rule in Russia as I see it now . . . and not only in a few exalted heads.[2]

How, one wonders, did the Witte system fit into such anti-Western orientation? Witte was quietly making arrangements for attracting large sums of foreign capital, for imitating Western capitalism and industrialism, for accelerating the silent revolution from without, while the government was trying to prevent any contamination by Europe.

The answer was that Witte himself, with his correct political conservatism and his sense of Russian destiny, had no understanding of the revolutionary implications of his system. How much less could his contemporaries see whither he was aiming! At the outset, indeed, his determination to finish the Siberian railroad, expand Russian industries, and improve Russian credit abroad seemed to confirm the official mood. He gave it both a new buoyancy and a sound economic underpinning. How confident and expansive the mood of the capital was may be gathered from Prince Radolin's report of conversations with high-ranking Russian officers. The official circles were full of talk about the cultural tasks of Russia in Asia, he stated in the dispatch already quoted. They looked forward to the time when Russia would be a *Kulturstaat* of the first rank. Witte had grasped this fact and worked with great skill, though perhaps too recklessly, for this project. Russia had at last awakened to new life after many years of sleep. She was expanding in all directions and making great strides in building railroads in order to open up the most distant regions and find new sources of production. Her credit had attained colossal, unprecedented proportions and she possessed resources greater than any other country. She need not shrink from any task; she was invincible. "In short," Radolin concluded, "in everything which I

[2] Radolin to Hohenlohe, July 14, 1895, *Grosse Politik,* IX, 357.

hear they proclaim with one voice that it is Russia's mission to gain in due time the mastery of the world." For the moment, however, Russian expansion was limited to the east and southeast, where European civilization and "the cancer to which it gave rise" had not yet penetrated. The officers to whom Radolin had talked were not exaggerating; Witte, so his comments on Badmaev's report showed, shared the imperialist exultation.

And yet, as an imperialist he was thwarted both by the backwardness of Russia and by his own principles. The incompatibility of traditional Russia and his modernism, of Russian poverty and his buoyant optimism, could not easily be glossed over. Late in 1895, when he was writing his budget report for the following year—the same report in which he so extravagantly praised the virtues of capitalist speculation and hailed the advent of capitalist agriculture—he was aware of a growing undercurrent of criticism that called attention to the discrepancies. The state, it was being whispered against him, was growing rich while the poor grew ever poorer. The government was siphoning the savings of the people into the Treasury, and, worse, it was becoming the agent of foreign bankers. In his report Witte proudly refuted these accusations, but his arguments only tended to sharpen the inevitable conflict. From 1896 the Witte system was under increasingly bitter attack. The present chapter, then, while tracing the evolution of the Witte system to the turn of the century, will deal also with the rising tensions that surrounded his work.

Nicholas II had succeeded his father in November, 1894. With Alexander III Witte had been fortunate, but the auspices for such excellent relations with his successor were hardly favorable. Alexander III had died in the prime of life. His heir was a young man of twenty-six, endowed with an unusually good head and exceptional charm, well educated beyond the run of the Romanovs, but with little experience in government. Most important, he lacked even a pittance of the innate sagacity and drive of leadership. As Nicholas himself confessed to his uncle the Grand Duke Vladimir

Aleksandrovich, in the year of his coronation; "I always give in and in the end am made the fool, without will, and without character." [3] Witte, in his *Memoirs*, ascribed to him the temperament of a woman.[4] Uncertain of himself and untried, he was suddenly given possession of the largest powers claimed by any European ruler. It was a tragedy that he could never hold his own in the interminable human contest for personal ascendancy; his personality was too small for the format of his office. How then could he dominate Russia as the autocrat must? How could he, who was determined above all to preserve autocracy, ever be master in his own government? Government, even under autocracy, requires team work. Nicholas, however, was never able to rally an effective official team to his leadership. Foreign diplomats were soon aware that his ministers wrangled among themselves for preferment and that even Pobedonostsev's influence waxed and waned with alarming rapidity.[5] There was no longer a steady hand to guide the ship of state. And before long Nicholas was leaning on unworthy advisers or even scoundrels.

It was unlikely, then, that this gentle, cultivated, sensitive, and prudish young man would be able to suffer for long the airs of the self-made industrial tycoon with his uncouth Ukrainian speech and rough manners. How could the Tsar assert himself against such a forceful, elemental presence? Witte had never learned to mince words; he would even bang his fist on the table and make

[3] In his letter of November 26, 1896, *KA*, XVII, 220.

[4] Witte, *Tsarstvovanie Nikolaia II,* II, 228. The sources on Nicholas II, unfortunately, are very limited. The Soviet edition of his diary, *Dnevnik Imperatora Nikolaia II, 1890–1906 gg.,* obviously omits many entries.

[5] Sir Frank Lascelles, for instance, reported from the British embassy on August 11, 1895, his impressions that the Emperor did not have central direction of affairs; each minister was on his own and was competing with the others. PRO, Foreign Office Series 65, Vol. 1491. In November, 1895, the German diplomats reported that the new course was progressive conservatism; a year later, that Pobedonostsev's influence was greater than even under Alexander III. In May, 1897, they said that he was losing influence fast, and in May, 1898, that his influence was great. In 1900 it was said to be low again. Bonn, Series 67, *Allgemeine Angelegenheiten Russlands,* Vol. LXX ff.

the Emperor wince.[6] Their relationship had some semblance to that between Bismarck and William II before Bismarck's fall, except that Witte was a straightforward and simple man and the Emperor less robust in his self-confidence than his German cousin. Witte also had to reckon with the Empress Alexandra, watching jealously over the respect paid to her husband. Even during his father's last illness and before their marriage, she had admonished him: "Don't let others be put first and you left out!" [7] She would instinctively turn the Emperor against Witte, who already was suspect in her eyes because of his wife.

Witte apparently did not realize at the outset how deeply he jarred the sensibilities of his young master. He was too much the self-made man to adjust his manner, with the quick grasp of the courtier, to Nicholas's feminine temperament. Only bitter disillusionment over the years taught him how deep the gulf was. And the incompatibilities, events were to prove, did not stop at matters of temperament but covered the entire range of Russian life. The polarity between the modernizer and the traditionalist is deeply embedded in Russian history. It had cropped up in the tragedy between Peter and his son, in the polemics between Westernizers and Slavophiles. Now—to speak only of the official circles—it came to permeate the relations between Witte and Nicholas II. The figure among his ancestors whom Nicholas II liked least was, typically enough, Peter the Great.[8] Through too much admiration for European culture, Nicholas once observed, "Peter had stamped out Russian habits, the good customs of his forebears, and the usages bequeathed by the nation." Witte, on the other hand, was driven on by that very same admiration. As he saw it, Russia had to conform to European ways if she wanted to hold her own. Catching up imposed brutal sacrifices on the Russian people, as

[6] Witte, *Tsarstvovanie Nikolaia II,* I, 10 ff. See also Dillon, *The Eclipse of Russia,* p. 113.

[7] *Dnevnik Imperatora Nikolaia II, 1890–1906 gg.,* p. 83.

[8] Mossolov, p. 16.

it had in the days of Peter. But Nicholas was temperamentally incapable of demanding such sacrifices from his subjects.

In his first years, to be sure, there was no inkling of the later clashes. Nicholas stood dutifully by his Minister of Finance, even against his mother, the Dowager Empress Maria Fedorovna (who later was Witte's principal ally in the Imperial family). In August, 1895, she wrote to her son—to cite an example of Nicholas's original loyalty to Witte (and also of the old-fashioned conception of state finance prevailing at Court)—asking him to cancel a loan of nearly 500,000 rubles paid to the husband of one of her friends, the Princess Lopukhin-Demidov, and begging him for a loan of another half million without interest.[9] She added the gratuitous complaint that Witte was enriching the Treasury at the expense of the landed proprietors. Nicholas answered for once firmly and in the negative: "It would be a fine state of affairs indeed at the Treasury, if in Witte's absence (he is at present on a holiday) I were to give a million to one, two million to another, etc. All that has been accumulated—and what forms one of the most brilliant pages in the history of dear Papa's reign is the sound condition of our finances—would be destroyed in the course of a few years." In this spirit Nicholas tried to continue his father's policies.

He was a conscientious and well-meaning ruler, applying himself diligently to his new duties and spending long hours secluded in his study. His exalted sense of responsibility and his political views appeared clearly in his annotations to the annual reports of his governors general, city commandants, and provincial governors.[10] He read their reports with obvious care, underlined what he considered significant, and commented in a lively manner. In the reports covering the year 1895, one finds, for instance, almost

[9] E. J. Bing, ed., *The Secret Letters of the Last Tsar,* his mother's letter of August 3, 1895; his reply of August 13.

[10] *Svod vysochaishikh otmetok po vsepodanneishim otchetam za 1895 g. general-gubernatorov, gubernatorov, voennikh gubernatorov i gradonachal'nikov* (available also for the years 1891–93, 1896–1900).

five hundred Imperial marginal jottings made during the rather busy year of 1896. By far the largest number of comments were concerned with education. Nothing seemed to touch him more deeply than the need of his people for schools. When he was told that only half of the school-age children in St. Petersburg were receiving elementary education, he jotted down: "And this in the capital of Russia!" Next in frequency among his comments stood his concern for better roads and medical service. The misery of the peasants likewise aroused his sympathies, as did the sufferings of colonists in Siberia. When he read of the plight of the nobility in the Vologda province he jotted down: "All this is very sad." Conversely, he rejoiced over every sign of popular piety. And he followed the welfare of the Orthodox Church with particular attention. His strongest single outburst occurred when he read of a delay in the construction of a new cathedral. By contrast, problems of administration or of trade and industry remained rather in the background.

This gentle and compassionate ruler was, however, quite strict when he scanned the order of his political household. Everything must be tidy under the Imperial rule. No zemstvo, town duma, or Assembly of Nobles was allowed to overstep its boundaries and discuss affairs not in its competence. But if it applied itself to its legitimate tasks humanely and diligently, the Emperor would write, "I am pleased to hear that" or "Praiseworthy," or suggest a decoration. In case of disorder or opposition Nicholas would bristle with righteous indignation and recommend the use of the police to the limit. But on the whole he shunned violence. When informed, for instance, of the irregularities among the Siberian gold miners, he ordered, "besides repression, the soonest possible measures for a new gold mining statute!" Only occasionally did a note of irritation creep into his observations. When he was told by the governor of Grodno that with more enlightenment strikes would cease, he objected: "That is not true. Strikes were invented by educated Europe." [11] Another time, when he read a complaint about the growing power of the Jews in Ekaterinoslav province, he sighed: "Unfortunately that is so, but what can one do?" And a report about the arrogance of foreign experts who caused strikes in the southern metallurgical industries provoked an indignant note. Underlying all these comments one senses an attitude basically anticapitalist, antimodern, and inwardly resentful of the changes in Russian life which he could not grasp. From the start, Nicholas lacked political understanding suited to his age. He harked back toward Muscovy.

But being the autocrat of Russia was indeed a superhuman task in those years. The traditional structure of the Empire was daily being weakened by the subversive Western examples in every aspect of contemporary life. It had barely held up in the reign of Alexander III; it collapsed before his son was fifty. By the claims of his resounding title the Tsar should have been master of the situation. But how could anyone caught in the insidious, only dimly realized disintegration of traditional Russia rise to political mastery? It was not the government but rather the revolutionaries who were in daily touch with the most crucial, yet largely invisible innovations of Russian life. Men like Lenin or Trotsky were groping for forms of leadership that would hold up under the strains of modern mass politics in a backward country. The person least capable of adjustment, by the very nature of his exalted station, was the Tsar.

Immured in privilege and ceremony, he spent his days in the quiet of the Imperial palaces and their fine parks. In the deeper layers of his mind he craved, like so many of his generation, the green pastures and still waters of nature. Detained indoors, he always had an eye open for the weather outside. His taste for society was simple. Increasingly his old comrades in the Guards and the narrow circle of his family sufficed for company. Beyond stood

[11] *Ibid.*, p. 41.

the serried ranks of officials, military and civil, who dutifully reported to him what they did and planned and what, no doubt, they thought would please "the Imperial Personage" of whom they stood in such awe. Thus the Tsar moved as in a vacuum, far removed from the new Russia that was emerging. His ignorance of reality reached preposterous dimensions even in the years when he was still flexible and open-minded. But he was merely following to the best of his ability the time-honored routine of absolute monarchy. The great silent revolution in contemporary Russian life, however, was no respecter of tradition. It transformed the splendor of autocracy into an invisible prison.

The outward isolation in which the Tsar lived might not, by itself, have proved fatal. What ruined Nicholas II was his inward seclusion, his withdrawal to the impregnable shelter of religious devotion. Adversity never caused him to reexamine his policies or his basic assumptions, for his religion taught him that all misfortune must be suffered meekly, in the spirit of Job. Thus he never profited from the best of all schools, that of hard knocks. The many blows which he received as emperor turned him ever more ardently to the solace of piety. And so, in an age preoccupied with money, machines, and power, his prayers completed the estrangement from contemporary reality. Alas for the futility of a religion which preaches the meekness of the dove but lacks the wisdom of the serpent! It is doubly catastrophic in the highest places.

Witte, on the other hand, although a pious man too, was master of the ways of the serpent. His task was to carry out the insight which he had shared with Alexander III that a modern state must be an industrialized one. This truth never struck home with Nicholas II. Thus, after only two years in office, Witte lost the security of unequivocal Imperial endorsement. He was increasingly forced to become a politician, maneuvering and intriguing at Court or among his ministerial colleagues, and appealing to public opinion in a vain search for a substitute for the steadfast support of

Alexander III. If of all the servants of Nicholas II he was the only one to criticize his master bitterly, it was because he had placed great hopes in autocracy. More than any other Russian statesman of that age he was brutally disillusioned.

II

The first open denunciation of the Witte system came from abroad, through the pen of Vyshnegradskii's apostate Paris agent, Tsion. His attack on Witte, published in 1895, was widely circulated in western Europe.[12] Yet it had its roots in Russia and represented more than Tsion's personal views. Before his departure he had been close to Katkov's circle in Moscow, combining an ardent Slavophilism with propaganda for the promotion of Russian industries unhampered by foreign competition.[13] Although residing in France, he still had excellent connections in both Moscow and St. Petersburg. With the information thus received he let fly from the sidelines of *haute finance* at Russian economic policy.

Here was a new variant in the long history of the pamphlet war against the Russian government. Tsion's main purpose, and his greatest threat to Witte, was the undermining of Russian credit in France. He had at his disposal some effective arguments. France, he pleaded with her *rentiers*, should not become involved in the economic collapse of Russia; the welfare of the French investor should be put above the politics of the Russian alliance. His description of economic conditions in Russia, indeed, was enough to frighten any holder of Russian securities. Ninety percent of the population was hungry, twenty million peasants were starving to death, Russian industries were in decay. The Russian government, moreover, was going deeper and deeper into debt and, worse, was passing on French savings to Germany. Russia, Tsion insisted, was becoming the economic hinterland of Germany, par-

[12] Tsion (E. de Cyon), *M. Witte et les Finances Russes.*

[13] Grüning, pp. 49–50. Tsion, however, was recalled to Russia in order to justify his conduct. When he refused, he was stripped of his rank.

ticularly after the Trade Treaty of 1894, and was swamped with cheap German goods. The villain in Tsion's eyes was Witte, the autocrat of Russian finance, who pushed aside experienced men like Bunge, terrorized the banks and the businessmen, and bought the press to sing his praises. He had transformed the State Bank into *une cuisine à assignats* for vain experiments in state socialism. Under him the state was becoming the sole banker, exporter, and master of trade and industry. He was snuffing out individual enterprise and—*grand ciel!*—ushering in communism.

It would have been in the best tradition of Russian autocracy to suppress such scurrilous propaganda at home and discredit it, through counterpamphlets, abroad. Witte, far shrewder, allowed it to circulate freely.[14] He did not let it go unanswered, to be sure, taking issue himself with the charges in his budget report for 1896. He realized that a free discussion of Russian economic development was a sign of strength. His enlightened approach more than offset the damage which Tsion inflicted upon Russian credit. But the agitation persisted. While Tsion continued his diatribes[15] with dire predictions as to whither the dictatorship of Monsieur Witte—he even called him a disciple of Karl Marx—was leading Russia, the opposition came to a head within the country itself, and from an unexpected quarter.

The occasion for the first public outcry against the Witte system was the great Exposition of Trade and Industry held in the summer of 1896 in the city of Nizhni-Novgorod, and the Third All-Russian Congress of Trade and Industry, which assembled there under government auspices in order to lend splendor to the occasion. Both these events formed an essential part of Witte's basic design.

Plans for a demonstration of Russian industrial skill and enter-

[14] Migulin, *Russkii gosudarstvennyi kredit,* Vol. III, Part II, p. 277.

[15] See his pamphlet *Où la dictature de M. Witte conduit la Russie*; also Oldenburg, I, 84.

prise had been laid soon after Witte's appointment.[16] It was part of the Witte system to call the world's attention to the fact that Russia was one of the great industrial powers. But it was only fitting that a demonstration of her economic progress should also be given at home. For the site of such an exhibit the choice of Nizhni-Novgorod was a clever one. With its great annual fair it was still the center of Russian trade. And its commercial intelligence system reached far into central and eastern Asia, where, for lack of other examples, Russian industry (and Russia in general) could still gain prestige from the triumphs of modern technology. At the same time it was not too far from Moscow, whence many visitors were expected; any location farther west might have invited invidious comparison and defeated the purpose of the Minister of Finance. Thus, since 1893, with many a tiff between the Ministry of Finance and the local governor, Nizhni-Novgorod had been groomed for the occasion and its sanitation system—always the weakness of Russian towns—modernized.

When the gates of the exhibit were finally opened on May 28, 1896, almost immediately after the coronation of Nicholas II, Witte in his welcoming speech sounded the keynote of his "system." The exhibit (unfinished as it still was) demonstrated, he said,[17] the spiritual and material expansion of Russia. "Russia grows, its productive forces grow, and with them grows the wealth of the country, its powers, and the recognition of its strength." Nor did he fail to draw the proper lesson: "The success of our industry is so considerable, the influx of capital so great, and the creation of new branches of industry so speedy that the protective system, introduced by the late Emperor, must be considered a measure of great political wisdom." The exhibit, which was furnished and maintained entirely at government expense, plainly

[16] For information on the Nizhni-Novgorod exhibit see *Albom uchastnikov vse-rossiiskoi promyshlennoi i khudozhestvennoi vystavki v Nizhnem-Novgorode v 1896 g.*; also the German diplomatic reports in the Bonn archives.

[17] *Albom*, p. 54.

served the aim of creating public enthusiasm for industrialization. As Mendeleev, one of the driving forces behind the scenes, observed with almost Bolshevik sternness: "To see our exhibit means to become acquainted, to learn, to study, to think, and not simply to look around." [18] That was why in the summer of 1896 students and workers were given free railroad transportation from any point in Russia to Nizhni-Novgorod.

Unfortunately, the Russian public was in no mood to fall in line with Mendeleev's industrial puritanism. In its original conception the exhibit made no concession to public frivolity. Only later, as attendance fell far below expectations, were public amusements and a theater added. Still the total number of visitors remained less than a million, fewer than had visited a similar exhibit in Moscow fifteen years earlier. The whole show was symbolic of the fate of the Witte system. He had spared no effort to give distinction to the exhibit; yet the results were disappointing. First the visitor was held up by a seemingly inextricable traffic snarl at the Nizhni-Novgorod railroad station, and when he reached the exhibit (on an electric trolley built by Siemens and Halske) he was appalled by the parched grass on the shadeless grounds, on which the displays stood bare and alien in the summer glare.

In July the Imperial couple arrived for a visit and were given an extraordinary and startling reception. In their honor, the *Volgar*, the leading newspaper of the middle Volga basin, published a bold editorial extolling the loyalty of the Russian *kupechestvo* to their Tsar.

Standing in the closest communion with the Russian people, constituting its strongest part, the *kupechestvo* has preserved the genuine Russian spirit more than any other *soslovie*. Nowhere else does the national feeling appear with such strength, conviction, and breadth. Of all groups in Russia it alone is strong also in an economic sense. There is nothing it cannot do. And behold, it is a Russian *soslovie* which has not betrayed the testament of its forebears; it is accustomed to love Russia hotly and without restraint, with all that is good and bad in it. The

[18] Quoted by Oldenburg, p. 63.

Russian *kupechestvo* is giving proof, to the pride of all Russia . . . of how much it supports the government. For the first time, the sons of the *kupechestvo* of Moscow and Nizhni-Novgorod have furnished an Honorary Body Guard for His Majesty.[19]

It was a remarkable appeal. The Russian merchant community suggested to the Emperor nothing less than that it take the place of the Russian aristocracy in the hierarchy of Russian society. It could make a strong claim, indeed. While the nobility had become Westernized, the *kupechestvo* had preserved its native traditions. Historically speaking, it was even more Russian than the nobility. It was also more loyal than the zemstvo gentry which so recently had indulged in the "senseless dreams" of a constitution. What counted even more in the present age, it alone could hold its own economically. It was a *soslovie* on which the future could be built. Its advance was a logical corollary of the Witte system. But would it find the approval of the Emperor?

After his visit the canard was circulated [20] that when Nicholas greeted the Moscow merchants' guard of honor as he entered the exhibition, he asked for their names. The first one answered to the name Von Einem, the next Schulz, the third Zenker, the fourth Knoop. After this, His Majesty abruptly stopped. (The wags observed that Russian was also admitted as an official language at the exhibit.) What the Imperial couple thought is not known. They were overtaken by a terrible hailstorm upon their arrival, and left soon after they had completed their tour. Witte recalled later that the Emperor had seemed somewhat aloof on this occasion, but he attributed the cause to a dispute over foreign policy.[21] Considering Nicholas's bent of mind, however, it was unlikely that he would be converted to Witte's faith in Russian industry or trust in the *kupechestvo*. As regards the Imperial couple, the demonstration had failed.

The climax of the exhibit came in August when the Third All-

[19] Quoted in Berlin, p. 138.

[20] This story was repeated many times. One source is Buryshkin, p. 66.

[21] Witte, *Tsarstvovanie Nikolaia II*, I, pp. 68–69.

Russian Congress of Trade and Industry assembled.[22] It was the first time that the government itself had taken the initiative in convoking such a gathering. It had wished to promote further industrial progress by an open discussion of the chief problems. For this purpose the Ministry of Finance had invited, somewhat indiscriminately, representatives of trade, industry, and agriculture, professors of economics and finance, scientists like Mendeleev, and various *chinovniki*. Its own senior officials acted as chairmen. The congress was an assembly of notables drawn from all important fields of Russian economic life.

Its agenda, as set forth by the chairman, Privy Councilor Kobeko, read like a summary of the contemporary economic problems of Russia.[23] Each of the five sections into which the congress divided itself for its deliberations was assigned a special area of economic activity. The reports laid before these sections and the subsequent discussions afford an excellent view of the many irritations engendered by the industrial impact. One small example: The chairman outlining the program of the fifth section remarked, "Russian goods cannot compete with Western goods, because of our lack of technical education." And then, pointing to one crucial dilemma of industrialization, he met head on, though hardly convincingly, the annoying reproach of the conservatives that Western education was subversive. "One must know that the Russian absorbs from his mother's milk a firm belief in the faith of his fathers and an immutable loyalty to his Tsar. True education will never and nowhere shake these foundations, which are inherent in the Russian people since time immemorial. On the contrary, it will confirm them." [24]

What matters in this context is not the self-delusion of the industrializers but the sudden rebellion against the Witte system which

[22] The records of the congress are found in the *Trudy vysochaishe uchrezhdennago vserossiiskago torgovo-promyshlennago s"ezda 1896 g. v Nizhnem-Novgorode,* 3 vols.

[23] *Ibid.,* Vol. I, the report on the session of August 4, 1896; *otkrytie s"ezda,* pp. 2–3.

[24] *Ibid.,* p. 7.

flared up at this congress. The agitation grew out of the discussions of the second section, which dealt with the tariff. As if by prearrangement, all enemies of the Witte system convened here for a joint attack. They carried a resolution, offered by V. I. Khodskii, professor of finance at the University of St. Petersburg, which went far beyond the tasks set for this section.[25] It charged that the economic policy of the government had an extremely inequitable effect. It had acted adversely on agriculture in all its branches. The resolution attacked in particular the high price of iron and steel, which made agricultural equipment expensive. As an alternative it proposed lowering the tariff on these items and granting credit to the small producers so that they could buy machinery. It also suggested special measures for the expansion of rural credit, the support of the rural handicrafts, and the improvement of rural roads. In short, it listed the essential points of the agrarian program. The supporters of this resolution succeeded in laying it before the entire congress and demanded a vote in the plenum. Thus the congress was transformed, spontaneously, into a parliament discussing basic government policy.

The debate started when one delegate complained that no one as yet had paid any attention at the congress to the difficult position of Russian agriculture.[26] The reason for the poor state of agriculture, he said, lay in the lack of agricultural machinery, which in turn was caused by the high tariff. This was the clue for Professor Khodskii, who then delivered a resounding attack on the government's tariff policy in general. He had come to the exhibit, he announced, to see the effects of the tariff on Russian agriculture. But unfortunately agriculture was barely represented. If it had made the same progress as other branches of Russian economy, it would stand squarely in the center of the exhibit. The reason why it did not prosper was the tariff on iron, which put metal goods out of reach of the peasant and the *kustar'*. Thus the tariff

[25] *Ibid., obshchee sobranie,* p. 1.
[26] *Ibid.,* pp. 2–41.

of 1891 was evil. Instead, the government should first protect "the basis of all national labor," that is, agriculture. When it flourished, all other branches of Russian economy would thrive too.

Professor Khodskii was followed by an industrialist, A. K. Alchevskii, who first protested against the provision that each delegate state whether he was manufacturer, agrarian, or *chinovnik* as he cast his vote on the resolution. This provision, he charged, had been cleverly inserted to prove that the agricultural interests had been badly underrepresented. His main point, however, was fundamental: The tariff was necessary because "in every respect, and for decades, we are behind western Europe; we cannot compete on the world market." Without a tariff, the metallurgical industries (Alchevskii came from Kharkov) would be destroyed and railroad construction would fail. The next speaker, a mining engineer, argued in the same vein, warning in addition, perhaps illogically, that making tariff concessions to Germany in the import of metal goods would create further difficulties for Russian agricultural exports. After him a *chinovnik* employed at the exhibit rose. He spoke frankly against the tariff, pointing out that the area under cultivation in Russia had shrunk by four million dessiatines since 1882 and that there was not enough bread for the local population, even in black-soil provinces like Kherson. Peasant welfare was declining. Yet he ended (tongue in cheek?) on a loyal note, praising the brilliant position of Russian economy as shown at the exhibit.

The next delegate, who hailed from Tambov province, claimed to speak from "the practical farmer" point of view. He first listed the many benefits of cheap iron to the peasant, then contended that even railway rates could be lowered if iron were cheaper. But the tariff made no difference to him; he preferred to work with peasants rather than machines, so as to give them employment. He also saw good reason for building up domestic industries, even at a sacrifice to the government. So he pronounced himself, no doubt to the merriment of the other delegates, in favor of both the Khodskii resolution and the rival one supporting the tariff offered by Mendeleev.

The following speakers, all *chinovniki,* took a more decided stand against the tariff on iron. One of them, stationed in Turkestan, maintained that soil conditions there required foreign-built equipment. Then a manufacturer from St. Petersburg put in a plea for the development of the Ural iron mines, with local wood for fuel. Thus far the hidden tension in the assembly had barely made itself felt. But when the next speaker arose, a flurry of excitement must have swept through the hall. He was Privy Councilor D. A. Timiriazev, director of the Bureau of Agricultural Statistics in the Ministry of Agriculture, who submitted some revealing figures in support of the Khodskii resolution. Grain prices, he said, had fallen 27 percent in the past three years, while iron prices had risen 13 percent. How then was Russian agriculture to benefit from industrialization? This speech from high quarters brought Mendeleev to his feet at last. In his brief but vehement remarks Mendeleev insisted on the need for national industries. The prosperity of all Russia depended on them, he shouted, and the prosperity of the peasants too, for they also bought industrial goods like kerosene and cotton fabrics. There was no use relying on foreign manufacturers. For a time they might dump their products cheaply on the Russian market, but when they had ruined their Russian competitors they would raise their prices again. "You can't plow all the Russian soil with German plows. No," he thundered, "I will never agree to that!"

When after some more exchanges of this sort the ballots were counted, it was found that Professor Khodskii's resolution had been carried by 140 to 63. It was an impressive triumph for the opposition. And it was a fully representative vote. If a popular election had been held on the Witte system at any time between 1895 and 1903, it would have been soundly defeated.

Yet in August, 1896, the censure of Imperial policy was a vain gesture. At a banquet of Moscow merchants held shortly after the congress, Savva Morozov, one of the biggest "wheels" among them, announced that this vote could be given no particular weight:[27] "We industrialists are accustomed to think twice before we grant credit to anybody." And Witte, who was the guest of honor, gave free rein to his autocratic instincts, blurting out: "What kind of government would turn for advice to a congress? Ten people can say something wise, but thousands say something stupid. Take the first but not the second. Here, pardon the expression, they'll skin us alive. We cannot think of lowering the tariff. One might think that this was said by people sent in from abroad." (Two years later, however, as a concession to the agrarian opposition, the tariff on agricultural machinery was indeed rescinded.)

On October 1, 1896, when the Exhibition of Russian Trade and Industry closed its gates, it could well be doubted whether it had been worth all the money and effort. Witte steadfastly maintained that it had been a great success. But State Controller Filippov, in his report for 1896, conveyed a different opinion to the Emperor.[28] He disputed the figures of government expenditure for the exhibit which Witte had submitted and questioned the validity of the entire project in view of the disappointing attendance. Certainly, as an effort to convert the Russian people to the ideal of industrialization, the exhibit had been a colossal failure.

III

If the exhibit and the Congress of Trade and Industry had shown the extent of public opposition to the Witte system, Witte's next move—and one of his most famous—was to reveal the intensity and depth of the opposition within the government. This move was the introduction of the gold standard, which took effect in January, 1897. The final steps were taken in 1896, the year of the coronation and the Nizhni-Novgorod exhibit. Indeed all three

[27] Quoted by Oldenburg, p. 65.

[28] See *Vsepodanneishii otchët gosudarstvennago kontrolera za 1896*, pp. 76 ff.

events—the coronation, the exhibit, and the introduction of the gold standard—had been designed to parade the strength of the Empire before the world. The last measure, hailed by one of Witte's associates as among "the most significant steps of cultural progress in our fatherland," [29] was the culmination of that demonstration. Yet it was one most bitterly resisted within and without the government. The debate at Nizhni-Novgorod was only part of a larger debate over the gold standard. The positions were identical, but the latter engagement was even more crucial.[30]

The conversion of the ruble to a gold basis had become, in the mid-nineties, more than ever a matter of national respectability and economic advantage. The major European countries, as well as India and Japan, had adopted the gold standard. For Russia (as for any civilized country at that time) it was a prerequisite for sound credit and economic progress in general. Above all it would encourage more foreign investment in Russian industry. Thus far foreigners had bought mostly government securities; the Treasury's large foreign debt was a political liability. Investment in private firms, on the other hand, would not only reduce the necessity of government support for industry but would also create a vested interest abroad in Russian prosperity and check hostile speculation with Russia's foreign debt. Furthermore, after a series of exceptionally good harvests, the conditions for carrying out the reform were auspicious, for the gold reserves in the Treasury were sufficiently high (amounting to 40 percent of the paper rubles in circulation).

Thus, in March, 1896, Witte moved toward formal adoption of the gold standard. His only technical problem lay in determining what value the new gold ruble should have. Should it redeem the paper ruble at the official par set a long time ago, or should it be recoined so as to equal in its gold content its current value,

[29] Gurev, p. 781.

[30] The literature on the introduction of the gold standard is quite extensive. See the bibliography in M. Saenger, *Die Wittesche Währungsreform.*

which the government for some years had tried to stabilize at two thirds of par? Witte decided in favor of the latter alternative. Although in theory it meant devaluation, in practice it left Russia's economy undisturbed; price levels had long ago been adjusted to the lower rate. In the technical details of conversion, incidentally, Witte was ably advised by the banker Adolph Rothstein, who had helped introduce the gold standard in Austria-Hungary. Now a Russian subject, he was one of the key figures among the St. Petersburg financiers. All told, no critic has ever found fault with Witte's handling of the technicalities of conversion. The big—and the only—question was: Could Russia afford the gold standard now?

The discussion of this issue was handicapped by the fact that the Russian public at large was completely unaware of the benefits of a gold standard. In December, 1895, when Witte had ordered the Treasury to accept payments in gold at the new rate, the Russian people had already shown considerable resistance. They had become so used to paper rubles that they saw no need for new money, especially when it contained less gold than was stipulated on the old bills. But public ignorance and inertia apart, there were good economic reasons for hesitation, which were aired in the public protest. On March 15, 1896, when the details of conversion were first announced, the Imperial Free Economic Society of St. Petersburg, the stronghold of agrarian opinion, called a public meeting for the following evening. There Professor Khodskii attacked Witte's plans before an unusually large and appreciative audience.[31] He started by calling devaluation an act of government bankruptcy. But his real concern was not with the rate of conversion but with the fact of it. The gold standard could be maintained, he argued, only with a continued active balance of payments, which in turn depended upon the general prosperity of the country. Neither of these vital prerequisites existed in Russia. The balance of payments was negative. If conversion were at-

[31] Migulin, *Russkii gosudarstvennyi kredit,* III, 240.

tempted, the government's heavy foreign debt would drive out the gold, thus depleting the gold reserve, and would soon force suspension of convertibility. He also tore into Witte's claims of Russian prosperity. Looking below the surface he saw only the growing indebtedness of the government and the increasing pressure of taxation which already curtailed consumption. In short, the standard of living was declining, ruining all chances of conversion.

After Professor Khodskii other antagonists arose, advocates of a silver standard like the economist Slonimskii, bimetallists like Isaev, and the partisan of the paper ruble, Sergei Sharapov. The leaders of the Legal Marxists, Peter Struve and Tugan-Baranovskii, also obtained a hearing. The supporters of the government, on the other hand, were shouted down. The best case for the reform was made by A. N. Gurev, the secretary of the Scientific Committee in the Ministry of Finance, who contended that the balance of payments was favorable because, in fact, the gold reserve in the Treasury was increasing. But the plea carried no weight. Under Sharapov's prompting, subsequent discussions in the Society for Assistance to the Improvement and Development of Manufacturing Industry were still more hostile. The official press, naturally, followed Witte. But among the Russian intelligentsia conversion stood condemned from the outset. As Witte himself wrote in his *Memoirs*: "Almost all thinking Russia was against me." [32]

How, then, did Witte's plans fare within the government? The first agency to consider the proposed reforms was the Finance Committee, whose function was the supervision of government credit operations.[33] That group, which included the leading financial experts of the State Council such as the heads of the Department of Economy and Finance and the Department of Legislation, the state controller, the minister of finance, his assistant, and the obligatory grand duke, took a favorable stand. The only danger

[32] Witte, *Tsarstvovanie Nikolaia II,* I, 82.
[33] Migulin, *Russkii gosudarstvennyi kredit,* III, 1082.

to the gold standard which these men could foresee was war or the aggravation of the agricultural crisis. But they felt that Russia could weather such emergencies more effectively with convertibility.

The reception of conversion in the State Council was quite otherwise. The reaction of that body, when it began its deliberations at the end of April, 1896, boded ill for enactment by regular legislative procedure.[34] Some members spoke of devaluation as fraudulent bankruptcy. Others admitted that the gold standard might score an initial success by attracting more foreign capital, but in the end, what with the growing burden of interest charges and increasing taxation, the gold would flow out again. The crucial point, as before, was the dubious state of the balance of payments. In reply to his critics Witte went so far as to admit that if it were really negative, he too would oppose conversion. Nor did he approve, he said, of preserving an active balance of payments through continued foreign loans. (All the same, he negotiated a hundred million ruble gold loan from the Rothschilds a few months later.) Whether he himself believed all he said or not, he exuded confidence: "Our condition is entirely solid, even from the point of view of those who attach so much significance to the balance of payments." [35] But this hardly convinced the State Council, which was more preoccupied with the depressed state of Russian agriculture than the promises of industrial prosperity.

While the State Council balked, Witte turned to foreign authorities for support, such as the German pundit Adolf Wagner, several Frenchmen, and the English Lord Goshen and even the venerable Gladstone.[36] The latter two both pleaded ignorance. The attitude of the French was mixed. P. P. Leroy-Beaulieu, the famous economist, approved. But more influential men like Alphonse Rothschild or Léon Say (a former minister of finance)

[34] The discussion of the State Council in *Otchët po deloproizvodstvu gosudarstvennago soveta za sessiiu 1896–1897 gg.*, pp. 261 ff.

[35] Migulin, *Russkii gosudarstvennyi kredit,* III, 261 ff.

[36] *Ibid.*, p. 266.

strongly advised in favor of a bimetallic currency. The French premier Méline even sent an urgent message to the Tsar to the same effect. The reason for the unexpected opposition of the French government was perhaps a rather selfish one. France, although herself on the gold standard, had much silver in circulation and tried her best to unload it upon her ally. Thus Witte drew little comfort from that quarter, and during the summer of 1896 his prestige seemed to deteriorate. He could discount Tsion's pamphlets, but the failure of the Nizhni-Novgorod exhibit was more serious. Moreover, in the autumn it became clear that the State Council would reject the currency reform. The criticism and delay already began to affect Russian credit abroad.

There was only one escape from this crisis: to bypass the State Council altogether by resorting to an Imperial ukase, the most extreme form of autocratic command. On January 2, 1897, the Finance Committee meeting at Tsarskoe Selo, enlarged by the presence of another grand duke and presided over by Nicholas in person, decided to issue the order for the coinage of the new five- and ten-ruble gold pieces, which were the symbols of the reformed currency. Thus the gold standard was put into effect. When the decision became known, a storm broke loose in the State Council. Through its chairman it sent a ringing protest to the Emperor.[37] "Of course," so the sentiments in the State Council ran, "as autocrat the Emperor can issue any ukase he pleases. But where then is the difference between a monarchical government and a despotic government of the Asiatic type? The difference is that the first observes but the latter destroys at its pleasure the laws of the country. To advocate such a doctrine to the Emperor means leading him on the road of the Emperor Paul." Not satisfied with this, a few months later the opposition, through a motion

[37] See the entry for January 6, 1897, in A. A. Polovtsev's diary, *KA,* XLVII, 116. I suspect that the version printed there is garbled. It would seem incredible that the Emperor was presented with these words. More likely, the quotation represents Polovtsev's version of the sentiments expressed in the State Council.

of fifteen members including the minister of war, tried to reopen the matter.[38] This, however, was voted down by a majority of twenty, among them the Grand Duke Konstantin Konstantinovich and Pobedonostsev. But of all the legal formalities connected with the adoption of the gold standard, the State Council approved only the necessary changes in the statutes of the State Bank, which now became a bank of issue. By July, 1900, however, tempers had sufficiently cooled to permit passage of the monetary statute consolidating all previous Imperial decrees.

As it turned out, Witte was justified and his enemies confounded by the subsequent course of events. The gold standard weathered such bitter calamities as the Russian defeat in the war with Japan and the subsequent revolution. The *Witte kinderi* and *matildori*, as hostile gossip dubbed the new coins,[39] sneering at both Witte's German descent and the reputation of his wife Matilda, created a stable currency with all its beneficial consequences for the economic development of the country. It served as a vehicle not only for foreign credit but for the Europeanization of Russia in general. Witte subsequently called it with characteristic exaggeration "one of the greatest successes in the peaceful cultural development of mankind." [40] Paradoxically, however, it had been achieved only by the most un-European assertion of autocracy, in defiance of public opinion and the orderly legislative process of the Empire. The State Council was not a reactionary but rather a liberal body, much concerned with popular welfare and the restraint of illegality. Yet, because of its sympathy with rural Russia, Witte could not expect much support from it, on the contrary. Given a free hand, it would have repudiated the Witte system at once. A goodly portion of the credit for the gold standard must therefore go to the Emperor, who was willing

[38] *Otchët po deloproizvodstvu*, p. 264.
[39] Oldenburg, p. 85.
[40] Budget report for 1897.

on this occasion to disregard all warnings and back his Minister of Finance to the hilt.

In 1896 and 1897 it was high time that the reform was achieved. Had Witte tarried longer, renewed poor harvests and thereafter a protracted industrial depression would have postponed conversion *ad calendas Graecas*. "If not done quickly, it would not have been done at all," he remarked in his *Memoirs*. "In Russia it is necessary to carry out reforms quickly and hurriedly. Otherwise they will not succeed for the most part or will be watered down." [41]

Yet his opponents had also been right in emphasizing the appalling costs of the gold standard. The gold reserve, which lay immobilized in the Treasury, was accumulated through brutal taxes and forced export, through hunger and back-breaking toil, through depriving the Russian population of the necessities of life. The Russian peasant could complain even more justly than the American farmer in these years that he was being crucified on the cross of gold for the benefit of bankers and industrialists and for the prestige of his country. It was not the muzhik's fault that the high price of the gold standard was also the high price of Russian backwardness.

Neither was it Witte's fault. In December, 1896, while the political struggle in the government over the gold standard rose to its acrimonious climax, he had written in his budget report for 1897 the ultimate refutation of his critics: "One can differ over the question which is preferable: the intensive development of industry over a short time or a weaker and thus also considerably slower forward movement. But one cannot deny that once the government adheres to the protective system for a rather long period and with undeviating strictness and determination, any premature interruption of it would be a serious political mistake and cause deep tensions in the economic organization of the country." And if he did not spell out the full implications of his ad-

[41] Witte, *Tsarstvovanie Nikolaia II,* I, 83.

herence to a rapid tempo of industrialization, P. P. Migulin, a contemporary economist to whom we owe the fullest account of Witte's work as minister of finance, did it for him a few years later. Witte's monetary policy, so he wrote,[42] was predetermined by the decision of Alexander II and Reutern, his minister of finance, to build Russia's railways with the help of foreign capital. "Of course," Migulin continued, "limiting ourselves to our own resources and working with the help of savings accumulated by our own labor, we could proceed more cheaply and gain more lasting results. But time does not wait. Life goes full steam ahead. Even so we are behind all the Western peoples. And by walking slowly one does not go far, despite our proverb to the contrary. We have to live in a more rapid tempo and, whether we want to or not, must resort to the service of foreigners." After the Crimean War, Russia could not afford to tarry. Witte told the Grand Duke Mikhail Aleksandrovich a few years later: "A great nation cannot wait." [43]

At the present time, Witte continued in his budget report for 1897, industrialization was mandatory. "In the history of the material culture of every state, the foundation of industries is rightly held to be an extremely important turning point in the economic life of a people. Purely agricultural countries are poorer than those with diversified labor and additional sources of prosperity." Thank goodness, Witte noted, Russia was no longer an exclusively agricultural country. Such a status would have been incompatible with her dignity as a great power.

IV

While Witte did his utmost to gird Russia for a position of equality among the great powers, he was at the same time deeply conscious, more so than his adversaries, of Russia's need for peace. If there was one serious danger to the gold standard, it lay in

[42] Migulin, *Russkii gosudarstvennyi kredit,* III, 324.
[43] Witte, *Konspekt lektsii,* p. 140.

costly military adventures. Thus his budget report for 1897 sounded an unusually pacifist note. He harped on the Emperor's love of peace and the Russian government's sincere desire to maintain friendly international relations, concluding: "May God give us similar peace-loving desires on the part of other peoples." While he wrote this passage, however, he must have prayed above all for a more peaceful attitude on the part of the Emperor, for during the Nizhni-Novgorod exhibit and the last stages of the gold standard controversy they were bitterly opposed over a risky venture of foreign policy.

As minister of finance Witte was consulted on any major move of Russian foreign policy. As the government's financier he had to consider the effects of any such move both on the Russian economy and on the international money market. However readily he might fall in with the mood of expansion and imperialism in the East, his responsibilities for Russian finance and industry always came first. While over the years he took an ever larger part in the shaping of Russian foreign policy, he never lost that vital touch with his primary duty.

By the nature of his "system," therefore, he could not accept a clear-cut boundary between domestic and foreign policy, between economics and politics. The logic of industrialization required that all government activities be directed toward this central goal. Thus the Minister of Finance was driven to trespass upon the domain of the Minister of Foreign Affairs. This, of course, was incompatible with the essence of autocracy. Every minister was supposed to stay within his jurisdiction and leave the central direction of affairs to the Tsar. As Nicholas, however, did not provide such leadership, his ministers were increasingly engaged in a wrangle for ascendancy. By virtue of his office (not to mention his temperament) Witte was fighting in the midst of it, and not always by fair means, as events in early 1897 were soon to show.

Throughout 1896 the Russian government, like all of Europe,

had been much aroused over the massacres of Armenian Christians by Turkish bands. By the end of the year the great powers seemed ready at last to coerce again the Sultan into reform. But while the Concert of Europe hesitated, divided as usual by suspicion and divergent national interests, the Russian ambassador in Constantinople, Nelidov, contemplated a daring scheme. He tried to persuade the Tsar that Russia, in unilateral action, should seize the northern entrance of the Bosporus and thus gain one of her oldest political goals, control of the Straits. Provided that this *coup de main* be carried out resolutely, it stood—in the judgment of a modern historian—an excellent chance of success.[44] In England Lord Salisbury was reconciled to the dismemberment of the Ottoman Empire, while Germany was then courting the Russian government. And the French foreign minister, Hanotaux, although opposed to the sudden demise of a country in which France had many interests, could hardly throw over the alliance with Russia because of the Near East. No serious opposition was to be expected and yet, when Nelidov appeared in St. Petersburg in November, 1896, to plead his cause, Witte adamantly opposed it.[45] The project would cause war, he predicted, and Russia's finances could not afford it. Besides, he argued, if the Ottoman Empire were carved up, a state weak and amendable to Russian pressure would be replaced by the far stronger European powers. He was overruled, however, standing alone in his pessimism. On January 11, Nicholas II, highly elated by the prospects of an easy triumph so early in his reign, granted the necessary emergency measures. The action hung in the balance until February, when Witte, with utter disregard for governmental discipline, decided to torpedo the scheme. Thoroughly alarmed, he leaked the

[44] Langer, *Diplomacy of Imperialism,* pp. 338 ff. Langer's admirable account of Witte's policy, like B. A. Romanov's and A. Malozemoff's, does not see Witte's policy in the proper perspective of his central needs as minister of finance.

[45] Langer, *Diplomacy of Imperialism*; see also Witte's account, *Tsarstvovanie Nikolaia II,* Vol. I, Chap. VI.

Russian plans to the British government.[46] The British, averse to unilateral action by Russia, strengthened their fleet in the Mediterranean, killing Nelidov's scheme. One can well imagine the Emperor's annoyance.

In the winter of 1896–97 Witte was even more deeply involved in foreign affairs on another and seemingly much safer front, the Far East, and with the Emperor's full approval. The desire of the government to complete the Siberian line according to plan had drawn the Minister of Finance deeply into Russo-Chinese relations and Far Eastern politics in general. Witte's ambition to give the Siberian line the greatest possible economic significance had left him no choice. He had, it will be remembered, stressed from the outset the economic advantages which would accrue to Russia from this venture. But he had since learned that in the Far East economics and politics could not be kept entirely separate. After the Treaty of Shimonoseki (concluded in April, 1895), which gave the Japanese the Liaotung peninsula and severed Korea from China, it was Witte who had insisted most forcibly that the Japanese gains be limited.[47] On his urging the governments of Russia, France, and Germany demanded the withdrawal of the Japanese from the Liaotung peninsula. Again it was he who negotiated the Franco-Russian loan which enabled the Chinese government to pay its indemnity to Japan and he who wrote into that loan special privileges for Russia. His aim was the painless and gradual economic penetration of China by her more advanced neighbor Russia. A friendly and weak but not unduly feeble China offered the

[46] See also Witte's conversation with the British ambassador O'Conor on January 24, 1897, in which he told the diplomat that "he did not desire one foot more of territory, for they already had more than they could possibly develop in a hundred or two-hundred years. What they wanted was peace to bring out the wealth of the country, foster trade, commerce, and industry, and improve the status of the people and make them in course of time self-sufficient. . . . He also said that he was not a politician in the ordinary sense, but that as Minister of Finance of a great country he could not remain indifferent to politics." PRO, Foreign Office Series 65.

[47] For the following see Langer, *Diplomacy of Imperialism,* p. 182, and A. Malozemoff, pp. 66 ff.

best opportunity. In all his subsequent interventions in Far Eastern affairs he never strayed far from this simple, rather innocuous, and increasingly unrealistic conception. Above all he was trying to find business for his railroad so that it could speedily pay for itself.

In no imperialist haste, Witte next organized the Russo-Chinese Bank, a masterpiece of financial strategy, as an instrument of peaceful economic advance.[48] Its purpose was the promotion of railroad construction in conjunction with the Siberian road, and of economic development in China in general. The capital, however, was not Russian (it could not be) but French. So strong was Witte's standing in Paris that a consortium of seven French banking houses willingly lent its funds as a tool of Russian economic expansion. The Russo-Chinese Bank operated with all the advantages of a private bank, although underneath its disguise it was but an adjunct of the Russian treasury. Prince Ukhtomskii and Adolph Rothstein, both close collaborators of Witte, played leading parts in it. Its statute was confirmed by the Siberian Committee.

While the Russo-Chinese Bank was being established, a crucial decision in regard to the Siberian line had to be taken.[49] The preliminary surveys of the proposed stretch from Sretensk to Khabarovsk, made in 1894, showed that construction along the Shilka and Amur rivers would be very costly indeed, because the roadbed had to be protected from floods. Why build such an expensive road when it would have to compete with the cheaper river transport? Witte, who had originally envisaged no more than a feeder line into China, now proposed to take the Siberian road straight through Manchuria, saving well over three hundred miles of track and immeasurably strengthening Russia's position in the Far East. After the Japanese victory over China, the rapid completion of a direct link seemed all the more mandatory. Thus Witte was

[48] Langer, *Diplomacy of Imperialism,* pp. 397 ff.; also Malozemoff, pp. 70 ff.
[49] Langer, *Diplomacy of Imperialism,* p. 403.

empowered, despite warnings that the new road was too far outside Russian territory and would cause complications, to negotiate with the Chinese government for the right of way through Manchuria, with connections to the existing Chinese railroads. He himself foresaw no dangers. His interest lay in a speedy channeling of the Chinese trade to the Siberian trunk line and forestalling European competition in the construction of Chinese railroads in or near Manchuria. That he was not anxious at that time to secure for Russia (and her French backers) an economic monopoly in China may be seen from the fact that he let the second indemnity loan to the Chinese government fall into the hands of an Anglo-German syndicate.[50]

In his *Memoirs* Witte, who was a connoisseur of character, has told with obvious relish the story of his negotiations with Li Hung Chang, the representative of the Son of Heaven at the coronation of Nicholas II. He even took him to the Nizhni-Novgorod exhibit and duly impressed his guest with Russia's industrial skills.[51] The record shows that it was not Prince Lobanov-Rostovskii, the foreign minister, but Witte who conducted the shrewd bargaining (eased by a very handsome bribe to Li) which led to the establishment of the Chinese Eastern Railroad as the final link of the Siberian railroad between Lake Baikal and Vladivostok. The terms of the eighty-year "lease" under which Russia controlled the new branch of the Siberian road were, according to Witte himself, "extremely favorable" to Russian interests.[52]

In the year 1896 Witte thus greatly extended his reach. Through both the Russo-Chinese Bank and the Chinese Eastern Railroad he acquired far-flung responsibilities. The bank opened branch offices throughout Asia; the railroad organized a steamship company plying the Yellow Sea and the Pacific; and in Russian diplomacy Manchuria was made the private preserve of the Ministry of Finance. Witte now was engaged in business on the

[50] *Ibid.,* p. 401.
[51] Witte, *Tsarstvovanie Nikolaia II,* I, 44, 68.
[52] Romanov, *Rossiia v Mandzhurii,* p. 89; Malozemoff, p. 81.

grandest scale. The secret defensive alliance between Russia and China, which Lobanov-Rostovskii signed at the same time, provided a convenient political framework for the economic settlement. Russia appeared as the sole protector of China.

Naturally Witte was eager to take advantage of the opportunities. While the new route was being surveyed, he negotiated with the Chinese government for the building of a connecting line to Shanhaikwan on the way to Peking. However, the most the Chinese would allow the Russians was a toe hold in the charter giving an American company the rights to the important Peking-Hankow line. They were resolutely opposed to a South Manchurian railroad under Russian control.[53] But, on the whole, Witte could be satisfied with the progress of his plans and his role in Russian Far Eastern policy. For a time his agents wielded the dominant influence in China; in Manchuria he seemed within reach of a Russian economic monopoly. As an envious English observer wrote in February, 1897: "The art of European diplomacy seems to have degenerated into the monotonous occupation of watching the progress of Russia in China."[54] Even in Korea Witte managed to establish a financial agent, after a palace coup in Seoul had ousted the Japanese advisers of the Korean emperor. He followed up this success by creating, after some hesitation, a Russo-Korean bank modeled after the Russo-Chinese Bank. The bold schemers who pushed Witte into this venture hoped that Korea would perhaps provide a better outlet for the Chinese Eastern Railroad than Vladivostok, which was icebound for four or five months.

It was only a question of time, however, before Russian expansion in the Far East, which so far had produced no international crisis, would be stalled by the intrusion of the other great powers. That intervention occurred all too soon. In November, 1897, the German government spoiled Witte's game by seizing Tsingtao. From the moment it became clear that Germany was in Tsingtao

[53] Langer, *Diplomacy of Imperialism,* p. 410.
[54] *Ibid.,* p. 412.

to stay, political considerations, which were the province of the Russian foreign minister, moved again into the foreground. Should Russia support the German seizure and claim another Chinese port for "compensation," or by opposing it under her treaty of 1896 alienate Germany and so endanger her own position in the European balance of power? Murav'ev (who had taken over the post of foreign minister after the death of Lobanov-Rostovskii) decided, with the Emperor's hearty approval, on the former course. Russia, after all, could not afford to pursue her Far Eastern policy at the expense of her position in Europe. Besides, she had long craved an ice-free port on the Pacific. Thus in March, 1898, Russian forces seized Port Arthur, in violation of the Russo-Chinese alliance, and the international scramble for Chinese ports began.

Nothing could have been more disastrous from Witte's point of view. As his *Memoirs* show, he protested vehemently, going to such lengths as sending, without Murav'ev's knowledge, a telegram to William II asking him to withdraw the German troops from Tsingtao. When the Emperor heard of his insubordination, he made a scene and Witte tendered his resignation. Nicholas, however, refused to accept it; Witte was still indispensable.[55] Witte, to whom the rules of diplomacy meant little, never forgave Murav'ev for having broken away from his own economically oriented policy. In his eyes the Russian occupation of Port Arthur was a fateful step. Later he never tired of insisting that it had led directly to the war with Japan. Moreover, by breaking her pledge to China Russia had lost the good will of the Chinese people upon which Witte had staked so much.

His attitude, somewhat reminiscent of his opposition to the Nelidov project, was summed up in his statement at the Crown Council of November, 1897, when the seizure of Port Arthur was first broached.[56] It was desirable, he conceded there, to have an ice-

[55] Witte, *Tsarstvovanie Nikolaia II,* I, 127.

[56] Langer, *Diplomacy of Imperialism,* p. 457; also Glinskii, p. 46, and Malozemoff, pp. 101 ff.

free base on the Pacific. But there should be no hurry about it. The eastward expansion of Russia would bring such a result in due time. First of all, the road through Manchuria had to be completed. Meanwhile patience was needed, not force. As Witte phrased it: "When that job is finished, and if we maintain the friendly relations which have always prevailed between Russia and China, then we can, on the basis of our economic interests which made possible the construction of the Manchurian railroad, find an outlet on the Pacific. . . . Our policy in the East has always been outstanding for its fairness. If we maintain our traditional friendship we will get better results than the European powers." If this was imperialism it was of a particularly subtle and patient variety. In his budget report for 1898, composed while the seizure of Port Arthur was pending, Witte further underlined his warnings to Nicholas: "The chief stay of Russian economic and financial progress is the long-standing peaceable and equitable policy of its Emperor; the heritage of the late Emperor Alexander III and Your Majesty's own true love of peace are guarantees that, for the good of the country, the foreign policy of Russia will always be averse to aggression and that no danger threatens our economic and financial position from this quarter."

Yet was it realistic to expect that Russia could forever enjoy the Chinese power vacuum as her special preserve? If other European powers carved out their ports and spheres of influence, was Russia to stand by China against all the West? There were certain implications in Witte's view which tended toward that conclusion. But as with other aspects of the Witte system, the time for such an alliance had not yet come. Besides, the Chinese government gave every indication that it would not interpret Russian economic penetration as a benefit to itself. So Murav'ev's wisdom prevailed over Witte's, and the balance of power over economics (and ideology).

Witte certainly proved again to be a realist when he drew the conclusions of Russia's new commitment in the Far East. While he remained convinced of the correctness of his original stand to the end of his life, he adjusted himself to the new circumstances. It was better that he remain to defend the economic interests of Russia and act as a moderating influence than give up his job altogether. And it was soon time for moderation. In the face of determined Japanese opposition Witte readily withdrew his agent from Seoul and surrendered Korea as a Russian sphere of influence. He had his hands full in Manchuria, adding to the Chinese Eastern Railroad a branch line southward to Port Arthur and building a commercial port adjacent to the military base to serve as its terminal. That commercial port, its name twisted by the Russian soldiers from its Chinese original into Dalny,[57] the "faraway place," became another symbol of Wittean planning and efficiency. As was stated in the ukase establishing the town: "Our Empire, covering vast areas of Europe and Asia, is called by Divine Providence to bring together peaceably the peoples of West and East. In our effort to fulfill this historic mission we have enjoyed the friendly assistance of the Chinese Empire."[58] Thus it arose, a model settlement, clean, rationally laid out around town hall and cathedral, inviting business. While Witte could not undo the seizure of Port Arthur, he at least held out conciliation to the Chinese through trade. For in 1898 peace was his motto more than ever before.

In the spring of that year the Russian minister of war, Kuropatkin, was faced with his professional share of the troubles stemming from the industrial impact.[59] In 1896 the French had introduced a rapid-firing field piece, the famous 75-mm. gun. The Germans had followed suit with a cannon that could fire six times more rapidly than its Russian equivalent. How was the Russian army to catch up now? As usual, the problem fell into Witte's lap. His response was of a piece with his system, in which industrial

[57] Witte, *Tsarstvovanie Nikolaia II,* I, 132.
[58] Wittschewsky, p. 199.
[59] Langer, *Diplomacy of Imperialism,* p. 582.

development had the first claim. Already at loggerheads with the army over appropriations and having just spent 150 million rubles for the introduction of the Mosin rifle,[60] he refused any further funds. From his point of view it seemed more realistic to try stopping the arms race altogether. So it was he who persuaded the Russian government to issue its famous call for the first disarmament conference, which opened at The Hague in 1899. In the text of its invitation the Russian government gave Witte's arguments a prominent place: "The economic crises, due in great part to the system of armaments *à outrance*, and the continual danger which lies in this massing of war materials are transforming the armed peace of our days into a crushing burden, which the peoples can bear only with more and more difficulty." [61]

The idealism of the Russian government has justly been doubted.[62] The poverty of its treasury was too plainly visible behind the fine words. But Witte's pacifism at any rate was sincere. He anticipated by a few years the gospel of Sir Norman Angell. Both men knew that war ruined finance and economic well-being, and that modern society required international cooperation rather than cutthroat rivalry. In 1898, during a visit of William II to St. Petersburg, Witte developed his thoughts still further.[63] Europe, so he prophesied, was a tottering old woman, soon to be treated like a fading beauty. To escape such fate Europe should unite and dispense with the armaments that were crippling her economic development.

These random thoughts clearly showed the character of Witte's ideas on foreign policy. He was fully aware of the exorbitant cost of contemporary power politics and wide awake to Russia's inability to pay it. But his own remedies (apart from making Russia

[60] Liashchenko, *Istoriia,* II, 211.

[61] Langer, *Diplomacy of Imperialism,* p. 585.

[62] Concerning Russian motives, see the comments of Bülow to William II, August 28, 1898, also Radolin to Hohenlohe, December 20, 1898, *Grosse Politik,* Vol. XV.

[63] Witte, *Tsarstvovanie Nikolaia II,* I, 109–10.

economically as strong as possible) were basically those of an amateur, of a businessman lost among the alien arts of diplomacy, and sometimes of a patriot carried away by imperialist ambitions.

V

Before returning to Russia's economic troubles it is necessary to look at two other aspects of Witte's work in these years, his opposition to the extension of the zemstvos proposed by Minister of the Interior Goremykin, and his views on the nature of autocracy as set forth in an exchange of letters with Goremykin's successor, Sipiagin.

The foregoing section has shown how Witte became for a time the dominant force in Russian foreign policy. The same logic that guided his actions there operated also in regard to domestic policy, leading him to trespass on the domain of the minister of the interior. Successful industrialization, to state the problem in general terms, required that all domestic policy be geared to that one aim. Thus Witte, aided by his abilities and temperament, again expanded his field of operations, although with less success than in foreign policy. In the end, the two occasions just mentioned only gave him an opportunity of stating his views. But they revealed in which direction he would have moved had he been given the chance.

Goremykin, who in later years as minister president proved such a comfortable foil to Nicholas II in the latter's feeble capacity for leadership, had a reputation of liberal views when he was given the Ministry of the Interior in 1895. His chief project in that role was the extension of the zemstvos, which had been instituted after the reforms in only thirty-seven provinces of European Russia. In 1898 he laid a project before the State Council under which zemstvos would be introduced into some of the western and southwestern provinces. His motives had indeed a liberal tinge.[64] "The

[64] Cited by Witte in *Samoderzhavie i zemstvo: Konfidentsial'naia zapiska Ministera Finansov stats-sekretaria S. Iu. Vitte (1899 g.)*, ed. P. Struve, p. 194.

basis of a state's true power," he argued, "no matter what its form of government, lies in the human personality, educated and conditioned to self-reliance. Only the habit of self-government can develop a people's capacity for organization and self-assertion. By emphasizing bureaucracy and governmental guardianship we create nothing but depersonalized and disunited mobs of people, mere human dust." But lest he be accused of disloyalty, he went on to the Slavophile argument that in Russia there was no danger whatever of the zemstvos developing into agencies of representative government. In this respect, he said, Russian development would not follow Western precedent. With her vast spaces, Russia past, present, and future was a country of local self-administration.

Unfortunately, Goremykin's laudable enterprise ran against the very grain of Witte's program. Witte had little use for the zemstvos. In 1895 he had already taken their funds under his control, to prevent mismanagement, he said.[65] And from the start he was irked by their outspoken opposition to his economic policy. In 1895, for instance, an all-Russian congress of Russian landowners under the leadership of the progressive wing of zemstvo leaders had petitioned the government for a lowering of the railroad rates and a review of the customs tariff in the interest of Russian agriculture.[66] In 1896 the zemstvo men in the Agricultural Council, an advisory body under the Ministry of State Domains and Agriculture, had stated their hope that the minister of agriculture would work for the revision of the tariff of 1891.[67] This was followed by attacks on the currency reform by members of the zemstvos and their allies. It was all too obvious: The zemstvos distrusted autocracy and waged a relentless campaign against the Witte system.

It was no wonder then that Witte was determined to stop Gore-

[65] *Ministerstvo Finansov, 1802–1902,* Vol. II.

[66] Veselovskii, III, 379.

[67] *Ibid.,* p. 377.

mykin's project. He did so in open argument. With expert assistance he drafted a lengthy memorandum, which leaked out and was first published abroad by Peter Struve in 1903 under the title *Autocracy and Zemstvo.*[68] Much of it testified to the ghostwriters' academic polish, but the basic views certainly were Witte's. They were remarkable indeed, for here Witte placed himself clearly in the tradition of Peter the Great, contending that Russia did follow the Western pattern.[69] The crux of his argument, so far as it matters here, was the assertion that Russia was a country of strict administrative centralization. A progressive bureaucracy had always taken the lead in reform and thereby made Russia a great power.[70] To be sure, he would not abolish the existing zemstvos, but would merely transfer, in a badly needed reorganization of local government, some of their functions to the state. Witte made much of the confusion in local government, pointing, for instance, to the divided control over elementary education: Church, zemstvos, and the Ministry of Education, each had its own schools. In such waste and duplication, Witte argued, lay one of the principal reasons for the slow development of Russia's resources. Besides, he argued craftily, bureaucratic centralization was cheaper than local self-administration; in the zemstvo provinces taxes were higher.[71]

But how did Witte counter Goremykin's liberal plea that bureaucracy killed the spirit of enterprise among the people? He agreed that independence and self-reliance were absolutely essential for a strong state; these qualities must not be sapped by ad-

[68] See Struve's introduction to *Samoderzhavie i zemstvo*; also Oldenburg, p. 153, who identifies A. N. Gurev as the ghostwriter. See also Witte's reply to Pobedonostsev ("Perepiska Vitte i Pobedonostseva [1895–1905 gg.]," *KA,* XXX [1928], 104), which makes his antipathy to the zemstvos still stronger and belies the pro-zemstvo interpretation of his pamphlet in his conversation with Shipov in 1902.

[69] Cf. p. 87 for his earlier assertion that Russia stood between East and West, as expressed in his comments on Badmaev's report.

[70] *Samoderzhavie i zemstvo,* p. 206; the authorities he cited were Mackenzie Wallace and Leroy-Beaulieu!

[71] *Ibid.,* p. 184.

ministrative tutelage. Did the Minister of the Interior, Witte slyly asked, always act on that principle? Moreover, Witte denied that the work of a progressive, modernized bureaucracy contradicted the spirit of free enterprise. "The full and many-sided development of social forces is not only *not* incompatible with the principle of absolute monarchy, but, on the contrary, gives it life and strength." [72] And again: "Arbitrariness, chaos, lawlessness, formalism, and delay" would be curtailed considerably if the government were "organized on a plan carefully thought out, strictly carried through, and based on new and vital principles." [73] Throughout, Witte emphasized the need for uniformity: "Whoever is master in the government must also be master in the administration." [74] At the same time he called for a progressive spirit within the ranks of the bureaucracy. If the government possessed a reliable civil service, it could safeguard personal security and independence by granting the necessary freedoms: freedom from arbitrary arrest, freedom of movement, work, creed, and speech. These were indeed essential for the orderly progress of society and the prosperity of the country. "A healthy policy in an autocratic empire," Witte stated, "should aim at the broadest possible development of lawful private enterprise." [75]

Witte's way of thinking will not convince the pupils of John Stuart Mill (its contradictions will be pointed out at the end of the book). But could he not show a reasonable contemporary demonstration of the validity of his views? In the German Empire science, business, industry, social welfare, and many other forms of nonpolitical private enterprise flourished under a government decidedly closer to absolute monarchy than to parliamentary rule. The German *Rechtsstaat* was the ideal which Witte had in mind. Here politics was largely reduced to administration by an efficient and honest civil service, and the individual was left free to pursue

[72] *Ibid.*, p. 209.
[73] *Ibid.*, p. 194.
[74] *Ibid.*, p. 197.
[75] *Ibid.*, p. 16.

his varied interests. "Where the government has established a firm and definite framework of laws," Witte concluded, "it can quietly allow the development of personal and social initiative with freedom of speech and thought. It must merely make sure that nobody, including the administration, transgresses the framework of laws and demand from all whole-hearted fulfillment and absolute compliance." [76] A constitution, he echoed Pobedonostsev, was the greatest lie of the time. But strict legality was not only not incompatible with, but was essential to, good autocracy.

It was another integral part of Witte's conception of good autocracy that the government should work closely with the public. He cited his own ministry as an example: It "always listened to public opinion and let the public take an interest in its activities." [77] If the government as a whole was not aware of the needs of the people or disregarded them, he warned frankly, it would be overthrown, as had happened in some well-known cases in western European history. If the government was bad, so Witte bluntly wrote to Pobedonostsev at this time, revolution was fully justified.[78] These were prophetic words in 1899, the first of the ever gloomier predictions of disaster made by Witte in later years.

Such, then, was the conception of enlightened autocratic government to which Witte had come after ten years in government service. Its essence was a streamlined, comprehensive, and thoroughly modern civil service in close touch with the needs of the people, not subject to the delays caused by parliamentary discussion or by ignorant public opinion, but still keenly responsive to the aspirations of the public and bound by a law common to all subjects. It was the form of government most suitable to industrialization because it could quickly remove "all the unfavorable conditions which cramped the economic development of the coun-

[76] *Ibid.*, p. 197.

[77] *Ibid.*, p. 16.

[78] *Ibid.*, p. 208. See also Witte's observation in the above-mentioned correspondence with Pobedonostsev that the rise of self-government in the West was due to the backwardness of the central administration.

try," and kindle, in the new atmosphere of civil security, the healthy spirit of enterprise which was to develop the natural riches of the country. It would lead the Russian people firmly, but patently in their own interest. Publicity, thus, was always essential. "In the difficult and responsible business of government one must above all be sincere" and "the government must give itself, before the eyes of the people, a clear account of what it is doing in each measure." [79] In his budget reports he was doing just that.

Prophetic as were Witte's arguments in *Autocracy and Zemstvo*, they bore little practical fruit. He did indeed succeed in persuading the Emperor that any extension of the gemstvos might lead to a constitution, and so contributed largely to Goremykin's fall. Subsequently he limited even further the *zemstvos'* financial responsibilities. But otherwise nothing was changed in the Ministry of the Interior, which was the inner fortress of tsarist bureaucracy. Goremykin's successor, Sipiagin, was a friend of Witte's. Socially both men were on excellent terms, and even in matters of domestic policy they cooperated to a degree. Yet how little even Sipiagin shared Witte's convictions may be seen from a minor dispute over principles reflected in their correspondence.[80]

The issue at stake was, as in the dispute over the zemstvos, the nature of autocracy. Sipiagin's interpretation, according to Witte, ran as follows: The Tsar, as autocrat, created laws for his subjects but not for himself. His ministers were nobodies, mere *rapporteurs*. The Tsar made all the decisions himself, he needed no rules. He who called for rules for the Tsar wished to limit his authority. And to suggest that the Tsar was incapable of making just decisions on the strength of his own wisdom was a sign of disloyalty. Witte naturally had no use for this theory, so typical of the old-fashioned tradition of the Russian bureaucracy. He contended that the Tsar was autocrat only in the sense that from him, and from him alone, proceeded the motive power for the entire

[79] *Ibid.,* p. 210.

[80] For the following see the letter in *KA,* XCIII (1926), 32; the letter is undated.

machinery of government. Ruling over a hundred and thirty million subjects, he could not do without advisory machinery. He could change the machinery at any time if he wished, but while it functioned he too had to submit to its rules. Sipiagin's theory resembled, in Witte's eyes, the theory of papal infallibility, but, he protested, "We are not Catholics." Even the Tsar, in other words, was under the law as long as he was not actually changing it. He had to work honorably with his ministers and comply with their recommendations, or else change the team. (But must he not also respect the views of his State Council?)

The foregoing fragments of Witte's views illustrated a set of convictions rather than a concrete program of reform,[81] but they constituted a landmark in his development. He was slowly awakening to the fact that his program of industrialization required a profound recasting of the Russian government. But such reorganization of the political structure implied a reaffirmation and not a denial of autocracy. Autocracy, in essence, was to be the vanguard of the Russian people in their efforts to create a better and stronger country. Of course vanguards, one might add parenthetically, often have their troubles with the main forces, and Witte's conception of autocracy as outlined above was shot through with inconsistencies. A government far ahead of public opinion in the interpretation of the best interests of the people is bound to tangle with legality and civil liberty; it cannot afford free discussion. And if the *Rechtsstaat* was a fact in Imperial Germany, it did not follow that it could be introduced into the much more rapidly moving and far weaker Russian Empire.

VI

By 1899 the incompatibility of the Witte system with traditional Russia had become patent. For the sake of rapid industrialization

[81] He did remark, however, to Pobedonostsev that he was confident that in two to three years he could reorganize the economic function of the provincial administration in the non-zemstvo provinces in accordance with the basic needs of Russian economy. See the aforementioned correspondence with Pobedonostsev.

Witte was driven into an ever-widening circle of reforms. Under him, industrialization developed a totalitarian grasp reaching into foreign policy, domestic policy, education, and agriculture. It even presumed on the prerogatives of autocracy. It may not be irrelevant at this point to cite a noted historian of the early Soviet period, M. N. Pokrovskii, on Witte's powers as minister of finance.[82] They were as extensive, Pokrovskii commented, as those of the Supreme Economic Council, which assumed control over Russian economy after the Bolshevik Revolution and undertook the first experiments in Soviet planning.

But what would happen if Witte's contemporaries did not share his sense of urgency or his standards of efficiency? Would they not see in his constantly expanding activities only the powerful appetite of an administrative "empire builder," a born intriguer, or a dangerous rival? Alexander Izvol'skii, one of Russia's leading diplomats in the decade before the First World War, has left us a good description of the reputation which Witte was creating for himself in these years.

Then a phenomenon strange and incomprehensible to the European mind was witnessed—that of a finance minister who had created little by little a state within a state, and who had superimposed, so to speak, upon the many different organs of government other organs of similar functions but deriving their powers directly and solely from his Ministry. In this way Count Witte had the control of an innumerable crowd of functionaries of all denominations and all ranks, a network of schools of lower and even higher grades, a vast territory—a veritable kingdom, in fact, of which he was the sole master—an army, a fleet, even a diplomatic service. Furthermore, on account of his constant tendency to extend indefinitely the power of the state to the detriment of personal initiative and activity which was still in its infancy in Russia, one may say that for some ten years he was the real master of the 160 million inhabitants of the Empire. Truth compels me to say that the greater part of the elements composing the system created by him were better organized, performed their function more perfectly,

[82] See his article on Witte in Vol. II of the *Bol'shaia Sovetskaia Entsiklopediia* (1st ed.).

and were imbued with a broader and more modern spirit than the corresponding government services.[83]

Witte's propensity for empire building became proverbial, and at the end of the 1890s rumor placed him not only in the Ministry of the Interior but also in a specially created prime ministership. As a result, he was increasingly feared and, perhaps as often, hated with an implacable fury.

How did his preeminence in the government appear to Witte himself? One day in April, 1899, he spoke his mind in his usual blunt fashion to the German ambassador Prince Radolin, who reported Witte's words while they were still fresh in his mind.[84] Witte's position, so Radolin wrote, was not an easy one. He had to battle with his colleagues; and the constant intrigues of people who were narrow-minded and stubborn made him at times quite discouraged. To be sure, he had recently won a victory over his enemies by obtaining the Emperor's sanction for his economic policy. But at every turn his difficulties were renewed.

The cause of all this trouble—one has to imagine clenched fists accompanying these words—was Pobedonostsev. He was a narrow-minded fanatic and a doctrinaire professor who was stirring up trouble in everything but left the responsibility to others. He would have liked to be minister of the interior and minister of education. He had wisely turned down the administrative positions, preferring to give them to puppets. Now they had to take the blame for the mistakes which he himself had caused. Quite abruptly—for such was his manner, wrote Radolin—Witte said:

If my colleagues and I were not ministers but, say, peasants, then Kuropatkin [the minister of war] would be a Cossack private. Maybe he would have advanced to corporal, and perhaps he would have been shot somewhere and no one would have given a hoot. I probably would have become a coachman, because I love horses. With luck I might have become a good coachman in Petersburg. That would have been the

[83] Izvolsky, p. 113.

[84] Radolin to Hohenlohe, April 18, 1899. Bonn, Series 67.

height of my ambition. Herr Pobedonostsev, he was born to be a grave-digger; and that indeed he probably would have become under normal circumstances. For even now he was doing nothing but dooming everything that was an inconvenience to him. He was digging the grave of every person who stood out among the rest; he destroyed and buried every idea which reached beyond his horizon. Everything he wants to level and suppress. The only success which I would concede him as a gravedigger is that he has buried the Constitution.

Would Pobedonostsev also succeed in digging the grave of the Witte system? Or rather, since the relationship between these two men remained one of personal respect if not admiration, would the old Russia, which Pobedonostsev wanted to preserve, defeat the new? In February, 1898, Witte's position was still exceedingly strong. The Emperor graciously issued a rescript praising his Minister of Finance for his successes.[85] On January 1, 1899, Witte was raised to the second highest *chin*, that of Real Privy State Councilor. From then on, however, the old Russia asserted itself against Witte. The battle for Russia's future was on.

[85] Migulin, *Nasha bankovaia politika,* p. 236.

5. The Turn of the Tide

Witte repeatedly affirmed that in a few more years Russia would be the first industrial country of the world. GURKO, Features and Figures of the Past

Russia will not become England's competitor for fifty years.
WITTE, *as reported by Sir Charles Scott to A. D. White*

I

THE YEARS 1898 to 1900 marked the high point of the Witte system. Witte's political powers were never greater than in 1899, when he unseated Minister of the Interior Goremykin and prevailed in the choice of his successor, Sipiagin, or again in the following year, when the Emperor selected for him a thoroughly cooperative minister of foreign affairs, Count Lamsdorff. At the same time, however, the opposition to his system was rising fast; it even reached the ear of the Tsar. Nor was the economic progress of Russia as rapid or complete as Witte had promised. An industrial depression was on its way, aggravating the endemic agricultural crisis. In short, the obstacles were mounting; the task proved more complex and difficult than had been anticipated.

Witte rose to the challenge. He submitted the most drastic proposals of reform, more radical than those discussed in the previous chapter, and at the same time made his most urgent plea for a forced pace of industrialization. At last he himself was beginning to realize the inexorable logic of his aims. The early optimism was replaced by a groping awareness of the hidden problems; the confidence in traditional methods gave way to a bolder search for new policies. The basic structure of the "system" remained, but its spirit hardened and became more heroic. The change showed the Minister of Finance in his most argumentative and prophetic mood.

In order to understand the transition it is necessary to return for a moment to the agrarian opposition in the aftermath of the currency reform. A petition of the Imperial Free Economic Society to the government, adopted in December, 1897, may illustrate the mounting resentment.[1] The Free Economic Society was, of course, the honored spokesman of the liberal agrarian viewpoint, the zemstvo leaders, the run of the professors of finance or economics, and the liberal intelligentsia in general. Its petition took up the public outcry against the tariff on metal goods and the Witte system where the All-Russian Congress of Trade and Industry had left off.

The high prices for iron goods, it announced, while affording some Russian industrialists outrageous profits ranging from 30 percent to over 80 percent, hurt everybody. They made the ironmongers concentrate upon the production of railroad equipment to the neglect of consumer goods. And they were building no lasting foundation for the Russian metallurgical industry because the rural consumption of metal goods was falling off owing to the decline of agriculture. As for the consumers, they had gained little. The high prices had not led to a sufficient increase in Russian production to keep up with the demand; the import of metal goods still increased more rapidly than their domestic production. In the meantime, Russian agriculture was suffering from lack of metal equipment; it was reduced to wooden implements while its competitors abroad used steel. As regards the per capita iron consumption in Russia, the petition further charged, the country stood far behind the other European powers.

The expansion of the railroad network likewise met with no sympathy among members of the Free Economic Society. The quality of Russia's railroads was inferior to those of other countries, they said, as was shown by the many accidents and the high casualty rate. As for nails, a consumers' item, the United States

[1] The text is found in *Trudy imperatorskago vol'nago ekonomicheskago obshchestva,* 1897, No. 6, pp. 125 ff.

produced 20 million poods more for a population only half of Russia's. It was as though the Free Economic Society took a special delight in publicizing the shortcomings of Russian industry and blaming them on the Minister of Finance.

The gravest charge against the Witte system was that Russian agriculture was deteriorating. The year 1897 had brought a calamitous crop failure; the next year, the forecast ran, would bring another one because of the shortage of seed. All this in Russia's primary source of livelihood which sustained three quarters of her population and furnished as much of her government revenues! By contrast, the boons of free trade stood out brilliantly. Increased consumption would yield greater revenue to the government, replace thatch on the roofs with sheet iron, thus preventing village conflagrations, improve crops through the use of better implements, provide more rural employment, make available cheaper raw materials to Russian industries and railways, reduce the need for foreign loans, improve the balance of payments, and even create a sounder currency. The petition, of course, never came to grips with the necessities which had foisted the tariff on the Russian government. But the truthfulness of its description of agricultural conditions was unimpeachable.

There rose in these years yet another and more rabid wing of agrarian opinion, one with close allies among the industrialists of the central industrial region. It spoke through the weekly magazine *Russian Labor* (Russkii trud), edited from 1897 to 1899 by Sergei Sharapov. Sharapov was the domestic counterpart of Tsion; he represented an extreme form of nationalism applied, in the Katkov tradition, to Russian economic development. The decline of Russian agriculture, according to Sharapov, was only one of the consequences of foreign economic penetration—the entire economy was headed for collapse as a result of the gold standard. He turned the available information more ruthlessly against the Witte system than the liberals of the Free Economic Society had, taking full advantage of the freedom of economic discussion that prevailed under the Witte system until Witte, in 1899, more alarmed than by Tsion's pamphlets, forced its suppression. (It was said, however, that at the same time he secured a subsidy for Sharapov's factory making steel plows.)

There was also angry talk in government circles. As a well-informed Russian official whispered to the Austrian ambassador, Baron Aehrenthal: "I am terribly frightened by the advancing atrophy and anemia of the central parts of the Empire and the heightened expansion at the periphery which accompanies it."[2] In the summer of 1898 Witte himself confided to Prince Radolin that his position was difficult. The Russian agrarians, he explained, were more powerful than their Prussian cousins. Most of the grand dukes were among them, for they owned large estates.[3] From the officials and the grand dukes the agitation penetrated into the Emperor's cabinet.

But even if Witte had been able to ignore the mounting clamor, he could not disregard the mute reproaches of agricultural statistics and insufficient revenue. Every autumn the plight of Russian agriculture was brought to his attention by the state of the harvest. In 1897, after four unusually ample crops, he was again faced with a crop failure, which reduced the harvest by more than one quarter. In the following year the prediction of the Free Economic Society was almost literally fulfilled. While the total crop was normal, some areas suffered worse than in the previous year.[4] The results also showed up in the declining balance of trade, which in 1899 turned negative by a small amount, and still more painfully in the reduced tax receipts. In 1898 the tax arrears of the peasants, always an index of their economic well-being, were enough to give the Minister of Finance serious concern.

Despite the relief granted at the time of the coronation (mostly

[2] Quoted by E. Walters, "Austro-Russian Relations under Goluchowski, 1895–1906," *Slavonic and East European Review,* XXXII, No. 78 (December, 1953), 205.

[3] Radolin to Hohenlohe, July 13, 1898, *Grosse Politik,* XIII, 184–85.

[4] See Veselovskii, III, 370.

by extending the period of payment), all peasant Russia was in debt to the government.[5] By 1899 the arrears in redemption dues were greater by 16 million rubles than the dues collected that year.[6] The causes of such appalling poverty could not be ascribed entirely to the decline in grain prices, since they were on the mend after 1895. Nor was the misery universal. In many regions the peasants were paying off their debts. But there was no question about the persistent decline of the central and east central provinces of Russia. "The impoverishment of the Center" became a standard complaint in these years. A special conference, the first of a series, was called in 1899 by the Emperor to investigate the reasons.

Peasant poverty naturally cut into the government's revenue. When the peasant was unable to pay his direct taxes, the indirect ones could hardly be increased. In 1896 the State Controller had already resumed the alarm about the exhaustion of the "paying powers" of the agricultural classes, particularly in the central provinces.[7] And the Emperor, always sensitive to rural welfare, had commented: "It seems so to me too." At the end of the following year Witte himself issued a serious warning. All local and central authorities were anxious to lighten the burden of taxation, he wrote in his budget report for 1898. But how could this be done in the face of constantly growing needs and requirements? "The desire to extend the activity of the government for the good of the population," he continued, "deserves sympathy, of course. It is excusable to some extent under the conditions in our country—a country comparatively young in culture and developing rapidly. *But if the needs are innumerable, the means of satisfying them are limited*" (italics added). Obviously, after five years even Witte was recognizing the stop signs which the poverty of Russia set in the path of his policy of rapid industrialization. Deficit financing could not be carried on ad infinitum. But while

[5] Polenov, p. 6.
[6] Taburno, p. 140.
[7] *Vsepodanneishii otchët gosudarstvennago kontrolera za 1896 g.*, p. 55.

he correctly read the danger signals, he was not willing to let them stand in his way. And thus Witte the industrializer was driven to conquer the next frontier, the backwardness of rural Russia.

It was typical of the tsarist regime that confronted with the plight of agriculture it should try to give priority to the needs of the rural nobility. Ever since the revolutionary crisis that killed Alexander II the government had strengthened its ties with the landed nobility. It was the only group outside the bureaucracy on which it thought it could rely. Unfortunately, however, even in that group "senseless dreams" about a constitution were being discussed. Moreover, the agricultural depression and the innate inability of the average nobleman to adjust his estate to the requirements of a modern economy were undermining the social prestige of that class. It was selling or leasing its lands to the peasants or the *kuptsy*. It was also deeply in debt; 42 percent of private agriculture was said to be in the red, on the average by 1028.70 rubles.[8] In short, the rural nobility could and would not serve as a strong base for autocracy. Yet there were powerful forces in the government which tried to stave off the decline. Thus the pressure for subsidies came to a head in 1896. First, a Conference of the Marshals of Nobility gathered in St. Petersburg. Next year a Special Conference on the Needs of the Landed Nobility was called under the chairmanship of I. N. Durnovo. Its driving spirit was the head of the Imperial Chancellery and a powerful figure in the Ministry of the Interior, V. K. Plehve.

As usual, the problem reduced itself to one of finance. Would Witte, a member of this conference, agree to transform the rural nobility into state pensioners and to subsidize the enemies of industrialization to the tune of 35 million rubles at the expense of, say, the Siberian railroad? Never![9] He said so, before this conference,

[8] Baturinskii, p. 54.

[9] See the correspondence between Witte and Pobedonostsev, as cited in footnote 68, p. 159, particularly the letters of 1895–98; also I. F. Gindin and M. Ia. Gefter, "Trebovaniia dvorianstva i finansovo-ekonomicheskaia politika tsarskogo pravitel'stva v 1880–1890-kh godakh," *Istoricheskii arkhiv,* No. 4, 1957, pp. 123 ff.

in a speech with a novel and positive twist, arguing that peasant welfare was a prerequisite to the prosperity of the rural nobility and therefore should have priority. He was concerned, so he maintained, with the well-being of all the people, not only of a privileged class.[10] Such sentiments, of course, intensified Witte's unpopularity among the rural nobility. The special conference eventually came to naught after four years of futile deliberations. More important, Witte himself, after the introduction of the gold standard, moved the peasant question into the forefront of his economic policy.

He took his first official stand in favor of peasant reform at a meeting of the Committee of Ministers called in April, 1898, to consider the declining "paying powers" of the agricultural population.[11] He admitted in that body that some areas of Russia were taxed more heavily than others. The black-soil provinces and the central industrial regions paid nearly two rubles per head, while the outlying areas paid not even one. In order to enable the peasants to bear their tax burdens more comfortably in the future, he argued in a familiar strain, their prosperity had to be raised. That could be done only if the property rights and the social framework of peasant life were entirely recast; the peasants had to enjoy full legal security. If there was one reason for the decline of the central provinces, he added, it was the "economic disorganization of the peasant population" that prevailed there. He did not elaborate the implications of these vague phrases. There could be no doubt, however, that he was striking at the peasant commune. Naturally,

[10] Cited in Witte, *Ob"iasneniia Ministera Finansov komitetu ministrov po povodu zaiavleniia gosudarstvennago kontrolera o naprazhenii platezhnykh sil naseleniia,* appended to the second edition of *Samoderzhavie i zemstvo,* p. 216. He did, however, make some concessions; for instance, he lowered the interest rate on government loans to noble landowners from 4 percent to 3½ percent. The nobility, incidentally, was allowed special credit facilities which permitted them to hold on to their grain harvest until spring, when the prices were highest. The peasants, it will be remembered, were forced to throw their grain on the market in the fall.

[11] *Ibid.,* p. 218.

peasant reform could be handled only at the highest governmental level. Witte therefore suggested the calling of a special conference to take up his project.

When the Emperor, despite these pleas, did not react for months, Witte sent him a letter (he was then at Yalta) urging peasant reform in the strongest possible terms. Since this missive contained the first full exposition of Witte's views on peasant reform, let us examine its contents in detail.[12]

The question with which Witte opened his letter was reechoed throughout the entire document. Was Russian power to increase, as it had done after 1861, or was it to weaken again? After the Crimean War, Witte wrote, it had been decided that serfdom must disappear if Russia's prestige in the world was to rise again. Thus serfdom was abolished and Russia grew powerful. Now again it was time to move forward. As Alexander III had not lived to complete his father's work, the responsibility rested with Nicholas. Witte then launched his main argument, a lengthy plea for a free capitalist peasantry. He started with the assertion that France and Austria yielded much higher revenues than Russia, a difference which he attributed to the social organization prevailing in those countries. Every individual, so he expounded his views of human nature, was seeking to improve his life; he must be given every opportunity. Only freedom aroused man's fullest capacities; slavery killed initiative. Let the Russian peasant therefore be liberated from the slavery of arbitrary interference; give him legal security. Too many authorities meddled in peasant affairs: the land captains, policemen, feldshers (rural medical aides), the elders of the volost and the commune, the teachers in the rural schools, and every *barin* in the neighborhood. Witte also condemned the use of the whip in peasant courts: "It killed God in human beings." Next he deplored the fact that the peasants were not masters of their land. They had no legal security over their property under the custom of collective tax responsibility. Fur-

[12] Witte, *Tsarstvovanie Nikolaia II,* I, 467 ff.

thermore, zemstvos and peasant communes were highly arbitrary in levying their taxes. Also, rural education was in a deplorable state: "It was behind not only Europe but some Asiatic and transatlantic countries as well." Perhaps education was corrupting the people, Witte added as an afterthought; but even if it were, it had to be promoted so that Russia could move forward. Still more vehemently he went on: "It is necessary to move energetically. A 'dark people' cannot be perfected. He who does not go forward will, for that very reason, fall back compared with the countries that do move forward."

After this show of passion, the letter proceeded more calmly, but not for long. It was necessary above all, Witte continued, to raise the spirit of the peasantry by giving them the freedom of true citizens. While their present condition lasted, the Russian state could not attain that significance in the world which belonged to it "by the nature of things, and perhaps by fate." The recurrent famines were sufficient warning. But the remedies did not lie in pampering the landed nobility. The throne must care for all subjects alike: "God preserve Russia from a throne not based on the entire nation, but on separate classes!"

Both the mission and the future development of Russia, Witte wrote in conclusion, demanded ever new expenditures. The financial drain was becoming unbearable, but not because of Russia's poverty. The reason, he contended, lay in "the Russian disorder." What was the Minister of Finance expected to do? Everybody asked him for more money and yet at the same time accused him of overtaxing the population. In case all these hard truths lacked persuasiveness, Witte, touching the Emperor's most vulnerable point, warned that the disorder of peasant affairs was a fertile field for subversive agitation. At the end he again suggested a special conference of top officials to consider the matter.

How the Emperor reacted inwardly to this outburst is not known. Outwardly he remained passive. Apparently he showed the letter to Pobedonostsev, who gave him no answer. Witte indeed had no allies among the Tsar's advisers. Goremykin, for instance, who was still minister of the interior, was known for his opposition to peasant reform; the others remained indifferent. The Tsar, who was of a divided mind on the question of the preservation of the peasant commune,[13] would not move while the majority of his ministers remained unsympathetic.

Witte, forced by such inaction to increase his agitation, then took his case before the public. In his budget report for 1899 he commented frankly on the hardships of the rural population, which in some areas were admittedly extreme and which caused him considerable anxiety. Voicing the prevalent mood, he cited the adversity of the Russian climate and the stagnation in the peasant economy. But the reasons—and here he shifted to the offensive—lay not in the heavy tax burden or the industrial development. After all, industry gave part-time employment to many peasants and increased their money income. The causes rather lay in "the undefined economic and social relations among the peasants," which gave rise to multifarious difficulties in every aspect of the peasants' economy and prevented the most profitable employment of their resources. The current system only caused a confusion in legal concepts. The present age required a firm code of civil law replacing the peasants' fluctuating common law. As before, Witte avoided mentioning the peasant commune by name, but he made it clear that the *mir* was incompatible with capitalist agriculture among the peasants. Again he concluded on a note of urgency: "The final arrangement of the social conditions and property rights among the peasantry is the task for our generation."

The time for peasant reform, however, had not yet come. Witte accomplished no more in these years than (1) the transfer of rural tax collection from the local authorities to special agents of the Ministry of Finance,[14] which assured a more effective and humane

[13] *Svod vysochaishikh otmetok za 1900 general-gubernatorov, gubernatorov, voennykh gubernatorov i gradonachal'nikov,* p. 81.

[14] *Ministerstvo Finansov, 1802–1902,* II, 359; also Robinson, p. 146.

approach, and (2) the abolition of collective tax responsibility for hereditary communes, a distinct minority in the countryside. Only in 1903 did he succeed in extending the abolition to all communes. Even that was no great gain.

II

While Witte tried to solve the agricultural crisis by a bold program of peasant reform, a more insidious threat developed—the attack on the influx of foreign capital—which aimed at both the heart of Witte's industrial policy and the source of his authority, the Emperor. Sharapov's agitation against foreign gold was having its effect as the adoption of the gold standard began to show the expected results. While Witte rejoiced, many Russian capitalists became frightened by the creation of so many new enterprises financed from abroad which threatened their own economic security. This sentiment was strongest in the central industrial provinces, which had always been most sensitive to foreign competition. Now they also found themselves in a new dependence upon Baku oil and the southern metallurgical industries, where foreign capital predominated. Early in 1899 the Stock Exchange Committee of Moscow accused the Baku oil companies of raising the price of crude oil. Supported by the conservative *Moscow News* (Moskovskiia vedomosti), it subsequently voted a resolution warning the Minister of Finance of the dangers of foreign capital. A similar committee in Saratov soon joined in the protest.[15] Obviously even some sections of the industrial community were turning against the Witte system.

What made this agitation effective, however, was its connection with the agrarian opposition. By themselves the *kuptsy* had little hope of influencing the Emperor. It was only natural, on the other hand, that the agrarians should try, through the grand dukes and

[15] As reported by *Zhizn'*, II (February, 1899), 148. See also Iu. B. Solov'ëv, "Protivorechiia v praviashchem lagere Rossii po voprosu ob inostrannykh kapitalakh v gody pervoyo promyshlennogo podëma," in *Iz istorii imperializma v Rossii*, p. 382.

other prominent members of the Court, to provoke Nicholas against his Minister of Finance. The Emperor's deep sympathy with his rural subjects, his antipathy to Jews and to foreign influences in general, assured such extragovernmental presentations a favorable reception. From 1898 onward the Emperor, well aware that he bore the final responsibility for the fate of Russia, began to waver in his loyalty to his father's economic policy. Was it wise to pursue industrialization at such obvious detriment to agriculture and at such a high price of foreign indebtedness? Taking advantage of these qualms, Witte's enemies at Court began to spin their intrigues.

The first of these intrigues came to a head early in 1899. According to A. A. Polovtsev, a dignified elderly member of the State Council and the keeper of an invaluable diary (its entries inspired, in this instance and others, quite possibly by Witte), Grand Duke Alexander Mikhailovich had recommended a certain Khlopov to his brother-in-law, the Emperor.[16] Khlopov, Polovtsev noted, wrote pessimistic accounts of the economic conditions of Russia in the manner of Sharapov's editorials and claimed that the state of Russia's economy was being kept from the Emperor. Nicholas had fallen in with Khlopov's mood and had denounced a Prince Belosel'skii who was financing a factory on his estate with Belgian capital. By February, 1899, Polovtsev recorded that the Emperor, under the influence of Khlopov's "kvas patriotism," had denied the desirability of foreign capital and that, as a result, the influx of foreign capital was stopping. Witte, in profound alarm, took a very firm attitude with the Emperor and forced the matter into the open. He asked Mendeleev to compose a memorandum for the Emperor and wrote another one himself. Witte even demanded that the Emperor submit his memorandum to the State Council and preside in person over the discussion. He had to take this drastic step, one may surmise, in order to offset the repercussions

[16] "Iz dnevnika A. A. Polovtseva," *KA,* XLVI (1929), 119–20; see also Witte's account *Tsarstvovanie Nikolaia II,* pp. 227 and 449.

abroad over the Emperor's unguarded remarks.[17] Most likely, however, he aimed much higher. Now was the time to give battle to all his enemies and establish his policies once and for all.

Witte's memorandum, "On the Necessity of Formulating and Thereafter Steadfastly Adhering to a Definite Program of a Commercial and Industrial Policy," [18] was the most effective and powerful statement of the Witte system yet undertaken. It was full of the vitality of the man and was of crucial significance in the history of the economic development of modern Russia. With its cumbersome redundancy of phrase and thought, its rough and occasionally abrupt force of argument, and its repeated emphasis upon strict plan and coherent economic system, it was a typical product of the Minister of Finance's mind and personality. Before the Emperor, Witte dropped the facile optimism which was part of his public duty. He was entirely frank about the economic effects of industrialization. It imposed, he wrote, a heavy burden on the impoverished landowners and peasants, particularly in a year of crop failure. The paying power of the population was strained to the utmost. The Russian people were paying for industrialization not from a surplus but out of current necessities, with a heavy sacrifice. Nor was he less candid about the results of industrialization thus far. Despite all efforts, he admitted, national industry was not yet capable of satisfying the needs of the people; imports

[17] Professor Gindin has found no noticeable drop in the influx of foreign capital in this period; Witte's apprehension most likely was somewhat exaggerated. Yet it was essential that he nip in the bud any intrigues against foreign capital before the news leaked out to be exploited by Tsion or Sharapov. See *Dokumenty po istorii monopolitisticheskogo kapitalizma v Rossii* (*Materialy po istorii SSSR*), VI, 161.

[18] A copy of this memorandum, signed by Witte himself, was given to the Library of Congress in 1931 as a gift accompanying a large order of books from the library of the Winter Palace. The full English text, from which the quotation that follows was taken, can be found in my article "A Secret Memorandum of Sergei Witte on the Industrialization of Imperial Russia," *Journal of Modern History,* Vol. XXVI, No. 1 (March, 1954). A Soviet edition has recently been published by Professor Gindin in *Dokumenty po istorii monopolisticheskogo kapitalizma,* pp. 173 ff., together with the other documents mentioned below.

were on the increase. Worse, the national industries were still a drain on the Treasury rather than an asset, for Russia lacked the essentials of quick industrial growth. All this showed how extremely difficult it was to create national industries in a country with a colonial form of economy, and how unavoidable the shortcut of inviting foreign capital.

Never before had Witte attached such crucial significance to foreign capital. In 1892 he had hoped that the government would be able to increase the tempo of economic development largely out of its domestic revenues. Now, as Russia's resources proved insufficient, he was driven to stress more than ever the creative role of foreign gold. It was to act as a seed. Counted in millions, it would give rise to billions of native capital, stimulate competition and enterprise, and break down the native monopolies of the unenlightened and inflexible Russian merchants. Was it not better indeed to import foreign capital than foreign goods? The former, rather than the latter, gave employment to Russian enterprise and enhanced the productivity of native industries, until both foreign capital and goods were no longer needed. Then the protective system would come to an end. And even if Russian goods could not compete with European goods in Europe, they would at least find a market in Asia, and Russia might thus be able to repay her debts to Europe from her earnings in Asia.

Taking issue with the accusation that the influx of foreign capital impaired Russian sovereignty, he made the countercharge that Russian conditions discouraged foreign investors and delayed industrialization:

> It must also be stated that the influx of foreign capital does not proceed as easily and freely as is necessary to assure its continuation until the demands of the country no longer require the help of foreign savings. On the contrary, there are in our country such obstacles to its influx as exist in no other civilized country. We do not have the corporation laws which are in effect in the majority of civilized countries. Under such laws, everyone who wishes can form a joint-stock company by fulfilling certain conditions stipulated by law. In Russia a foreign

company can be opened only by a special decree of the Committee of Ministers, which requires the confirmation of Your Imperial Highness. Russian joint-stock companies in which foreigners are shareholders are permitted to have only a minority of foreigners on their board of directors. In ten provinces of Poland, in eleven provinces of the western regions of Russia, in Turkestan, the steppe regions, and the Amur district, neither foreign companies nor Russian companies with foreign participation are permitted to acquire property or exploit natural resources. A new company is admitted into Russia only with the permission of the local administration; and the acquisition of the right to exploit natural resources for a stated period is decided entirely on an individual basis and then only after preliminary investigation by the local administration into the actual needs of such enterprise. All foreign companies are subject to Russian laws and regulations as well as to ordinances and rules *which may be subsequently issued.* In permitting the activities of foreign companies in Russia, the government retains *the right to revoke at any time that permission and to demand the liquidation of any company.* Obviously, every detail of the influx of foreign capital into Russia is kept under strictest control by the central and local authorities. Whether this influx will be increased, decreased, or stopped altogether depends on their estimate and their interpretation of public welfare. Under these circumstances one should rather speak of an excess of government control of foreign capital, which takes its chances in going to Russia, and of unnecessary limitations imposed upon its freedom of investment. One should not forget that in a country which has the right at any time to close down foreign companies there are no safeguards against the harmful effects of sudden closure. Furthermore, because of the difficulties and tribulations which a foreign entrepreneur has to go through in Russia, because of all kinds of petitions and applications which he has to submit to provincial and central authorities, and because of constant interference not only by the law but also by administrative regulations, the influx of foreign capital into Russia is not yet copious enough. That, despite the invigorating effects which foreign capital has upon the productive resources of our entire national economy!

Considering the fact that the influx of foreign capital is the chief means for Russia in her present economic condition to speed up the accumulation of native capital, one should rather wish that our legislation concerning foreigners might be simplified. Historical experience shows that those human energies which accompany foreign capital are a useful creative ferment in the mass of the population of the most powerful nation and that they become gradually assimilated: mere economic ties change into organic ones. The imported cultural forces thus become an inseparable part of the country itself. Only a disintegrating nation has to fear foreign enslavement. Russia, however, is not China!

Russian nationalism, of course, was Witte's trump card. Russia did not want an economy befitting a colonial country, she wanted to be a "metropolis" herself. (This proved, incidentally, that Witte, like List, did not aim at complete autarchy. All he wanted to achieve for Russia was the same degree of economic independence and security which the other great powers enjoyed.)

The dominant note in this memorandum was the emphasis upon plan and system. Russia's economy, he recognized, was a highly complex organism. Every part of her economy was related to every other part. Consequently, the government's economic policy must be comprehensive. Witte's terminology for the scope of economic control varied. Sometimes he spoke of "a definite plan" or "a firm and strict economic system," sometimes of "a comprehensive commercial and industrial policy" or a "carefully planned system." It was clear, at any rate, that he recognized that industrialization required rational planning by the state. And besides rationality, planning called for continuity over years and decades. But as to the degree of control, his emphasis upon foreign capital privately invested (and upon private initiative in general) indicated that he thought essentially in terms of a capitalist society. He was convinced that the Russian people would succeed by themselves in promoting Russia into the ranks of the "metropolises," as long as the state provided the proper conditions.

It was in such powerful terms and with such novel perspective that Witte argued with his enemies in the government. At the same time he also took his case before the public in a major address to the Commission on the Regulation of the Grain Trade, which happened to meet on March 1, 1899.[19] Here, too, he was disarmingly

[19] Printed in *Vestnik finansov* for 1899, pp. 768 ff. Also in *Dokumenty,* pp. 195 ff.

frank. He endorsed the various proposals made by representatives of the grain merchants from the entire Empire. But he warned that all these technical measures would not make Russian agriculture more prosperous. For that a profound change in the legal structure of peasant life was necessary so that capitalism could spread in the countryside. Capitalism was necessary for industrialization, and industrialization was necessary for the creation of a strong domestic market and independence from high-priced foreign products. Once economic independence had been attained, he assured his listeners, the protective system would have outlived itself. At the present moment, he conceded, the protective system imposed a very heavy burden upon the population. It was all the more important, therefore, that Russia pass through that phase of her development as rapidly as possible. That could be done, however, only with the help of foreign capital. Thus, if the Minister of Finance did his utmost for the development of Russian industry, he did so not "out of personal sympathy with the capitalists, but from higher considerations," for reasons of state.

Witte—in a remarkable departure from his usual statements—then denounced those Russian capitalists who under the guise of patriotism resented the competition which foreign capital was introducing into the Russian business community. Such resentment, he said, only helped to prolong the agony of Russian agriculture. Yet it was not foreign capital alone that mattered. Russian economic development also demanded better technical schools, the removal of "various hindrances upon industrial initiative" (a vague phrase hinting at more reforms), and improved conditions for Russian workers. At the end he warned in a ringing phrase that "only work, work, not dreams" would help Russia to pass rapidly through the hard school of protectionism and liberate her eventually from foreign dependence. It was a fighting speech widely quoted in the Russian press.

In early March, 1899, Witte, with uncommon assertiveness, had thus stated his case within and without the government. On March

17 his position was at last debated on the highest level, before a special ministerial conference presided over by Nicholas II himself.[20] Before this tribunal Witte's alarms over Russian backwardness sounded even more shrilly. The per capita consumption in Russia, he said, stood at only one fourth or one fifth of what was considered the minimum in western Europe. If Russia merely wanted to preserve her present level of consumption, the value of her industrial production had to rise from the present 2.7 billion rubles to 11 billion per year within the next twenty years. It should, of course, grow even faster. And he added a pithy warning. "It is not only the possibility that the government will have to face stormy moments that forces us to attempt the quick development of our industry. There are also other reasons. Above all one has to take into consideration that the population cannot for very long sustain the protectionist system, because high prices inevitably follow from it and the masses grow poorer while a few individuals grow rich."[21] By 1904, perhaps, when the commercial treaty with Germany was due for renewal, the tempo of industrial development might again be reduced, but not before. He hoped that God would grant Russia peace in the meantime, so that she could fully develop her native riches. "That is our greatest task. But if we waste the propitious moment, and threats from without confront a Russia that has not strengthened her economy, then posterity will rightly reproach us for not having made use of the peace and set the country on its feet." (Prophetic words, which did not save him from just that accusation by the Bolsheviks.) While thus figuratively pounding the table, Witte at the same time revealed the weakness of his position when he admitted that "in view of the drift of opinion in some circles" he did not dare demand categorically that all restrictions be lifted from the influx of foreign capital, at least not until 1904.

[20] *Dokumenty,* pp. 200 ff.

[21] *Ibid.,* p. 201. Witte here used a phrase frequently employed by the opposition: "obednenie massy naroda pri obogashchenii edinits." This part of his speech, incidentally, he omitted from the official report.

The discussion before the special conference fully confirmed Witte's apprehensions. True, Minister of Foreign Affairs Murav'ev, whose relations with Witte were anything but cordial, endorsed the Witte system in general terms. But he too warned of the uncontrolled influx of foreign capital which threatened to turn "whole regions of our fatherland" into economic dependencies of foreigners. He suggested that all foreigners be barred from the exploitation of Russia's mineral riches and only be admitted into manufacturing. Obviously he resented the position which the foreigners had attained in metallurgy or the oil companies. Minister of War Kuropatkin likewise expressed himself in favor of excluding foreigners from acquiring land in Cossack districts, which was another way of saying that he agreed with Murav'ev.[22]

The Emperor's decision, published two days later, confirmed the status quo.[23] He, too, commended the Witte system, but on the crucial point he stood by the existing restrictions. Furthermore, he injected a new note, forewarning Witte of more difficulties, as he called for legislation to satisfy the moral and material needs of "the factory people" through contributions by their employers. On this issue Witte had for some time been clashing with the Ministry of the Interior. Now the "labor problem" and the exploitation of Russia's riches by foreign capitalists were being linked. In the inner citadel of power Witte was thus held at bay. Foreign capital was not excluded, but neither was it invited more cordially or on more liberal terms.

At this point a less determined official would have relinquished the struggle. Not so Witte. At the end of March, pressing his offensive still further, he wrote to the secretary of the Committee of Ministers, Kulomzin, protesting the many disadvantages to Russia's economy resulting from the discrimination against foreigners.[24] Not enough qualified native personnel were available; expensive and unsuited Russian stand-ins for foreign advisers had

[22] *Ibid.,* Murav'ev's speech, p. 203; the views of Kuropatkin, p. 220, note 9.
[23] *Ibid.,* pp. 205 ff.
[24] *Ibid.,* pp. 209 ff.

to be hired. And the few expert industrial managers of Russian origin were overburdened by the many roles they had to fill. Moreover, interlocking directorates were multiplying, with close and corrupting ties to the bureaucracy, which contradicted the civil service regulations issued under Alexander III. All this held up rapid industrial progress. Kulomzin, however, would not budge. He conceded that hard and fast rules dealing with foreign enterprises were lacking and that, as a result, administrative practice had fluctuated. As a remedy for such uncertainty he suggested that the Ministry of Finance codify all relevant decisions during the past forty years, which was cold comfort to Witte.

At this point, it appears, Witte finally dropped the fight. But within a year he returned to the attack once more. There was no chance, he argued at that time, of carrying out a concerted drive for rapid industrial development as long as each ministry and each branch of the government insisted on its own approach to economic questions. If industrialization was to succeed, the paramount need was for central direction. This was the gist of another great memorandum on industrialization which Witte submitted to the Emperor in February, 1900.[25] The impressive phrases of this memorandum have already been quoted at the beginning of the first chapter. Like the opening sentences of Witte's letter on peasant reform, they showed how much he tried in these years to impress the Emperor with the political dangers of economic and cultural backwardness, whether in agriculture or industry. "International competition does not wait. If we do not take energetic and decisive measures so that in the course of the next decades our industry will be able to satisfy the needs of Russia and of the Asiatic countries which are—or should be—under our influence, then the rapidly growing foreign industries will break through our tariff barriers and install themselves in our fatherland."

The memorandum repeated the earlier plea for the infusion of foreign capital into "our extremely backward industries" and

[25] Quoted on pp. 1 ff.

cited the obstacles put in the way of "foreign and Jewish" capital by local and central government agencies. Too many authorities in the towns and provinces of Russia were in charge of industrial affairs, and too few of them were convinced that industrialization was a state necessity. Witte therefore made the bold suggestion that the Emperor himself furnish effective leadership. "Only the sovereign master of the fate of the Empire, in his love for his humble and devout people, can draw up the bright guiding views which will lead to the common goal and inwardly harmonize all activities of the central and local government agencies." As the will of the sovereign prevailed unquestioned in the administration of justice or in foreign affairs, so it should prevail also in economic matters. The throne should make it clear that it considered industrialization of primary importance for the spiritual and political welfare of the country. Therefore, all economic policy should be concentrated in the Minister of Finance, and all departments, "by their friendly and coordinated efforts in their own spheres," should give their fullest support.

This document never had any practical consequences. But it testified further to the progressive clarification of Witte's thought. It showed not only his impatience with red tape, local obstruction, and indifference, but above all his insight that rapid industrialization demanded a single-minded leadership and a common program for the entire government. It confirmed the conclusions of his tract on *Autocracy and Zemstvo*, but applied them specifically to his own field of responsibility. Moreover, it resumed the tradition of authority established by Peter the Great and pointed ahead in revealing the comprehensive, not to say totalitarian, consequences of any policy aimed at catching up fast. Obversely, it made the weaknesses of Nicholas's regime all the more patent. For no matter how vehemently Witte might plead, tsardom could not achieve the unity of purpose necessary for its task. It could not even understand the urgency.

III

At this point it might be well to round out Witte's view of Russia's economic conditions. In 1900 his "system" was passing its peak. The industrial depression was fully under way. In the Far East the Boxer Rebellion and the subsequent turmoil in Manchuria imposed heavy expenditures on the Treasury and undermined Witte's control over Russian policy in an area vital for the success of the Siberian railroad. At home, student riots, strikes, and peasant uprisings indicated a growing political unrest. Witte's pleas for reform, his letter to the Emperor, and the two memoranda on industrialization had sprung from his realization of the strength of the opposition which he was encountering. All these measures had remained pleas; their very urgency foreshadowed failure. After 1900 Witte was beginning to be cornered by the forces which in 1903 brought about his fall. Thus, his visions of Russian economic development, sharpened by his awareness of impending disaster, assume special significance.

Circumstances gave him a final opportunity to state his ideas. In 1900, when Nicholas II fell sick of typhoid fever and the succession of his brother, Grand Duke Mikhail Aleksandrovich, became a possibility, Witte was asked to give the heir presumptive lessons in economics, state finance, and fiscal policy.[26] Naturally these lectures, delivered in 1901–2, when he was exceedingly busy, were not written by the Minister of Finance himself. He had an able staff, including the secretary of the Scientific Committee of his chancellery, to prepare them for him. But the crucial ideas—only a few of which can be related here—were his own (as derived from Friedrich List).

In the dialectics of economic development, Grand Duke Mikhail was told, society advanced from the primitive nomadic stage to an agricultural stage, and eventually to a mixed agricultural-

[26] They were made available to the public in 1912 under the title *Konspekt lektsii o narodnum i gosudarstvennom khoziaistve.*

commercial-industrial level. The ladder was a universal one; the economic order of all civilized societies was becoming identical. There was then, the Grand Duke was given to understand, no economic order peculiar to Russia. But while the western European states and the United States had already reached the final state of a well-balanced economy, Russia had barely made a beginning. There were good historical reasons for her economic backwardness; in the past the state had swallowed up all available resources. Like her Western models, particularly the United States, Russia therefore had to resort to foreign capital in order to start a modern economy. But if Russia was behind, her aim was the same: "Every nation must develop all its faculties in order to contribute, in the free give and take with other nations, as much as it can, to the treasure chest of mankind." [27]

Russia even had her own civilizing mission:

> Spread over a huge expanse, on contiguous territory, equipped with all that is necessary for reaching the highest state of economic development, Russia represents a market unique in its magnitude. Her international trade is not a matter of survival for her, but the means of a natural and therefore peaceful exchange of her surplus.

Russia, therefore, did not have to turn colonial exploiter.

> Russia's tasks abroad carry not only a pacific but even a highly cultural character in the best sense of the word. In contrast with the Western powers, which aim at economic and frequently even political subjugation of the peoples of the East, Russia's mission in the East must be a protective and educational one. It is Russia's natural task to guard her neighboring Eastern lands which lie in her sphere of influence against the excessive political and colonial claims of the other powers.[28]

This, the Grand Duke must have recognized, was the guiding principle of Witte's Far Eastern policy.[29]

Witte left no doubt in the Grand Duke's mind of the extraordinary effort required to bring Russia into the foreground of the

[27] *Ibid.,* p. 200.

[28] *Ibid.,* p. 203.

[29] Cf. Witte's comments on Badmaev's report, cited on p. 87 above.

leading civilized nations. The Russian masses lived in enforced unemployment because the natural wealth of the country was not being exploited. "On the shoulders of the present generation has fallen the task of making up what the empire has missed in two hundred years of economic sleep." [30] And the task brooked no delay: "A great power cannot wait." [31] Protectionism therefore was a necessity; the greater the country's backwardness, the higher the tariffs had to be, until at last the Russian economy had caught up with the economy of the leading countries. And for the same reason, Russia had to resort to foreign capital. These "artificial" measures were not peculiar to Russia; the other great powers had used them in their time. So did the United States at present, whose rapid economic progress was always before Witte's eyes.

Witte not only instructed the Grand Duke on the benefits of protectionism and of foreign capital; he covered the full range of Russian economic life. Starting with the condition of Russian agriculture, he deplored the obstacles to economic individualism created by the communal life of the peasants and praised the economic benefits of a system of small individual holdings, such as could be found in Tula province and parts of the Ukraine. Throughout he impressed upon his pupil the advantages of free labor and the respect of individual dignity;[32] nothing raised a country's productivity more. Next he criticized the zemstvos for their lack of initiative and efficiency. Nor did the city dumas receive any praise; they were charged with lukewarmness, unscrupulousness, and inefficiency. Witte blamed their shortcomings on the limited suffrage which excluded the educated classes.[33] Like a Russian Colbert, Witte criticized the business community for its lack of initiative and its habit of relying on government orders

[30] *Konspekt lektsii,* p. 60.

[31] *Ibid.,* p. 140.

[32] Particularly in Lecture X, pp. 101 ff.

[33] *Konspekt lektsii,* p. 26.

and taking subsidies.[34] On the other hand, he left no doubt that in a modern economy this class, emancipated from the narrow traditions of the *kupechestvo,* occupied the most important position, socially as well as politically.

Nowhere, by contrast, did Witte mention the landed nobility as an economic asset; it did not exist from an economic point of view. But he did refer to that class indirectly when he discussed the best form of society. "The accumulation of wealth in a country is the more fruitful the more harmoniously the various branches of production cooperate, and the more the social structure is of the kind in which no excessive efforts are squandered upon the satisfaction of irrelevant demands."[35] The waste of labor power and resources was a national loss, he said, citing the example of Spain, where monks, beggars, and officials ate up the national substance. (One wonders, did the Grand Duke draw the proper parallel?) At the same time Witte minced no words when he came to the economic results of militarism. "Militarism creates a class interested in war and thus promotes the likelihood of war."[36] The economic interdependence of the modern world drew everybody into a war; and even in peace militarism undermined the economic life of modern states. Strange doctrines indeed to be preached to a potential autocrat!

It was natural that Witte should speak at length about railroads and their economic and cultural contributions. "The railroad is like a leaven, which creates a cultural fermentation among the population. Even if it passed through an absolutely wild people along its way, it would raise them in a short time to the level prerequisite for its operation."[37] In Russia, of course, railroads were of still greater importance than in western Europe,

[34] *Ibid.,* p. 183.

[35] *Ibid.,* p. 80.

[36] *Ibid.,* p. 81. Witte attributed the prosperity of the United States to the fact that it had no standing army.

[37] *Ibid.,* p. 344.

and their construction had to be supervised by the state according to the needs of Russian trade and industry. In this context, too, Witte stressed the advantages of Russian trade with China and Persia, where her products enjoyed a competitive advantage over the superior Western goods, and enlarged upon the need for access to the open seas and for a merchant marine of her own.

But lest the Grand Duke put too much emphasis upon state initiative, Witte warned that the state may inspire but does not create: "The true creators are the citizens."

> The more society progresses, the more complex become all the functions of the productive process and the more difficult will be the role of the people involved in it. In order to fulfill their role they must have not only capital but also the necessary personal qualifications, the spirit of enterprise, and energy. These grow only on the soil of self-reliance. Not to stifle independent action, but to develop its strength by creating favorable conditions for its application, that is the true obligation which in our time the state must discharge toward our ever more complex national economy.[38]

That the Russian people possessed the necessary qualities he never left in doubt. Looking back over the economic progress made in recent years, he observed: "I am utterly amazed when I see how much has happened in this relatively short time and how great are the creative powers of the Russian people." [39] The natural talents and the diligence of the Russian people combined with the immeasurable wealth of their country always inspired Witte to a magnificent vision of Russia's economic future. His detractors in Russia indeed claimed he believed that Russia would eventually become the leading industrial country in the world.

The Grand Duke, in contrast to his brother, could have considered himself thoroughly up to date in political economy, assuming that he studied his lessons. Under Witte's tutelage he had been introduced to the rudiments of economic theory, even of

[38] *Ibid.*, p. 132.
[39] *Ibid.*, p. 139.

Marxism. He was made aware of the complexities of the international balance of payments and of the government's credit operations. And he knew which way Russia had to travel in order to catch up with the advanced nations of the West.

Was Russia ready for that race? Prince Meshcherskii's bittersweet words, composed after Witte's speech to the Commission on the Regulation of the Grain Trade in March, 1899, hinted at the plain truth:

It would seem offensive on my part, as well as on that of all of us Russians, to say about the Minister of Finance—in his praise—that he is by virtue of his activities and his qualities an insufficiently Russian minister of finance. But it may seem possible to say that he is an insufficiently contemporary minister of finance and too much a future one. Impatient, clear-sighted, and with a fanatically believing mind, he marches way ahead of his economic army.[40]

In contrast to the host of his fellow *chinovniki*, the Prince continued, Witte decided the big problems of the day by faith in the future self-sufficiency of Russia and her ability to help herself. But the trouble was that the economic life of Russia was not following rapidly enough behind its leader, because it was overburdened with the baggage of the ages from which his own mind was free. "Therefore I believe in his mind and in all his creative powers. Yet, sinful man that I am, I don't believe in the ability of our economy to stand on its own feet."

Unfortunately, the government and the highest spheres were full of such sinners. What the Prince meant in his honeyed condemnation was that Russia was not ready.

[40] In *Grazhdanin,* 1899, No. 17, in the column "Dnevnik."

6. Depression and a Change of Policy

Our present economic situation is difficult—crop failures, many bankruptcies. On this ground, then, they persuade the Tsar that it is necessary to change drastically our financial policy and that it was my fault. But how to change it they don't know. WITTE TO SIPIAGIN, *July, 1901*

Witte is a gambler by nature, full of talent and spirit, full of energy—yet a gambler. His entire policy has an element of gambling in it.

A GERMAN DIPLOMAT, *reporting from St. Petersburg, November, 1898*

I

THE STORY of the decline and fall of the Witte system may best be introduced by surveying the standards of public service which prevailed in the highest spheres of tsarist Russia during these years. For in the last analysis Witte's dismissal from the Ministry of Finance in August, 1903, resulted not only from the fact that he disagreed with the Emperor over Russian policy at home and abroad or even that his "system" seemed ruinous to popular welfare. It resulted equally from the constant reminder that in the ranks of the government he represented an alien force. Prince Meshcherskii had said that Witte stood too far ahead of his environment. He made enemies among the *sanovniki* just because his standards of governmental actions were different. And the fact that he was different spurred him on to remake Russia—all of it, if he could—according to his own conceptions of efficiency. The discrepancy between his ideals and Russian realities transformed every issue which he touched into a struggle for power between the forces of tradition and the Minister of Finance. As a result he was constantly enmeshed in petty wrangles. "What could I not do, had I not to waste two thirds of my time on intrigues," he exclaimed in these years.[1] Eventually he began to be feared even by people who were in basic agreement with him, on no other ground than his seemingly limitless ambition.

The growing weakness of his position lay, of course, in the uncertain support of Nicholas II. The incompatibility of the Emperor's outlook with that of his Minister of Finance was becoming more obvious as the Emperor's attitudes hardened under the burden of his solitary responsibility. These were harrowing years for the young tsar. His chief calamity was that as autocrat he could ask no one for the simple truth. He was surrounded by a welter of conflicting views which became more confusing as the need for action increased. Witte pleaded for drastic reforms in state and society; Goremykin and others advocated the strengthening of the zemstvo. Witte wanted to revise the peasant institutions, but the nobility on which autocracy had rested so long insisted that its own position be safeguarded first. Witte based his hope for progress on industrialization. But A. A. Polovtsev, who also had close connections to industry, sent the Emperor a memorandum advocating a return to "the wise policy of Catherine II," who had given, he asserted, private property in land to all classes.[2]

The spokesmen for agriculture brought Nicholas irrefutable evidence of rural impoverishment and unrest. Some of these counselors pleaded for the abolition of the peasant commune; others rejected this idea. Furthermore, while industrial growth strengthened the Treasury, strikes in the cities, towns, and factory-villages of Russia threatened public order. Education, though highly desirable, seemed to promote subversive attitudes and activities. The intelligentsia was already hopelessly hostile, although in the Tsar's eyes it was an isolated group despised by the Russian people.

[1] Propper, p. 241.

[2] Polovtsev's diary, entry for June 12, 1901, *KA,* III, 95.

Witte always advocated more freedom for private initiative and a secure and uniform legal order for all Russians. But what would become of the authority of the government if it did not possess an effective police? And why could not the Tsar's ministers agree more easily? Nicholas loathed their constant competition for his favor; but really good men, he complained, were very scarce. Fortunately, there were still "the people," the peasants of Russia, who would always stand by their Tsar. But it was often impossible to hear their voice.

Where in this maze of contradictory tendencies was the Emperor to turn for an answer? The traditionalists replied: To himself and to God. Thus preached not only his wife but also important dignitaries and friends like Sipiagin or Prince Meshcherskii. "God ruled all," they told him, "and God's anointed tool was the Tsar. The Tsar should not listen to anyone but counsel exclusively with God. And if his contemporaries did not like his acts, it did not matter; for only history would prove their validity." [3] To Nicholas, unfortunately, turning to God meant turning against his official advisory bodies, chiefly the State Council, which thwarted his will. He barely took notice when the State Council celebrated its hundredth anniversary in 1902.[4] And he began to distrust his ministers as well. Counseling with God soon came to mean heeding all sorts of irresponsible advice and even consulting obscure men pretending to speak in the name of God. In 1900 the Montenegrin Princess Militsa, who was married to Grand Duke Peter Nikolaevich, introduced at Court a professional soul doctor and proven charlatan, Monsieur Philippe, whom she had met in France. When the Russian police agent in Paris reported him as a fraud, the agent was dismissed. Monsieur Philippe then obtained, with the help of Kuropatkin (since the

[3] Entry for April 2, 1902, *ibid.*, p. 136. See also Witte's story about Grand Duke Konstantin Konstantinovich (*Tsarstvovanie Nikolaia II,* I, 248), who believed that Nicholas II was a demigod, standing halfway between God and man.

[4] Entry for May 18, 1902, *KA,* III, 162.

minister of education, in charge of the medical schools, would not stoop to illegality), a medical license from the Imperial Academy of Medicine, a highly respectable institution, and was appointed Privy State Councilor, a rank one *chin* below that held by Witte. Soon strange rumors began to circulate that under his guidance spiritualist séances were being held in the Winter Palace at which the spirit of Alexander III was being invoked. The stage was being prepared for Rasputin, who made his appearance at Court toward the end of 1903.[5]

It was a situation presaging disaster, and a witness recording the evil omens was not lacking. The diarist A. A. Polovtsev, who as a member of the State Council was well acquainted with the "highest spheres," confided in June, 1899, these laments to posterity:

> Moral forces are nowhere to be felt. The Emperor does not possess the necessary education or the political experience; he particularly lacks strength of character. Everybody can convince him and change his mind. Among the members of his family the majority pursue their personal advantage. Even Vladimir and Aleksei, who stand above the others, the one by probity and the other by brains, are surrounded by contemptible and suspicious characters because of their passion for distraction; they . . . have no influence. His uncle Sergei has the greatest influence over the Emperor, but he is a wretched fellow in the fullest sense of the word, and in his soul there is not a shred of clear and high feeling.

Polovtsev then reviewed some of the other grand dukes. Alexander Mikhailovich, who was married to the Tsar's sister, was "a child without any understanding" and therefore all the more dangerous. Konstantin Konstantinovich, who led an honorable private life, thought himself a genius and therefore was also a menace. Mikhail Nikolaevich took an interest, as far as the government was concerned, in the artillery and hence always quarreled with the minister of war. The rest Polovtsev considered second rate, "very ordinary people without education or habits of work, only con-

[5] Pares, *The Fall of the Russian Monarchy,* pp. 130 ff.

cerned with satisfying their appetites and capable of no spiritual uplift."[6]

According to the standards prevailing in Western urban-industrial life the Russian grand dukes and duchesses were indeed a plague upon the House of Romanov.[7] Of the sons of Nicholas I, the "first generation" of grand dukes, only Grand Duke Mikhail Nikolaevich was still alive at the beginning of the reign of Nicholas II. He was president of the State Council, but lived mostly on the Riviera. One of his sons was the Emperor's brother-in-law, Alexander Mikhailovich, a dangerous busybody; another was Sergei Mikhailovich, equally incompetent but fortunately less energetic.

Of the sons of Alexander II, Vladimir and Alexei belonged, as Polovtsev indicated, among the more respected members of "the second generation" of grand dukes. Vladimir was president of the Academy of Fine Arts. By his vigorous personality he struck terror into his Imperial nephew; hence Nicholas wisely abstained from any unnecessary contact with him. His wife, Maria Pavlovna, was a beautiful woman possessed, as she was fully aware, of all the charms of royalty which the Empress so conspicuously lacked. Many actions of her court were motivated by spite toward "the Grand Court." Their son Cyril later married a German princess who had been divorced from the Empress's brother, for which crime he was permanently banished from Russia. Aleksei Aleksandrovich was high admiral of the Russian navy and bore his share of responsibility for the disaster at Tsushima. Afterwards he retired to Paris until his death. A third uncle, Paul, had created a scandal by marrying a Mme Olga von Pistolkors; he lived abroad deprived of all his functions and revenues. The fourth uncle, and the most influential, was Sergei, of whom Polovtsev had such a low opinion, the most reactionary member of the Romanov family and a mystic

[6] Entry for June 17, 1899, *KA*, XLVI, 122.

[7] My account here follows A. A. Mossolov, *At the Court of the Last Tsar.* See also the autobiography of Grand Duke Alexander Mikhailovich, *Once a Grand Duke,* which gives an excellent picture of his state of mind.

of dubious charity. Until his assassination in 1905 he occupied the position of governor-general of Moscow, sponsoring a host of men and measures hostile to Witte. By contrast, the most innocuous grand duke of note was the Emperor's brother Mikhail, who was his heir until 1904. The only irregularity that could be held against him was his morganatic marriage. The younger set of grand dukes again were no better than their fathers. They all used and abused with a lordly air the privileges and sinecures with which their birth had provided them.

Witte, of course, loathed the wasteful, undisciplined ways of the grand dukes even while he sometimes bowed to the pretensions of their title. They harassed him with constant requests for money; they meddled in his affairs and corrupted the Emperor. To Witte they were part of the backward Russia. But he also hated the lesser nobility that had access to the Court, and for similar reasons. The worst of them, unable to earn their living legitimately, begged for subsidies and abused their position by intriguing against him. Some of this group he considered downright scoundrels, even more despicable than the professional revolutionaries.[8] These men, Witte knew, understood nothing of the mode of life which he represented; and what they saw of it, they generally scoffed at. What valid counsel could they give the Tsar?

As they expanded their influence at court, Polovtsev, in July, 1901, penned another gloomy prophecy in his diary:

> Those circles upon whom the care for the fate of the fatherland rests are devoid of any clear and firm sense of direction. All measures are without inner connection, casual, the creations of the moment. The young Tsar, under the influence of the place-seekers in his environment, becomes ever more contemptuous toward the executive organs of his government and only believes in the benevolent power of his personal rule, which he sporadically asserts. . . . We live under conditions reminiscent of the terrible times of Paul I. They are out for Witte's head, accusing him of giving away the riches of the country to foreigners. Logically it follows from this that he should give them

[8] Witte, *Detstvo,* p. 255.

to those parasites at court. At the head of these intrigues one finds the grand dukes, whose influence expands beyond all measure; they recognize no law. The State Council represents in their opinion an assembly of the most radical elements, which wish to limit the Imperial power by parliamentary methods. The Senate is a council of senescent men. The Tsar wants to hear the voice of the people and turns to those worthless nonentities who cheated their way into his confidence.[9]

But, to descend now to the lower ranks of the highest circles, the caliber of the chief officials was frequently not much superior to that of the grand dukes and the backstairs influences whom Polovtsev so deplored. Witte's successor as minister of communications, Krivoshein, was convicted of large-scale bribery and managing state railroads for his own pocket and was dismissed. A. A. Abaza, minister of finance for a brief spell after Reutern and, as head of the Department of Economics and Finance in the State Council, one of the most capable advisers of Alexander III, was notorious for his marital infidelities and his insatiable gambling at Monte Carlo. He was also playing the stock market on the basis of confidential information. Brought before a special court of honor presided over by Bunge, he was stripped of his office.[10]

The State Controller, Tertii Ivanovich Filippov, whose task consisted of auditing all but the most secret accounts of the government, likewise had his heart set on other matters. His ambition was to become Oberprokurator of the Holy Synod, replacing no less a figure than Pobedonostsev. Thus he wrote treatises on mysticism rather than on state finance.[11] After his death a general of the infantry and professor of military science, General Lobko, was given his place. Of him Polovtsev remarked that "he never saw the slightest reason for having the faintest doubt about anything he was officially told." [12] Witte once complained that Lobko

[9] Entry for July 22, 1901, *KA,* III, 99.

[10] Witte, *Detstvo,* p. 194, also pp. 207, 263.

[11] *Ibid.,* p. 277.

[12] Polovtsev's diary, entry for April 4, 1900, *KA,* XLVI, 126.

was in favor of giving Russian oil wells to the poor people rather than to the rich (as he himself reputedly did), adding: "I insist on my conviction . . . that the *chinovniki* are the original socialists."[13] Lobko proved a ready tool for all of Witte's enemies.

Another general of the same ilk was the commandant of St. Petersburg, N. V. Kleigels, who together with Grand Duke Sergei Mikhailovich and the ballerina Kshesinskaia engaged in sordid financial speculations.[14] None were so bad, however, as a third general, E. V. Bogdanovich, a member of the Council of the Ministry of the Interior, who had retired to Paris and sniped from there at Witte by feeding adverse reports on Russia's economy to the French press.[15]

Goremykin, the minister of the interior, was known to be incurably lazy. His motto was "It's a trifle"; nothing was worth getting excited about. One of his subordinates went so far as to assert that "his policy was based upon personal rather than state interests, and when these two clashed, he had allegiance to the former."[16] Sybarite that he was, however, he was credited with scrupulous personal honesty.

His successor, Sipiagin, was credited with more firmness of character, which endeared him to Witte. He was a good soul, an old-fashioned country squire, loyal, jovial, but also vain and self-satisfied, without any idea except that the Tsar was absolute master and he his unquestioning servant. As Witte put it, "He could see no further than this," and shut his eyes. He also loved his cups; one night he fell drunk under the table at the Imperial Yacht Club, the finest in St. Petersburg.[17] As minister of the interior he freely made use of the police and arrested even respected persons at the slightest pretext; he too was fighting the changes which were occurring in the country. As a result, he

[13] *Ibid.,* p. 129.

[14] *Ibid.,* III, 91, 94.

[15] See "S. Iu. Vitte, frantsuzskaia pressa i russkie zaimy," *KA,* X, 39.

[16] Gurko, *Features and Figures of the Past,* p. 75.

[17] Polovtsev diary, January 2, 1902, *KA,* III, 109. See Plehve's letter to A. A. Kireev of August 31, 1903, *KA,* XVIII, 202–3.

consolidated the moderate opposition and aroused the wrath of the revolutionaries; he was promptly assassinated. His successor (likewise assassinated) was V. K. Plehve, who more than any other single man was responsible for Witte's downfall. He embodied all the forces that opposed the Minister of Finance.

Plehve was an unusually able product of the Russian bureaucracy, highly intelligent and successful in whatever he touched. His career, therefore, had not only been rapid but had also carried into the innermost citadels of the government. After the assassination of Alexander II he was given charge of the police department in the Ministry of the Interior. In 1894 he became head of the Imperial Chancellery for nearly a decade; in 1899 he was also State Secretary for Finland. In addition, he served on every government committee of importance. He thus possessed an excellent knowledge of the bureaucratic apparatus. Unfortunately, however, bureaucracy and, at its center, the police circumscribed his intellectual horizon. By training and conditioning, as well as by his sarcastic and withdrawn temperament, he was no more than a "superlative clerk." [18]

Yet it would be unfair to deny him a touch of vision. After his appointment as minister of the interior in April, 1902, he set forth a broad program of reform. He vaguely realized that Russia was rapidly changing and that the administrative machinery was badly in need of adjustment. He admitted that with a few exceptions the population was dissatisfied (his police reports told him so). It was his intention, therefore, to reduce the internal tensions by bringing about closer cooperation between the government and the public through a reform of local administration. In the provinces the governors were to consult with zemstvo and town duma, which were to receive greater independence. The opposition was to be granted creative outlets in local work, under autocratic leadership to be sure.[19]

[18] Gurko, *Features and Figures of the Past,* p. 111.

[19] Polovtsev diary, January 5, 1903, *KA,* III, 169; also Witte, *Tsarstvovanie Nikolaia II,* I, 193.

But Plehve let his bureaucratic instincts get the better of his good intentions. After his assassination, for instance, letters were found in his office which the police had intercepted from persons whom not even the wildest imagination could have suspected of conspiracy. Like other ministers of the interior before him, he loved to spy on the private correspondence of people who interested him. Or take his attitude toward the Jews. While himself no hater of Jews, as even Witte admitted, he nevertheless lent his support to anti-Semitic outrages. Kuropatkin noted in his diary after the hideous Kishinev pogrom at Easter, 1903: "I heard from Plehve, as from the Emperor, that the Jews must be taught a lesson, that they gave themselves airs and were the leaders in the revolutionary movement." [20] No wonder that Pobedonostsev called Plehve a scoundrel[21] (but then Pobedonostsev, who knew too well how the rapid changes in Russian life cut the ground from under any conviction, also remarked to Witte: "Who is not a scoundrel nowadays?").[22]

Witte attributed Plehve's bureaucratic inflexibility to the fact that he was a convert of Polish origin.[23] A kinder critic has argued that Plehve was convinced autocracy would fall but that he thought neither the Emperor nor the country as a whole was ready for constitutional government. Thus he fought all liberal reforms with the grim resolve of a wounded warrior, unwilling to cede an inch, even if it cost him his life.[24] The truth was that he could not adjust himself, except with a policeman's frown, to the silent revolution occurring in Russia. When the change challenged his conception of autocratic government, he struck back. In this he was very much like the Emperor himself. His final and most disastrous recourse for the internal pacification of Russia was, if one can trust Witte's testimony, "a victorious little war." [25]

[20] "Dnevnik A. N. Kuropatkina," *KA,* Vol. II, entry for April 14, 1903.

[21] Maklakov, p. 287.

[22] Witte, *Tsarstvovanie Nikolaia II,* I, 31; also *Detstvo,* p. 278.

[23] Witte, *Tsarstvovanie Nikolaia II,* I, 194.

[24] Maklakov, p. 290.

[25] Witte, *Tsarstvovanie Nikolaia II,* p. 262.

As it happened, Minister of War Kuropatkin was bitterly opposed to a little war in the Far East. He was a loyal and conscientious servant of the Tsar, always demanding larger appropriations than Witte would grant him, often opposing him in matters of foreign policy, yet preserving an instinctive liking for him as a man who, he recognized, stood several feet above the rest.[26] Their deepest disagreement concerned Witte's economic policy. Kuropatkin had no use for what he called the untimely industrial development of Russia. Over Witte's protest he bought military equipment abroad rather than at home, saving money rather than developing Russian industries.[27] He, too, thought that the Witte system would end in a frightful crash. Meanwhile he observed its alarming effects on the health and morale of his peasant recruits. And, like the rest, Kuropatkin had his own panacea for the ills of Russia. It consisted of the harmonious development of the three main forces in Russian life, the bureaucracy, the aristocracy, and the zemstvo.[28] (Where, one may wonder with Witte, did the *narod* fit into his scheme?)

But the most incredible thing about the Minister of War was his reply to Witte's argument that military preparedness must be backed by industrial preparedness. He told the Emperor in Witte's hearing that at present all wars were caused by the immoderate industrial development of the European countries which forced their governments to compete for markets. In view of the inescapable war, therefore, Russia should put a brake on the successes of her industry. "That's what a very clever man said who has no education fit for a member of the government," Witte sputtered as he told this story to Polovtsev.[29]

Kuropatkin was another of the many honorable specialists in the government, competent in all matters to which his career had given him access, but without comprehension of the larger setting.

[26] Kuropatkin's diary, entry for January 19, 1903, *KA,* II, 26.
[27] Polovtsev's diary, entry for February 18, 1901, *ibid.,* III, 83.
[28] Kuropatkin's diary, entry for November 29, 1902, *ibid.,* II, 11.
[29] Polovtsev's diary, entry for March 16, 1899, *ibid.,* XLVI, 121.

And he, too, lacked the least political sense. That, of course, was the basic charge to be laid against the tsarist regime—or any autocratic government at a time of rapid change—that it bred bureaucrats and specialists of frequently excellent caliber, but not men of comprehensive vision and a deep experience of national life. The most representative figures in the government remained "superlative clerks." The lesser *chinovniki,* in the rigid routine of their bureaus, were too often timeservers without principles, engrossed in their daily chores, and working at cross-purposes with other departments. At best they were motivated by a common desire to preserve the glory and the power of the state as embodied in its bureaucracy and cared little for the needs of the people at large. A glimpse into the inner cabinets of the Ministry of the Interior, as caught by one of the department heads, V. I. Gurko, reveals an odd assortment of individualists proceeding with astounding inefficiency, unexpected mutual tolerance, and an arrogant ignorance of the subject with which they were dealing.[30]

Finally, there was the phenomenon of Pobedonostsev. Like Witte he stood out among the servants of the Tsar. He possessed character, erudition, and a truly cultured mind. Witte, fume as he might against Pobedonostsev, never ceased to admire him for these qualities, the latter two of which he himself so conspicuously lacked. Both men, despite their disagreements, shared many convictions. Both were stanch proponents of autocracy. Witte also sympathized with Pobedonostsev's concern for the welfare of the Orthodox Church, although he came to realize how superficial the official religion had become in the Oberprokurator's hands. And he willingly granted state funds for parochial schools, since he felt that "without religion the Russian people would become like a beast."[31] But beyond that point they parted company. By temperament Pobedonostsev was hostile to the new world encroaching

[30] These are the impressions derived from reading Gurko, *Features and Figures of the Past.*

[31] Witte, *Detstvo,* p. 350.

upon Russia. Wiser in many ways than Witte, he realized the incompatibility of the old and new orders. He was a pessimist and, like Plehve, tried to stave off the inevitable subversion of Russian tradition by the foreign models, knowing that in Russia they only caused chaos. Witte, on the other hand, was an optimist, ready to master the chaos by the modernization of Russia from above. It was a tribute to both men that in such contrast of instinct and principle they continued to recognize each other's genius.

But to advance now from men to measures, how did the chief policies of the other ministries articulate with the Witte system? The basic trend of Russian autocracy was toward consolidation, toward the creation of a greater unity within the administration as well as within the deeper layers of popular consciousness in language, religion, or loyalty to the Tsar. Witte could not but sympathize with the effort to give to the Russian Empire the same internal cohesion which her Western competitors possessed. But he found himself almost alone in deploring the brutal measures employed to achieve these aims. He opposed the compulsory Russification of national or religious minorities and the attacks on the autonomy of Finland; he loathed the persecution of the Jews. These acts, he knew, were bound to arouse profound indignation. "Nothing undermines the prestige of authority more than the frequent and wide application of repression," he had written in his pamphlet *Autocracy and Zemstvo.*[32] His own instincts were rather for mutual accommodation and smoothing over the difficulties by mutual respect and consideration. It was he who recommended leniency toward the rebellious students, saying that neither a scholar nor a policeman, but only a gentleman and an aristocrat with good manners, was fit to deal with them.[33] These were the

[32] Cited from *Samoderzhavie i zemstvo* by Oldenburg, p. 155.

[33] Reported by Lamsdorff to Tschirschky, who reported these words to the German Foreign Office on November 6, 1899, Bonn, Series 61, Vol. LXX ff. There is one discordant note in the testimony about Witte's attitude toward rebellious students. A. S. Suvorin reported in his diary on March 25, 1899, that Witte had favored such strict measures that Pobedonostsev had cried out:

standards of successful business; he applied them profitably in his own ministry.

Typical of his political sense in these last years was the founding, under his ministry, of the St. Petersburg Polytechnical Institute, an institution specially designed to overcome the dearth of experts in metallurgy and electrical engineering and of trained economists suitable for government service. He granted its professors a degree of self-government unheard of in Russia.[34] He even confirmed as a professor of economics one of the Legal Marxists, M. I. Tugan-Baranovskii, whom the minister of education had recently dismissed from his position as *Privatdozent* at the University of St. Petersburg (he had participated in a student demonstration). What Plehve was preaching, Witte was practicing, giving the opposition a constructive outlet for their energies.

The government, however, was driven by its incomprehension to carry matters to a break. It arrested students and scholars, recruited Finnish soldiers for the Russian army, confiscated the lands of the Armenian Church, restricted the rights of Polish schools, and always resorted to extreme methods at the smallest sign of disloyalty. After Sipiagin's assassination Witte told the Emperor to his face that revolutionary violence was the result of the lawlessness of the government. "Where the government proceeded with administrative violence rather than under law, the population responded in kind."[35]

As the domestic scene grew darker and Plehve turned toward repression, Witte, by instinct, veered in the opposite direction. Soon after Plehve's appointment he called for decisive changes. A ukase was to be issued that all laws were to be obeyed by the

"No, Sergei Iulevich, that is impossible." On February 24, 1900, Suvorin asserted that Witte was the author of the decree drafting arrested students into the army. If these assertions are true, one has to ascribe the vacillation to Witte's divided nature, as sketched below.

[34] *Ministerstvo Finansov, 1802–1902,* II, 608; also Witte, *Tsarstvovanie Nikolaia II,* I, 230.

[35] Polovtsev's diary, entry for April 2, 1902, *KA,* III, 136.

government (*sic*) and the independence of the courts restored. The Senate was to regain its authority, all "temporary measures" were to be reviewed by the State Council, and a special commission was to review the roster of administrative exiles.[36] At the same time Witte consulted specially constituted local groups about the needs of agriculture, trying to unite government and society in a crucial reform of the peasant order.

Whether through industrialization, peasant reform, the organization of the bureaucracy, or the grant of civil liberties, he wanted autocracy to undertake the recasting of Russian society after the Western model. The Tsar should be the chief "revolutionary from above" and in this way prove again the time-honored merits of autocracy as the vanguard of the Russian people. Autocracy was to be master of the changes occurring in Russia, not its victim. Instead, the government frittered away its energies in vain repressions. Here lay the deepest core of the disagreement between Witte and his opponents.

It is not to be assumed, however, that in these years Witte was a paragon of administrative efficiency or even legality. He too could not deny his role as a minister of the Tsar. Once, for instance, he let drop the remark that in a contract between the government and a private firm only the latter was bound by the law if a conflict arose.[37] The state, in other words, could break any contract at will. Likewise, when it was a matter of aiding a private firm whose survival he considered essential, Witte would readily ignore the law.[38] And in his dealings with the State Council he would occasionally flout its opinions, as he had done in the introduction of the gold standard. The arrogance which ruined autocracy in these years was at work also in him. Having a vision of a better Russia, he was sometimes inclined to fight it out rather than argue it through. To be sure, like autocracy at its best, he had an excuse: Russia could not wait for the slow process of public en-

[36] Entry for April 18, *ibid.,* p. 138.

[37] Korostowetz, *Graf Witte,* p. 34.

[38] Polovtsev's diary, entry for April 21, 1901, *KA,* III, 90.

lightenment; speedy action was necessary to preserve her security and power. These shortcomings in Witte did not materially diminish the disagreements between him and his colleagues, but they proved that he too shared the weaknesses of character caused by the autocratic regime.

Considering their differences, it was remarkable how well Witte managed to work with his colleagues, with Sipiagin, Kuropatkin, Pobedonostsev, or even so slippery a man as Prince Meshcherskii. But inevitably he became involved in strange inconsistencies. On the surface he would express opinions that did not set him too far apart from his colleagues. On a deeper level, however, the discord would be more pronounced. It is extraordinarily difficult to fathom Witte's mind in these years. Statements showing how he disagreed with his colleagues can be matched by others proving how close he stood to them. The contradiction can only be resolved by assuming, as his associates did who knew him well, that he was really two men at the same time.[39] First he was a minister of the Tsar bound to work with his fellow officials and by nature gregarious enough to do so gracefully, and, second, a man with a vision who knew that the very Russia with which he was cooperating was doomed unless he could put his own vision into effect. He would say to Sipiagin, for instance, that the latter's policy of drafting rebellious students into the army was better than treating them with the knout, and yet in another context bitterly condemn Sipiagin's entire approach to the student problem. He cooperated with his enemies, for he could not afford to antagonize them or the Tsar by saying what he really thought. Otherwise his work would have been made impossible (and he did love the power that he wielded as minister of finance). Neither could he jettison his deepest convictions and conform lightheartedly to the official views. The frustrations began to poison his good sense.

[39] See Kovalevskii's judgment in *Istoricheskii vestnik,* CXL (April, 1915), 257; also Alvensleben's report on the excellent relations between Witte and Plehve dated July 9, 1903, and his report of August 25, 1903, where he commented on Witte's "Methode sich mit Gegnern zu arrangieren." Bonn, Series 82, No. 2.

In order to understand his complex mind one must also remember the incredible provocations from which he suffered in these years. The wrath of his enemies knew no bounds. It was small matter that they denounced him as a "German," but more important that they blamed him for every abuse that came to light in the Ministry of Finance.[40] Unable to discredit his integrity, they spread rumors about his jealousy of a potential rival, V. I. Kovalevskii, the head of the Department of Trade and Industry, whom he was forced to dismiss suddenly because of a private scandal (in order to protect him he could give no reasons in public). They gossiped about a cancer in his nose, or a collapse he had suffered during an audience with the Tsar; they tattled about the syphilis which was undermining his reason. As neither his good health nor continued mental vigor would oblige them, his enemies then settled with malicious glee on Mme Witte, spinning out the tales of her former liaisons or her present financial machinations behind her husband's back.[41] The defamation of the Minister of Finance was another reflection of the moral corruption of the Russian *haute volée*. The tragedy was that there could be no effective defense; public opinion was basically hostile to the Witte system. Only within his own ministry did he continue to enjoy the fullest loyalty. On the tenth anniversary of his appointment as minister his collaborators even arranged for a celebration. But the sums raised by public subscription for this occasion were conspicuously disappointing, and many of the congratulatory articles in the press bore all too distinctly the character of paid work.[42]

The strain of these years inevitably affected Witte's personality.

[40] Tschirschky's report of October 17, 1899, on the scandal concerning the head of the railway department in the Ministry of Finance, Maximov, and Maron's report of December 16, 1902, on the dismissal of Kovalevskii, are here of interest. Bonn, Series 82, No. 2.

[41] *Ibid.*, Alvensleben's report on Witte's syphilis, December 14, 1901; Radolin on his cancer in the nose, July 8, 1895. On Matilda Ivanovna's past see Radolin's dispatch of May 28, 1897, also Romberg's report of September 14, 1903.

[42] See the report on Witte's anniversary by the German Consul-General in St. Petersburg, Maron, dated September 17, 1902. Bonn, Series 82.

His early humility and all the efficiency in dealing with people resulting from it were disappearing. The many battles over domestic and foreign policy left their scars, and his extensive powers as minister of finance corrupted his soul. He grew short-tempered, and the innate contradictions in his nature stood out more nakedly. But there was also a new sense of desperation. His counsels went unheeded; there would be a frightful crash. These were trying years for Witte, and his personal difficulties aggravated the adversities which his system encountered after the turn of the century.

II

By the turn of the century Witte's policies had been in operation for seven years. Was his "system" working according to theory? As far as the state of Russian agriculture was concerned, the answer according to a great majority of his contemporaries was a resounding no. First there was the adversity of a string of bad harvests. Both 1897 and 1898 had been very poor years, 1899 was satisfactory, but 1900 again was only mediocre. The year 1901 was disastrous, but fortunately the next two harvests were normal or better. But other indices of agricultural welfare showed no improvement. On the contrary, the number of horses and farm animals declined;[43] rural wages, slightly on the rise before, fell after 1900.[44] The persistent poverty undermined the health of the rural recruits, which worried the minister of war.[45] The hidden unemployment in the villages remained high. To be sure, from the viewpoint of the Minister of Finance the rural situation was not entirely hopeless, as will appear subsequently. But the lot of the peasants, especially in the central black-soil provinces, sank even below the normal level of misery. And the landlords were hardly doing better.

The central black-soil provinces particularly stood out as a depressed area. They remained largely untouched by the growing

[43] Maslov, I, 295; II, 7.

[44] Robinson, pp. 105–6.

[45] Kuropatkin's diary, entry for January 19, 1903, *KA*, II, 26.

industries; nor did they furnish industrial labor to the new mills and factories. Their social structure also had changed least since emancipation. Yet, as Witte himself had admitted, they were saddled with a considerable part of the tax bill. In the eyes of many contemporaries the stricken areas constituted the heart of peasant Russia. Their plight evoked a profound response and was the subject of several official investigations. In late March, 1902, their misery was suddenly revealed in its full measure when, after a long period of unusual calm among the Russian peasants, the villagers of the Poltava and Kharkov gubernias, a region with many "poverty lots" and a general land shortage, rose up to burn and loot the manors. Their rebellion was widely interpreted as a popular indictment of the Witte system. It caused, in turn, additional hardships for the Treasury, as a new rural police had to be created in an effort to prevent further violence.

While in the eyes of contemporaries the agricultural crisis deepened with the years, how did industry, Witte's chief concern, fare? For several years his sanguine predictions seemed to have come true. Particularly after the currency reform Russian industry experienced a phenomenal boom. And yet, starting in 1899, industrial development suffered a serious setback, which lasted, in some ways, until after the Revolution of 1905.

The industrial crisis, to describe it briefly, started in late 1898 as a tightness in the international money market, on which Russia had come to depend more than ever in the wake of the currency reform.[46] The Fashoda crisis, the Spanish-American War, the conflict in South Africa, the events in the Far East, all the wars and rumors of wars at the turn of the century diverted the flow of capital away from peaceful industrial investment. The scarcity of money, Witte wrote as early as November, 1898,[47] ended for

[46] On the effects of the depression see the works by Wittschewsky, Migulin, and also Iakovlev, Chap. VII.

[47] B. A. Romanov and B. V. Anan'ich, "Popytki S. Iu. Vitte otkryt' amerikanskii denezhnyi rynok dlia russkikh zaimov (1898–1902 gg.)," *Istoricheskii arkhiv,* 1959, No. 1, p. 128.

the time being the "planning and carrying out of new large-scale measures that demanded loans," such as the expansion of the Russian railway network and the granting of extensive state orders to the heavy industries. With the slowing of pace, Russian business, in many instances carried away by the boom, suddenly found itself in straitened circumstances. Already in August, 1899, two respectable firms with extensive industrial and financial interests, those of Mamontov and Von Derviz, went bankrupt. They had overexpanded their operations, counting on a continued boom. Soon after, on September 23, the crash hit the St. Petersburg stock exchange as it became clear that Russian industry shared to some extent the predicament of these giants. Thereafter the depression wore on month by month and year by year, hitting first at the textile industry and then, in greater force, at the heavy industries.

In the fall of 1901, after the poor harvest, a new low was reached. Among the firms ruined that year, Poliakov's in Moscow was the most famous. Poliakov's distress, to be sure, made the Emperor rejoice, for it would help to eradicate, so he said, "that Hebrew nest in Moscow." [48] But many other firms also tottered, for the Poliakovs had widespread connections. In Kharkov the metallurgical firm of Alchevskii collapsed, dragging down with it several St. Petersburg banks, among them A. J. Rothstein's International Commercial Bank. In the following year (1902) the depression descended in full weight upon the iron and steel industry in the Ukraine, while there were some signs of recovery in other industries. During the course of the depression altogether some 2,400 enterprises closed, and nearly 90,000 workers were thrown out of work. Of the 64 Krivoi Rog iron mines operating in 1900, only 40 were at work in 1903; 18 of the 70 joint-stock corporations in metallurgy disappeared from the scene.[49] In these years syndicates and trusts, as usual in bad times, began to make their

[48] Romanov, *Rossiia v Mandzhurii,* p. 453.
[49] Iakovlev, p. 271.

appearance in Russian industry. The smaller companies were squeezed out; the remaining ones protected themselves by marketing agreements. Nearly everywhere production fell off, most significantly in the smelting of pig iron and the mining of manganese.

There were, to be sure, a few exceptions. Coal mining, benefiting from the fall of prices, even gained at the expense of imported coal. In the oil industry, despite price falls and output restrictions, profits continued. The light industries as a whole actually advanced more rapidly than in the three years before 1900, although the textile industry suffered a slight setback. The Ural industries, likewise, which had barely shared in the boom, hardly suffered from the depression. All told, if one takes the fall in prices as an index of the severity of the depression, Russia was apparently no worse off than England, the United States, or Germany during the same years.[50] Yet the loss of economic momentum was unmistakable. The marked ascent of the industrial growth curves in the late 1890s suddenly leveled off, settling here and there even into a slight trough.

But why measure the impact of a depression only in economic terms? What counted far more heavily were the psychological effects of firms going bankrupt, factories closing, and unemployed workers slinking back to their villages. The self-confidence of the industrial and commercial community was undermined, the intelligentsia's aversion to capitalism deepened, workers and peasants were thrown into greater despair, and whatever buoyancy had thus far upheld the prestige of the Witte system (if not of the tsarist regime) was lost forever. What more triumphant proof could Witte's enemies wish to find for their we-told-you-so's? In short, Russia had less resilience than the Western countries long entrenched in their capitalist economies, which also experienced a recession at the time. In the West, industrial capitalism could

[50] *Ibid.*, p. 267.

stand the strain of a depression. In Russia, on the other hand, the jolt was bound to be profound.

In this adversity Witte, like other statesmen in similar circumstances, tried to salvage as much as he could. He aided stricken banks, transferred some enterprises to state management, and, contrary to the statutes of the State Bank, subsidized others (like Poliakov's, so that the owner might wind up his affairs without harm to the Moscow business community). These extraordinary loans of the State Bank, amounting to more than 200 million rubles between 1900 and 1903, were a disagreeable business which caused considerable criticism. Witte also valiantly strove to preserve a bold front, invoking even the testimony of the Finance Committee and an Imperial rescript to support his denials that Russia had encountered economic difficulties. At times he even stooped to blustering, saying that the government's condition was so strong that it did not need any foreign loans and that he was turning down the many offers he had received. All the while, however, he explored the possibilities of loans from English, American, and German bankers,[51] obtaining in the end only one from the Mendelssohns in 1902. At the same time he took precautions in order to prevent a fatal outflow of gold. As there was unrest and criticism also among the French *rentiers,* Witte did not shrink from exploiting the Emperor's state visit to France in 1901 to strengthen Russian credit and obtain a loan (after he had just denied the necessity for one). The Emperor, incidentally, was much offended by being made a tool of financial policy. But most important of all, refuted by the turn of events, Witte vigorously defended his policy and his management of state finances in the budget reports published every New Year's Day, each one a clever

[51] On Witte's efforts to obtain loans from Britain and the United States see the articles by B. V. Anan'ich, "Russkoe samoderzhavie i vneshnie zaimy v 1898–1902 gg.," and A. A. Fursenko, "Iz istorii russko-amerikanskikh otnoshenii na rubezhe XIX–XX vv.," in the volume *Iz istorii imperializma v Rossii,* Trudy leningradskogo otdeleniia Instituta Istorii, No. 1.

mixture of propaganda, economic analysis, and *apologia pro domo sua*.

In his report for 1900, for instance, he admitted the international shortage of credit and the existence of a world-wide depression, from which Russia was no exception. He further conceded, as he had many times before, that peasant welfare lagged behind, although he contended that the picture was not uniformly black. As for the harvests, the good years made up for the bad ones. On the positive side he cited the strong development of Russian industry. To be sure, it could not yet satisfy the domestic demand for iron and coal. But the figures for the growth of industry in the twenty years between 1877 and 1897, measured in the ruble value of the total industrial output, showed, so he argued with a flourish of statistics, the most brilliant results of the protective system. The average annual increase over the previous years had been 26.1 million rubles between 1878 and 1887, 41.6 million between 1888 and 1892, and a breath-taking 161.2 million rubles between 1893 and 1897 while he was minister of finance. Then followed a long dissertation on Russian railroad development, particularly on the tremendous undertaking of the Siberian line and its new South Manchurian outlet at Dalny, and a defense of its cost of more than 750 million rubles, defrayed, he said, almost entirely from current revenues. Fortunately, the period of greatest expenditure was already past. All sacrifice would surely be repaid by the tremendous eventual earning capacity of the new road.

The next year's report (for 1901) was primarily designed to reassure Russia's creditors abroad. It cited the calamities that had lately befallen Russia's economy, such as the poor harvests and the heavy expenses of the Chinese crisis. Under those circumstances it was a great financial success for the government, he asserted (making a virtue of necessity), that it did not have to conclude a new foreign loan. While he urged continued prudence in the management of Russia's finances, he was all optimism: the money market would rally slowly, Russian expenditures in the

Far East taper off, the balance of trade improve. At any rate, the present embarrassment would have been much worse had it not been for the currency reform of 1897. Witte then explained a measure which aroused strong domestic opposition during these lean years—the government's hoarding of a large cash reserve amounting to over 500 million rubles. Would it not be better to reduce taxation than perpetuate this cache of gold? But Witte defended it as an absolute necessity for a country with a large foreign-held state debt; it had to be on hand as a safeguard for the gold standard and the foreign debt, and as an emergency fund for unforeseen events like the Boxer uprising. Such large sums, he might have added, also served as a demonstration of Russian financial soundness, although the average Russian could well object that this wealth did not fill his empty stomach.

Witte's report for 1902 had to face a more disillusioned public. He had to admit at the outset that there had been no improvement in the international money market. And yet, despite the bad harvest in the previous year, he insisted that Russia's economic condition was sound. Again he glorified the triumphs of Russian industry with a new set of statistics, revealing how production in the heavy industries had doubled in the years 1892–1900. If there had been overexpansion in industry, it was caused by undue speculation, of which he as minister of finance had given official warning (this did not sit well with the Russian industrialists). And, again putting the best possible interpretation on unpleasant facts, he said that the sudden fall of prices, although constituting a temporary setback to producers, was beneficial to the consumer; it was a guarantee of further growth. Had he not always favored lower prices?

Furthermore, the fact that the budget of the previous year, as well as for the past ten years, had been so well balanced showed that "the general prosperity of the country as a whole had not undergone any change for the worse." If the country were poor, the state finances would not be so sound. In fact, he asserted,

Russia was growing more prosperous, for the revenues had increased. To bolster his point he quoted the increased per capita consumption of various items. But he also admitted that the current process of redistributing the wealth of Russia was causing hardships for some groups and regions, particularly as the transition from an agricultural barter economy to a money economy was so rapid. Yet why not look at the prosperous regions? All told, despite the triple strain of a crop failure, the money shortage, and the industrial depression, the prosperity of the country as a whole showed no decline.

Witte's last budget report, looking back over the year 1902 and forward into 1903, began with a clarion call—the budget had soared over the two billion ruble mark. It had nearly doubled in the ten years of his term as minister of finance. What could prove Russian prosperity better than the increase in government outlays, matched, since the budget was balanced as usual, by her revenues? Witte also listed lesser blessings. After years of depression there had been a good harvest, the money market was improving, Russian foreign trade had picked up. But here he ran out of good news. He admitted that the state had subsidized certain firms, but only those vital to national interest, that is, the defense industries. For, he argued, "at the present we are in the grips of an iron law which decrees that the requirements of civilization may be satisfied only from what remains after the expenditures of defense have been met." It was guns before education, roads, health, and all manner of consumer goods. Despite his heroic efforts, he had not managed to supply Russia with both a purse becoming to a great power and adequate pocket money for her citizens. Was it a wonder that Witte's last budget report ended on even a stronger note of pacifism than his previous ones?

While in public Witte maintained a brave front in order to preserve Russia's credit and the prestige of her government at home and abroad, in private and behind the closed doors of the government he sounded much more apprehensive. He was driven into a corner. In the spring of 1899 he had confidently fought the intrigue against his system and its reliance upon foreign capital. In February, 1900, he had even pleaded with the Emperor for a unified direction of all economic activities of the government. Then had come the heavy expenses of the military occupation of Manchuria, which he tried to offset by an over-all increase in import duties and the further raising of some taxes. At last, in the summer of 1901, he was quite pessimistic. "The harvest is bad," he wrote to Sipiagin. "What calamity! Even if it passes without food distribution at state expense, it will be a hard year economically. And even without the bad harvest it has been a bad year. The harvest might have put many things right. Now that hope is gone." [52] Yet in two years, he thought, everything would be normal again. In the same year, however, and despite his previous boast, he concluded a French loan on rather disadvantageous terms, for the French stipulated that it be applied to a strategic railroad without economic prospects.

Worst of all, he was now under the heaviest fire from within the government. In 1901 the state controller, General Lobko, reported to the Emperor that the industrial crisis had hit Russia with special force, because the growth of Russian industries had not been accompanied by an increase in the purchasing power of the domestic market, and that Witte had disregarded the statutes of the State Bank in granting loans to ailing enterprises.[53] The same official administered a stinging defeat to Witte late in December of that year during the final hearings on the budget for 1902 in the plenum of the State Council. Witte had just referred to the large cash reserve in the Treasury as proof of the brilliant financial condition of the government, when Lobko curtly announced that according to his calculations the cash on hand resulted merely from the French loan recently contracted.[54]

[52] Witte's letter to Sipiagin, July 7, 1901, *KA,* XVIII, 44.

[53] *Vsepodanneishii otchët gosudarstvennago kontrolera za 1900 g.*, p. 64.

[54] Polovtsev's diary, entry for December 29, 1901, *KA,* III, 106.

In his next annual report the State Controller even launched a well-reasoned attack on the Witte system as a whole.

At present there is no more doubt that the crisis is caused by the artificial and excessive growth of industry in recent years. Industry, based on the protective tariff, extensive government orders, and the speculative increase of cheap foreign capital, has grown out of proportion to the development of the consumers' market, which consists chiefly of the mass of the agricultural population to which 80 percent of our people belongs. An entirely sound existence for industry is guaranteed only by a corresponding development of the domestic market representing a sufficiently broad and constant demand for manufactured goods. That condition is particularly important for a young industry developing under the influence of protective tariffs, as it is in no position to count on the international market. Furthermore, the economic condition of our agriculture cannot be called satisfactory. The strenuous efforts of the government to plant industries has not been accompanied by equally intensive measures for the support and raising of the agricultural base of the welfare of the Russian people.

In view of the inadequacy of the government measures the negative sides of the protective system show up all the more strongly in the agricultural population. The chief burden of that system rests undoubtedly upon the agricultural masses, seriously impairing their purchasing power. They have to bear almost the whole burden of direct and indirect taxes. As a result, the demand of our domestic market cannot keep up with the excessive growth of our industry. The equilibrium between industry and the domestic market has been destroyed and with it the basis of a successful economic development. This, according to my deepest conviction, constitutes the chief cause of the present difficulties.[55]

In Lobko's office the opposition to Witte had found a convenient perch from which to broadcast the weaknesses of Witte's policy.

The most dramatic clash between Lobko and Witte occurred in the plenum of the State Council late in December, 1902, when the budget of 1903 was under consideration.[56] Witte proudly re-

[55] *Vsepodanneishii otchët . . . za 1901 g.*, pp. 55–56.

[56] Polovtsev's diary, entry for December 30, 1902, *KA*, II, 164; also Kuropatkin's diary, entry for the same date, *ibid.*, II, 17. Witte's report was published

ported that his budget had passed the two billion ruble mark, rising in his ten years in office from 1.050 billion to 2.0717 billion. Then the State Controller submitted his own analysis, which showed that Witte's conclusions had been based on garbled figures. According to Lobko's statistics the increase in government expenditures had been only from 946 million rubles to 1.348 billion, 42 percent instead of the nearly 100 percent claimed by Witte. Furthermore, Witte had succeeded in making ends meet only by constantly increasing the taxes.

This session of the State Council turned into a resounding demonstration of Witte's decline. He who had always maintained an optimistic front was now forced to admit, at least in the relative secrecy of this body (whence his report leaked out and was published in Austria), that after three years of the industrial depression and after a decade and more of an endemic agricultural crisis, "the paying powers of the population" were exhausted. Not that he blamed his own work for this. The reason lay in the construction of strategic railways insisted upon by Kuropatkin, the minister of war. Now he pleaded that all government departments exercise the strictest economy, because further taxation was inadmissible. This had also been the conclusion reached by Vyshnegradskii before his fall.

Speaking of economy, had Witte himself always practiced it? As the Controller reported to the Emperor in 1903, Witte had spent more than 8 million rubles for the construction of the St. Petersburg Polytechnical Institute.[57] When the Emperor read this sentence he underlined it and remarked on the margin, "Truly a monstrous sum." Nicholas also underlined two other sentences: "The reduction of the tax burden laid on our peasants would undoubtedly have a very great influence over our agriculture. It would lead to an improvement of our agricultural production, and

by P. Struve in Germany under the title *Finanzminister Witte und der russische Reichsrat über die Finanzlage Russlands: Protokoll der Plenarsitzung des russischen Reichsrats vom 30 Dezember 1902.*

[57] *Vsepodanneishii otchët . . . za 1902,* p. 55.

the question of lowering our taxes to a level corresponding with the paying powers of the peasantry should be moved to first place." [58]

After ten years of the Witte system, Russia had not escaped from the old impasse. Witte had finally come to face the obstacle which no minister of finance had yet been able to surmount—"the exhaustion of the paying powers of the population," which was synonymous with the misery of the Russian peasantry. Here the Witte system had reached its limits. Unless he could satisfy the clamor of the agrarian population, he could not continue his policy of rapid industrialization.

III

While the ground was thus giving way under the Witte system, Witte himself did not remain idle. He took the lead in adjusting his policy to the changing circumstances. He had long realized the weaknesses of Russian agriculture and had often enough alluded to the obstacles which they put in the way of Russia's economic progress. Yet as for accomplishments in this field, Witte had little to show. In addition to the measures mentioned in earlier chapters, he raised the question in the State Council of canceling the redemption dues altogether, but without success. The prevailing fear of an increase in the indirect taxes resulting from such a step prevented further exploration of this matter.[59]

The basic issues of peasant reform were, of course, political. They involved deep-reaching decisions at the very top level of the government, among the ministries most directly concerned and above all in the mind of Nicholas. And here Witte had made the least progress. As will be remembered, his letter of 1898 to the Emperor on the peasant question had been without result. While Goremykin was at the Ministry of the Interior—and that was the ministry most directly in charge of peasant affairs—any tamper-

[58] *Ibid.*, p. 50.
[59] Witte, *Tsarstvovanie Nikolaia II*, I, 478.

ing with the *obshchina* was out of the question. Under prodding, however, his successor proved more amenable, but at first even Witte was reluctant to take advantage of the change. In April, 1900, when Polovtsev confronted him with the facts of peasant poverty, Witte retorted that they had been much exaggerated. But when Polovtsev reminded him that he himself had urged peasant reforms, Witte shot back: "I can't get involved in everything. They already accuse me too much of that." He went on, however: "But I doubt whether a man can be found who could carry through the change from the *obshchina* to the individual farm basis so necessary for economic progress." Polovtsev then proposed Sipiagin, but Witte vetoed this suggestion.[60] He himself was obviously the man to do it, and, as subsequent events showed, he was willing.

The Minister of Finance, however, was barred from the central jurisdiction over peasant affairs, which lay in the Peasant Section of the Ministry of the Interior. The interministerial conflict over peasant reform could thus be resolved only by the Emperor. By 1901, Nicholas was under pressure from many sides to take measures for the improvement of Russian agriculture, and at last he began to act. In November of that year he appointed a new commission under the chairmanship of V. I. Kokovtsov "for a thorough analysis of the question of the economic decline of the Center in comparison with the economic conditions of the other parts of the Empire"—the second commission in two years to deal with that problem.[61] In January, 1902, he instructed Sipiagin to revise peasant legislation so as to "coordinate it with the real needs of the population and the well-being of the Empire." [62] The peasant order as established by Alexander II was to be brought up to date, a project already long under consideration.

Two weeks later, in an even more significant move, Nicholas made Witte chairman of a Special Commission on the Needs of

[60] Polovtsev's diary, entry for April 14, 1900, *KA,* 46, 128.

[61] It did not meet until after Witte's fall.

[62] Gurko, *Features and Figures of the Past,* p. 131.

Agricultural Industry, thus conferring on him the authority over rural economy. He told Witte: "I made you chairman, for if you don't do this job, nobody else can."[63] It was a weighty interdepartmental commission, including the ministers of the interior and of agriculture, other officials selected by the Emperor, and experts called by the chairman. It thus possessed more authority than the Peasant Section of the Ministry of the Interior. Yet would Witte's commission be able to bring about a coordinated reform of peasant society when the Ministry of the Interior was charged with an almost identical task? It seemed that Nicholas in his usual indecision had avoided the basic issue of a central jurisdiction.

Witte was not slow to bring the flaw to Nicholas's attention. In his first audience after his appointment he held out little hope for success. In outlining what might be done for the improvement of rural economy he rejected the obvious fiscal remedies that lay in his province. In view of the international arms race, lowering the taxes was not feasible, nor was tariff reduction. The foremost need, Witte repeated, was freedom and independence of action among the peasants. The legal issues had to be settled before any economic improvement could be expected, and this could not be done under the present divided jurisdiction. He therefore urged the Emperor to preside in person, as Alexander II had done in preparing the emancipation decree. Nicholas replied that Witte should repeat these arguments in Sipiagin's presence.[64] But in the subsequent meeting with Sipiagin, and later at the first session of the commission, the Minister of the Interior insisted upon his own prerogatives. Thus Witte's efforts were crippled at the outset even by the good-natured Sipiagin. After the latter's assassination in early April, following which Witte's sworn enemy Plehve was appointed to the post, his task was made still more difficult.

Whatever the prospects, the fact was that the year 1902 wit-

[63] Polovtsev's diary, entry for January 26, 1902, *KA,* III, 114.

[64] Entry for January 2, *ibid.,* p. 115.

nessed a marked revival of interest in peasant affairs. The uprisings in Poltava and Kharkov accelerated the trend. With Plehve's appointment domestic politics veered decidedly toward rural Russia and away from industrialization. In the fall of 1902 the Emperor, attending the army maneuvers near Kursk in the heart of the impoverished Center, summed up the new domestic policy:

> I know that village life demands careful attention. The landed gentry is experiencing hard times. There are defects also in the organization of peasant life. It is in order to do away with these latter defects that the Ministry of the Interior, in accordance with my orders, is taking much-needed measures. In due time we shall ask the gubernia committees, attended by the nobility of the *zemstva,* to participate in this work. And as for the landed gentry—the ancient stronghold of order and the moral strength of Russia—it will be my constant concern to consolidate it.[65]

This, then, was the new course born of the depression: concentration upon rural welfare, particularly in the economically most backward areas of European Russia, and support for the rural nobility. Both were to be accomplished through the reform of local administration and through greater cooperation between local forces and the bureaucracy. This change of policy was Nicholas's first major independent decision in domestic policy and, in view of the depression, not an entirely unreasonable one. The agitation among the peasants was rising. The nobility—to judge by the opinions of the zemstvo spokesmen (not to speak of their staffs, the so-called third element)—was becoming increasingly restless. Everywhere the opposition was hardening. Something had to be done. Witte, whatever the validity of his arguments, offered no remedy for placating the public, at least none which inspired the Emperor with confidence. Yet having made the change, the Emperor did not adjust all phases of his domestic policy to the new trend. Witte remained in office, clashing with Plehve over a thousand issues, chief among them the direction of peasant reform.

The indecision was accentuated by the fact that from the very

[65] Cited in Gurko, *Features and Figures of the Past,* p. 228.

start of the new course Witte still held the initiative. Sipiagin had tarried in carrying out his orders, while Witte proceeded with his usual dispatch. His commission held its first meeting on February 2, 1902, and soon thereafter, in a major move, he decided to enlist the support of the public by a consultation of committees of "local men," convened first within the confines of the *uezd* and later of the gubernia. These local bodies were especially constituted for this purpose. They were not identical with the zemstvos—there were obvious objections to consulting these outright—but they were closely associated with them, both being presided over by the local marshal of the nobility. These "local men," numbering more than 11,000 (including a handful of peasants), were asked not only to give their advice on rural economy but also to discuss "certain questions pertaining to law and order and to general administration so far as they have a bearing on agriculture and local life." [66]

With such a broad mandate the deliberations of the local men could hardly be limited to purely agricultural matters. Inevitably, the whole range of peasant problems would be raised and through their recommendations referred back to Witte's commission. By the time the Ministry of the Interior had prepared its proposals, the minds of the local men would already be made up and the guidance of rural reform placed in Witte's hands. There is no evidence to decide whether this flanking maneuver was planned by Witte or whether it developed accidentally through his energy. At any rate, in the summer and fall of 1902 his commission, through the public attention given to its local committees, had the advantage over the projects of the Minister of the Interior. It was made clear subsequently that the proposals of the Ministry of the Interior (now under Plehve's leadership) would also be submitted to gubernia conferences attended by "deserving persons who enjoyed public confidence." Nothing ever came of this plan except in-

[66] *Ibid.*

creased agitation among rural liberals for a central representative body under a constitution. But it was obvious that both ministers were bidding for public support.

At first sight one wonders if Witte had not made a fatal miscalculation by calling the local men, whose opinion would be largely identical with zemstvo opinion. For the most part they stood for free trade and the preferment of agriculture over industry. Plehve, who in July, 1902, talked to D. N. Shipov, the leader of the Moscow zemstvo, with notable kindness, especially admonished his visitor regarding this point. "I believe it exceedingly useful to stress, in the memoranda which the representatives of the zemstvo boards intend to present to the local committees, the weak points of our financial and economic policies." [67] Had not Witte been a declared enemy of zemstvo activity?

On the other hand, he was visibly changing his attitude toward the zemstvos, perhaps under the influence of liberal zemstvo representatives like Prince A. D. Obolenskii and M. A. Stakhovich, of whom he saw much in these months, or perhaps more generally under the impact of the rising discontent. He now sensed in their ranks a kindred attitude toward society and government (although hardly toward industry), a spirit of independence and initiative which he had always respected; he was thus more tolerant of their aspirations than was Plehve.

During these months of half measures and indecision there thus occurred a subtle transformation in Witte's political philosophy. Or rather, certain liberal elements in it became strengthened. As in the past he had drawn support from the representatives of trade and industry, so he now hoped for another ally among the public for the modernization of rural society. The zemstvos in these years had undertaken much laudable work for the promotion of agriculture. In the five years before 1900 they had more than doubled their expenses for agronomy, established special commit-

[67] *Ibid.*, p. 695.

tees and commissions on rural improvements, and even created a network of weather stations.[68]

In two respects particularly, Witte's bold move for local consultation proved wise. The crucial issues at stake in all planning for peasant reform were (1) the future of the commune and (2) the question of the legal equality of the peasants. As for the latter, the Congress of Zemstvo Workers held in Moscow during May, 1902, adopted the demand for equality as one of the points in its program.[69] As for the commune, the majority of the local committees, particularly on the *uezd* level, proved either downright opposed to the *obshchina* or, more frequently, at least in favor of free exit from it.[70] The stanchest defenders of the commune, apart from the northern province of Vologda, were found in central Russia, in the Moscow, Nizhni-Novgorod, and Tambov gubernias, and generally in the northern and central provinces of the black-soil area, the same Center which had so signally declined in recent years. But they were heavily outnumbered by the local committees of the peripheral parts of European Russia. Rural Russia, at least as represented by the areas that held their own economically, was ready, in a cautious way, for a more comprehensive experiment in capitalist agriculture and individual ownership. Witte's appeal to the grass roots sentiment had been justified. Yet here too he stood ahead of public opinion. Few committees matched the firmness of his belief that the commune should be abolished outright. In May, 1902, he was impatiently proposing that as an experiment single household farms be created in a few *uezds*.[71]

But certainly the main forces of the government also lagged behind public opinion. Sipiagin was a supporter of the commune. Plehve, although he conceded the advantage of introducing the concepts of private property among the peasants, was of two

[68] Veselovskii, III, 393.

[69] Veselovskii, "Dvizhenie zemlevladel'tsev," in *Obshchestvennoe dvizhenie,* I, 310.

[70] Oldenburg, p. 185 and the map on that page.

[71] Polovtsev's diary, entry for May 2, 1902, *KA,* III, 144.

minds. His assistant, V. I. Gurko, the head of the Peasant Section, was, like Witte, opposed to the commune, but having no use for Witte on other grounds, would lend him no assistance. The Emperor, like Plehve, wavered. The government's absurd ambiguity was glaringly illustrated in a statement of the Imperial *ukase* of February 3, 1903.[72] Here one could read that the project of peasant legislation "shall be based on the inviolability of the communal organization of peasant landownership, and at the same time shall endeavor to establish means whereby individual peasants may more easily leave the commune." One can only marvel at the skill with which two diametrically opposed policies were coupled in the same sentence. The ambiguity demonstrated the bankruptcy of autocratic leadership: "The bowsprit got mixed with the rudder sometimes."

No one would question the fact that Witte's novel enterprise in public relations set a dangerous precedent. Although zemstvo opinion had at first held that the zemstvos should have been more directly consulted, it was soon ready to use the local committees as a forum for all its grievances. Thus many local committees—and many zemstvo assemblies discussing their instructions to them—succumbed to the temptation and ventured into the prohibited area of politics. Here and there even the word "constitution" was heard. Witte was willing to look the other way in such cases; these excesses did not belong in his province. But Plehve became increasingly incensed over the obstinacy of disloyal zemstvos. Naturally he blamed the rising discontent on Witte, who had originated the local committees, and undermined Witte's position with the Emperor by denouncing him as an accomplice of revolutionaries.

Thus in the field of peasant reform the Witte system again had reached its limits. The depression had brought to prominence the problem of Russian agriculture. From 1902 onward it stood in the foreground of Russian domestic policy, remaining there until the advent of the Soviets. Witte had valiantly tried to take the lead

[72] Gurko, *Features and Figures of the Past,* p. 217.

in the work, hoping to adjust Russian agriculture, and peasant society with it, to his "system." But the task could not be successfully directed from the Ministry of Finance. Since Nicholas was not willing or able to assume leadership himself, Witte's projects became hopelessly mired in the mounting domestic crisis. To be sure, even after his removal from the Ministry of Finance he continued as chairman of the Special Commission on the Needs of Agricultural Industry, but its work did not prosper. Hostile intrigues and the Revolution of 1905 prevented any results. Part of Witte's aims was eventually accomplished by Stolypin. The grant of complete legal equality to the Russian peasants, however, had to wait until after the fall of tsarism.

7. The Fall of the Witte System

For time is the greatest innovator; and if time of course alters things to the worse, and wisdom and counsel shall not alter them to the better, what shall be the end?
FRANCIS BACON, Of Innovation

Apart from the rather strained conditions of her finances, Russia is undergoing too rapidly a change big with meaning. Like her mighty rivers, which when the ice breaks, inundate the land with a sudden column of water, like her spring which comes with a rush, instantly changing the general aspect of nature, the Russian industrial revolution has been probably too rapid. Agriculture is and will be for many years Russia's chief stay, but the government eager to be up with the West has forced on an industrial development which has done much to break up Russian life and sow the seeds of discontent.
The Economist, March, 1901

I

WAS THERE NOTHING in the progressive disintegration of the Witte system to withstand the adverse trend, no accomplishment which remained untarnished? The great strides made in the expansion of the Russian railroad network would seem to constitute such an exception. In these years Russian construction went ahead at a phenomenal rate, not only in the routine work of double-tracking, improving, and adding to the existing lines in European Russia, but in the more spectacular enterprises in Asiatic Russia. The railroad linking Tiflis with Kars on the Turkish border was completed in 1899; it was extended to Erivan in the following year. In 1901 the Orenburg-Tashkent line was begun; it was to bring cotton from Central Asia directly to the Moscow mills. All of these roads were expensive to construct and maintain; they would yield little revenue for years to come. But they were indispensable for the economic development of the country and the promotion of a sense of political and administrative unity. They also strengthened the military power of Russia on its Asiatic frontiers.

None of these roads, however, could compete in promise and problems with the great Siberian line which neared completion at the turn of the century.[1] It was opened to traffic according to the original plan. The West Siberian section from Cheliabinsk to the Ob River, together with its link to Ekaterinburg and the Ural network, had been completed as early as October, 1896; in 1899 the line also received its outlet to Archangel via the new Perm-Kotlas road. The next lap from the Ob to Lake Baikal was opened January 1, 1899, and, a year and a half later, the route from Lake Baikal to Sretensk, whence water transportation to the Amur River system began. On the far eastern end the rail link between Vladivostok and the Amur River at Khabarovsk had already been in operation since 1897. After the summer of 1900 there existed a continuous line of communications by water and rail between the Baltic ports and Vladivostok running entirely through Russian territory.

Work on the direct connection between Lake Baikal and Vladivostok via the Chinese Eastern Railroad had begun in earnest only in 1898. During the Boxer uprising in the summer of 1900 much destruction took place, delaying completion. Yet despite these unforeseen interruptions the rails advancing westward from Vladivostok and eastward from the Manchurian boundary met in the fall of 1901. On October 21 the last spike was driven into the longest railroad line of the world. Taking the fastest train, one could now travel from Moscow to Vladivostok in thirteen days or, over the South Manchurian line then also opened, to the port of Dalny on the Yellow Sea in eighteen and a half days.

It was not until the summer of 1903, to be sure, that regular through traffic was established. The unsettled conditions of Manchuria and the temporary character of much of the construction

[1] See, in addition to the books on Russian railway developments mentioned in Chap. IV, also E. Ames, "A Century of Russian Railroad Construction, 1837–1930," *ASEER*, Vol. VI, No. 18–19 (1947).

along the Chinese Eastern Railroad would not permit full use at an earlier date. And one particular weakness remained—the ferry linking the shores of Lake Baikal. Every spring the ice pressure during the thaws caused considerable damage to the docks, and the interruption of traffic lasted almost two weeks. In 1901 it was decided, therefore, to construct a railway around the southern shore, a lengthy and costly detour not completed for a number of years. Yet for all practical purposes, by the end of October, 1901, the great venture had been accomplished according to plan, ten years and a half after the Tsarevich Nicholas had driven the first spike at Vladivostok. Considering the fanfare at the opening and the high hopes subsequently expressed by Alexander III and his son Nicholas, this surely called for a celebration.

Instead, the dominant note was dejection and criticism. For one thing—perhaps inevitably at a time of economic stagnation—it was objected that the railroad had cost too much. The expenditures had been persistently running ahead of the estimates, so much so that in 1899 a special conference under Count Solskii had been appointed to study the reasons. Another commission under the engineer Mikhailovskii was sent out for local investigations.[2] Even the State Controller took part in the examination, pointing out, for instance, that the mid-Siberian section had exceeded the estimates by 18 percent and the trans-Baikal section by 19 percent. This was blamed on insufficient preliminary surveys and technical miscalculations, on local disturbances, crop failures, epidemics, floods, and similar unforeseen events, and even on faulty engineering caused by the rapidity of construction. One engineer was indicted, but blame was also cast upon subcontractors and suppliers of building materials.[3] The total cost of construction of the Siberian and the Chinese Eastern railroads was estimated by an economist close to the Ministry of Finance to have run between 780 and 844 million rubles, somewhat higher than the figure given

[2] Migulin, *Nasha noveishaia,* p. 291.
[3] *Ibid.,* p. 292.

by Witte in his budget report. And it was charged that these figures represented an increase of 150 percent over the original estimate.[4]

Common sense would consider such an error (assuming these figures to be roughly correct) by no means excessive. In the 1880s American railroad builders did indeed accurately forecast the costs of construction when they dealt with the level territory of the Great Plains; for the Rocky Mountains they made no such claims. In the 1870s one finds the Missouri division of the American Central Railway estimated at a cost of $640,000, bonded for $800,000, and finally built for $1,375,000.[5] Siberia and Manchuria, with their adverse climate and territory and the ignorance and hostility of their population, certainly constituted a far more difficult terra incognita for railroad men than the American and Canadian West. But against the current of Russian opinion, aroused over the misery of the peasantry, such common sense made little headway.

There was another argument belittling the merits of the Siberian railroad—the imperfections of its service. As already said, the road had to be built on a shoestring. The emphasis had been on the benefits of through traffic rather than of local service; only the barest essentials of equipment had been allocated. When railway operations commenced, however, it was found that the three daily trains in each direction permitted by the light roadbed were not enough. By 1899 more than one million crowded passengers had traveled over the lines open to traffic. Freight, particularly after a good harvest, rotted on the sidings. The speed, likewise, was too slow for Russian taste. And along certain sections, as between Tomsk and Irkutsk, so Witte himself admitted,[6] construction was so flimsy as to make travel unsafe. In short, the Russian public, eager to find fault, was already complaining about the

[4] *Ibid.*, p. 299.

[5] Cochran, p. 112.

[6] Polovtsev's diary, entry for January 1, 1903, *KA*, III, 169.

results of their finance minister's parsimony. Apparently they would have liked to spend more rather than less.

A third complaint appealed to Russian nationalism. It was said that the low fares from Moscow to Vladivostok (or Shanghai) amounted to a subsidy to foreigners.[7] A maritime passage from London to Shanghai via the United States lasted about one month. or thirty-six days through the Suez Canal, costing between 650 and 900 rubles. Going by train across Russia, however, took only three weeks and cost between 130 and 319 rubles. Few Russians would use the express trains; they benefited mostly the foreigners.

Moreover (and inevitably), it was pointed out that the Siberian railroad operated at a deficit, despite the heavy demand. Witte had bad luck here, too; the benefits of the through traffic from the Pacific into Europe were not forthcoming as rapidly as he had anticipated, in part at least because of the Boxer Rebellion and the political uncertainty in the Far East. Witte did his best to counteract these factors by strenuous efforts to channel freight over the Chinese Eastern Railroad. But he did so at the price of undercutting the maritime interests of Russia's Black Sea ports.[8]

Another blemish on his Far Eastern ventures was the conspicuous failure of the port of Dalny. Despite Witte's grandiose planning, it withered rapidly. By the end of 1903 it was clear that its functions would be entirely usurped by the naval base of Port Arthur. And finally, whatever economic opportunities he had provided, statistics proved that for the time being at any rate they benefited British and American rather than Russian subjects; there was no market for Russian goods in Manchuria to relieve the depression in Russia. All told, Russia's earnings in Asia were not helping to pay her debt in Europe.

Nearer home, meanwhile, the Siberian Committee had made many efforts to increase the population of Siberia. It had dis-

[7] Migulin, *Nasha noveishaia,* p. 301.
[8] Malozemoff, p. 193.

tributed thousands of information booklets and undertaken a well-organized effort to give direction to the eastward movement. Between 1894 and 1902, 900,000 settlers were counted, by a conservative estimate.[9] They found their railroad fares reduced by one fourth and government officials ready to assist them in the choice of a location, to look after their health, or to build schools and churches for them. Yet it was also discovered that the supply of easy lands was limited.[10]

The industrial potential of the Urals came under specially close scrutiny. Why were the Ural industries lagging behind those of the Ukraine? In the summer of 1899 Witte sent Mendeleev to find an answer. Mendeleev's report was to the point.[11] The Urals, he wrote, particularly the Magnet Mountain, had enough iron ore to supply all of Europe at prices below those currently prevailing. And yet Russia supplied only half of even her own iron consumption from domestic sources. But the patent need notwithstanding, Mendeleev held out no hope for an immediate improvement. The industrialists of the area were set in their ways; they wanted no newcomers. The protective system curtailed competition which would force them to modernize their production. Certain relics of serfdom, some outdated and confusing laws on property rights, and the obstructionist attitude of the Department of Mining in the Ministry of Agriculture also hampered improvements. Mendeleev was particularly indignant at the Ministry of Agriculture. All government agencies, he admonished, should cooperate in the "fulfillment of the over-all government plan by strengthening and broadening the domestic production of pig iron and cast iron."[12] He also held that the entire future of the Ural industries lay in the hands of the government; their development justified many sacrifices. He especially recommended that the Department of Mining

[9] Krypton, p. 103.

[10] Migulin, *Nasha noveishaia,* p. 303.

[11] D. I. Mendeleev, *Ural'skaia zheleznaia promyshlennost' v 1899 g.,* Part III, Chap. III, pp. 97 ff.

[12] *Ibid.,* p. 98. This memorandum may have inspired Witte's of February, 1900.

undertake a new geological survey and that the metallurgical works be put under the care of the Ministry of Finance. The latter, however, should not take charge directly. Mendeleev's concern, like Witte's, was with capitalist enterprise. Progressive capitalism was to modernize the Ural industries. Hence the need was also for new laws facilitating the organization of private enterprise.

Witte himself, after a secret trip over the new Siberian and Manchurian line in the fall of 1902—taken, according to rumor, because he had not been invited to accompany the Tsar to the Crimea—wrote a comprehensive report on the new road in order to refute the criticism.[13] He again stressed its benefit as a grand artery of international trade, promoting commercial exchange between East and West. Its benefits to Russia he considered of only secondary importance. Yet even for Russia, he wrote, the gain was enormous despite the sacrifices made during the construction, which prevented "a fair appraisal" at the moment. Siberia, for instance, would serve as a safety valve for Russian overpopulation and prevent peasant uprisings. The yearly population increment in the Empire was 1.3 million. Agriculture in European Russia could not hope to absorb the surplus; too large a percentage of the rural population was already now without land. Granted that the good lands of Siberia were being filled, Witte still saw new opportunities along the Amur and in the Khirgiz steppes, although admittedly life out there would be a harsh struggle at first. As in 1893, Witte still complained about the hostile attitude of many officials in European Russia, who would not expedite resettlement. Besides social and economic considerations, power politics also entered his plea; Russia had to resist the population pressure of "the yellow race" by shifting its own population to the East.

His recommendations for future action were in his usual grand manner. What was needed for the development of Siberia was (1)

[13] Reprinted for the most part in Glinskii, pp. 190 ff.

the "planned and systematic investigation" of its vast spaces so as to make them available for settlement, (2) the linking of Central Asia with Siberia by a railroad from Tashkent to Omsk and with western China by another one, (3) the drafting of a "basic plan" of Siberian settlement "according to state need," and (4) the increase of the industrial population of Siberia. The present generation of Siberian monopolists, he wrote, did not possess enough capital for the founding of local industries, despite their enormous profits. Neither was the labor supply sufficient. Such, in Witte's eyes, were the tremendous tasks and efforts ahead. They were so vast, he admitted in a characteristic Russian flourish, that their final scope could not be predicted. In short, Witte's achievement could not prosper before the next seven-league stride was taken. Thus the present generation, and Witte foremost, were cheated of their glory by the poverty and imperfection of contemporary Russia. The real benefits lay hidden in coming ages.

For all these reasons the completion of the Siberian trunk line did not lead to the driving of a golden spike and the ringing of bells. It was hardly mentioned in the Russian press; the Emperor sent a perfunctory telegram, and it was left to Witte himself to write, many years later, a fitting memorial: "I do not exaggerate when I say that that great enterprise was completed thanks to my energy, supported, of course, at the outset by Alexander III and then by Emperor Nicholas II." [14] The foreign press, on the other hand, took more enthusiastically to the new transcontinental road, and the accounts of the first foreign passengers were generally favorable. The American Senator Albert J. Beveridge, for instance, who traveled through Manchuria over the new Chinese Eastern Railroad, found it a model of efficiency and comfort.[15]

II

It would be wrong, however, to ascribe the conspicuous lack of

[14] *Detstvo,* p. 392.

[15] Beveridge, pp. 81 ff.

rejoicing over the completion of the Siberian railway entirely to the depression. The fact was that the event coincided with a crisis in Russian foreign relations as well. Ever since the Germans seized Tsingtao—so at least Witte said, although the crisis might just as well be traced to the Treaty of Shimonseki or the Russian decision to strike through Manchuria on the way to Vladivostok—the Far East had become a political storm center. The agencies of the Ministry of Finance in the area—the Chinese Eastern Railroad and the Russo-Chinese Bank with all their subsidiaries—stood in the very eye of the controversy.

Their fortune was inseparable from the fate of Manchuria in general, as events proved all too soon. The Boxer uprising not only constituted an unexpected, highly unwelcome complication in the completion of the Chinese Eastern Railroad but also superimposed an alien element of power politics upon a venture which Witte had originally conceived largely as a commercial enterprise. Since the foreign diplomats refused to adopt his interpretation, Witte was propelled, in order to safeguard his economic policy, into the uncongenial field of diplomacy. As the moving spirit behind Russia's commercial ventures, he was forced more than ever to take charge of Russian foreign policy in the Far East. And although he refused to realize the fact, this move implied responsibility for Russian foreign relations in general, as the Far East could not be torn out of the context of *Weltpolitik*. After Murav'ev's death at the height of the Boxer crisis, Witte unwittingly became the central force in Russian foreign policy. In contrast with the appointment of Murav'ev, with whom he had not been on speaking terms after their tiff over Port Arthur, the new foreign minister, Lamsdorff (a retiring personality who never had courage enough to speak out in ministerial conferences), was installed at Witte's behest.

Inevitable as the assumption of the new burden was under the logic which had driven Witte into many activities outside his original jurisdiction, it invited failure. For despite his awareness of the pressure of power politics in general, Witte was never more than an amateur diplomatist. Moreover, he was overburdened with other responsibilities, particularly in these years of economic crisis. He could never give foreign affairs his continuous and undivided attention or reexamine his basic assumptions about the nature of his policy in the Far East. Perhaps his greatest asset in his new role was his caution, stemming from the realization that Russia was less capable than ever of waging war.[16] Yet at the same time he was under great pressure from the more acquisitive segments of the government, the army and navy, and the Court; he had to adjust to their point of view as well. While his own power waned, he was more than ever at the mercy of the conflicting wills in the government. It is therefore impossible to determine how much he was guided in these years by conviction and how much by expediency. He became involved in an insoluble dilemma. Intending to pursue a policy of peaceful, even nonpolitical economic expansion, he drifted into a storm center of power politics.

The external dilemma, however, was aggravated by the unresolved confusion in his own mind. His original plan had been to make the Siberian railroad, and subsequently the Chinese Eastern Railroad, a viable business venture and thus to ease the strain upon the Imperial treasury. How much these financial calculations were still present in Witte's mind may be seen from his report to the Emperor after his return from his inspection trip in the fall of 1902. "It is possible," he wrote apropos of the current tension with Japan, "that thanks to the Chinese Eastern Railroad a rapprochement between Russia and Japan may occur in the not too distant future, on the basis of economic and industrial interests. Such close mutual relations between peoples in that sphere appear as one of the most powerful factors in the avoidance of armed conflicts." [17] For these reasons he believed a peaceful settlement with Japan possible, provided that Russia made concessions

[16] See particularly Witte's statement on Russian foreign policy reprinted under the title "Tsarskaia diplomatiia o zadachakh Rossii na vostoke v 1900 g.," *KA,* XVIII, 22 ff.

[17] Glinskii, p. 215.

in Korea. If, on the other hand, these hopes should prove false, he added with a nod to the expansionist, the conflict should at least be postponed until Russia had strengthened her position in the Far East through the economic development of Manchuria.

The afterthought revealed the weakness of his starting point; there was no guarantee that the other powers, or even the military in Russia, would interpret Russian activities as harmless commercial ventures. And how could they, when even Witte was forced, in a moment of panic, to safeguard his investments against the Boxers by calling in Russian troops? Threatened with the destruction of his railroad, he himself was driven to abandon his purely economic approach and rely on force. But when subsequently, forewarned by Lamsdorff, he realized the dangers of Russia's isolated position among the great powers and of Japanese hostility, he was again ready to sound the alarm. Then his pacifism would reassert itself.

Certainly he did nothing in these years to help prepare Russia for war. The army budget was kept to a minimum, so much so that later Kuropatkin blamed Witte's parsimony for the Russian defeat at the hands of Japan.[18] Many times in these years Witte acknowledged that a war would be a great calamity, although he was bound to insist that in case of a conflict Russia would be the winner. The point was that he was ready for withdrawal and compromise; he dreaded an incident which might inflame Russian (or Japanese) passions to the fever pitch. Curious as it may seem, he had no sense of diplomatic "face." He did not even seem to realize the gravity of the political setback which Russia had suffered from the conclusion of the Anglo-Japanese alliance in January, 1902. It was as though, having become involved in the competition of power politics, he refused to accept the rules of the game.

The logical goal of his position would have been to provide the

[18] See *Zapiski generala Kuropatkina o russko-iaponskoi voine: Itogi voiny* and Witte's reply *Vynuzhdennyia raz"iasneniia po povodu otcheta General-adiutanta Kuropatkina o voine s Iaponiei.*

Chinese Eastern Railroad and the Russo-Chinese Bank with the greatest volume of business by opening the door to all comers. The American policy of the "open door" was not without potential benefit to Russia as well. This implied, however, a surrender of a market reserved for Russian industry to international competition, and he was naturally reluctant to retreat thus far. Would his colleagues in the government have permitted it? Yet in the end—and too late—he did indeed adopt this solution.[19]

From his own perspective, at least, he was essentially right when he later absolved himself of all responsibility for the war which broke out; his instincts had always been for withdrawal in the face of danger. As he put it in his picturesque speech, while he had only wished to take his friends to the aquarium, they had got drunk, dragged him to a brothel, and kicked up a row there.[20] But the image also demonstrated his incomprehension. In the first place, he should have known what company he kept and acted accordingly. In the Russian setting of the 1890s the heady wine of expansion in the Far East was bound to loosen the restraints of caution which guided the Minister of Finance. Had he not, in a moment of weakness, himself helped to serve that potent brew? And secondly, owing to the jealousy of the great powers, the Far East had long ceased to be an "aquarium." Here lay the cardinal mistake in which Witte persisted to the end of his days. He never realized how serious the opposition of the powers had become, particularly that of the Japanese.

At the outset of the Boxer Rebellion in the spring of 1900 the events in China seemed to favor his original approach. For a few months no Russian interests were harmed by the Righteous Har-

[19] Romanov, *Rossiia v Mandzhurii,* p. 308. Romanov's works (*Rossiia v Mandzhurii* and *Ocherki diplomaticheskoi istorii russko-iaponskoi voiny 1895–1907,* 2d ed., 1955) contain the most detailed account of Witte's policies in the Far East, yet the author is far too eager to prove Witte's responsibility for the Russo-Japanese War. By contrast, the British ambassador in St. Petersburg, Sir Charles Scott, always believed Witte to be a man of peace.

[20] Kuropatkin's diary, entry for December 3, 1903, *KA,* II, 91.

monious Fists. Russia even seemed able to demonstrate her friendship with the Chinese people. Soon, however, the violence spread north, and Witte, aroused over the damage done to the work on the Chinese Eastern Railroad, called for the troops. Throwing his usual thrift to the winds, he recommended the concentration of a large force. He wrote to Sipiagin, "It is better to lose money than prestige." [21] Thus the Russian army, in a move which amounted to the bankruptcy of his earlier position, entered Manchuria, not to leave again until forced out by the Japanese.

Quickly, however, the disadvantages of the occupation became apparent to Witte. It not only antagonized the Chinese government and mobilized the opposition of the other powers, especially the Japanese; it also spoiled the monopoly which the Ministry of Finance had enjoyed over the direction of affairs in Manchuria. Henceforth the Russian army, an institution very alien to Witte's purposes, had to be taken into account. It was not surprising then that Witte reverted to his former policy and pressed, together with Lamsdorff, for an early withdrawal of the troops. He hoped to provide the necessary security by an increase in the Railway Guards, a police force organized by the Chinese Eastern Railroad and presumably nonpolitical. But Kuropatkin was not easily persuaded; he preferred to retain at least northern Manchuria for Russia. Official Russian policy was thus divided at the source.

At this point wise statesmanship would have called for an overall settlement with the powers, for the Russian occupation of Manchuria constituted primarily an issue of concern to all and only secondarily conflict between China and Russia. Yet for many months Witte negotiated with the Chinese government alone, trying to make the most of its current weakness, as though conditions had not changed since 1896. He drove a hard bargain with his old partner Li Hung Chang (until Li's sudden death) for substantial economic concessions that would have amounted to a Russian monopoly over the exploitation of the mineral resources

[21] Witte's letter to Sipiagin, July 7, 1900, *KA*, XVIII, 32.

of Manchuria. At the same time he tried to substitute the Russo-Chinese Bank for the Chinese Eastern Railroad as a less obtrusive agent of Russian penetration. He was stubbornly determined to defend Russia's economic privileges.

As these negotiations dragged on, however, he became vaguely aware that he could not disregard the Japanese government altogether. For that reason he was at last willing to make concessions in Korea if Japan promised Russia a free hand in Manchuria. When the Japanese statesman Prince Ito visited St. Petersburg in early December, 1901, Witte and Lamsdorff were ready to negotiate a mutually agreeable compromise. Yet the Russian government was by no means unanimous in this matter, and what was more important, the Japanese government had already decided in favor of the English alliance, which was announced on January 30, 1902. Nothing came, therefore, of the bargain suggested by Witte and Lamsdorff except, indirectly, an evacuation agreement with China concluded in April, 1902, more favorable to the Chinese government than any previous draft.

In the spring of 1902 Witte thus suffered a considerable setback in his Far Eastern policy. As a result of the occupation of Manchuria, Russia had been isolated among the great powers. Great Britain, in an unusual step, had even concluded with Japan an alliance obviously directed against Russia. Witte's plans for a Russian monopoly in the economic exploitation of Manchuria had also failed. The evacuation agreement with China contained none of the sweeping privileges which he had originally envisaged. Here, too, he had come to the end of his tether. He had pushed his plans for the economic development of Manchuria as far as he could; they had been a costly failure. The question now before the Emperor and the government was this: Should Russia cut its losses and retreat under foreign pressure or, in a change of mood, resist that pressure and make sure of her gains at the increased risk of war?

The decision emerged in a curious roundabout way, again indicative of the disintegration of autocratic leadership. It involved, and even brought to a climax, the old struggle between Witte and his reactionary antagonists, the Sharapovs and their protector in high places, Grand Duke Alexander Mikhailovich. The ringleaders this time were two aristocrats of the very type which Witte despised. One was a retired officer of the Guards, Vladimir Mikhailovich Vonliarliarskii, who, after squandering his wife's fortune on a number of commercial failures, now advanced to sacrificing other people's funds as well.[22] In his memoirs, incidentally he blamed his business failures on Witte's factory inspection, which aggravated "the workers' question." [23] More dangerous because of his ambition was Alexander Mikhailovich Bezobrazov, likewise a retired officer of the Guards, who had speculated on the St. Petersburg stock exchange and taken a special interest in the Far East.

As early as 1897 these men had been lured by the prospects of a timber concession on the Yalu River and Russian expansion in Korea generally. Backed by others of their type and supported by dignitaries like Count Vorontsov-Dashkov, the former minister of the Court, and even by the Emperor himself, they founded the East Asiatic Company, which was to defend Russian interests in Korea against foreign capitalists, representing moreover, under the Emperor's aegis, the "true Russian" element, not, as Bezobrazov put it, "the Jews and the Poles whom Sergei Iulevich had commissioned to be our color bearers in Manchuria." [24] This group, in other words, challenged Witte's monopoly over Manchuria and deplored his Manchurian orientation at the expense of Russian designs in Korea. At the same time they stormed against the Witte system in general. "Sergei Iulevich," Bezobrazov wrote to Grand Duke Alexander Mikhailovich in 1900, "created a system which did not work even in peace, lay heavy on the productive

[22] See the characterization in Gurko, *Features and Figures of the Past,* pp. 259–60.

[23] Vonliarliarskii, p. 123. This autobiography reflects well the mentality of the reactionary opposition to Witte.

[24] Romanov, *Rossiia v Mandzhurii,* p. 273.

forces of the country, and bred a mass of malcontents and dispossessed persons, while in war it evoked fear of the possibility of state bankruptcy."[25] Again it was Bezobrazov who a few months later whispered into the Tsar's ear the preposterous lie that Witte had pledged the entire mineral wealth of Siberia to the Rothschilds as collateral for a loan.[26]

Against such intrigues Witte did not remain idle. Several times he managed to stop the commercial venture on the basis of legal technicalities, each time, however, spurring the determination of its backers. In the spring of 1902, just as the East Asiatic Company was about to collapse for lack of business, the setback suffered by Witte in the Far East provided Bezobrazov and his group with their opportunity. For implicitly Bezobrazov represented the alternative to Witte's inclination to retreat under foreign pressure. As he had stated in the letter already cited: "The ground is being prepared for future success or failure in the Far East and prepared irrevocably. We shall either come out on top and consolidate the Russian cause politically and economically or we shall fall prey to the Jewish *consistorium* and the tricks of European diplomacy."[27] Bezobrazov wanted to make sure that Russia—the true Russia—would come out on top. Nicholas, ever since his visit to the Far East as Tsarevich, was of the same opinion. In the summer of 1902, at his meeting with William II at Reval, where the German Emperor greeted him as "Admiral of the Pacific," Nicholas predicted, in William's recollection, that in 1904 he would declare war on Japan.[28]

The new course in foreign policy, however, did not come into effect until May, 1903. Meanwhile a stalemate between Witte and Bezobrazov emerged which was reminiscent of that between Witte and Plehve. After his failure to secure from the Chinese govern-

[25] *Ibid.,* p. 274.
[26] Witte to Sipiagin, July 12, 1901, *KA,* XVIII, 45.
[27] Romanov, *Rossiia v Mandzhurii,* p. 274.
[28] Trautmann, p. 142.

ment a blanket monopoly for the exploitation of Manchuria's mineral riches through the Russo-Chinese Bank, Witte tried to secure similar privileges through negotiations with local authorities. For this purpose the Bank created a subsidiary, the Manchuria Mining Association, which was to take charge of the mining of gold, iron, and coal in the vicinity of the railroad. At the same time Bezobrazov tried to obtain similar industrial concessions in Manchuria, aiming especially at the economic opportunities near the Yalu River. Neither side made much headway toward actual operations; the local conditions were too difficult. While these projects hung fire, Witte in the fall of 1902 made his inspection trip to the East, warning of Japanese hostility upon his return and advising the surrender of all of Korea lest war result.

In Witte's wake, Bezobrazov left on a similar errand. Once in Manchuria he set out at a reckless pace gathering concessions, antagonizing the local authorities with whom Witte had been careful to cooperate, and ruthlessly eliminating foreign competitors. Even the commander in chief of the Far Eastern force, Admiral Alexeev, was alarmed by Bezobrazov's brazen methods. Throughout, Bezobrazov intrigued for an aggressive policy of securing concessions along the Yalu as a springboard for penetration into Korea. Witte, Lamsdorff, and even Kuropatkin (who deplored the tying down of Russian forces in the Far East) tried to ward him off, again informing Nicholas of the Japanese hostility to Russian designs on Korea and advocating concentration upon Manchuria alone. In view of the local insecurity they then delayed the withdrawal of Russian troops scheduled for April, 1903, and even considered, contrary to the agreement with China, retaining certain key points such as Kharbin. Whether they would have done so without the strong pressure of the Emperor and Bezobrazov for a tough front must remain an open question. Witte certainly seemed ready during his last months in office to please the Emperor even at a considerable sacrifice to his convictions.

At all events, the stalemate was suddenly ended in early May, 1903, and the central direction taken out of the hands of the "triumvirate" of Witte, Lamsdorff, and Kuropatkin. The alternate policy of self-assertion, which Witte had dreaded, became the official one. For now the Emperor instructed Admiral Alekseev, without even consulting his ministers, that "in minimal time and without balking at the necessary expenditures, our fighting power in the Far East . . . be brought up to the level of our politico-economic tasks, giving a demonstration visible to all of our determination to defend our rights . . . in Manchuria." [29] On May 7 Bezobrazov emerged as state secretary, and at the end of July, in an unprecedented step, Alekseev was appointed viceroy of the Russian territories on the Pacific. Witte's Far Eastern preserve had come to an end.

It was small consolation that the Emperor heeded his advice on Korea and soon dropped Bezobrazov from all positions of influence there,[30] limiting the new tough policy to Manchuria alone. On the essential point, Russian determination to defend her influence in Manchuria by arms if necessary, the breach was irreparable. In August, a few days before his dismissal (and at a time when the Japanese government may already have decided on war), Witte at last drew the consequences of his original policy and spoke out in favor of the free admission of foreign enterprise into Manchuria. At this point that was all the Japanese government was officially asking.

In short, under the aggravated danger of war, Witte surrendered his former goal of a Russian monopoly in Manchuria; his vacillation came to an end. Having reached the limit of his Manchurian venture, he was ready to retreat to his ideal of peaceful economic cooperation between nations. When the domestic conflict was at its peak, Witte and Nicholas II parted company in foreign policy as well.

[29] Romanov, *Rossiia v Mandzhurii,* p. 284.
[30] Malozemoff, pp. 221–22.

III

How different the political scene in Russia looked at the beginning and at the end of Witte's career as minister of finance! In 1892, in the aftermath of the great famine, Russia was quiet. The public had done its share in alleviating the suffering, often with inward reproaches against the government. But public order had never been threatened. As in the country at large, so in the government itself the authority of the Emperor prevailed; Witte could start his work under a firm mandate. Ten years later the deluge that eventually toppled the tsarist regime was rising fast. It was not only the sporadic strikes harassing the government since the mid-nineties which sounded the first warning, but also the student riots in the capitals and lesser cities in 1899 and after. In their wake came the assassination of the minister of education in 1901, then the attempt on Pobedonostsev's life. In the spring of 1902 the peasants of several southwestern gubernias rose against their landlords, and the minister of the interior was shot to death. Next year worse things befell, at Easter the infamous pogrom at Kishinev and in the summer industrial unrest culminating in the great strikes of southern Russia.

Underneath these elemental eruptions of violence, opinions, tempers, and loyalties were in ferment. The revolutionary parties were forming as fighting units, in both the Marxist and Social Revolutionary camps. The liberals of all shades were organizing under a hundred pretexts—as zemstvo spokesmen, physicians, or agronomists meeting at professional congresses. Agitation was stalking the country, through the statisticians who compiled data for the zemstvos, the teachers in the schools, or the professors talking to workers' study circles, through the teen-agers tasting the thrills of underground work by dropping leaflets in streets and factories, or through workers returning to their villages.

Even the loyalty of the *kupechestvo* began to waver. Having relied too heavily on the favors of the state, they now blamed their current difficulties on their benefactor. The business circles of Moscow and the Volga towns had always been suspicious of Witte's policies. Suddenly even they hankered for greater freedom from government interference. Business opinion fell in step with the critical trend among the Russian public, preparing the stage for the foundation of the Octobrist party. In short, the poverty of the peasants, the plight of the workers, and the distress of industry all served as an incentive to further opposition and obstruction. A defeat in foreign policy would have made matters worse yet.

The more thoughtful officials were painfully aware of the change. Polovtsev, after a conversation with Pobedonostsev in June, 1901, lamented the student riots and strikes: "That is the end of the Russia we knew and which we worshiped with all our hearts. What is to be done? Where lies salvation?" [31] A year later he confided still greater anguish to his diary: "The Russian people are coming more and more to an oppressed, disastrous condition. Their patience weakens. The ground of anarchism becomes ever more fertile. . . . Russia is facing great calamities." [32] In January, 1903, Plehve, talking to Polovtsev, admitted that the situation was serious, although not without hope. There was no denying that, with a few inconsequential exceptions, the entire population was dissatisfied. Then he went on to complain that no agreement among the various ministries existed as to how this deplorable situation could be met.[33] Plehve had pointed out the weakest spot in the tsarist regime: There was no hope of a common program.

And how could there be, considering the multitudinous crosscurrents of official advice, backstage intrigue, or family influence continuously washing over the Tsar's bewildered mind? It was perhaps not surprising that in these years of mounting discontent he should have lost confidence in his official staff of ministers. Why had they not been able to prevent it? He had plainly told

[31] Polovtsev's diary, entry for June 12, 1901, *KA,* III, 94.
[32] Entry for September 22, 1902, *ibid.,* p. 161.
[33] Entry for January 5, 1903, *ibid.,* pp. 169–70.

them to stop the unrest in a special conference held after the attempted assassination of Pobedonostsev.[34] If they failed, it was obviously owing to their incompetence. So argued the reactionaries who worked through the Empress, the grand dukes, their unscrupulous wives, and their favorites who gained access to the Court through the Guard regiments. It was not only Witte who suffered from such interference; the other ministers had their troubles too. In the spring of 1903 it was an open question as to which set of advisers on Russian Far Eastern policy would prevail, the official ones of the "departments" or the unofficial clique around Bezobrazov; the latter even won out for a time. Needless to say, the quality of the advice proffered by the outsiders was dubious at best; they possessed neither the experience nor the formal responsibility of the regular *sanovniki.* The Tsar, however, was incapable of distinguishing between the experts and the amateurs.

His task, of course, was made difficult by the fact that, as Plehve had said, even his experts in the "departments" could not agree. A typical case of such disagreement was the role played by Colonel Zubatov in Moscow. A former revolutionary and now member of the secret police, Zubatov was the protégé of the governor general of Moscow, Grand Duke Sergei. He thus had the highest possible sanction for his efforts to organize the industrial workers under the auspices of the police. Competing with the Marxists, he offered the workers higher wages, better working conditions, and—under "Russian" symbols—an anticapitalist ideology. The victims of this agitation, as also of the revolutionaries', were the industrialists, particularly foreign ones. It was no accident that the first strike staged by Zubatov's men was directed against a foreign firm. In their distress the Moscow *kupechestvo* turned to Witte for protection against this officially sponsored labor movement which ran so counter to the Witte system. In

[34] Reported by Charles Scott, April 1, 1901, from the British embassy in St. Petersburg, PRO, Foreign Office, Series 65, Vol. 1602.

addition, the French ambassador protested on behalf of the French investors. Yet Witte, enraged though he was, proved powerless to interfere with Zubatov's activities. Other cases of interdepartmental strife, involving again the ministries of the Interior and of Finance, concerned the Nobles and Peasant Land banks, factory inspection, peasant affairs, the treatment of minorities, or the building of an elevated electric railway in St. Petersburg—in short, the entire gamut of domestic issues. The Ministry of the Interior stood for the traditional Russia of landlords and bureaucracy, for Muscovy; the Ministry of Finance, for a modern capitalist Russia, for Europe. Both believed in autocracy, but with almost mutually exclusive connotations.

Each of these key departments also quarreled with lesser ones. The minister of war deplored the tendency of the Ministry of the Interior to make the army into a penal institution or to use it as a police force against strikers and rebellious peasants. The minister of war also quarreled with the minister of finance over the army budget, foreign policy, and the purchase of war materials abroad. And which minister in these years did not complain about the interference of the minister of finance in affairs that did not belong to his jurisdiction? The minister of education was upset by Witte's ventures into higher education; the minister of state domains and agriculture, over his investigation of rural economy.

Clearly the Russian government was in need of basic administrative reform. As Nicholas II was incapable of assuming the central leadership, who would take over? The Committee of Ministers was never allowed to presume upon the Imperial prerogative, nor was the much more rarely convoked Council of Ministers. A prime minister then? But that again meant an end of Nicholas's personal rule. To that he would never consent, not even after 1905. For a while it seemed that he contemplated another step, splitting up the big ministries so as to make them more amenable to his weak will. After Witte's fall, for instance, he spoke of dismembering the Ministry of Finance or dividing the Ministry of War.[35] In 1901 he had already made a move which was highly disagreeable to Witte, reducing the latter's administrative empire by taking away the control over Russia's merchant marine. Instead he established it, without even consulting the State Council, as a chief administration under no less a nonentity than Grand Duke Alexander Mikhailovich, Witte's old enemy. The Emperor did not, however, elevate the Department of Trade and Industry into a separate ministry, as was also suggested by Witte's enemies.

Underneath the anarchy in the highest spheres one can discern a major change of mood. It hardly deserves being called a policy, yet it was of the Emperor's own making and permeated into the ranks of his officials. Trying to fathom the state of the Tsar's mind or his political motives is, of course, an elusive task. Soviet historians have published neither official documents allowing a direct insight into the Emperor's daily work nor even his diaries for this crucial period, when he made a valiant though fatal effort to assert his authority. None of his ministers, so a study of the available materials shows, possessed more than a partial view of their master's policy. Nevertheless, the following outline of the Emperor's course emerges from the investigation of the last years of the Witte system.[36]

After his accession Nicholas had sincerely desired to continue his father's policies for the economic development of Russia. He had backed Witte to the full in the currency reform and the encouragement of industry, and had even consented to the extensive utilization of foreign capital. With the years Witte's authority in the government had even grown. After Goremykin's fall in 1899 and Murav'ev's death in the summer of 1900, Witte was indeed the strongest of all the Tsar's ministers. Yet this very fact aroused

[35] Romanov, *Rossiia v Mandzhurii,* p. 309.

[36] The best account is found in Oldenburg, Vol. I, Chap. VIII. Yet what Oldenburg describes belongs rather to the year 1902 than 1903.

suspicion. Was he not becoming more influential than the Tsar himself?[37] And was not he, whose policies were unpopular, also undermining the prestige of autocracy? After 1900 his work was obviously not prospering.

At the end of March, 1902, the Emperor suddenly saw the handwriting on the wall. First had come the Anglo-Japanese alliance, next the peasant uprisings in the South, and a few days later the assassination of Sipiagin. Now was the time to assert himself. The crisis thus brought to the fore his deepest convictions, on the positive side his belief in autocracy, in the traditional Russia of the Orthodox Church, of landlord and peasant, and in the mission of Russia on earth; on the negative side his aversion to industry, capitalism, the Jews, the press, social mobility, and rapid technological change. It was then that he appointed Plehve and gave Bezobrazov a freer hand. In the summer the new mood appeared even more clearly when he showed a firm air in his talks with William II, made much of the necessity of fighting anarchism, and harped on the tasks of propagating Russian influence in the East. In September, in his speech at Kursk, he laid down the new trend in domestic policy as well: aid to the landlords and peasants, the victims of the Witte system. It was this orientation, so preposterously unrealistic from Witte's point of view, which led to the war with Japan and the Revolution of 1905.

These decisions did not sit lightly upon the Emperor's conscience. In these months the signs of inward anguish increased. It was the summer of Monsieur Philippe's influence at Court, of the Empress's mock pregnancy, and of the precipitous order for the canonization of Seraphim of Sarov, a saintly hermit whose memory brought special solace to the Imperial family. The last-named event clearly revealed the strange tensions that so often surrounded Imperial policy. In July, 1902, when Nicholas gave that order, saying it had to be completed within six days, on the anniversary

[37] So Witte reported on the talk among his enemies. See his letter to Sipiagin, July 12, 1901, *KA,* XVIII, 45.

of Seraphim's death, Pobedonostsev, as Oberprokurator of the Holy Synod, protested against the unsanctimonious hurry. The Tsaritsa was reported to have tried to overrule him: "The Emperor can do anything."[38] The canonization, nevertheless, was postponed for a year.

Against this tide of obscurantism Witte could make little headway; he was losing the Emperor's confidence. He complained that Nicholas would brook no contradiction and was commanding him to take measures with which he did not agree.[39] The anarchical absolutism preached by Sipiagin or Prince Meshcherskii was reaching an extreme form. And Polovtsev burst out in despair a few weeks later. The Russian people were losing patience, he wrote, "thanks to the unbridled license of the bureaucrats, their thoughtless fantasies, thanks to the regimentation, which was reaching ridiculous limits, and to the capricious interference in every conceivable affair, but particularly thanks to the unfortunate choice of companions by the Empress, the grand dukes and duchesses, and the crowd of rotters surrounding them."[40] By the end of the year, after the fateful budget session in the State Council, Witte's fall seemed imminent. The order for his dismissal, it was said, was to be signed by the first of the new year.

Great must have been the astonishment of the official circles, however, when they read a few days later the Emperor's rescript to his Minister of Finance, congratulating him on his tenth anniversary in office and expressing his fullest confidence in the man and the future. Why had the Emperor changed his mind? Was it on the pleading of his mother, the Dowager Empress Maria Fedorovna, who loyally stood by Witte, or because of apprehension over the effects of Witte's fall on Russian credit abroad, or as a rebuff to the State Council? Thus the indecision continued for another seven months.

[38] Witte, *Tsarstvovanie Nikolaia II,* I, 242.

[39] Polovtsev's diary, entry for September 1, 1902, *KA,* III, 157.

[40] Entry for September 22, 1902, *ibid.,* p. 161.

In the new year 1903, since Witte could score no economic or diplomatic victories and the domestic agitation mounted, the scales tilted still further against him. The manifesto of February 23 again emphasized the government's concern for the traditional pillars of Russia—the Orthodox Church, the landed gentry, and the peasants. The concessions which it made, in the vague guarantee of religious tolerance and the promise to consult "deserving men enjoying public confidence," were bows to public opinion rather than to Witte; they meant nothing. In domestic policy the worst instincts of Plehve were winning the upper hand, which meant less reform and more repression. In May, Witte's position was further undermined by the appointment of Bezobrazov as state secretary and the dispatch of new instructions to Admiral Alekseev for a firmer policy in the Far East.

Yet two more events, occurring simultaneously in mid-July and leaving their mark on the Emperor's mind, were needed to dislodge Witte from his post: the great strikes in the south and the canonization of Seraphim of Sarov. Labor unrest had been simmering since the spring. Suddenly on July 1 the oil workers of Baku struck, followed by those in Tiflis and Batum. On July 17 the agitation reached Odessa, where it assumed the proportions of a general strike, then spread to the industrial centers of the Ukraine, where the depression had made its worst and most recent inroads, and finally encompassed Kiev, before it died out at last around August 15, the Feast of the Assumption. It was the worst strike wave which had yet afflicted tsarist Russia and demonstrated the extent of the domestic crisis. Whether or not the Emperor blamed the strikes directly on Witte or whether they merely strengthened his determination that something drastic must be done, they could not but cast additional doubt upon the wisdom of Witte's domestic policies.

The other events supplied the Emperor with the moral courage needed for breaking with his powerful Minister of Finance. While large-scale industrial and political warfare raged in Odessa and elsewhere in the south, the Emperor went on a pilgrimage, together with three hundred thousand pious subjects from all over Russia, to the monastery of Sarov, in the dense woods between Nizhni-Novgorod and Tambov.[41] The Tsar was accompanied by the Tsaritsa, his mother, the Grand Dukes Sergei and Nikolai Nikolaevich, and lesser members of his family. They were joined by the metropolitan of St. Petersburg and the bishops of Nizhni-Novgorod, Kazan, and Tambov. The morning after their arrival the Emperor walked humbly to the cell where the holy Seraphim had lived and died. On his way he was cheered by the multitude of pilgrims. After the service in the Cathedral of the Assumption, all walked to the hermit's grave in the Zosimo-Savvatievskaia Church. Thence in the evening, in the dense worshipful silence, Nicholas, the grand dukes, and the priests carried the coffin back to the cathedral amidst the hundred thousand flickering candles of the pilgrims who lined the road. When they reached the cathedral the choir broke out in its beseeching hymn, uniting in one common reverence the ruler and the ruled. The "Sarov days" were a profound religious experience to all who participated in them. In his concluding prayer Innokentii, the bishop of Tambov, joyfully spoke of the close communion of the Tsar with his people. After all the doubts and the isolation of the Imperial palaces, here the Emperor was at one with his *narod*, with the simple peasants from the heart of Russia, and all was right with the world. Never has religion been a more fatal opiate to an autocrat!

Thereafter matters developed rapidly, as the Emperor's mind was resolved. By the end of July Alekseev was appointed viceroy for the Far East, and Witte's ascendancy in Manchuria ended. And on August 16, at the conclusion of their routine weekly conference, the Emperor informed Witte in the kindest words that he had just promoted him to the position of chairman of the Committee of Ministers in order to relieve him of his pressing anxieties as minister of finance. When Witte, dumbfounded, made a sour

[41] Oldenburg, p. 210.

face, Nicholas assured him that the Empire could offer no higher honor.[42] During this quiet meeting in the Tsar's cabinet, the Witte system came to its end.

Nicholas had not been entirely wrong, to be sure, in saying that a greater honor awaited Witte. Nominally the chairman of the Committee of Ministers ranked higher than a minister. But Witte did not possess the privilege of regular access to the Tsar and was shorn of the executive powers which he had wielded as minister of finance. Not that his usefulness was entirely ended, however. In 1904 he assumed command of the negotiations with Germany over the renewal of the trade treaty of 1894, and he retained until early in 1905 the chairmanship of the Special Commission on the Needs of Agricultural Industry. The Emperor, furthermore, eased the blow by a very generous financial arrangement.[43] But as for executive power in a crucial position, Witte was condemned for the next two years to a frustrating inactivity, sitting on the sidelines during the disasters of the Japanese War and the ascending phase of the revolution. Only in the fall of 1905 did he once more return to power, but by then the political problems raised by the revolution took precedence over any policy of industrialization.

Not all elements of the Witte system came to an end with their author's fall. The tariff remained because the fiscal necessities which had brought it into existence were perennial. So did the gold standard, the liquor monopoly, the tax structure, and the urgency of expanding the Russian railroad network and her industries in general. But gone was the industrial tycoon's zeal and experience, gone the passionate plea to make rapid industrialization the order of the day. Witte's successors were again products of the bureaucracy; Pleske was a colorless, aged official who lasted but two months, and Kokovtsov was a very capable and honorable but conformist *chinovnik*, not to mention later incumbents who

[42] Witte, *Tsarstvovanie Nikolaia II,* I, 218. See also Kokovtsov, pp. 5 ff.

[43] See Romberg's account of Witte's fall in his dispatches dated August 31 and September 14, 1903. Bonn, Russland Series 82, No. 2.

left even less permanent marks. Never again under the tsars did the ideal of industrialization find such a powerful and clear-sighted protagonist as Sergei Witte.

Plehve's version of how the Emperor arrived at his final decision may permit a last, if irreverent, glimpse into Nicholas's thought processes. The Emperor, Plehve said, had made up his mind suddenly, during a Te Deum at the launching of a new battleship. "The Lord put into my heart the thought," so Plehve recalled Nicholas's words, "that I must not delay that which I was already persuaded to do." [44] The reasons that swayed Nicholas were given by Kuropatkin. Three mines had been planted against Witte, he wrote, the first by Grand Duke Alexander Mikhailovich, who had told his brother-in-law that Witte was becoming too powerful; he arrogated to himself the function not only of several ministries but even of the autocrat. The second mine was laid by Bezobrazov; Witte's policy in the Far East was contrary to Russian interest. The third and most powerful charge, however, was devised by Plehve and possibly also by Murav'ev, the minister of justice, in league with Pobedonostsev. They told the Emperor that all dissatisfied elements among the public were finding encouragement in Witte: the Finns, the Armenians, the Jews, and the students.[45] In August, 1903, all three mines exploded simultaneously, apparently under an unsuspecting victim.

A historian reflecting on the last years of Witte's activities as minister of finance will go even further than Kuropatkin. He will say no less than that the entire "system" had prepared Witte's downfall. His efforts to remake not only Russian economy but the Russian state and society as well had mobilized all the latent forces of tradition against him. And when, on economic grounds alone, his task turned out to be much bigger than he had expected, when he was harassed by agricultural discontent, industrial depression, strikes, and by all the familiar ogres of Russian poverty and

[44] Gurko, *Features and Figures of the Past,* p. 225.
[45] Kuropatkin's diary, entry for August 19, 1903, *KA*, II, 59.

public rebellion against them, his usefulness had ended. To go beyond his present work and solve, one by one, the basic problems of Russian backwardness, to force the population to tighten their belts still further for distant and dubious benefits, was obviously impossible under the present regime. There remained only the alternative—falling back into the traditional sloth, muddling along, and trying to resolve the crisis by a "victorious little war." But, as Witte had warned, nothing would lay bare still more cruelly the flaws of contemporary Russia.

Looking back over the events of these years, over the Tsar's attitude, that of his advisers, and the mentality prevailing at Court and in the government generally, a Western observer cannot but shake his head. "What he would inevitably feel," Bernard Pares reflected when looking at the Imperial quarters at Tsarskoe Selo after they were opened to visitors by the Soviets, "would be that all this happened far back in the Middle Ages, when it was still thought possible to regard a sixth of the world as a personal estate and to govern a hundred and seventy million of humanity from a lady's drawing room. Then he would say to himself that all this was gone far, far away, never to come back again." [46] In 1903 Russia numbered not quite as many inhabitants, and among the places where Imperial policy was made the Emperor's study, chapel, and cathedral also have been mentioned. But medieval the setting was, all the same.

It is easy for foreigners to dismiss this spectacle of Russian governmental medievalism at the beginning of the twentieth century as something incredible or characteristically Russian. But what would have been the reaction of the patriotic subjects of Nicholas, as acutely aware as Pares of the incompatibility of this obscurantism with the demands of a modern world, but unable as patriots to disengage themselves from their Russian realities? Would it not be choking despair and bitter resentment? Thus one

[46] Pares, *The Fall of the Russian Monarchy*, p. 502.

comes within reach of understanding the pent-up fury of Witte's *Memoirs*—or the ferocious righteousness of a Lenin.

The reaction of most contemporaries, however, was quite different when they heard of Witte's fall. They breathed a sigh of relief. There was no voice of protest. The stock market did not flatter the fallen minister by a sharp drop. The well-known journalist A. S. Suvorin of the *New Times* summed up the prevailing feeling when he penned the following lines under the fresh impression of the news:

> There is nothing left for Sergei Iulevich to do now in the realm of government finance. . . . Financial policy must now give way, if one may say so, to political policy. Much has been done; much has been begun which was necessary according to European financial science to which Sergei Iulevich so loved to appeal. But from now on it is necessary to adjust all that has been recently done to the foundations of Russia, where life is in ferment and begins by itself to search for new paths. We need creative activity, and not only in finance or railroads, in trade or industry. The truth is that the financial policy of S. Iu. Witte encroached too much upon Russian policy in general. He forced it into close dependence upon its material basis. He was therefore not only minister of finance but also first minister. Thanks to his supreme intellectual gifts he spread his influence over all sides of government life. He was carried away, and he dragged Russia after him where he wanted to go and where, in his firm conviction, it was best for his fatherland and the glory of its ruler.[47]

It was obvious that all Russia had resented the strait jacket of the Witte system. Now it wanted to be free and go its own way, each group in its own direction, and turn, as Suvorin had said, from economic policy to the fundamentals of political power. A Russia which had advanced so rapidly in its economy was now eager to catch up politically as well. Thus the Witte system had helped to set the stage for the Revolution of 1905.

[47] Cited by *Promyshlennyi mir,* No. 36, 1903.

8. *Sic et non*, and a Conclusion

As minister of finance I was also in charge of our commerce and industry. As such I increased our industry threefold. This again is held against me. Fools! It is said that I took artificial measures to develop our industry. What a silly phrase! How else can one develop an industry? . . .

It was imperative to develop our industries not only in the interest of the people but also of the state. A modern body politic cannot be great without a well-developed national industry. WITTE, Memoirs

Russia is at the parting of the ways, one eye fixed on her simple agricultural past, the other gazing forward into what the government believes will prove her great industrial future. Such times are always trying for nations, especially when they are imperfectly prepared. . . . A suddenly expanding and not altogether unified Power cannot act in the simple familiar way of a Power which has many centuries behind it and simple tasks to perform.

The Economist, March, 1901

I

FROM A POLITICAL point of view, the Witte system was a failure. Too many Russians, confronted with rural poverty and the protracted industrial depression, thought that the country was even poorer after the experiment than it had been before. As a result, Witte himself had been dismissed from his post as director of Russia's national economy. Yet was there no truth in his vehement insistence that Russia had greatly benefited from his policies?

Any analysis of the economic effects of the Witte system must start by looking at the size of the investment made in the field of railroad expansion. The record shows that it was very considerable indeed. Between 1890 and 1900 the government paid on the average more than 120 million rubles a year for railroad construction.[1] This was no mean sum, when in the entire decade it spent only 150 million rubles for elementary education.[2] The outlay amounted to about one tenth of its total income in the year 1894, although the percentage decreased in subsequent years. To the government expenditures must be added foreign loans for railroad construction by private companies, to the tune of another 341 million rubles.[3] Altogether, it was estimated, nearly 1.7 billion rubles were invested in all *new* construction (including the Chinese Eastern Railroad).[4] As for the grand total of *all* outlays for Russian railroads in this period, by the government or by government-guaranteed private financing, it was said to amount to slightly more than 3.5 billion rubles, or as much as the government's revenue for the years 1898 and 1899 combined.[5] Of the sums, incidentally, which the government applied to new construction, more than two thirds stemmed from Russian sources, that is, taxation, domestic loans, and other forms of government income. As for the private lines, which added considerably less than one half of the new construction, foreign lenders supplied slightly more than half of the funds.[6] Thus the Russian people themselves paid for the better part of their new railroads.

Of the additions to the Russian network, the great peripheral lines have already been mentioned. The bulk of the increase, however, took place within European Russia, intensifying and speeding the traffic between the various economic centers—more than 1,300 versts of existing lines were double-tracked[7]—extending their reach into new territories or creating new outlets. Moscow—to mention only the major additions—emerged more than ever the

[1] Liashchenko, *Istoriia,* II, 155.
[2] Migulin, *Nasha noveishaia,* p. 324.
[3] *Ibid.,* p. 323.
[4] *Ibid.,* p. 322.
[5] Liashchenko, *Istoriia,* p. 155.
[6] Pogrebinskii, *Ocherki,* p. 160.
[7] Migulin, *Nasha noveishaia,* p. 322.

rail hub of Russia.[8] It received access to Archangel, which provided also a White Sea outlet for northern lumber, another link to Riga in the west, and several shorter connections with the industrial center of Ivanovo-Voznesensk, with Kazan, Simbirsk, and Samara, and, via Ranenburg in the southeast, with Tambov and the Don region. Moscow was also the beneficiary of a new connection between Elets, Voronezh, and Volchansk on the Kharkov-Penza line, which speeded its traffic to the Donets area, and of the direct link with Briansk, which shortened the journey to Gomel and southern Poland. The northern capital, St. Petersburg, bettered its communications by the construction of a trunk line through Vitebsk directly to the Ukraine (it was finished only in 1904). Kiev was given direct access to the Donets basin by a line running through Poltava. The Baltic ports improved their inland reach, first through a northern route from Pskov to Bologoe on the Moscow–St. Petersburg line, and thence to the upper Volga, with the aid of a new link farther east between Rybinsk and Kostroma, and secondly to the middle Volga through a new connection between Smolensk and Ranenburg. In order to develop Windava as an outer harbor to Riga, a road connecting these ports was built. New seaports hitched to the rail net were Mariupol on the Azov Sea, which thus became an outlet for the Donets basin, and Kerch, which was hooked up with the Crimean railroad at Feodosia.

Interior communications, furthermore, were improved with the construction of a line from Kharkov to Penza, which speeded traffic between the industrial Ukraine and Siberia, or another one between Nizhni-Novgorod and Ruzaevka on the Moscow-Samara line, which tied Nizhni to the Siberian railroad, and a third one between the textile city of Vladimir and Riazan. Briansk was connected with the Kiev-Kursk line, and an additional track was laid linking the coal of the Donets basin with the iron of Krivoi Rog. More peripheral but no less important was the connection of

[8] The following is largely based on the map in *Statisticheskii atlas putei soobshcheniia Rossii k nachalu XX veka,* compiled by the Statistical and Cartographical Section of the Ministry of Communications.

Rostov-on-the-Don with Baku, which provided a rail link from the central provinces to the trans-Caucasus system, completed earlier for the oil haul from Baku to the Black Sea. A short spur, incidentally, was added to the latter railroad, giving access to the Chiaturi manganese mines. Another significant addition in southeastern Russia was the trunk line from Tsaritsyn at the bend of the Volga to the port of Novorossiisk; it delivered Volga timber to the Black Sea. At Tsaritsyn timber was loaded on freight cars going to the Donets basin on still another new road, which brought back Donbas coal for shipment upstream. Finally, a costly strategic road of little economic value but considerable length must be mentioned, the Bologoe-Sedlets road traversing the thinly populated areas of Belorussia from central Poland to the halfway point on the Moscow–St. Petersburg line.

Needless to say, railroad mileage soared. Between 1892 and 1902 the length of the Russian network grew by 46 percent, the fastest increase occurring in the years of maximum activity, between 1897 and 1901.[9] The Minister of Finance had reason to be proud; never under the tsars did railroad construction reach a faster pace, and nowhere else in Europe was such speed attained in these years. (The United States, a Soviet authority acknowledged, exceeded even the Russian rate.)[10]

At the end of Witte's career as minister of finance Russia still lagged behind the other great powers in the density of her railroad grid, but she owned, according to a Russian source,[11] more rolling stock per mile of track than France, Italy, or Holland, where short hauls prevailed, and also more than the United States. Because of government subsidies she boasted the cheapest passenger rates in Europe, even for first-class accommodations;[12] and long-distance travel was generally considered the most comfortable in Europe. Customers, too, were not lacking. In 1902

[9] These figures from Khromov, p. 462.

[10] Neopikhanov, p. 99.

[11] Migulin, *Nasha noveishaia,* pp. 348 ff.

[12] *Ibid.,* p. 366.

over 127 million tickets were sold, almost twice as many as five years before. And passengers traveled longer distances, too.[13] Freight movement increased proportionally; the existing facilities were barely able to handle the demand. By 1900 the Russian railroads had long ceased to be carriers of agricultural products exclusively. More than four fifths of the freight (by value) consisted of nonagricultural goods.[14]

The general benefits which the new railways added to Russian economy and Russian life are, of course, impossible to estimate precisely. Certainly all of Russia profited. Her widened arterial network allowed an increased mobility of people and goods. The new roads fused all of Russia into an economic unit as her far-flung borders were linked through a system of effective interior communications. Surely, what had been built under Witte remained forever as part of the country's working equipment.

These general benefits apart, railroad construction had been planned to make a specific contribution to economic expansion. The demand for building materials and equipment constituted, so Witte's theory ran, a powerful incentive for the creation of heavy industry. The gigantic expenditures for railroad construction were, in fact, cash payments for orders from mines, steel mills, and machine shops, and for those industries which, in turn, equipped the makers of railroad materials. The phenomenal emergence of the Ukraine as the foremost center of Russian metallurgy was inseparable from the railroad boom of the Witte period.[15]

Yet the tremendous increase of heavy industry in Witte's time was not entirely financed out of state orders, magnificent though they were. They merely provided the incentive for extensive investment by private enterprise. Where did that capital originate? As will be remembered, in 1894 Witte had released in a single gigantic credit operation over a billion rubles to the domestic

[13] Neopikhanov, p. 77; also *Ezhegodnik Rossii za 1904*, p. 342.

[14] Liashchenko, *Ocherki*, p. 271.

[15] In 1898, for instance, over one half of all finished metal products of the southern metallurgical industry consisted of rails. See Shpolianskii, p. 38.

investors. Here was ample working capital for industrial expansion in many fields. Yet it was mostly foreigners, French and Belgians, who invested in the development of the heavy industries of the Ukraine, where the fastest growth occurred. The foreign-owned companies were the leaders in raising the output of Russian heavy industry.

Whatever the source of investments, the results were remarkable. Russian coal production as a whole more than doubled between 1892 and 1902; in the Donets basin it tripled.[16] In pig iron, it has been estimated, the output of European Russia grew almost threefold, but in the Ukraine fivefold. The supply of cast iron and steel increased two and a half times, nearly five times in the Ukraine. Even so, in neither coal, iron, nor steel could the domestic production satisfy the demand. Yet at the end of the Witte period Russia had advanced over France in the output of pig iron, standing at fourth place in world production, and fifth in steel.[17] In the process she was creating a modern industrial center in the Ukraine, where she was working with up-to-date techniques and business methods, in contrast to the tradition-ridden Ural industries, which were now deposed from their preeminence. In southern Russia the blast furnaces had the highest output per unit in all of Europe (the American furnaces, as usual, outdistanced even the Russian ones).[18]

While the heavy industries stood in the foreground of the advance, the tempo of expansion (nicely measured by contemporary or Soviet percentagemongers) was shared by related industries. The ceramics industries, for instance, making the bricks and cement for railroads and factories, are said to have raised the value of their output by 184 percent between 1887 and 1898.[19] In the chemical industries the output increased by 177 percent. In

[16] These figures from Khromov, pp. 456 ff.

[17] V. E. Motylev, "Ob osobennostiakh promyshlennogo razvitiia Rossii v kontse XIX—nachale XX veka," *Voprosy istorii,* No. 7, 1955, pp. 11 ff.

[18] Mendelson, p. 688.

[19] Liashchenko, *Istoriia,* II, 146.

1900 Russia listed 276 chemical enterprises, with a product worth 40 million rubles.[20] A third group, the metalworking industries producing tools, equipment, and implements (numbering about 1,700 in 1887 and over a thousand more ten years later), bettered the value of their output by 175 percent in the same period.[21] Of these establishments, 585 were building machines, "the manufacturers of manufactories." These figures do not even include the peak years of the boom. Again, the domestic production of machines did not match the growing demand. And to conclude the success story: Oil production from Baku (and after 1896 also from the Grozny fields) registered a 243 percent increase between 1892 and 1901, for a brief moment surpassing even the total American output.[22]

It is easy to trace the specific effect of railroad construction upon the growth of the heavy industries. The depression bore out the interdependence, for the southern mines and metallurgical works which had relied most heavily on state orders suffered most when these orders declined; there was no other market for their wares. But the next step in Witte's theory, the stimulation of the light industries, is more difficult to evaluate. The link between railroads and the consumer industries was a more tenuous one, the causal connection between policy and the volume of production less certain. But taking the cotton industry, the biggest employer of industrial labor in Russia, as an index, one can again record a significant expansion. Unlike the southern steel mills, the textile manufacturers produced for the mass market; they weathered the depression rather well. Thus the near-doubling of the consumption of raw cotton in the country and of the production of cotton goods in the 1890s[23] would indicate a corresponding gain and a justification of Witte's theory. The growth of production also led to the modernization of equipment. Some of the new textile machinery

[20] Lukianov, p. 177.
[21] Liashchenko, *Istoriia,* II, 146.
[22] Khromov, p. 459.
[23] *Ibid.,* pp. 460–61.

was indeed destined to last until 1955 (if not longer).[24] The least improvement among the light industries was registered by the food-processing industries.[25] On the whole, consumer goods were apt to lag behind capital goods.

The conclusions suggested by the foregoing figures are confirmed by a highly respectable Soviet calculation of the increases in the over-all industrial production.[26] If total industrial production of Russia in 1913 is set at 100, it stood at about 31 in 1892. Eleven years later, after Witte's dismissal, it had risen to nearly 64. In short, it had fully doubled during these years at a pace of development unequaled in tsarist Russia or, for that matter, among other European countries except Sweden. Russia was indeed catching up. Whereas in 1870 she had produced only 3.7 percent of the world's manufactured goods, in 1900, according to a League of Nations survey, she accounted for 5 percent. And while England had outproduced her by more than eight times at the earlier date, Russia had more than halved her lag at the later date.[27] Witte's boast in his *Memoirs* that he had increased Russian industry threefold[28] was exaggerated or applicable only to a few industries, yet it was not entirely unjustified. And Russia's new ability to produce helped to kindle the "healthy spirit of enterprise" which Witte tried to foster among the Russian people.

It is impossible, of course, to indicate the volume of entrepreneurial energy in terms of statistics, but some rough estimates are in order showing how the Russian people responded to the challenge. An estimated four billion rubles were privately invested in transport and industry between 1893 and 1902.[29] The results

[24] At the Moscow *Trekhgornaia manufaktura* the average age of mechanical looms in 1955 was sixty years, of the cloth-printing machines sixty-one years. *Voprosy ekonomii,* 1957, No. 7, p. 49.

[25] Liashchenko, *Istoriia,* II, 146.

[26] Cited by A. Gerschenkron, "The Rate of Industrial Growth in Russia since 1885," *Journal of Economic History,* 1947, Supplement VII.

[27] League of Nations, *Industrialization and Foreign Trade,* p. 13.

[28] Witte, *Tsarstvovanie Nikolaia II,* I, 226.

[29] Mendelson, p. 689.

of this golden rain were quite remarkable. In 1893, 648 joint-stock companies were registered; in 1900, 1,369, more than twice as many.[30] The increase was particularly marked after 1894. Whereas formerly the capital of newly formed joint-stock companies had rarely risen above 60 million rubles a year, it now stood, according to Soviet figures, at nearly 130 million in 1895, between 230 and 256 million in the following three years, and at a record height of 430 million in 1899.[31] The number of new corporations licensed by the Committee of Ministers[32] ran to 63 in 1894, 95 in the following year, 138 for two years thereafter, not quite 200 in 1898, and 318 in 1899. By 1903 the number of new ventures had sunk again to the 1895 level, but the total increase for the years 1894 to September, 1902, 1,520 companies in all (227 of which were foreign), represented a spectacular gain. Not every company so licensed commenced operations, but even so the figures testified to a very considerable increase in entrepreneurial activity. A goodly share of the expansion was due, admittedly, to foreign capital. But was the economic effect in such cases significantly different from that of the firms owned by Russians?

How much the new volume of capitalist activities benefited the growth of industry appears from the fact that almost three quarters of the new capital invested in joint-stock companies between 1889 and 1899 went into industrial enterprises; the remainder turned to transport, insurance, or banking.[33] The increase of new capital was greatest, of course, in the heavy industries—eightfold in metallurgy, fivefold in the chemical industries, sevenfold in brick and cement, more than threefold in mining—while the light industries did not even double theirs.[34] Foreign capital, taken by itself, showed the same preferences still more emphatically.

[30] Cited from L. E. Shepelev, "Aktsionernoe uchreditel'stvo v Rossii," in *Iz istorii imperializma v Rossii,* p. 148.

[31] Khromov, p. 463.

[32] *Istoricheskii obzor deiatel'nosti komiteta ministrov,* p. 19.

[33] Liashchenko, *Istoriia,* II, 156.

[34] *Ibid.,* p. 157.

In the light of these facts, it does not seem surprising that of all varieties of industrial establishments existing in 1900 as many as two fifths were founded during the *Gründerzeit* between 1891 and 1900.[35] In the face of the Soviet emphasis upon the tendency toward bigness in Russian industry it should be stressed, furthermore, that three quarters of the new enterprises employed 50 workers or less; it was the small ones which multiplied most rapidly. And new firms employing no more than 99 workers constituted nine tenths of the total.[36] The largest works, to be sure, added greatly to their labor force and augmented their output spectacularly, but most of them had already been in existence in 1891. This proves sufficiently that the spirit of enterprise was by no means limited to a few big capitalists, but extended into the depths of the Russian population.

It also penetrated into the outlying areas of European Russia.[37] The old industrial centers like Moscow, Vladimir, or St. Petersburg shared least, percentagewise, in the new growth. At the turn of the century, the new ventures founded in these areas since 1891 amounted to only a quarter or a third of all existing enterprises. The central black-soil provinces like Tula or Orlov characteristically added no more than one quarter. But Smolensk, Vitebsk, and Minsk were doing better; one half of their industries were new. As for the south, the industries of the provinces of Taurus, Bessarabia, Poltava and most of all Ekaterinoslav were also expanding. Almost two thirds of the industrial enterprises of the last-named were born during the 1890s; it registered the largest increase in all of Russia. Among the provinces which scored a 50 percent increase could be found, in the southeast, Voronezh, Saratov, Penza, Simbirsk, Astrakhan, Orenburg, and Ufa; to the north, Archangel. The old industrial centers still retained their preeminence, but industrialization spread throughout Russia. As

[35] Pogozhev, *Uchet chislennosti i sostava rabochykh v Rossii,* p. 76.
[36] *Ibid.*
[37] *Ibid.,* Chart 16 for the following.

in agriculture, so in industry—the more peripheral regions, less hamstrung by tradition, advanced more rapidly.

The foregoing data, whether of production or the number of enterprises, encompass only the measurable aspects of economic enterprise. The shortcomings of Russian and Soviet statistics notwithstanding, they still indicate the magnitude of the boom of capitalist and industrial activity. Beyond them lay the unrecorded and unmeasured world of small partnerships, family firms, and the kulaks' petty ventures. Did these businesses not share in the boom, at least to some extent? They probably suffered worst from the depression, but they must have had their slice of the benefits which preceded it.

How did Witte's theory of economic development prove itself in the still more peripheral realm of agriculture? The connection between railroad construction and the improvement of agriculture was rather tenuous and indirect. The industrial prosperity would, according to the theory, tend to relieve the hidden rural unemployment by enticing the peasants into the factories. It would provide new urban markets, encourage the application of machinery to agriculture and the adoption of more rational methods of cultivation. All this, however, would presumably take more than a single decade.

There is no hiding the fact that during its relatively short duration the Witte system did not score striking victories in agriculture. Yet in the face of the almost universal contemporary condemnation, certain positive aspects should be kept in mind. The new railways provided better and cheaper transportation for Russian crops. And industrial expansion did relieve, if only to a small extent, the hidden rural unemployment. Witte's own claim that railway construction and industry diverted 4–5 million people from Russian agriculture, thus increasing the land supply by 20–25 million dessiatines, was certainly an overstatement.[38] But the industrial side-earnings did keep many peasant families from starvation. The

[38] Witte, *Tsarstvovanie Nikolaia II,* I, 226.

urban market also grew and gave rise to truck gardening and to a new flourishing dairy industry in Siberia which even produced for export.[39] Industrial demand for alcohol and starch led to an increase in potato raising and under license from the liquor monopoly to the profitable operation of local distilleries. Sugar production doubled between 1892 and 1903,[40] providing an invaluable export item, while domestic consumption also increased, although slightly. Flax was in demand for the linen industry and, more significantly, for the makers of margarine. In many ways the growing industries called for industrial crops; only a capitalist mode of production could raise them efficiently. Wheat production, too, made great progress on the large estates of the south, where machinery, mostly imported from the United States, enabled the capitalist landowners to raise large cash crops for export. In the 1890s virgin lands east of the lower Volga were successfully brought under cultivation, again on a capitalist basis.

There was no basic reason for the Minister of Finance to worry about the Russian food supply. In the forty-year period between 1865 and 1905 the percentage increase in the food supply (that is, grain and potatoes) was double the percentage increase in the population.[41] As a whole, it would seem then that the Russian people were eating better, for not all of the increased crop went for export. The landlords with their improved methods produced big harvests, on the average a quarter more than the peasants did in good years, and up to 80 percent more, it was estimated, in years of famine.[42] The encouraging aspects of Russian agriculture unfortunately did not receive sufficient publicity at the time. Why should the modern producers, who could manage by themselves, advertise their success?[43] Thus, as Witte had pointed out in his

[39] Karnaukhova, p. 131.

[40] Khromov, p. 453.

[41] Liashchenko, *Istoriia,* II, 71.

[42] Lokhtin, p. 186.

[43] It was Lenin who in his book on *The Development of Capitalism in Russia* gave the fullest contemporary account of the development of capitalist agriculture.

budget reports, certainly not all agriculture was in distress. And at least one eminent modern authority on Russian agriculture has agreed with him. Improvement could come only through the growth of industrial capitalism.[44]

As for the Russian consumer, his lot was not entirely hopeless either, at least if measured by Russian standards and not by Westernized expectations. As evidence Witte cited in his budget report of 1902 the annual consumption of tea—and everybody drank tea—which had risen between 1893 and 1900 from 0.73 to 0.94 pound per person; of sugar, which was a luxury, from 8.28 to 11.2 pounds; of cotton, from 3.52 to 4.32 pounds; of kerosene, from 10.6 to 13.4 pounds. Or one might point to the more easily verified increases in the deposits in Russian savings banks, which grew from 239 million rubles in 1892, representing 1.1 million savers, to 861 million rubles representing 4.8 million savers.[45] These figures would seem to refute the charges of an increasing impoverishment of the Russian population, although, admittedly, five million savings accounts in a population of over 130 million constituted a small percentage; in Russia, as elsewhere in the world, the poorest did not save.

Finally, one might invoke the increasing tax receipts of the government to prove that if the government budget could be doubled, the prosperity of the Russian people could not lag too far behind. This, indeed, was the punch line in Witte's theory. If through railroad construction the entire economy of Russia had been given new life, the government in the end would profit through the increased tax yield. Filling the Treasury and improving the financial strength of the government had been one of the strongest single motives behind the whole policy of industrialization; it was the proof of the pudding. Government receipts, not counting the extraordinary sources of income, had risen from about 970 million rubles in 1892 to slightly over two billion in 1903, roughly by 110

[44] Pavlovsky, pp. 112, 321.
[45] Khromov, p. 540.

percent.[46] He had even saved the government a surplus of 1.8 billion rubles in his eleven years.

Moreover, through his successful financial management he had mastered most of those problems which had defeated his predecessors. He had stabilized the currency by introducing the gold standard; he had buttressed it by the accumulation of a large cash reserve. True, he had raised the government debt by slightly more than one third. But he had kept the increase in interest and amortization payments down to one ninth by refunding the state debt from an interest rate running between 4.2 and 5 percent to an average of 3.86 percent (which, incidentally, persuaded many Russian investors to put their money into industrial stocks rather than government bonds).[47] The annual debt charges, amounting to 27 percent of the yearly government income in 1892, drew only 15 percent of it in 1903.[48] As a result of his management, the 3 percent Russian government bonds enjoyed for a time an even better reputation than those of Germany or Prussia.[49] Russian credit, in general, stood firmer than for many years before or after his term in office. Through the establishment of the gold standard he had also opened the way for the free influx of foreign capital into private enterprise. And the problem of preserving the balance of payments was now transformed into one of guarding the gold reserve. Even here he was weathering the depression remarkably well, against all predictions of the pessimists.

He had also made considerable progress over his predecessors in the field of public relations. Through his annual budget reports and public speeches he had campaigned vigorously against the deep-seated public ignorance and incomprehension of Russian economic realities. He had enlisted the aid of the professors and thus given scientific depth to his contentions. It was due to him, more-

[46] Migulin, *Russkii gosudarstvennyi kredit,* Vol. III, Part V, "Itogi ministerstva Vitte," p. 119.

[47] In the budget report for 1902.

[48] Migulin, *Russkii gosudarstvennyi kredit,* III, 1084.

[49] Migulin, *Nasha bankovaia politika,* p. 236.

over, that the censors permitted a relatively free public debate of the government's financial policy. Although he failed to rally any appreciable public support to his side, it was most remarkable that a tsarist minister should lay the issues squarely before the "thinking people" of Russia. If the public, like the Tsar, refused to be educated in a matter extremely vital to their future, it was not Witte's fault.

Judging by the criteria usually applied to Russian ministers of finance, Witte's regime as a whole had been a remarkable accomplishment. He had made ends meet in state finance and, in addition, through industrialization had strengthened and expanded the economy of Russia. Even by modern standards, his work for the economic advance of Russia, though eclipsed by the Soviet drive, stands out as a monument to Russian state ambition.

This was the way in which he longed, so vainly for the remainder of his life, to have his accomplishments viewed. But how enduring was the gloss of success?

II

Among the most influential political salons in St. Petersburg at the turn of the century was that of Konstantin Fedorovich Golovin. The host, a paralyzed and blind gentleman who was moved about in a wheelchair, was a personage of some note both as a novelist—he had written fifteen volumes of fiction—and an economist.[50] His attitudes and manners were those of a landowner and nobleman with close ties to the central provinces, his political views those of the moderate zemstvo spokesmen, liberal but far from radical. His guests were mostly men of the same mold: Count P. I. Heiden, the venerable president of the Free Imperial Economic Society; a group of zemstvo representatives, some of them au-

[50] The following characterization is taken from Gurko, *Features and Figures of the Past,* pp. 229–33. See also Golovin's works (which I have found only in German translations), *Russlands Finanzpolitik und die Aufgaben der Zukunft* (1900), and *Meine Erinnerungen* (1911).

thorities on peasant affairs; and a handful of high-ranking *chinovniki*. Among the last-named were P. K. Shvanebakh, a member of the Council of the Ministry of Finance much admired for his erudition in all fiscal matters, and V. I. Gurko, whom Plehve appointed head of the Peasant Section in his ministry. The group disagreed sharply on the merits of the peasant commune (Golovin himself favored its abolition), but it was of one mind when the discussion turned, as it often did, to the work of the Minister of Finance. None of these men concealed their bitter hostility toward Witte; they even stated their reasons in public. Once Shvanebakh tore into Witte's budget at a meeting of the Association for the Furtherance of the Interests of Trade and Industry, until the discussion was interrupted by order of the authorities.[51] Shvanebakh, Gurko, and Golovin each published books denouncing the Witte system even before its fall, and with their assistance a memorandum was prepared on the plight of Russia's economy for Plehve's perusal, providing him with ammunition in his fight against Witte.

The starting point of all attacks on the Witte system made in Konstantin Fedorovich's salon was the assumption, or rather article of faith, that agriculture was the permanent basis of Russian economy.[52] The vast majority of Russians were peasants. By their side stood the landed nobility, acting as mediator between the peasants and the authorities and also representing the peasants' economic interests. In the name of rural Russia Golovin's circle demanded that the government concentrate its solicitude on agriculture, particularly in those areas where it was suffering most, in the central black-soil provinces. Golovin himself, in one of his economic treatises, described the misery of the Center in doleful terms. He was a pessimist. The soils of Russia were becoming exhausted through erosion and excessive exploitation, the water table was falling as a result of the destruction of the forests, and

[51] Gurko, *Features and Figures of the Past,* p. 232.

[52] The following is paraphrased from Golovin, *Russlands Finanzpolitik.*

the climate was deteriorating.[53] All this called for quick action by the government.

Among his remedies, tax relief stood foremost. The government should not mop up every kopek for its own needs and leave nothing for rural improvement. The tariff, too, was under fire, for the familiar reasons. In addition, Golovin's circle demanded that the government extend cheap credit to peasants and landowners so that they could undertake much-needed improvements on their land. The local crafts particularly needed official encouragement. Furthermore, the government should construct grain elevators and regulate the grain market in the interest of the producers. In short, the government should, by every available means, rebuild the prosperity of rural Russia. Only when the village was flourishing could—and should—industries arise; their markets would then be ready. But ever since Vyshnegradskii, Golovin charged, the government had put the cart before the horse. It had tried to develop a manufacturing industry artificially, without relation to the daily needs of the Russian people. And it had succeeded, up to a point, because the state was a "mechanical apparatus with huge powers, capable of putting into motion millions of rubles and millions of men." [54] But Russia remained poor, and even grew poorer. Moreover, the peasants drawn from the villages were transformed into proletarians, their dignity and creativity as human beings crippled by the heartless factories.

The hostility toward industry took many forms among the members of Golovin's circle. But they bore a special grudge toward foreign capital and foreign capitalists. It was asserted that the foreigners who invested in Russian industries cared only for their dividends and not for the economic advance of Russia. When they had made their fortune, they let their enterprises collapse. Occasionally they merely wanted to speculate on the stock market and

[53] *Ibid.*, p. 82. This, however, was denied by Gurko in his book *Ustoi narodnogo khoziaistva Rossii,* p. 7.

[54] Golovin, *Russlands Finanzpolitik,* pp. 5–6.

never bothered to visit Russia in person.[55] A goodly portion of what little wealth industrial Russia was producing was exported, Golovin charged, for the benefit of foreigners. It is only fair to add, however, that Golovin's group also bemoaned the loss of rubles spent abroad by Russians, estimated at about 69 million a year. Gurko suggested that, by order of the government, the volume of foreign travel be allowed to expand no further.[56]

Another target of criticism in Golovin's salon was Witte's statistics proving the rapid advance of Russian industry. It was said, for instance, that the official *Handbook for the Department of Trade and Industry for 1896* deliberately overestimated the value of the annual cotton textile production by adding the full value of the raw materials, semifinished goods, and finished articles. This naturally produced a much higher figure than the sales value of the final product, which, in the opinion of these men, was the only one that counted.[57] They also disputed Witte's figures showing that the industrial product of Russia outweighed in value her agricultural product; this simply was not so.[58] Statistics, according to Bentham, are king-size lies, and it was inevitable that the battle over Witte's statistics, the genesis of which was never adequately explained, should rage over an extended front. As the statistics were used to prove a point, so they invited contradiction to prove the opposite point.

The most trenchant criticism emanating from this group was levied against Witte's budgets.[59] Under Shvanebakh's withering scrutiny the glamour of Witte's accomplishments faded away. While Witte had contended, for instance, that the increased revenue of the government had reflected the increased prosperity of

[55] Gurko, *Ustoi*, pp. 76 ff.

[56] *Ibid.*, p. 129.

[57] Reported from G. Butmi, *Itogi finansogo khoziaistva s 1892 k 1903*, by Paul Rohrbach, *Preussische Jahrbücher*, CIX, 103.

[58] Wittschewsky, p. 280; also Golovin, *Russlands Finanzpolitik*, p. 133.

[59] For the following see Shvanebakh, *Nashe podatnoe delo* and *Denezhnoe preobrazhenie i narodnoe khoziaistvo*.

the country, Shvanebakh maintained that it was due, in large measure, to increased taxation. Witte had started his regime by raising existing taxes and asking for new ones; almost every year thereafter he had added to them. The Chinese troubles in 1900 had brought a further turn of the screw. Altogether, tax yields in Russia increased by 49 percent between 1893 and 1902, while the population had risen only 13 percent;[60] in some areas of Asiatic Russia the tax increase even amounted to 200 percent.[61] The indirect taxes on certain items, Shvanebakh wrote, had soared even faster than the general tax rate. Between 1889 and 1902 the tax on sugar had gone up more than twofold, likewise the tax on matches, and it had increased by one half on kerosene.[62] Five sixths of the tax revenue, according to Shvanebakh,[63] stemmed from indirect taxes that weighed particularly on the rural poor, inasmuch as matches, kerosene, tea, sugar, and even vodka were items of necessity. By contrast, Golovin and his friends were convinced that the urban-industrial population was taxed much less proportionally.

Among the other forms of revenue, Shvanebakh subjected the liquor monopoly to close scrutiny.[64] It was true that its receipts exceeded the income from the old liquor tax by nearly a quarter. But it was not the efficiency of the new agency, this *chinovnik* charged, but higher liquor prices which were responsible for the gain. As for the whole institution, despite the fine talk about the prevention of drunkenness and the government's concern for the spiritual and material welfare of the population, it was a simple fiscal "gadget" for increasing the government revenue,[65] without any effect whatever on the frequency of drunkenness. In addition, the added yield for the government was not an absolute benefit,

[60] Miliukov, *Russia and Its Crisis,* p. 442.
[61] Pogrebinskii, *Ocherki,* p. 198.
[62] Cited by Rohrbach, *Preussische Jahrbücher,* CIX, 99.
[63] Shvanebakh, *Nashe podatnoe delo,* p. 31.
[64] *Ibid.,* Chap. III.
[65] *Ibid.,* p. 66.

for the liquor monopoly deprived certain local administrative bodies, such as the peasant volost, of the revenue derived from licensing the taverns.

If from a fiscal point of view the liquor monopoly was a dubious enterprise, Russian railroad economy as reflected in the budget was still more so. Despite the reforms of the 1880s, Shvanebakh charged, the government still had to pay subsidies to inefficient private railroads. Its own roads, too, barely profitable in the latter part of the 1890s, began to operate at a loss when the long overland stretches of the Siberian road were opened. Altogether the deficit of all railroad operation in Russia under both private and state management amounted, in Shvanebakh's estimate, to some 70 million rubles between 1892 and 1899 alone.[66] It is safe to say that it rose toward the end of Witte's regime. Although Witte had promised that railroad expansion would provide an additional source of income to the government, it proved a constant drain. From an economic point of view, in short, it was a failure.

Shvanebakh clinched his point by his analysis of the budget for 1900.[67] He found that among certain nonrecurrent sources of income, valued at 127.2 million rubles, several were entirely fictitious and others considerably exaggerated. He thus reduced the entry to 85 million rubles. He then checked the figures given for the revenues from state enterprises, state railways, post and telegraph, state forests, and the vodka monopoly, the total revenue of which was listed as 597.6 million rubles. Upon examination it turned out that the 374 million rubles listed as revenue from the state railways consisted entirely of operating costs and had to be discounted. As a matter of fact, the state railways had had a deficit that year of 31.6 million rubles. In a similar manner Shvanebakh calculated the net revenue from post and telegraph at 15 million rubles (rather than the 50 million listed), from state forests at 40 million (instead of 55.7), and from the liquor mo-

[66] Shvanebakh, *Denezhnoe preobrazhenie,* p. 182.

[67] Shvanebakh, *Nashe podatnoe delo,* Chap. II, *passim.*

nopoly at 30.3 million (instead of 117.9). The relatively high net profit of the state forests, he discovered, was the result of unpardonable parsimony in their upkeep, for which future generations would have to pay. At the end, Shvanebakh had reduced Witte's impressive figure of 597.6 million rubles to a mere 54.2 million. Adding this figure to the 85 million from other sources mentioned above, he obtained the sum of 139.2 million rubles instead of Witte's 724.8. The total revenue recorded in the budget for 1900 had thus shrunk from 1.7041 billion to 1.1142 billion rubles.

It was no wonder, then, that the impressive increase in government revenues claimed by Witte was received with grave mistrust by his enemies. Sergei Sharapov, who was more reactionary than Golovin's friends, went even further and argued that the official figure for the increase of government revenue, given as 73 percent between 1890 and 1900, should be pared down to a mere 22 percent.[68] And that small rise was easily explained by the increase in taxation that had taken place in the meantime. That these figures were not computed by entirely irresponsible figuremongers may be seen from the fact, mentioned above, that the state controller likewise pared down from 110 percent to 42 percent Witte's claim of the increase in government revenue during his regime.

But then, if the government's revenues were not so great as Witte had claimed, how did he manage to balance the budgets? He did so, according to his enemies, partly by the simple bookkeeping device of unloading every conceivable expense from the ordinary into the extraordinary budget, and conversely by placing every conceivable item of income into the ordinary budget. The charges for new railroad construction, for instance, the acquisition of private roads by the state, and loans to private railroad companies were carried in the extraordinary budget, while the income from the new roads and the repayment of the loans were listed in the ordinary budget. The same applied to the acquisition

[68] Sharapov, Chaps. II, IX, and X.

of private liquor stores by the state monopoly. Why was the cost of acquiring them listed as an extraordinary expense, while the profits from them were entered as ordinary ones?[69]

The real reason for the balanced budgets, however, so Golovin's circle asserted, was that Witte constantly borrowed at home and abroad. In other words, underneath the brilliant façade of solvency the government operated at a permanent deficit. It avoided bankruptcy only by going ever deeper into debt. Between 1893 and 1902, Shvanebakh emphasized, the government debt had increased by one third. The gold obtained abroad was kept in foreign banks and through them paid out again as dividends to the holders of Russian stocks and bonds without ever reaching Russia.[70] But how could Witte obtain more and more new foreign loans to pay for the old ones? Shvanebakh replied that it was done on the basis of new railroad construction and the anticipated (though spurious) future earnings. As seen from this angle, railroad construction, and even industrialization as a whole, were no more than a huge hoax born of an inexorable fiscal necessity. Only with their aid could the budget be balanced.[71]

Foreign loans pledged for railroad construction had also a second and no less significant use. Considering the constant outflow of gold, the balance of payment sufficient for maintaining Russia's gold reserves could be preserved, even with an excessively high tariff, only by a constant influx of gold through such loans. Railroad construction and industrialization were thus indispensable accessories to the luxury of the gold standard.[72] Golovin and his friends preferred silver or at the most bimetallism as the basis for Russian currency.

If the government did not use its foreign loans for railroad con-

[69] See, for instance, the comments on the Russian budget in *Russkii trud* for the issues of January 18, 1902, or January 24, 1903. They follow closely the views of Shvanebakh.

[70] Shvanebakh, *Denezhnoe preobrazhenie,* p. 92.

[71] Migulin, *Russkii gosudarstvennyi kredit,* pp. 379–80; also Golovin, *Russlands Finanzpolitik,* pp. 54, 124.

[72] This view was also adopted by Pasvolsky and Moulton, p. 35.

struction, how did it pay for the tremendous growth of the railroad network that took place? The answer heard in Golovin's salon was that it was paid out of current domestic revenue and loans. Naturally his circle deplored the excessive mobilization of domestic capital for the purposes of the state. They called attention to the fact, for instance, that by forcing the savings banks to purchase government bonds Witte very largely preempted the savings of the Russian people for his ends. In 1900 more than half of the savings banks' deposits were invested in government securities and railway bonds.[73] These funds were spent by the government regardless of the wishes of the people who had earned that money by the sweat of their brows.

The condemnation of the Witte system in Golovin's salon ran the gamut of the objections heard among the opposition. But there were a number of other groups offering variations upon the common theme. While the temper of Golovin's circle was fairly reasonable, the defenders of the "Russian way" in industry and agriculture, who gathered around Sergei Sharapov's weekly *Russian Labor*, represented the voice of the old Russia threatened to its marrow and provoked to the point of desperation. In October, 1899, Sharapov himself accused Witte, to judge by a memorandum found among the papers of Nicholas II, not only "of making mistakes, but of deliberately committing crimes." [74]

The mentality of this group may best be gathered from their program. They aimed at "the cultivation of a clear and healthy form of Russian economic thought and the creation of a Russian theory based on the facts, figures, and conditions of Russian life and the true psychology of the Russian people" [75]—the old will-o'-the-wisp. The group's thinking on economic problems was outlined

[73] Pogrebinskii, *Ocherki,* p. 123; also Liashchenko, *Istoriia,* II, 155–56.

[74] *Materialy po istorii SSSR,* VI, 217.

[75] *Russkii trud,* 1897, No. 1. After the suppression of *Russkii trud* in 1899, Sharapov received a subsidy for his plow factory until his death in 1911. See I. F. Gindin, "Neustavnye ssudi gosudarstvennago banka i ekonomicheskaia politika tsarskoi pravitel'stva," *Istoricheskie zapiski,* No. 35, 1950, p. 8711.

in an article by Prince Aleksei Shcherbatov.[76] He proposed that the "popular forces" of Russia be developed through the "proper exploitation of Russia's national wealth." By this he meant that the labor of the peasants and craftsmen be improved with the help of all local authorities, starting with the marshal of the nobility and running through the land captains, priests, teachers, doctors, feldshers, and ending with the volost and village elders. Needless to say, strict order was to be maintained in the countryside and "the moral foundations of society" strengthened.

Naturally Sharapov and his associates were violent protagonists of the village commune and the privileges of the landed gentry. For the big capitalist landowners they had no sympathy. But Sharapov also drew on the fears of the reactionary industrialists of Moscow and elsewhere. The tariff did not provoke him —although he too compared the high Russian prices with those prevailing in London!—but factory legislation aroused him all the more. He loathed the new terminology, heard even in the government, which distinguished between capital and labor. In Russia, he wrote, there was only the *khoziain*, the boss, who dealt with his mill hands as of old, on the basis of the "moral foundations" of society.[77] (And yet, why does one find among the advertisements in his paper foreign firms spreading their wares in Western tongues?)

In the name of Russian tradition Sharapov even doubted the wisdom of Witte's railroad program. Just witness, he exclaimed,[78] the dire consequences of a new railroad intruding into the village. The value of the forests rose, the woods were cut down to the detriment of the local population. The price of grain increased, the poor suffered. The prosperity caused by the demand for local labor and goods during construction was short-lived. The enterprising people moved away, but syphilis, brought in by the con-

[76] *Russkii trud,* 1898, No. 13, p. 7.

[77] *Ibid.,* 1899, No. 18, p. 12.

[78] *Ibid.,* 1899, No. 18, Sharapov's editorial.

struction crews, stayed on. Some peasants tried to improve their business, but nine times out of ten they failed for lack of capital. In short, the locomotive brought nothing but destruction to the natural order of society. Western European society, Sharapov reflected (not unjustly), was ready for the railroad, but the Russian village was not. "In economic life," he mused, "the chief and unconditional demand is for economic harmony, for planned relationships, for the proportionality and conformity of all parts." This harmony was being destroyed by Witte's policies. They flouted the traditional Russian yearning for an orderly and secure universe.

"What a terrible moment in the history of Russian culture!" Sharapov once cried out in an editorial.[79] "How will our great *narod* emerge from it?" The foundations were giving way under his eyes, and the machine of Russian economy was stopping completely. "Our well-organized neighbors thirst for the cultural collapse of the Russian colossus. And at home every kind of economic chicanery of Jews and foreigners has reached a new height." They sucked the blood from rich and poor alike and ruined Russian agriculture and industry. A crowd of foreigners were looting, as after a fire, the most important national riches. All this was made doubly easy by the "so-called sound money system." Sharapov was as fierce an enemy of the gold standard as William Jennings Bryan, whom he honored with a full-page picture and a lengthy eulogy. While some of his friends, like the economist Butmi, at least favored bimetallism, Sharapov held out uncompromisingly for a paper currency as the best medium for providing cheap credit to Russian agriculture and industry. It would keep out the foreigners and make Russia mistress again in her own household.

To Sharapov the Witte system appeared still more fraudulent than to Golovin. His own analysis, or that of his contributor Butmi, was more devastating, his picture of Russian realities gloomier, and his forecasts of disaster still shriller. He also ex-

[79] *Ibid.*, 1899, No. 1, the opening editorial.

pressed more vehemently than other critics two popular prejudices which were powerful political facts: the deep-seated dislike of foreign capital (which he shared with Golovin's circle) and anti-Semitism. Both Jews and foreign capital embodied the spearhead of the alien, subversive force of capitalism. They represented rationality, flexibility, cosmopolitanism, the ability to ferret out new opportunities, money-mindedness, materialism, the restlessness of modern life—all the virtues of an urban-industrial way of life, and also, no doubt, its faults. In his attacks on foreign capital, incidentally, Sharapov combined forces with the economist P. V. Ol', whose work is taken to this day as the most authoritative estimate of the penetration of foreign capital into Russia. Apart from his contributions to *Russian Labor*, however, Ol' never published his work under the tsarist regime. It was left to the Soviets to reveal the full extent of foreign economic penetration as compiled by one of tsarist Russia's most reactionary economists.[80]

There was no controversy over the quantity of Russian government bonds held abroad. The fact was that Russia was saddled with the largest foreign-owned national debt among the great powers. But what especially aroused Ol' and Sharapov was the increase in the private foreign investments. The figures cited by Ol' on the penetration by foreign capital in 1900 are indeed impressive. Of the securities of all metallurgical companies, 67 percent were foreign-owned; among the southern pig iron and steel producers it was 85 percent.[81] These were the highest figures, to be sure. In other branches the foreign component ran a trifle less than one half; for instance, among the biggest Polish metallurgical firms or the Donbas anthracite companies. Among the joint-stock companies engaged in transportation (principally railroads) it was 40.6 percent. In the textile industry, on the other hand, the foreign share was less than one fifth. In certain banks, too, according to a modern source, the foreigners owned consider-

[80] Ol', *Inostrannye kapitaly v khoziaistve dovoennoi Rossii,* also *Inostrannye kapitaly v Rossii.*

[81] Raud, p. 19.

able capital. In 1901, for instance, foreign banks held more than 20 percent of the capital in the St. Petersburg International Commercial Bank, a powerful institution headed by A. J. Rothstein.[82]

How much the new Russian industries were controlled from abroad was revealed by an article in *Russian Labor*[83] dealing with the Societé générale pour l'Industrie en Russie, which had been founded in Paris in 1896. Although not permitted to conduct business in Russia, this organization still controlled the fate of 47 of the biggest Russian companies in heavy industry. Among the members of this embryo syndicate were found such industrial giants as the Briansk Company, the Putilov works, the Russo-Belgian Company, the Sormovo factories, the Lena Gold Mining Company. The total capital assets of its members amounted to over 265 million rubles. More than one third of the directors and board members of the participating companies were foreigners. To Sharapov this was undeniable proof that Russia's national resources were shamefully exploited by outsiders.

From foreign financiers and Jews it was a short leap of the argument to the Russian Jews. They, too, Sharapov claimed, were increasing their power.[84] Of the 421 members of the First and Second Guild in St. Petersburg listed for 1896, so an article in *Russian Labor* explained, only 148, that is, 37 percent, were pure Russian; 18 percent were Jewish and the rest of foreign extraction. Since 1870 the Jewish element had increased by two thirds. In Moscow[85] matters were still worse: 37 percent of the members of the First Guild entitled to vote belonged to that faith. As an illustration of the influence of one of them—Poliakov—*Russian Labor* duly listed his vast holdings in real estate, railroads, industries, and banks. Anticapitalism, in short, also signified anti-Semitism.

[82] *Ibid.*, p. 23.

[83] In the article by Spiridon Bol'shakov in *Russkii trud,* 1898, No. 30, pp. 10 ff.

[84] *Ibid.*, 1898, No. 2.

[85] *Ibid.*, 1898, No. 46.

But to shift now from the reactionaries to the opposite camp and complete this survey of the anti-Witte arguments. P. P. Migulin, a professor of financial law at the University of Kharkov, compiled during Witte's term as minister of finance a detailed, stupendously dull study of the actions of the Russian ministers of finance since Reutern. The tone of his volumes was sympathetic; he even argued that all of Witte's foreign loans were necessitated by the crop failures which he encountered. But at the end an undercurrent of criticism broke through. By 1903 Migulin—after 1905 he emerged as an Octobrist—had ceased to defend the Witte system. Now he voiced many of the arguments heard in Golovin's salon, but added also a complaint of his own: Witte had not been doing enough for Russia.[86] Her means of communications were poorly developed, new railroad construction was badly planned, feeder lines were inadequate, and highway and water transportation was neglected. In agriculture, reforestation and irrigation were required to counteract the droughts. As for industry, a central industrial bank should provide credit for the exploitation of Russia's resources by Russian enterprise; foreign credit must be used with more caution and system. But above all, private enterprise was to be liberated from the tutelage of the government. Witte, "that true pillar of bureaucracy," [87] had killed what little spirit of private initiative existed. Industry in Russia had always been subject to interference by the government, but Witte had carried that tradition to an extreme.

While Migulin spoke for the industrialists of the Ukraine, Professor I. Kh. Ozerov of the University of Moscow, a true liberal, represented the interests of the Russian people as a whole, whether agricultural or industrial. His book *Economic Russia and Her Financial Policy* (1905), written with a fine awareness of the price paid for rapid economic change, was an excellent survey of Russian economic life at the end of the Witte era. Its theme was the

[86] Migulin, *Russkii gosudarstvennyi kredit,* Vol. III, Part II, pp. 413 ff.
[87] *Ibid.,* Part V, p. 1001.

common one: "Russia had wanted to take over the best of European industries, but they could not take hold" because of the basic poverty of the Russian people.[88] Industrialization, Ozerov warned, should not be hurried but must proceed organically, as in England, gradually expanding from small crafts into big industries as markets improved. The one aspect worth stressing amid the arguments already considered was Ozerov's denunciation of the tariff. While it benefited a few industries, he contended, the bulk of Russian enterprise was shielded from the necessity of improving its operations; the tariff thus slowed down or stifled industrial growth. It raised the price of new factories as much as 50 percent, Ozerov argued, over that prevalent in western Europe.[89] The tariff also encouraged trusts and syndicates and kept badly needed manufactured goods out of the reach of the villages. Let it be lowered by all means.

The views held among still more radical circles need not be cited here in detail; they added nothing new to the debate. Sentiment more than economic analysis determined the verdict, which may best be stated in the formulation of A. V. Peshekhonov, a *narodnik* writer: "No one has done more for the centralization of economic power in the hands of the government than Witte, and no one has done so much for the destruction of the *narod*."[90]

Such, then, were the conclusions of Witte's enemies. The government had channeled the earnings of the Russian people into industrial development to an unprecedented degree; it had also borrowed too freely abroad. But even with the utmost effort—an effort ruinous to the welfare of the people—it could not establish the new industries on a sound economic basis. What it bestowed on one branch of Russian economy it extorted from the others. It was engaged in a desperate gamble. Would the growing indebtedness and poverty of Russia be offset by her growing industrial productivity? Inasmuch as productivity depended on a widely

[88] Ozerov, *Ekonomicheskaia Rossiia,* p. 143.

[89] *Ibid.,* p. 61.

[90] Peshekhonov, *Ekonomicheskaia politika samoderzhaviia,* p. 5.

dispersed prosperity, on the development of new skills throughout the length and breadth of Russia—and inasmuch as all this was stifled by the Witte system—the gamble was bound to fail. Woven into these arguments was the outcry that Russia was a backward country, sometimes uttered as a reproach to the government which despite its exertions had made no headway, sometimes as a warning lest it speed up still further the unhealthy pace. And underlying all these accusations lay the yearning for a slow, organic economic development without sharp contrasts and dissonances. Thus from the hands of the opposition Witte's accomplishments emerged lusterless and battered, inspiring aversion and revolution.

And what, finally, do the Soviets think of the Witte system? Let it merely be said that Soviet historians, with due emphasis on the suffering of the toiling masses, have reiterated almost all the earlier criticisms, often confusing Witte's policies with the very conditions which they were to remedy. They resumed, more fiercely, the reproach first sounded by Migulin—not enough was done for the development of Russia's wealth; the Ural industries and Siberia were neglected, no rational plan for regional diversification was evolved, basic industries were left unfounded—and similar charges galore. Yet one finds bits of fairness as well. The most discriminating among the economic historians of Stalinist Russia, the late Professor Liashchenko (who printed one of his first scholarly articles in the *Russian Economic Review* published by the Ministry of Finance), has admitted, among his strictures, that Witte's policy not only played into the hands of the bourgeoisie or the Court but served "the broad needs of national economy and of the entire population." [91] All writers were bound, following a penetrating observation in Lenin's work on *The Development of Capitalism in Russia*, to point out that the dialectical incompatibility of Witte's progressive capitalism with the surrounding feudal-agrarian relationships in state and society acted as a brake upon industrialization.

[91] Liashchenko, *Istoriia,* II, 184.

The most rabid attack on the Witte system, characteristically enough, was contained in the general criticism of tsarist economic policy set forth in Stalin's *Short History of the Communist Party.* It asserted that the backwardness of Russia was intensified through its dependence on foreign capital. Stalin resumed the tradition of Sharapov when he called tsarism "the agent of Western imperialism for squeezing hundreds of millions of dividends from the population" and accused it of giving foreign capital "free access to such crucial branches of Russian economy as fuel and metallurgy." [92]

With such directives Soviet historians could hardly do justice to the great precursor of Stalinist industrialization. In more recent years, however, one can notice a perceptible softening in their views. Yet their basic grudge remains: The tsars did not raise Russia from her backwardness.

III

In evaluating the rival claims of Witte and his opponents, the modern historian has the saving advantage of hindsight. He cannot but recognize that the victorious expansion of the Western urban-industrial mode of life over the entire globe and the not unjustified fear among the "underdeveloped" countries of falling behind have decided the dispute over the priority of industry or agriculture in favor of the former. A League of Nations report of 1945 accepted as an incontrovertible truth "the fact that a country can usually secure a high degree of economic well-being only with the aid of domestic industry." It took for granted that "almost all countries should be anxious to possess a manufacturing industry." [93]

With this basic question categorically disposed of, adjudicating the various points of dispute between Witte and his opponents has become easier. To start with the controversy over statistics:

[92] Stalin, "Ob osnovakh leninizma," *Sochineniia,* VI, 75.

[93] League of Nations, *Industrialization and Foreign Trade,* p. 35.

Whatever the truthfulness of the data—finality, unfortunately, has been irretrievably washed down the river of time—one vital fact stands out. In the early and difficult phases of industrialization the announcement of favorable results is an indispensable morale builder. The small voice of Witte's budget reports with their figures on the high tempo of industrial growth was the prelude to the fanfare of statistics blared forth during the early five-year plans. In both cases it was necessary to convince the Russian people that the government's policy bore fruit and that their sacrifices were not in vain. In Witte's case, moreover, the all-important foreign creditor had to be reassured. Finally, Russia's rivals in the global struggle for power had to be shown that their gloating over her weakness was premature.

Considering all these inducements to put the best foot forward, there is no need to deny that Witte was tempted to adjust his statistics accordingly. But there was no evidence that they were deliberately fraudulent. The reproach, for instance, that he had overestimated the value of Russia's industrial product by adding the full value of raw materials, semifinished goods, and final product overlooked the fact that this was, in part, a matter of method. Computing such large aggregates is a difficult problem, but, by a Soviet admission, Witte's procedure was followed even in the Soviet Union.[94] As for the veracity of his budgets, informed contemporary opinion was divided. Henri Germain, the founder of the Credit Lyonnais, believed (so he at least told Bompard)[95] that the Russian budget was "perhaps the only sincere one in Europe, certainly more honest than the French budget"; he was loyal to Witte. The London *Economist*, on the other hand, treated all such claims with derision; it reflected the views of the opposition. The truth inclined perhaps toward the *Economist*. Yet, as with the offi-

[94] *Dinamika rossiiskoi i sovetskoi promyshlennosti,* Vol. I: *Svod statisticheskikh,* p. 45. This work was published in 1929. In 1960, however, S. G. Strumilin, in a book entitled *Ocherki sotsialisticheskoi ekonomii SSSR,* admitted the exaggerations resulting from this method.

[95] Bompard, pp. 35–36.

cial statistics, so with the budgets, political necessity forced the Russian Minister of Finance to radiate boundless optimism.

Next, let us examine the criticism of Witte's railroad management. Was it his fault that traffic was slow, the equipment poor and insufficient? The answer lay in two facts, as he himself pointed out after his retirement. First, Russia was a vast country with many empty spaces, and, second, many lines had a political and strategic rather than a purely commercial purpose—they could not produce a surplus.[96] Even the commercial lines did not always run through densely populated areas. Witte could have made an even stronger case by asking whether the Russian public wished to pay the higher fares necessary for making their railroads profitable within a short time after their construction. To be sure, the subsidy which the government paid to the users of the railroads (it was estimated to amount to 12 million rubles for Russian agriculture)[97] came from the taxpayers' purses. But who could deny that it was spent in a highly productive manner? It was a necessary investment for economic development in every respect. If Witte's railroad construction was costly and the results still inadequate—and if to this day Soviet rail transportation has been a troublesome bottleneck to further progress—the chief culprit is the fact, of which Russians have never ceased to boast, that their country covers one sixth of the world's land surface. Long distances and extensive wastelands made everything more costly, transportation as well as industrial production in general.

Speaking of industry and particularly heavy industry, should the government have let slip the timely opportunity of expanding these crucial branches of domestic industry? In the charters granted to the transcontinental railroads the Congress of the United States decreed that they use American steel. Was the Russian government not entitled to the same expedient? This was all

[96] Witte, "Prichiny ubytochnosti russkikh zheleznykh dorog," *Vestnik finansov,* 1911, No. 16, pp. 101 ff.

[97] Zagorskii, p. 19.

the more logical since in Witte's theory these heavy industries occupied a central place as the "manufacturers of manufactories." To judge by the experience of the other great powers, self-sufficiency constituted an asset. And even though during the depression the market for these industries had temporarily shrunk, the equipment and skills had become a part of Russian economy destined to serve long into the Soviet period (sometimes even to the present day). If the prices of their products remained high, the fault lay by no means with the rapacious foreigners alone but with more impersonal factors such as the distances between Russia and western Europe and between the economic centers within Russia, with the ignorance of Russian labor, the sluggishness of her business community, the undeveloped state of her credit facilities, the red tape encountered in opening and running a factory, and with a thousand other peculiarities of state and society. The high prices for manufactured goods (and often shoddy ones at that) were but the cash measurements of Russian backwardness.

We come, then, to the charge that taxation under the Witte system was excessive. Assuming again that rapid railroad construction and industrialization were necessary, the first question was how to finance them. Was there any other way than through heavy taxation? Taxation transferred the earnings of the people to the government and allowed the investment in capital goods of the highest priority. Given the agrarian orientation of the Russian people and their propensity for buying imported articles of consumption, they themselves, it is safe to say, would never have chosen the same productive investments. Heavy taxation also dried up all excess purchasing power and prevented the inflation usually associated with boom periods. The "protective tariff" constituted another inevitable impost, reducing Russian purchases abroad to a minimum and permitting the creation of a stable currency. What if, as Professor Ozerov had said, the tariff retarded industrial progress! It was the lesser evil as compared with the miseries of a paper currency and the waste of much scarce capital on foreign delicacies. Was it realistic to expect that poverty should have no penalties?

Next, let us examine in some detail the reproaches about the influx of foreign capital. There was indeed evidence of an unwelcome dependence. The debtor always surrenders some freedom of action to his creditor; the Russian government was no exception. Under Witte this dependence inevitably deepened. It increased in two ways, (1) through the sale abroad of state bonds and (2) through the power of foreign investors and their governments over private enterprise. Both heaped complications on the Russian government. In 1897 and again in 1899, for instance, the French government protested the sale of a Russian loan on the Paris bourse. In 1900 it refused all listings of Russian securities. The decision was changed only when Witte, much against his conviction, consented to the construction of strategic railroads which strengthened Russia's defenses but also constituted a liability to the Treasury.[98] In the same tradition, Bompard, the French ambassador after 1903, accused Witte of claiming too freely the French money market as his special reservoir for Russian needs.[99] In order to overcome such resentment the Russian Treasury had to pay a high price in constant subsidies to the French press and fat commissions to the Paris bankers.

The depression, of course, further deepened the dependence of the government on its foreign creditors. When, for instance, several foreign-owned southern metallurgical companies ran into difficulty, their French stockholders undertook a press campaign against Witte, charging that the debacle of these firms suited him because he could acquire them cheaply for Russian owners. In the wake of the Dreyfus affair Russia's economic conditions, indeed, temporarily became an issue in French domestic politics. The anti-Semitic press under Drumont, stung by the victory of the Dreyfusards, accused the Waldeck-Rousseau government of irresponsi-

[98] See Feis, pp. 140, 219; also Anan'ich, p. 196.
[99] Bompard, p. 34.

bility toward the French investors in Russian securities. Against this hostility—or was it blackmail?—Witte was forced to raise the subsidies to the French press by 160,000 francs.[100] At the same time the French ambassador conveyed to Witte the wishes of Caillaux that the Russian government provide a subsidy for the Briansk Company, one of the big southern metallurgical enterprises founded by French capital. Witte, after protesting at first, heeded these costly commands "for the sake of good relations with the French government." [101] He again swallowed his objections when French bankers in the Société Générale pour l'Industrie en Russie organized the syndicate Prodameta, which became one of the first big industrial syndicates of tsarist Russia.[102] (The creation of a similar organization for the marketing of coal, Produgol, was likewise engineered from Paris in 1904.) Witte, it seems, would have preferred to let matters take their course toward a much needed drop in metal prices, but under French pressure he promised to leave the syndicate alone unless it took actions flagrantly prejudicial to Russian interests.

These examples show that while it is easy to exaggerate the degree of foreign domination, the moments of weakness when the Russian government was forced to bow to its creditors were neither infrequent nor inconsequential. In those years the Russian government, and not least the Tsar himself, found their freedom of action painfully restrained by Russia's dependence upon her foreign creditors. Above all, the reactionary elements, anti-Semitic and antiforeign, revolted against this bridle upon their spontaneity. Witte, on the other hand, who spoke in his *Memoirs* of Baron Alphonse Rothschild, the senior member of the House of Rothschild, as of an old friend, seems to have felt no emotional aversion to the indirect controls exercised by western Europe. But even he

[100] "S. Iu. Vitte, frantsuzskaia pressa i russkie zaimy," *KA*, X, 40.

[101] See particularly O. Crisp, "Some Problems of French Investment in Russian Joint Stock Companies," *Slavonic and East European Review*, Vol. XXXV, No. 84 (December, 1956); also Anan'ich, pp. 210 ff.

[102] Crisp, *Slavonic and East European Review*, XXXV, 224.

protested the presumption of the French government in meddling in the internal affairs of Russia.

Obviously, reliance on foreign capital had its patent and humiliating disadvantages. But considering the scarcity of Russian capital, was it not wise under the circumstances to take the utmost advantage of foreign savings and know-how while they were available on good terms? According to Professor B. F. Brandt, whom Witte commissioned to compile a scholarly justification,[103] foreign capital employed Russian labor, which otherwise would go idle. Through contact with foreign experts and equipment, Russian technicians acquired new skills that became a national asset. Foreign-owned factories were built with Russian bricks and timber; hence these branches of Russian industry quickened. Land values in the vicinity of the new factories increased, shopkeepers found new customers. Even if the foreigners spent their fat profits abroad—after all, they had to be given some incentive for investing in Russia—the impetus imparted to the economic life of the country was invaluable and lasting.

And to extend the argument: Would the industries of southern Russia have risen so soon without the help of John Hughes and the French and Belgian investors, or the Baku oil wells without the Nobel Brothers? Or, to refute a Stalinist sneer, was it not to the interest of the foreign investors to use the most advanced techniques suitable to Russian conditions? For the sake of their profit alone (not to speak of the political advantages which France derived from a prosperous Russia) they had no incentive for retarding the industrial development of Russia. It was not their fault if Russian conditions did not always permit the application of the latest technical innovations or if some of the new equipment soon became outdated in the rapid advance of Western technology. Thus it would seem that Russian pride rather than sound economy waged war against foreign capital.

What of those fat profits of foreign-owned companies which

[103] B. F. Brandt, *Inostrannye kapitaly,* Part I *passim.*

aroused so much comment in the Russian press? Here, as in other issues, the facts have been interpreted to confirm preconceived conclusions. The economist Taburno, moderately critical of Witte, assumed the profits of foreign capital to range from 5 to 9 percent in the years 1890 to 1899.[104] A Soviet writer citing contemporary sources on foreign enterprises in the Donets and Krivoi Rog regions put them much higher, between 51 and 84 percent in the years 1894 to 1896.[105] Pro-Witte sources gave a different impression. According to figures released by the *Financial Messenger* for the years 1897 and 1898, out of sixty foreign enterprises in mining and metallurgy, three paid dividends of more than 20 percent, five between 10 and 16 percent, eighteen between 5 and 10 percent. The remaining thirty-four enterprises either operated at a loss, disappeared after one year, paid no dividend, or, in the case of three of them, paid only between 1.3 and 3.5 percent.[106] Another set of figures was issued by the Statistical Bureau of the Congress of Southern Mines and Metallurgical Enterprises[107] for the years 1898 to 1900, good years again. They showed that in 1898 the average dividend paid by coal mines of both foreign and domestic ownership was about 4½ percent (the maximum was 13 percent). In metallurgy the rate was higher: 16 percent on the average, with a maximum of 40 percent. The next year dividends in coal fell to a mere 1.97 percent, although one company (a Russian one) paid 30 percent; in metallurgy they remained about the same. In 1900 profits fell to 1.14 percent in coal (with a maximum of 10 percent) and to 11.6 percent in metallurgy (with a maximum of 30 percent). The company with the fattest dividends in metallurgy, the South Russian Dnieper Metallurgical Company, was indeed a foreign one; the single instance proved the accusations.

[104] Taburno, p. 121.

[105] Nesterenko, p. 29.

[106] Quoted by Brandt, *Inostrannye kapitaly,* Part II, pp. 236–37.

[107] Statisticheskoe biuro soveta s"ezda gornopromyshlennikov iuga Rossii, *Balansy* (*otchët*) *gornozavodskikh aktsionernykh i paevykh predpriiatii iuzhnoi Rossii* (*1898, 1899, 1900, 1901 gg.*), Part I, 1903, p. 16.

The truth, perhaps, lay closest to the estimates of the economist Ol', who could not be accused of any sympathy for foreign capital (or Witte). He computed the average yearly return on foreign capital as follows: between 6.1 and 7.4 percent for the years 1890 to 1893, and between 4.8 and 8.9 percent for 1894 to 1900, which would not seem excessive.[108]

The resort to foreign capital logically justified the introduction of the gold standard. It was the best lubricant for the transfer of Western savings and skills to Russia. The alternative of complete financial isolation, suggested by Sharapov and eventually carried out by the Soviet government, was unthinkable at the end of the nineteenth century. The basic decision to employ foreign capital had already been made under Alexander II. It could not be repudiated in Witte's time without disastrous consequences. Furthermore, when all Russians, and not least the reactionaries like Sharapov, were absorbing, with spongelike eagerness, European standards in all phases of their lives, they would hardly have condoned the cultural isolation imposed by an economic curtain. The fact was that, from any angle, the gold standard was a sign of international respectability. The Russian state could not ignore it, even though it could barely afford the luxury of this particular kind of economic efficiency.

The Russian capitalists themselves are often held to have been the sole beneficiaries of the Witte system. Who else could have been trusted to invest capital where it contributed most, surely not the peasants or the landed nobility? The Witte system was, in a way, a gigantic wager on the capitalists. No wonder the Ministry of Finance tried its best to strengthen their position. If it wanted to encourage native capital accumulation, the business community was the logical repository. That Witte's policy rapidly bore fruit may be gathered from the increased rate of domestic capital accumulation in the first decade of the twentieth century. The more

[108] Ol', *Inostrannye kapitaly v khoziaistve dovoennoi Rossii,* p. 25.

wealth was created within Russia, the more the country could free itself from its foreign creditors.

But what about the backwardness of Russia? With this accusation Witte's critics charged through an open door. Within the decorum set for a minister of finance he openly admitted the fact. He constantly cited statistics (or had them compiled)[109] proving that Russia, despite the rapid tempo of her industrial growth, was still far behind the western European countries or the United States. The conclusion which he drew from these dismal proofs was the obvious one that Russia should exert itself to the utmost. It was the most powerful argument which Friedrich List had taught him. It justified the forced tempo of industrialization to all those who would have preferred a slow, organic growth. "Under the present conditions of economic development in various countries," Witte's spokesman, Professor Brandt, wrote in 1898, "the 'natural course of events' will only widen the gap which separates the economically backward countries from the advanced ones and will lead to the full economic subjugation of the former by the latter." [110] But even with the utmost exertions, Brandt conceded, Russia had little chance of catching up because the advanced countries were developing even more rapidly. Only the employment of additional capital from abroad gave Russia its chance—and a slim chance at that.

Nor was Witte deterred by the poverty of his country; he was fully aware of it. But he realized that the popular remedy, which was to lower taxes and the tariff, would not work. It was fair to assume that the increased spending would largely go to European imports, and after a brief spree the penalties of living beyond the country's means would have to be paid in full. Russia would be left still further impoverished.

On sober thought there was only the paradoxical and grim

[109] See the various books by Gulishambarov.

[110] Brandt, *Inostrannye kapitaly,* pp. 69–70.

choice between remaining poor by spending the available national income according to the wishes of the majority of the Russian people, and spending it wastefully, or, on the other hand, remaining poor by investing, under autocratic control, every available kopek in the development of the means of production. Neither alternative held out much hope. The former might for a time permit the illusion of Europeanization; the latter offered at least a chance of action, the opportunity for a heroic effort to win lost ground in the future. But even at best—and this much may readily be conceded to Witte's opponents—the utmost effort did not guarantee that the gap between an underdeveloped Russia and the rapidly advancing countries of the West could ever be closed. The more she tried to catch up, the more she fell behind.

IV

In conclusion let us touch on a few basic problems transcending purely economic analysis. Could a capitalist Russia, such as Witte envisaged, build up the necessary industrial base for Russian power? As noted above, the Witte system was a gigantic wager on the part of the Russian capitalists. Would they—or the population at large—be able to acquire the quick grasp, the willingness to take risks, or the dynamic mentality of, say, the American entrepreneur and voluntarily undertake what was necessary to advance Russian industries? Would the Russian capitalists, as they gained wealth and power in the community, also be able to earn, let alone retain, the goodwill of all the other groups of Russian society, so that the necessary social harmony in the body politic could be preserved? And, finally, could the government, concerned with the insufficient power of Russia in an age of imperialism, really permit the fullest development of private initiative?

The relationship of the capitalist elements, kulaks, *kuptsy*, and the various groups of foreign businessmen and experts to Russian society at large cannot be discussed here in detail. Suffice it to say that, judging by Russian literature in general and the press of the 1890s in particular, they were highly unpopular, and for reasons which their success was likely to aggravate. Given the peculiarities of Russian society, there was little hope of a reconciliation in the foreseeable future. On the contrary, the tensions were bound to increase.

The role of the government, however, calls for more specific comment. Was not the Witte system itself—quite apart from the negative attitude of the Tsar and most officials—an obstacle to free enterprise, as Professor Migulin had charged?

This raises the theoretical problem as to where the boundary between state action and private enterprise should lie. John Stuart Mill, in his *Essay on Liberty*, wrote:

> A government cannot have too much of the kind of activity which does not impede, but aids and stimulates, individual exertion and development. The mischief begins when, instead of calling forth the activities and powers of individuals and bodies, it substitutes its own activity for theirs; when instead of informing, advising, and, upon occasion, denouncing, it makes them work in fetters, or bids them stand aside and does their work instead of them.

Witte, too, subscribed to this ideal. He had told Grand Duke Mikhail Aleksandrovich that the true creator in modern society was the citizen. "Not to stifle independent action, but to develop its strength by creating favorable conditions for its application, that is the true obligation which in our time the state must discharge toward our ever more complex national economy." [111] The protective tariff, better communications, public works of all sorts, subsidies, the promotion of technical education, and all the other well-meant efforts of the Witte system were designed "to aid and stimulate individual exertion and development."

But did the mischief of state intervention not arise in the very process of carrying out this encouragement? Witte foisted the competition of foreign capital upon unwilling Russian merchants,

[111] Witte, *Konspekt lektsii,* p. 132.

granted subsidies to favored industries while slighting others, licensed the establishment of new industries, placed his men on the boards of banks, railroads, and industrial companies. Rather than let Russian capitalists make their own mistakes and learn by themselves, he predetermined the nature of their experiments by his policy of rapid industrialization. In short, at the very moment when the Minister of Finance began to exhort the Russian *kupechestvo* to modernize their ways, he interfered with their spontaneity. He steered the economic development of Russia into an alien channel, substituting state activity for private initiative. He was thus caught in the basic paradox of a backward country that wanted to catch up to the "capitalist" model. In order to prepare the opportunities for private initiative he had to limit them. While he tried his best to recreate the conditions of Western capitalism in Russia, he made the capitalists the servants of the state. As long as any disparity between the views of the *kupechestvo* and the government remained, the government always had the last word.

Mill's philosophy thus did not express the purpose of a Russian minister of finance. Witte might more aptly have quoted Jeremy Bentham: "Whether government should intervene should depend on the extent of the power, intelligence, and inclination and therefore the spontaneous initiative possessed by the public." [112] In Russia, the public (including the *kupechestvo*) would not spontaneously accomplish the modernization of Russian economy; the state had to do that. "In Russia under Nicholas II," so one might amend another of Bentham's dicta, "the list of *sponte acta* being a blank, that of *agenda* was proportionally abundant." Witte, in contradiction to his liberal theory, had to take over the agenda on behalf of the state. But in doing so he crippled the sense of independence and dynamic initiative which is such an essential ingredient of Western urban-industrial society.

The lessons to be drawn from this digression are two: first, that

[112] Quoted by Nurkse, p. 16.

the Imperial government, charged with the preservation of Russia's sovereignty, could never become a mere mouthpiece of the bourgeoisie; second and more significant, that the Witte system suffered from a profound contradiction. The freedoms of the Western model were incompatible with government initiative in the Russian tradition. Only socialism could avoid, in theory at least, the incompatibility (without, however, removing the basic flaw).

Witte's experiment was foredoomed to failure in still another sense. In essence, as the foregoing will have made clear, his policy of industrialization was undemocratic. It could not be otherwise, because the gulf between his own knowledge of modern economy and that of the bulk of the Russian people was too wide to be bridged by simple argument. All Russians were drawn into the charmed circle of European standards, even the most reactionary adherents of "the Russian way." But while they craved the goods and services which western Europe offered, they also wanted to keep their native tradition—an agrarian tradition. They refused to change their ways, blind to the incompatibility between their mode of life and that which produced these goods and services. Witte, whose eyes were wide open to these discrepancies, was almost alone in advocating the necessary reforms. His chief measures, the tariff and the gold standard, were carried through by authority of autocracy. Like his policy of industrialization in general, they would never have found majority support under a parliamentary regime. His system broke down the moment the Tsar was forced to make concessions to public opinion. How, one wonders, could his policy of industrialization have been carried out long enough to take effect?

Could it have been joined to the contemporaneous process of political Europeanization, to the desires of many Russians for constitutional government? To Witte Westernization meant forced industrialization, to the Russian liberals a Russian parliament. But constitutional government, as has just been said, precluded rapid industrialization; Russian liberalism was largely agrarian in orientation and opposed to foisting economic sacrifices upon the population. Thus List's dictum that constitutional government favored industrialization did not apply to a backward country like Russia. Sooner or later the incompatibility would break into the open. It was clear, then, that under Russian conditions the Western model could not be adopted in its entirety, with both its industrial and constitutional components. Russians had to choose between freedom and power.

If industrialization was incompatible with the ideal of popular government, it was so also with autocracy, at least as practiced by Nicholas II. It demanded, as Witte had sensed, a more virile authority able to accomplish drastic reforms within the government itself. What was needed first of all, it would seem, was stricter centralization and a unity of purpose, which would throw the weight of the entire government behind industrialization. By the same logic, industrialization called for an all-out effort by the government to enlist the energies of its subjects, to arouse their enthusiasm for the new way of life, and, most basically, to mold their habits and values so as to make them conform, voluntarily or involuntarily, to its discipline. In order to achieve this the government had to obtain a firmer hold over the minds and actions of its subjects and overcome their deep-seated suspicion of government authority in any form. In other words, the new autocracy toward which Witte groped was to rally both government and people to one common, almost superhuman effort. This was the lesson which linked the Witte system with the Soviet regime. It ruled out spontaneity not only in domestic politics but also in the economy. It was a lesson which Witte himself, in his conscious mind, would certainly have rejected.

Yet, in the last analysis, it was the only one that accorded with his deepest motives. "If . . . threats from without confront a Russia that has not strengthened her economy, then posterity will rightly reproach us for not having . . . set the country on its feet." In the face of such threats there was no time for spontaneity, no security for giving priority to social welfare. Witte's case, in contrast to that of his critics who thought in terms of popular well-being, was squarely based on the exigencies of power politics. On that ground it is indeed difficult to refute him. As Thucydides had observed, societies like individuals are engaged in a constant wrangle for ascendancy. The great powers in the late nineteenth century vied with each other for domination in Europe and throughout the globe. In their rivalry they reduced empires like China or Ottoman Turkey to spheres of influence or reservoirs of territorial booty. A weak Russia was exposed, as two world wars were soon to prove, to a profound challenge to its existence.

Few Russians were able to understand the logic of Witte's pleas. It was another tragedy of Imperial Russia that its subjects did not comprehend the long chain of necessities relating their personal well-being to the sovereignty of their government. Russian opinion was misled by the Western model. In the relative security of the Western powers all too few theorists of democratic welfare have kept in mind the truism that being ruled by native masters is a primary ingredient of popular happiness.

In his last budget report, when all other arguments had failed him, Witte fell back upon this truth as his ultimate justification:

> What requirement is the most pressing? Obviously that on which the very existence of the country depends, its invulnerability from without. For this purpose the people give their personal service and pay most of the taxes, receiving in return the priceless consciousness not to be measured by material benefits that under the guidance of their Imperial Ruler every one of Your Majesty's faithful subjects, his family, his property, and his native land, are safe from foreign foes. From an economic, humanitarian point of view it is to be regretted that mankind is not imbued with the high ideal of universal peace. Nevertheless, at the present age we are in the grip of an iron law which decrees that the requirements of culture may be satisfied only from what remains after the expenditures for defense have been covered.

If the Russian government did not heed that iron law and failed to put the country on its feet, Witte's argument implied, then its subjects would have no chance whatsoever of catching up and rebuilding that deeper sovereignty, that native originality, which would permit their country to hold its own in the cultural, economic, and political competition of the modern world. Without power, native creativity in any field of human endeavor could not unfold to its fullest potential. And yet, any "artificial" effort to hasten these results was bound, as these pages have shown, to lead to more suffering, ill will, and renewed weakness.

What citizen of the great powers of the West, immensely favored by prosperity and easily maintained power as he is, dare gloat over the abysmal tragedies inherent in Russian backwardness?

Glossary of Russian Terms

chinovnik — a holder of a rank (*chin*) in the Imperial bureaucracy

duma — an agency of self-government for the larger towns, elected by the wealthy property owners but closely supervised by the government (not to be confused with the Imperial Duma after 1905)

kupets (pl. *kuptsy*) — a member of the merchant community (*kupechestvo*), organized in two guilds, the industrialists belonging, generally, to the second guild

kustar' — a peasant craftsman

mir — the peasant commune, also called *obshchina*

narod — the people, the peasant masses

narodnik — a member of the Russian intelligentsia who identified himself with the *narod*

obshchina — the peasant commune

sanovnik — an officeholder of the highest rank in the Imperial bureaucracy

soslovie — social class or category. Russian law classified every Russian subject (except Jews and nomads, who stood outside the law) by their *soslovie*. To mention only the most important: the peasants, the *kupechestvo,* and the landed nobility.

uezd — an administrative unit within the province, comparable, say, to a county or township

volost — an agency of peasant self-government comprising a number of peasant communes, supervised by local agents of the government

Measures:

one dessiatine	2.7 acres
one pood	36.11 lbs.
one ruble	about 50¢ in American currency (as of 1900)
one verst	0.66 mile

Bibliography

Admiralteiskie izhorskie zavody: Kratkii istoricheskii ocherk [The Izhorsk Factories of the Admiralty: A Brief Historical Sketch], ed. G. Gorodkovyi. St. Petersburg, 1903.

Adresnaia kniga fabrichno-zavodskoi i remeslennoi promyshlennosti vsei Rossii [Directory of Industries and Crafts in All Russia], ed. A. V. Pogozhev. St. Petersburg, 1905. The data are for the years 1900–1902.

Ainzaft, S. *Zubatovshchina i Gaponovshchina* [The Zubatov and Gapon Movements]. 4th ed. Moscow, 1925.

Akademiia Nauk SSSR. *Istoriia Moskvy* [The History of Moscow]. Vol. V: *Period imperializma i burzhuaznodemokraticheskikh revoliutsii* [The Period of Imperialism and Bourgeois-democratic Revolutions]. Moscow, 1955.

—— *Ocherki istorii Leningrada* [Essays on the History of Leningrad]. Vol. III: *Period imperializma i burzhuaznodemokraticheskikh revoliutsii* [The Period of Imperialism and Bourgeois-democratic Revolutions]. Moscow, 1956.

—— Institut istorii. *Materialy po istorii SSSR* [Materials on the History of the USSR]. Vol. VI: *Dokumenty po istorii monopolisticheskogo kapitalizma v Rossii* [Documents on the History of Monopoly Capitalism in Russia]. Moscow, 1959.

—— —— Leningradskoe otdelenie. *Monopolisticheskii kapital v neftianoi promyshlennosti Rossii, 1883–1914: Dokumenty i Materialy* [Monopoly Capitalism in the Russian Oil Industry, 1883–1914: Documents and Materials]. Moscow-Leningrad, 1961.

—— Trudy leningradskogo otdeleniia instituta istorii. *Iz istorii imperializma v Rossii* [From the History of Imperialism in Russia]. Moscow-Leningrad, 1959.

—— —— *Monopolii i inostrannyi kapital v Rossii* [Monopolies and Foreign Capital in Russia]. Moscow-Leningrad, 1962.

Akademiia Nauk SSSR, Institut Ekonomii. *Ocherki razvitiia narodnogo khoziaistva Ukrainskoi SSR* [Essays on the Development of the Economy of the Ukrainian SSR]. Kiev, 1954.

—— Istoricheskii institut. *Ocherki razvitiia narodnogo khoziaistva Ukrainskoi SSR* [Essays on the Development of the Economy of the Ukrainian SSR]. Moscow, 1954.

Aksenov, S. S. "Polozhenie fabrichno-zavodskoi promyshlennosti i rabochikh Ekaterinoslavskoi gubernii v 1899–1900 gg." [The Condition of Industry and the Workers in Ekaterinoslav Province in 1899–1900], in *Pamiatnaia kniga Ekaterinoslavskoi gubernii za 1903* [Notebook for Ekaterinoslav Province for 1903]. Ekaterinoslav, 1903.

Albom uchastnikov Vserossiiskoi promyshlennoi i khudozhestvennoi vystavki v Nizhnem Novgorode [Album of the Participants in the All-Russian Industrial and Artistic Exhibit at Nizhni-Novgorod]. Nizhni-Novgorod, 1896.

Alexander, Grand Duke of Russia. *Once a Grand Duke*. New York, 1933.

Almanakh sovremennykh russkikh gosudarstvennykh deiatelei [Almanac of Contemporary Russian Government Officials]. St. Petersburg, 1897.

Ames, E. "A Century of Russian Railroad Construction, 1837–1936," *American Slavic and East European Review,* Vol. VI, Nos. 18–19, 1947.

Anan'ich, B. V. "Russkoe samoderzhavie i vneshnye zaimy v 1898–1902 gg." [Russian Autocracy and Foreign Loans, 1898–1902], in Akademiia Nauk SSSR, Trudy leningradskogo otdeleniia instituta istorii, *Iz istorii imperializma v Rossii.*

Annenskii, N. "Obshchiia techeniia finansovoi politiki gosudarstva" [The General Course of the Government's Financial Policy], in *Nuzhdy derevni: Sbornik* [The Needs of the Village: A Collection]. St. Petersburg, 1904.

Anspach, A. *La Russie économique et l'oeuvre de M. de Witte*. Paris, 1904.

Antropov, P. A. Finanso-statisticheskii atlas Rossii, 1885–1895 [Financial-statistical Atlas of Russia, 1885–1895]. St. Petersburg, 1898.

Arkhiv istorii truda [Archive of Russian Labor]. Moscow, 1921–24; continued under the title *Trud v Rossii* [Labor in Russia], 1924–25.

Aulagnon, S. *La Sibirie économique*. Paris, 1901.

Babey, A. M. *Americans in Russia, 1776–1917*. New York, 1938.

Badmaev, P. A. *Desiatyi doklad Ministera Finansov S. Iu. Vitte i vzgliady teoretikov i praktikov po voprosam sel'sko-khoziaistvennoi zhizni v Rossii* [The Tenth Report of Finance Minister S. Iu. Witte and the Views of Theorists and Practitioners on the Questions of Agricultural Life in Russia]. St. Petersburg, 1902.

Baedeker, K. *Russia with Teheran, Port Arthur, and Peking.* Leipzig, 1914.

Balov, A. "Sanitarnye nedochety nashei derevni" [Sanitary Deficiencies in Our Village], *Russkaia mysl',* Vol. II, January, 1903.

Baring, M. *What I Saw in Russia.* London, 1927.

Baturinskii, D. A. *Agrarnaia politika tsarskogo pravitel'stva i krest'ianskii pozemel'nyi bank* [The Agrarian Policy of the Tsarist Government and the Peasant Land Bank]. Moscow, 1925.

Baykov, A. "The Economic Development of Russia," *Economic History Review,* Vol. VII, No. 2, December, 1954.

Belokonskii, I. P. *Zemskoe dvizhenie* [The Zemstvo Movement]. 2d ed. Moscow, 1914.

Benckendorff, Count Constantine. *Half a Life: The Reminiscences of a Russian Gentleman.* London, 1954.

Berard, V. *L'empire russe et le tsarisme.* Paris, 1905.

Berdaev, N. *The Russian Idea.* New York, 1948.

Berlin, P. A. *Russkaia burzhuaziia v staroe i novoe vremia* [The Russian Bourgeoisie Past and Present]. Moscow, 1922.

Bernshtein-Kogan, S. *Chislennost', sostav i polozhenie peterburgskikh rabochikh* [The Number, Composition, and Condition of the St. Petersburg Workers]. St. Petersburg, 1910.

Beveridge, A. I. *The Russian Advance.* New York, 1904.

Bezrukov, A. *Sormovo, 1848–1908* [Sormovo, 1848–1908]. Nizhni-Novgorod, 1925.

Bilimovich, A. D. *Tovarnoe dvizhenie na russkih zheleznykh dorogakh* [Freight Movement on Russian Railroads]. St. Petersburg, 1902.

Bill, V. T. *The Forgotten Class.* New York, 1959.

—— "The Morosovs," *The Russian Review,* Vol. XIV, No. 2, April, 1955.

Bliumin, I. G. *Ocherki ekonomicheskoi mysli v Rossii v pervoi polovine XIX veka* [Essays on Russian Economic Thought in the First Half of the Nineteenth Century]. Moscow, 1940.

Bloch, J. *Les Finances de la Russie au XIX siècle.* Paris, 1899.

Blum, J. *Lord and Peasant in Russia from the Ninth to the Nineteenth Century.* Princeton, 1961.

Blum, M. L. *Industrial Psychology and Its Foundations.* New York, 1956.

B——o, N. *Zur Kritik der Kritik des Systems des russischen Finanzministers.* Berlin, 1902.

Bochkareva, A. E. *Iz istorii agrarnoi politiki tsarizma v gody pervoi russkoi revoliutsii* [From the History of Agrarian Policy in the Year of the First Russian Revolution]. Leningrad, 1947.

Bompard, M. *Mon ambassade en Russie, 1903–1908.* Paris, 1937.

Borzunov, V. F. "Rabochie sibirskoi zhelezhodorozhnoi magistrali v 1891–1904 gg." [The Workers of the Siberian Railroad in the Years 1891–1904], *Istoriia SSSR,* 1959, No. 4.

Botkin, P. S. *Kartiny diplomaticheskoi zhizni* [Pictures of Diplomatic Life]. Paris, 1930.

Brandt, B. F. *Inostrannye kapitaly, ikh vliianie na ekonomicheskoi razvitie strany* [Foreign Capital, Its Influence on the Economic Development of the Country]. 3 vols. St. Petersburg, 1899.

—— *Torgovo-promyshlennyi krizis v zapadnoi Evrope i v Rossii, 1900–1901* [The Business Crisis in Western Europe and Russia, 1900–1901]. St. Petersburg, 1902.

—— "Vitte" [Witte], in *Entsiklopedicheskii slovar'* (Brockhaus-Efron), Supplementary Vol. I. St. Petersburg, 1905.

Brüggen, E. von der. *Das heutige Russland: Kulturstudien.* Leipzig, 1902.

Brutskus, B. D. *Agrarnyi vopros i agrarnaia politika* [The Agrarian Question and Agrarian Policy]. Petrograd, 1922.

Brzheskii, N. *Nedoimochnost' i krugovaia poruka sel'skikh obshchestv* [Arrears and the Collective Tax Responsibility of Rural Communes]. St. Petersburg, 1897.

Bulgakov, S. N. *Kapitalizm i zemledelie* [Capitalism and Agriculture]. St. Petersburg, 1900.

—— *O rynkakh pri kapitalisticheskom proizvodstve* [On Markets under Capitalist Production]. St. Petersburg, 1897.

Buryshkin, P. A. *Moskva kupecheskaia* [The Moscow Merchant Community]. New York, 1954.

Butmi, G. V. *Itogi finansovago khoziaistva s 1892 po 1903* [The Results of Financial Economy from 1892 to 1903]. St. Petersburg, 1904.

Bykov, A. N. *Fabrichnoe zakonodatel'stvo i razvitie ego v Rossii* [Factory Legislation and Its Development in Russia]. St. Petersburg, 1909.

Byrnes, R. F. "Pobedonostsev on the Instruments of Russian Government," in *Continuity and Change in Russian and Soviet Thought*, ed. E. J. Simmons. Cambridge, Mass., 1955.

Capitalism and the Historians, ed. F. A. Hayek. Chicago, 1957.

Chermenskii, E. D. *Burzhuaziia i tsarism v revoliutsii 1905–1907* [The Bourgeoisie and Tsarism in the Revolution of 1905–1907]. Moscow, 1939.

Chernyshev, I. V. *Agrarno-krest'ianskaia politika Rossii za 150 let* [150 Years of Peasant Policy in Russia]. Petrograd, 1918.

Chuprov, A. I., and A. S. Posnikov. *Vliianie urozhaev i khlebnykh tsen na nekotoryia storony russkago narodnago khoziaistva* [The Influence of Harvests and Grain Prices on Some Aspects of Russian Economy]. St. Petersburg, 1897.

Clairmonte, F. *Le libéralisme économique et les pays sous-developpés: Etudes sur l'évolution d'une idée*. Geneva-Paris, 1958.

Claus, R. *Das russische Bankwesen*. Leipzig, 1908.

Cleinow, G. *Aus Russlands Not und Hoffen*. 2 vols. Berlin, 1909.

Cochran, T. C. *Railroad Leaders, 1849–1890: The Business Mind in Action*. Cambridge, Mass., 1953.

Continuity and Change in Russian and Soviet Thought, ed. E. J. Simmons. Cambridge, Mass., 1955.

Crisp, O. "Russian Financial Policy and the Gold Standard at the End of the Nineteenth Century," *Economic History Review*, 2d Series, Vol. VI, No. 2, December, 1953.

—— "Some Problems of French Investment in Russian Joint Stock Companies 1894–1914," *Slavonic and East European Review*, Vol. XXXV, No. 84, December, 1956.

Crist, D. S. "Russia's Far Eastern Policy in the Making," *Journal of Modern History*, Vol. XIV, No. 3, September, 1942.

Cultural Patterns and Technical Change, ed. M. Mead. Mentor Book, 1955.

Curtiss, J. S. *Church and State in Russia*. New York, 1940.

Danilevskii, V. Ia. *Narodnyi Dom* [The People's House]. Kharkov, 1915.

Danilevskii, V. V. *Russkaia tekhnika* [Russian Technology]. Moscow, 1948.

Daniloff, I. N. *Grossfürst Nikolai Nikolajewitsch*. Berlin, 1930.

Danilov, F. "Obshchaia politika pravitel'stva i gosudarstennyi stroi k nachalu XX veka" [The General Policy of the Government and the Governmental Structure at the Beginning of the Twentieth Century], in *Obshchestvennoe dvizhenie v Rossii*, Vol. I.

Delquist, J. "Graf Wittes Memoiren," *Preussische Jahrbücher,* Vol. CXCI, 1923.

Dement'ev, E. M. *Fabrika, chto ona daet naseleniiu i chto ona u nego beret* [The Factory, What It Gives to the Population and What It Takes from It]. Moscow, 1893.

Dillon, E. J. *The Eclipse of Russia.* New York, 1918.

—— "Two Russian Statesmen," *The Quarterly Review,* Vol. CCXXXVI, 1921.

—— *See also* Lanin, E. B.

Dinamika rossiiskoi i sovetskoi promyshlennosti v sviazi s razvitiem narodnogo khoziaistva za 40 let (1887–1926) [The Dynamics of Russian and Soviet Industry in Connection with the Development of the Economy for Forty Years, 1887–1926], eds. V. A. Bazarov, V. E. Varzar, V. L. Groman, L. B. Kafengaus, *et al.* Vol. I: *Svod statisticheskikh dannykh po fabrichno-zavodskoi promyshlennosti 1887–1926* [The Course of Statistical Data on Factory Industry, 1887–1926], Part I, *Promyshlennost' 1900 g.* [Industry in 1900]. Moscow, 1929.

"Dnevnik A. N. Kuropatkina" [The Diary of A. N. Kuropatkin], *Krasnyi arkhiv,* Vol. II.

Dnevnik imperatora Nikolaia II, 1890–1906 gg. [The Diary of Emperor Nicholas II, 1890–1906]. Berlin, 1923; also in *Krasnyi arkhiv,* Vols. XX–XXII.

Drage, G. *Russian Affairs.* New York, 1904.

Durban, W. "The Trans-Siberian Railway," *Contemporary Review,* Vol. LXXI, 1897.

"Dva dokumenta iz istorii zubatovshchiny" [Two Documents from the History of the Zubatov Movement], *Krasnyi arkhiv,* Vol. II.

Dvadtsatipiatiletie Aleksandrovskago kommercheskago uchilishcha, 1885–1910 [The Twenty-fifth Anniversary of the Alexander Commercial School, 1885–1910]. Moscow, 1911.

Eason, W. W. "Population Changes," in *The Transformation of Russian Society since 1861,* ed. C. E. Black. Cambridge, Mass., 1960.

Eckhart, H. von. "Die Kontinuität der russischen Wirtschaftspolitik von Alt-Moskau bis zur USSR," *Archiv für Sozialwissenschaft und Sozialpolitik,* Vol. LV, No. 3.

Egorov, P. I. *Inostrannye kapitaly i russkie tekhniki* [Foreign Capital and Russian Technologists]. St. Petersburg, 1900.

Engelmann, J. *Das Staatsrecht des Kaisertums Russland.* Berlin, 1889.

Engels, F. *Internationales aus dem Volksstaat, 1871–1875.* Berlin, 1894.

Epstein, E. *Banques de commerce russes.* Paris, 1925.

Ermanskii, O. A. "Krupnaia burzhuaziia do 1905 goda" [The Upper Middle Class to 1905], *Obshchestvennoe dvizhenie v Rossii,* Vol. I.

Eventov, L. Ia. *Inostrannye kapitaly v russkoi promyshlennosti* [Foreign Capital in Russian Industry]. Moscow, 1931.

Ezhegodnik Rossii [The Russian Yearbook]. St. Petersburg, annually.

Fadeev, A. M. *Vospominaniia Andreia Mikhailovicha Fadeeva, 1790–1867 gg.* [The Reminiscences of Andrei Mikhailovich Fadeev, 1790–1867]. 2 vols. Odessa, 1897.

Fedorov, V. "Pis'ma o russkoi promyshlennosti i inostrannykh kapitalov" [Letters about Russian Industry and Foreign Capital], *Russkoe ekonomicheskoe obozrenie,* Nos. 11–12, 1898.

Feis, H. *Europe the World's Banker, 1870–1914: An Account of European Foreign Investment and the Connection of World Finance with Diplomacy before the War.* New Haven, 1930.

Fenin, A. I. *Vospominaniia inzhenera: K istorii obshchestvennago i khoziaistvennago razvitiia Rossii (1883–1906 gg.)* [The Reminiscences of an Engineer: A Contribution to the History of the Social and Economic Development of Russia, 1883–1906]. Prague, 1938.

Finansovaia entsiklopediia [The Financial Encyclopedia]. Moscow-Leningrad, 1927.

Finn-Enotaevskii, A. *Kapitalizm v Rossii, 1890–1917* [Capitalism in Russia, 1890–1917]. Moscow, 1925.

——*Sovremennoe khoziaistvo Rossii, 1890–1910* [The Contemporary Economy of Russia, 1890–1910]. St. Petersburg, 1911.

Fischer, G. *Russian Liberalism from Gentry to Intelligentsia.* Cambridge, Mass., 1958.

Flegel, K. *Die Montanindustrie Russlands und Polens.* Leipzig, 1920.

Fomin, P. I. *Ocherk istorii gvozdarnoi promyshlennosti v Rossii* [An Essay on the History of the Nail Industry in Russia]. Kharkov, 1897.

Frankel, S. H. *The Economic Impact on Underdeveloped Societies.* Oxford, 1953.

Fursenko, A. A. "Iz istorii russko-amerikanskikh otnoshenii na rubezhe XIX–XX vv." [From the History of Russian-American Relations at the Turn from the Nineteenth to the Twentieth Century], in Akademiia Nauk SSSR, Trudy leningradskogo otdeleniia instituta istorii, *Iz istorii imperializma v Rossii.*

—— "Parizhskie Rotshildy i russkaia neft'" [The Paris Rothschilds and Russian Oil], *Voprosy istorii,* No. 8, August, 1962.

—— "Pervyi neftianoi eksportnyi sindikat v Rossii (1893–1897 gg.)" [The First Oil Export Syndicate in Russia, 1893–1897], in Akademiia Nauk SSSR, Trudy leningradskogo otdeleniia instituta istorii, *Monopolii i inostrannyi kapital v Rossii.*

Gaister, A. "Produgol (k voprosy o finansovom kapitalu v Rossii)" [Produgol (On the Question of Finance Capital in Russia)], *Krasnyi arkhiv,* Vol. XVIII.

Galperin. A. *Anglo-Iaponskii soiuz 1902–1921* [The Anglo-Japanese Union, 1902–1921]. Moscow, 1947.

Galprin, D. *Die russische Bauernbank in Rahmen der russischen Agrarpolitik.* Bern, 1920.

Garnett, D. *The Golden Echo.* London, 1951.

Gefter, M. Ia. "Tsarizm i zakonodatel'noe 'regulirovanie' deiatel'nosti sindikatov i trestov v Rossii nakanune pervoi mirovoi voiny" [Tsarism and the Legal "Regulation" of the Activities of Syndicates and Trusts in Russia on the Eve of the First World War], *Istoricheskie zapiski,* No. 54, 1955.

Gernet, M. N. *Istoriia tsarskoi tiurmy* [The History of Tsarist Prison]. Vol. III, 1870–1900. Moscow, 1957.

Gerschenkron, A. *Economic Backwardness in Historical Perspective.* Cambridge, Mass., 1962.

—— "The Rate of Industrial Growth in Russia since 1885," *Journal of Economic History,* Supplement VII, 1947.

Gessen, I. *V dvukh vekakh* [In Two Centuries]. Berlin, 1937.

Gessen, V. Iu. *Istoriia gornorabochikh v SSSR* [The History of Miners in the USSR]. Moscow, 1929.

Gil'bert, M. "K voprosu ob ekonomicheskom polozheniem rabochikh zavoda 'Serp i Molot'" [On the Economic Condition of the Workers in the Factory "Hammer and Sickle"], *Istoriia Proletariata SSSR,* No. 6, 1931.

Gindin, I. F. *Banki i promyshlennost' v Rossii* [Banks and Industry in Russia]. Moscow, 1927.

—— *Gosudarstvennyi bank i ekonomicheskaia politika tsarskogo pravitel'stva, 1861–1892 gg.* [The State Bank and the Economic Policy of the Government, 1861–1892]. Moscow, 1960.

—— *Russkie kommercheskie banki: Iz istorii finansogo kapitala v Rossii* [Russian Commercial Banks: From the History of Finance Capital in Russia]. Moscow, 1948.

—— "K voprosu ob ekonomicheskoi politike tsarskogo pravitel'stva v 60–80 godakh XIX veka" [On the Economic Policy of the Tsarist Government from the 1860s to the 1880s], *Voprosy istorii,* No. 5, 1959.

—— "Neustavnye ssudy gosudarstennogo banka i ekonomicheskaia politika tsarskogo pravitel'stva" [Non-statutory Loans of the State Bank and the Economic Policy of the Tsarist Government], *Istoricheskie zapiski,* No. 35, 1950.

—— "Ob osnovakh ekonomicheskoi politiki tsarkogo pravitel'stva v kontse XIX-nachale XX v." [On the Bases of the Economic Policy of the Tsarist Government at the End of the Nineteenth and the Beginning of the Twentieth Century], in Akademiia Nauk SSSR, Institut istorii, *Dokumenty po istorii monopolisticheskogo kapitalizma v Rossii.*

Gindin, I. F., and M. Ia. Gefter. "Trebovaniia dvorianstva i finansovo-ekonomicheskaia politika tsarskogo pravitel'stva v 1880–1890-kh godakh" [The Demands of the Nobility and the Financial-economic Policy of the Tsarist Government in the 1880s and 1890s], *Istoricheskii arkhiv,* No. 4, 1957.

Glavnoe arkhivnoe upravlenie. *Rabochii vopros v komissii V. N. Kokovtsova v 1905 g.* [The Worker Question in the Commission of V. N. Kokovtsov in 1905]. Moscow, 1926.

Glavnoe upravlenie po delam pechati. *Spisok knig vyshedshykh v Rossii 24 Marta 1884–30 Iiuna 1907* [A List of Books Published in Russia from March 24, 1884, to June 30, 1907]. St. Petersburg, 1907.

Glinskii, B. B. *Prolog Russko-Iaponskoi voiny: Materialy iz arkhiva S. Iu. Vitte* [The Prologue of the Russian-Japanese War: Materials from the Archives of S. Iu. Witte]. Petrograd, 1916.

—— "Graf Sergei Iulevich Vitte (Materialy dlia biografii)" [Count Sergei Iulevich Witte (Materials for a Biography)], *Istoricheskii vestnik,* Nos. 140–42, 1915.

Glivits, I. *Zheleznaia promyshlennost' v Rossii* [The Iron Industry of Russia]. St. Petersburg, 1911.

Goebel, O. *Der Entwicklungsgang der russischen Industriearbeiter bis zur ersten Revolution.* Leipzig, 1920.

——*Russische Industrie.* Berlin, 1913.

Gogel, S. *Die Ursachen der russischen Revolution vom Jahre 1917.* Berlin, 1926.

Goldshtein, I. *Russki-Germanskii torgovoi dogovor i zadachi Rossii*

[The Russo-German Trade Treaty and the Tasks of Russia]. Moscow, 1912.

Golovin, K. T. *Meine Erinnerungen.* Leipzig, 1911.

—— *Muzhik bez progressa i progress bez muzhika* [The Muzhik without Progress and Progress without the Muzhik]. St. Petersburg, 1896.

—— *Russlands Finanzpolitik und die Aufgaben der Zukunft.* Leipzig, 1900.

Gordon, M. "Rabochie na obukhovskom staliteinom zavode" [The Workers of the Obukhov Steel Mill], *Arkhiv istorii truda v Rossii,* No. 9, 1923.

Gornozavodskii listok [The Mining Gazette]. Kharkov, 1899—.

Granovskii, E. L. *Monopolisticheskii kapitalizm v Rossii* [Monopoly Capitalism in Russia]. Moscow, 1929.

Grazhdanin [The Citizen], ed. V. P. Meshcherskii. St. Petersburg, 1883—.

Greenberg, L. *The Jews in Russia.* Vol. II, 1881–1917. New Haven, 1951.

Grigorevskii, M. *Politseiskii sotsializm v Rossii* [Police Socialism in Russia]. St. Petersburg, 1906.

Grimm, C. *Graf Witte und die deutsche Politik.* Freiburg, 1930.

Die Grosse Politik der europäischen Kabinette: Sammlung der diplomatischen Akten des Auswärtigen Amtes, im Auftrag des Auswärtigen Amtes, eds. J. Lipsius, A. Mendelssohn Bartholdy, T. Thimme. Berlin, 1922–27. Vols. VII, IX, XIII, XV.

Grüning, I. *Die russische öffentliche Meinung und ihre Stellung zu den Grossmächten, 1878–1894.* Berlin, 1929.

Gulishambaraov, S. O. *Rossiia v mirovom khoziaistve i v riadu velikikh derzhav pri vstuplenii na prestol imperatorov Aleksandra III i Nikolaia II, 1881 i 1894 gg.* [Russia's Place in the World Economy and among the Great Powers at the Accession of Emperor Alexander II and Nicholas II, 1881 and 1894]. St. Petersburg, 1911.

—— *Sravnitel'naia statistika Rossii v mirovom khoziaistve i v riadu velikikh derzhav v tsarstvovanie imperatora Aleksandra III* [Comparative Statistics of Russia's Place in the World Economy and among the Great Powers in the Reign of Alexander III]. St. Petersburg, 1905.

Gurev, A. *Reforma denezhnago obrashcheniia* [The Reform of the Currency]. St. Petersburg, 1896.

Gurko, V. I. *Features and Figures of the Past.* Stanford, 1939.

—— *Nashe gosudarstvennoe i narodnoe khoziaistvo* [Our Government and the Economy]. St. Petersburg, 1900.

—— *Ustoi narodnago khoziaistva Rossii* [The Foundations of Russian Economy]. St. Petersburg, 1902.

Gushka, A. *Predstavitel'nye organizatsii torgovo-promyshlennogo klassa v Rossii* [The Representative Organizations of the Business Class in Russia]. St. Petersburg, 1912.

Gvozdev, S. *Zapiski fabrichnago inspektora (iz nabliudenii i praktiki v period 1894–1908 gg.)* [Memoirs of a Factory Inspector, from Observation and Experience, 1894 to 1908]. Moscow, 1911.

Habbakuk, H. J. "The Historical Experience on the Basic Conditions of Economic Progress," *International Social Science Bulletin*, 1954.

Hagerman, H. J. *Letters of a Young Diplomat.* Santa Fe, 1937.

Hancock, W. K. "The Underdeveloped Economies," *Economic History Review*, Vol. VI, No. 3, April, 1954.

Hare, R. *Portraits of Russian Personalities between Reform and Revolution.* Oxford, 1959.

Haumant, E. *La culture Française en Russie, 1700–1900.* Paris, 1913.

Hauptmann, P. *Die russische Eisenindustrie und die Kartellbewegung.* Zurich, 1913.

Häusler, E. *Der Kaufmann in der russischen Literatur.* Königsberg, 1935.

Hazlewood, A. *The Economics of "Under-developed" Areas: Annotated Reading List of Books, Articles, and Official Publications.* New York, 1954; 2d ed., 1959.

Hedenström, A. von. *Geschichte Russlands, 1878–1918.* Berlin, 1922.

Hodgetts, E. A. *The Court of Russia in the 19th Century.* 2 vols. London, 1908.

Hoffmann, W. *Stadien und Typen der Industrialisierung.* Jena, 1931.

Holtzman, F. *The Young Maxim Gorky, 1868–1902.* New York, 1948.

Humau, A. *Der Deutsch-Russische Handelsvertrag vom 20 März 1894.* Leipzig, 1900.

Iakovlev, A. F. *Ekonomicheskie krizisy v Rossii* [Economic Crises in Russia]. Moscow, 1955.

Ianzhul, I. I. *Iz vospominanii i perepiski fabrichnago inspektora* [From the Memoirs and Correspondence of a Factory Inspector]. St. Petersburg, 1907.

—— *Vopros o gosudarstvennom vmeshchatel'stve v oblast' promyshlennosti* [The Question about Government Intervention in the Field of Industry]. St. Petersburg, 1895.

—— *Vospominaniia I. I. Ianzhula o perezhitom i vidennom v 1864–1909 gg.* [The Memoirs of I. I. Ianzhul of His Experiences and Times, 1864–1909]. St. Petersburg; Vol. I, 1910; Vol. II, 1911.

Isaev, A. A. *Nachala politicheskoi ekonomii* [The Bases of Political Economy]. 4th ed. St. Petersburg, 1898.

—— *Nastoiashchee i budushchee Russkago obshchestvennago khoziaistva* [The Present and the Future of Russia's Social Economy]. St. Petersburg, 1896.

—— *O sotsializme nashikh dnei* [About the Socialism of Our Days]. Stuttgart, 1902.

—— *Zur Politik des Russischen Finanzministeriums seit Mitte der 80ger Jahre.* Stuttgart, 1898.

Ischchanian, B. *Die ausländischen Elemente in der russischen Volkswirtschaft.* Berlin, 1913.

Istoricheskii obzor deiatel'nosti Komiteta Ministrov pod glavnuiu redaktsiiu stats-sekretaria Kulomzina: Komitet Ministrov v pervaia vosem' let tsarstvovaniia gosudaria imperatora Nikolaia Aleksandrovicha (1894–1902 gg.) [Historical Survey of the Activities of the Committee of Ministers under the Chief Editorship of State Secretary Kulomzin: The Committee of Ministers during the First Eight Years of the Reign of Nicholas Aleksandrovich, 1894–1902]. St. Petersburg, 1902.

Istoriia proletariata SSSR [The History of the Proletariat]. Moscow, 1930–35, being the continuation of *Arkhiv istoriia trudy* and *Trud v Rossii.*

Istoriia SSSR: Ukazatel' sovetskoi literatury za 1917–1952 gg. [The History of the USSR: Guide to Soviet Literature for 1917–1952]. Vol. I: *Istoriia SSSR v period kapitalizma (1861–1917)* [The History of the USSR in the Period of Capitalism, 1861–1917]. Moscow, 1958.

Istoriia torgovli i promyshlennosti v Rossii [The History of Trade and Industry in Russia], ed. P. Kh. Spasskii. St. Petersburg, 1910.

Istorik Marksist [The Marxist Historian]. Moscow, 1936–41, being the continuation of *Istoriia proletariata SSSR.*

Iubileinyi sbornik tsentral'nago statisticheskago komiteta, 1863–1913 [Anniversary Collection of the Central Statistical Committee, 1863–1913]. St. Petersburg, 1913.

Ivanov, L. M. "K voprosu o formirovanii proletariata Ukrainy" [On the Formation of the Proletariat of the Ukraine], *Voprosy istorii,* No. 6, 1957.

—— "K voprosu o formirovanii promyshlennogo proletariata v Rossii" [On the Formation of the Industrial Proletariat in Russia], *Istoriia SSSR,* No. 5, 1958.

—— "Sostoianie i zadachi izucheniia istorii proletariata Rossii" [The Condition and Problems of the Study of the History of the Russian Proletariat], *Voprosy istorii,* No. 3, 1960.

Izdanie pereselenskago upravleniia glavnago upravleniia zemleustroistva zemledeliia. *Atlas aziatskoi Rossii* [Atlas of Asiatic Russia]. St. Petersburg, 1914.

Iz istorii rabochego klassa i krest'ianstva SSSR: Sbornik statei [From the History of the Working Class and the Peasantry in the USSR: A Collection of Articles]. Moscow, 1959.

Izvestiia gornykh inzhenerov [The Gazette of the Mining Engineers]. St. Petersburg, 1892—.

Izvestiia obshchestva dlia sodeistviia ulushcheniiu i razvitiiu manufakturnoi promyshlennosti [Gazette of the Society for the Improvement and Development of Manufacturing Industry]. Moscow, 1902.

Izvolsky, A. *Reflections of a Foreign Minister.* New York, 1921.

The Journal of Leo Tolstoi (1895–1899). Translated by R. Strunsky. New York, 1917.

Jurowsky, L. *Der Russische Getreideexport: Seine Entwicklung und Organisation.* Munich, 1910.

Kadomtsev, B. P. *Professional'nyi i sotsial'nyi sostav naseleniia Evropeiskoi Rossii po dannym perepisi 1897 goda* [Professional and Social Composition of the Population of European Russia According to the Data of the 1897 Census]. St. Petersburg, 1909.

Karnaukhova, E. S. *Razmeshchenie sel'skogo khoziaistva Rossii v period kapitalizma (1860–1914 gg.)* [The Distribution of Agriculture in Russia, 1860–1914]. Moscow, 1951.

Karpov, F. I. *Ob otkrytii i soderzhanii zavedenii obrabatyvaiushchei promyshlennosti: Spravochnyi sbornik dlia promyshlennikov* [About the Opening and Maintaining of Industrial Establishments: Reference Book for Industrialists]. St. Petersburg, 1901.

Karyshev, N. A. *Material po russkomu narodnomu khoziaistvu* [Material on the Russian Economy]. St. Petersburg, 1898.

Kaufman, A. A. *Pereselenie i kolonizatsiia* [Migration and Colonization]. St. Petersburg, 1905.

K dvadtsatipiatiletiiu soveta po zheleznodorozhnym delam [The Twenty-fifth Anniversary of the Council on Railway Affairs]. St. Petersburg, 1911.

Khachaturov, T. S. *Puti razvitiia transporta SSSR* [The Development of Transport in the USSR]. Moscow, 1941.

—— *Razmeshchenie transporta* [The Distribution of Transport]. Moscow, 1939.

Khramoi, A. V. *Ocherk istorii razvitiia avtomatiki v SSSR—dooktiabrskii period* [Essay on the History of Automation in the USSR—the Prerevolutionary Period]. Moscow, 1956.

Khromov, P. A. *Ekonomicheskoe razvitie Rossii v XIX–XX vekakh* [The Economic Development of Russia in the Nineteenth and Twentieth Centuries]. Moscow, 1950.

Khrulev, S. S. *Finansy Rossii v sviazi s ekonomicheskim polozheniem eia naseleniia* [The Finances of Russia in Connection with the Economic Condition of Its Population]. St. Petersburg, 1908.

Kizevetter, A. A. *Na rubezhe dvukh stoletii: Vospominaniia, 1881–1914* [On the Border of Two Centuries: Memoirs, 1881–1914]. Prague, 1929.

—— "Sumerki monarkhii (Dnevnik Polovtseva)" [The Twilight of the Monarchy (The Diary of Polovtsev)], *Na chuzhoi storone,* No. VI. Prague, 1924.

Kleinmichel, Countess Marie von Keller. *Memoirs of a Shipwrecked World.* New York, 1923.

Knoop, W. A. *Die verzinsliche russische Staatsschuld.* Berlin, 1907.

Kohler, S. *Die russische Industriearbeiterschaft von 1905–1907.* Leipzig, 1921.

Kokovtsov, V. N. *Out of My Past: The Memoirs of Count Kokovtsov.* Stanford, 1935.

Kolosov, A. *Aleksandr III, ego lichnost', intimnaia zhizn' i pravlenie* [Alexander III, His Personality, Intimate Life, and Government]. London, 1902.

Koltsov, D. "Rabochie v 1890–1904 g." [The Workers in 1890–1904], in *Obshchestvennoe dvizhenie v Rossii,* Vol. I.

Komar, I. V. *Ural: Ekonomiko-geograficheskaia kharakteristika* [The Urals: Economic-geographic Characterization]. Moscow, 1959.

Koni, A. F. *Sergei Iulevich Vitte: Otryvok vospominanii* [Sergei Iulevich Witte: A Fragment of Memoirs]. Moscow, 1925.

Kononenko, K. *A History of the Economic Relations between the Ukraine and Russia (1654–1917).* Milwaukee, 1958.

Korostowetz, V. K. *Graf Witte, der Steuermann in der Not.* Berlin, 1929.

—— *Neue Väter, neue Söhne.* Berlin, 1926.

Koshkarov, M. P. *Denezhnoe obrashchenie v Rossii* [The Currency in Russia]. St. Petersburg, 1896.

—— *Finansovye itogi poslednago desiatiletiia, 1892–1902* [The Financial Results of the Last Decade, 1892–1902]. St. Petersburg, 1903.

Kotelnikov, A. *Istoriia proizvodstva i razrabotki vseobshchei perepisi naseleniia 28-go ianvaria 1897 g.* [The History of the Census of January 28, 1897]. St. Petersburg, 1909.

Kovalevskii, M. M. *Ekonomicheskii stroi Rossii* [The Economic System of Russia]. St. Petersburg, 1900.

Kovalevskii, V. I. *Rossiia v kontse XIX veka* [Russia at the End of the Nineteenth Century]. St. Petersburg, 1900.

Kozmin, B. P. *Zubatov i ego korrespondenty* [Zubatov and His Correspondents]. Moscow-Leningrad, 1928.

Kozminykh-Lanin, I. M. *Fabrichno-zavodskoi rabochii Vladimirskoi gubernii (1897 g.)* [The Factory Worker of Vladimir Province, 1897]. Vladimir, 1912.

Krasin, A. N. *Istoricheskie osobennosti formirovaniia russkogo proletariata (1861–1895* [The Historical Peculiarities of the Formation of the Russian Proletariat, 1861–1895]. Moscow, 1953.

Kratkii ocherk istorii s''ezdov gornopromyshlennikov iuga Rossii [A Brief Essay on the History of the Congresses of the Mine-operators of Southern Russia]. Kharkov, 1908.

Kravchinsky, S. M. *King Stork and King Log: A Study of Modern Russia.* London, 1896.

Krest'ianskoe dvizhenie v Rossii v 1890–1900 gg. [The Peasant Movement in Russia, 1890–1900]. Moscow, 1959.

Krypton, C. *The Northern Sea Route: Its Place in Russian Economic History before 1917.* New York, 1956.

K stoletiiu Putilovskago zavoda. 1801–1901 gg. [The Centenary of the Putilov Factory, 1801–1901]. St. Petersburg, 1902.

Kucherov, S. *Courts, Lawyers, and Trials under the Last Three Tsars.* New York, 1953.

Kuczynski, J. *Die Deutsch-Russischen Handelsbeziehungen in den letzten 150 Jahren.* Berlin, 1947.

Kulomzin, A. N. *Le Transsibérien.* Paris, 1904.

—— *Nasha zheleznodorozhnaia politika* [Our Railroad Policy]. St. Petersburg, 1902.

Kuropatkin, A. I. *Zapiski generala Kuropatkina o russko-iaponskoi voine: Itogi voiny* [The Reports of General Kuropatkin about the

Russo-Japanese War: The Results of the War]. Berlin, 1909; 2d ed., 1911.

L. G. *S. Iu. Vitte i padenie gosudarstennago kredita* [S. Iu. Witte and the Fall of Russian Credit]. St. Petersburg, 1907.

Lavrinovich, Iu. N. *Obrazovanie rabochikh v Rossii* [The Education of the Workers in Russia]. St. Petersburg, 1900.

Lambsdorf, V. N. (V. N. Lamsdorff). *Dnevnik V. N. Lambsdorfa 1886–1890* [The Diary of V. N. Lambsdorf, 1886–1890]. Moscow-Leningrad, 1926.

Langer, W. L. *The Diplomacy of Imperialism.* 2d ed. New York, 1951.

—— *The Franco-Russian Alliance, 1890–1894.* Cambridge, Mass., 1929.

Lanin, E. B. (pseud. of E. J. Dillon). *Russian Characteristics.* London, 1892.

—— *Russian Traits and Terrors: A Faithful Picture of the Russian of Today.* Boston, 1891.

League of Nations, Secretariat. *Industrialization and Foreign Trade.* New York, 1945.

Lebedev, N. *Opyt izucheniia v sanitarnom otnoshenii byta sel'skokhoziaistvennykh rabochikh* [An Inquiry into the Sanitary Condition of Agricultural Workers]. Moscow, 1901.

Léger, L. *Russes et Slaves.* Series III, Paris, 1899.

Lehmann, C., and Parvus. *Das hungernde Russland: Reiseeindrücke.* Stuttgart, 1900.

Lenin, V. I. *Razvitie kapitalizma v Rossii: Protsess obrazovaniia vnutrennego rynka dlia krupnoi promyshlennosti* [The Development of Capitalism in Russia: The Process of the Formation of the Domestic Market for Heavy Industry]. Moscow, 1952.

Leontief, W. *Die Lage der Baumwollarbeiter in St. Petersburg.* Munich, 1906.

Leontowitsch, V. *Geschichte des Liberalismus in Russland.* Frankfurt-Main, 1957.

Leroy-Beaulieu, A. *The Empire of the Tsar and the Russians.* 3 vols. New York, 1893–96.

Levitov, I. *Sibirskie monopolisty* [Siberian Monopolists]. St. Petersburg, 1892.

Lewery, L. J. *Foreign Capital Investment in Russian Industries and Commerce.* Washington, 1923.

Lewis, W. A. *The Theory of Economic Growth.* London, 1955.

Liadov, M. *Istoriia Russkoi sotsial-demokraticheskoi partii* [The History of the Russian Social-Democratic Party]. St. Petersburg, 1906.

Liashchenko, P. I. *Istoriia narodnogo khoziaistva SSSR* [The History of the Economy of the USSR]. 2d ed., Vol. II. Moscow, 1950.

—— *Ocherki agrarnoi evoliutsii Rossii* [Essays on the Evolution of Agriculture in Russia]. St. Petersburg, 1908.

List, F. *The National System of Political Economy*. Translated by G. A. Matile. Philadelphia, 1856.

Litvinov-Falinskii, V. P. *Fabrichnoe zakonodatel'stvo i fabrichnaia inspektsiia v Rossii* [Factory Legislation and Factory Inspection in Russia]. 2d ed. St. Petersburg, 1904.

—— *Nashe ekonomicheskoe polozhenie i zadachi budushchago* [Our Economic Condition and the Problems of the Future]. St. Petersburg, 1908.

Liubomirov, P. G. *Ocherki po istorii metallurgicheskoi i metallo-obrabatyvaiushchei promyshlennosti* [Essays on the Metallurgical and Metal-working Industry]. Leningrad, 1937.

—— *Ocherki po istorii russkoi promyshlennosti XVII, XVIII, i nachalo XIX veka* [Essays on the History of Russian Industry in the Seventeenth, Eighteenth, and Early Nineteenth Centuries]. Moscow, 1947.

Livshin, Ia. I. *Monopolii v ekonomike Rossii* [Monopolies in Russia's Economy]. Moscow, 1961.

—— "K voprosu o voenno-promyshlennykh monopoliiakh v Rossii v nachale XX veka" [On the Monopolies in the Russian War Industries at the Beginning of the Twentieth Century], *Voprosy istorii*, No. 7, 1957.

Livshits, R. S. *Razmeshchenie promyshlennosti v dorevoliutsionnoi Rossii* [The Distribution of Industry in Prerevolutionary Russia]. Moscow, 1954.

Lokhtin, P. *Sostoianie sel'skago khoziaistva v Rossii sravnitel'no s drugimi stranami* [The Condition of Russian Agriculture in Comparison with Other Countries]. St. Petersburg, 1901.

Lokshin, E. Iu. *Ocherk istorii promyshlennosti SSSR (1917–1940)* [An Essay on the History of Industry in the USSR, 1917–1940]. Moscow, 1956.

Long, R. E. C. "Russian Railway Policy in Asia," *Contemporary Review*, Vol. LXXII, 1899.

Lopukhin, A. A. *Otryvki iz vospominanii* [Fragments from the Memoirs]. Moscow, 1923.

Lorimer, F. *The Population of the Soviet Union: History and Prospects.* Geneva, 1946.

Lorini, E. *La réforme monétaire de la Russie.* Paris, 1898.

Los', F. E. *Formirovanie rabochego klassa na Ukraine i ego revoliutsionnaia bor'ba* [The Formation of the Working Class in the Ukraine and Its Revolutionary Struggle]. Kiev, 1955.

—— "K voprosu o formirovanii rabochego klassa na Ukraine" [On the Formation of the Working Class in the Ukraine], *Voprosy istorii,* No. 2, 1954.

Lossky, N. C. *A History of Russian Philosophy.* New York, 1951.

Lukashevich, S. L. "The Holy Brotherhood: 1881–1883," *American Slavic and East European Review,* Vol. XVIII, No. 4, December, 1959.

Lukianov, B. V. "Rabochii vopros v russkoi dvorianskoi i burzhuaznoi politiko-ekonomicheskoi literature poslednei chetverti XIX veka" [The Social Question in the Politico-economic Literature of the Russian Nobility and Bourgeoisie in the Last Quarter of the Nineteenth Century], *Voprosy istorii,* No. 5. 1960.

Lukianov, P. M. *Istoriia khimicheskikh promyslov i khimicheskoi promyshlennosti Rossii do kontsa XIX veka* [The History of the Chemical Crafts and the Chemical Industry in Russia to the End of the Nineteenth Century]. Vol. I. Moscow-Leningrad, 1948.

Lunts, M. *Sbornik statei iz istorii fabrichnago zakonodatel'stva, fabrichnoi inspektsii, i rabochego dvizheniia v Rossii* [A Collection of Articles on the History of Factory Legislation, Factory Inspections, and the Workers' Movement in Russia]. Moscow, 1909.

—— "Rabochii vopros i fabrichnoe zakonodatel'stvo v Rossii" [The Social Question and Factory Legislation in Russia], *Russkoe bogatstvo,* Nos. 4 and 5, 1904.

Lur'e, E. *Organizatsiia i organizatsii torgovo-promyshlennykh interesov v Rossii: Podgotovitel'nye materialy i etiudy dlia kharakteristiki predprinimatel'skago dvizheniia* [Organizations and the Organization of the Business Interests in Russia: Preparatory Materials for the Study of the Characteristics of the Entrepreneurial Movement]. St. Petersburg, 1913.

Lutokhin. D. A. *Graf S. Iu. Vitte kak ministr finansov* [Count S. Iu. Witte as Minister of Finance]. Petrograd, 1915.

Machat, J. *Le développement économique de la Russie.* Paris, 1902.

Maiakovskii, I. L. *Ocherki po istorii arkhivnogo dela v SSSR* [Essays on the History of Archives in the USSR]. Vol. I. Moscow, 1941.

Maklakov, V. A. *Vlast' i obshchestvennost' na zakate staroi Rossii* [Government and the Public at the Decline of the Old Russia]. Moscow, 1936.

Malozemoff, A. *Russian Far Eastern Policy: 1881–1904.* Berkeley, 1958.

Malynski, E. *Alexandre III, Artisan de la Révolution.* Paris, 1933.

Mandelbaum, K. *The Industrialization of Backward Areas.* Oxford, 1945.

Manus, I. *Politicheskie, ekonomicheskie i finansovye voprosy poslednego vremeni* [Political, Economic, and Financial Questions of Recent Times]. St. Petersburg, 1906.

Martin, R. E. *Die Zukunft Russlands und Japans.* Berlin, 1905.

Maslov, P. *Agrarnyi vopros v Rossii* [The Agrarian Question in Russia]. 2 vols. St. Petersburg, 3d ed., 1906; 4th ed., 1908.

Materialy dlia torgovo-promyshlennoi statistiki: Svod tovarnykh tsen na glavnykh russkikh i inostrannykh rynkakh za 1890–1901 gg. [Materials for Business Statistics: The Course of Commodity Prices for the Chief Markets in Russia and Abroad from 1890 to 1901]. St. Petersburg, 1902.

Mavor, J. *An Economic History of Russia.* Vol. II. London and New York, 1914.

Mead, M., and R. Metraux. *The Study of Culture at a Distance.* Chicago, 1953.

Meien, V. F. *Rossiia v dorozhnom otnoshenii* [The Roads of Russia]. 3 vols. St. Petersburg, 1902.

Melgunov, S. *Na putiakh k dvortsomu perevorotu* [On the Road to the Palace Coup]. Paris, 1931.

Mendel, A. P. *Dilemmas of Progress in Tsarist Russia, Legal Marxism and Legal Populism.* Cambridge, Mass., 1961.

Mendeleev, D. I. *K poznaniiu Rossii* [Getting to Know Russia]. St. Petersburg, 1907.

—— *Sochineniia* [Works]. Leningrad, 1947–51. Vols. XVIII–XXV deal with questions of public policy.

—— *Tolkovoi tarif, ili issledovanie o razvitii promyshlennosti Rossii s sviazi s eia obshchem tamozhennym tarifom* [A Reasonable Tariff, or an Investigation of the Development of Russian Industry in Connection with Its General Customs Tariff]. St. Petersburg, 1891–92.

—— *Uralskaia zheleznaia promyshlennost' v 1899 g.* [The Ural Iron Industry in 1899]. St. Petersburg, 1900.

—— *Zavetnyia mysli* [Intimate Thoughts]. St. Petersburg, 1902–5.

Mendel'son, L. *Ekonomicheskie krisisy i tsikli XIX veka* [Economic Crises and Business Cycles in the Nineteenth Century]. Moscow, 1929.

Mertens, O. *30 Jahre russischer Eisenbahnpolitik und deren wirtschaftliche Rückwirkungen.* Berlin, 1919; Russian edition, 1912.

Meshcherskii, V. P. *Moi vospominaniia* [My Memoirs]. Part III, 1881–94. St. Petersburg, 1912.

Mezhenko, Iu. A. *Russkaia tekhnicheskaia periodika 1800–1916* [The Russian Technical Periodical Press, 1800–1916]. Moscow, 1955.

Migulin, P. P. *Nasha bankovaia politika 1729–1903* [Our Bank Policy, 1729–1903]. Kharkov, 1904.

—— *Nasha noveishaia zheleznodorozhnaia politika i zheleznodorozhnye zaimy* [Our Newest Railway Policy and Railway Loans]. Kharkov, 1903.

—— *Nastoiashchee i budushchee russkikh finansov* [Russian Finances at Present and in the Future]. Kharkov, 1907.

—— *Reform denezhnago obrashcheniia v Rossii i promyshlennyi krizis* [The Reform of the Currency in Russia and the Industrial Crisis]. Kharkov, 1902.

—— *Russkii gosudarstvennyi kredit* [Russian State Credit]. Kharkov, 1901–3.

—— *Vozrozhdenie Rossii* [The Revival of Russia]. Kharkov, 1910.

Mikulin, A. A. *Fabrichnaia inspektsiia v Rossii* [Factory Inspection in Russia]. Kiev, 1906.

Miliukov, P. M. *Russia and Its Crisis.* Chicago, 1906.

—— *Vospominaniia, 1859–1917* [Reminiscences, 1859–1917]. 2 vols. New York, 1955.

—— "Vitte," *Entsiklopedicheskii slovar'* (Granat), 7th ed., Vol. X.

Miliutin, V. P. *Istoriia ekonomicheskogo razvitiia SSSR* [A History of the Economic Development of the USSR]. 2d ed. Moscow, 1929.

Ministerstvo Finansov, 1802–1902 [The Ministry of Finance, 1802–1902]. 2 vols. St. Petersburg, 1902.

Ministerstvo Finansov. *Ezhegodnik Ministerstva Finansov* [Annual of the Ministry of Finance]. St. Petersburg, annually.

—— *Okrainy Rossii* [The Outlying Districts of Russia], ed. P. P. Semenov. St. Petersburg, 1900.

—— *Periodicheskiia izdaniia Ministerstva Finansov, 1865–1915* [The Periodical Publications of the Ministry of Finance, 1865–1915]. Petrograd, 1915.

—— *Spisok fabrik i zavodov Evropeiskoi Rossii za 1900–1903 gg.* [List of Factories and Mills in European Russia for 1900–1903]. St. Petersburg, 1908.

—— *Statisticheskiia svedeniia o fabrikakh i zavodakh po proizvodstvom neoblozhennym aktsizom za 1900* [Statistical Information on Factories and Mills Not Covered by the Excise Duty, for 1900]. St. Petersburg, 1903.

—— *Vestnik Finansov* [The Financial Messenger]. St. Petersburg, weekly.

—— Departament torgovli i manufaktur. *Fabrichno-zavodskaia promyshlennost' i torgovlia Rossii: S prilozheniem obshchei karty fabrichno-zavodskoi promyshlennosti Rossiiskoi imperii* [Factory Industry and Trade in Russia: With a General Map of Factory Industry in the Russian Empire]. St. Petersburg, 1896.

—— Departament zheleznodorozhnykh del. *Kratkii otchet o deiatel'nosti tarifnykh uchrezhdenii i departamenta zheleznodorozhnykh del za 1889–1913* [A Brief Account of the Activity of the Tariff Agencies and of the Department of Railway Affairs from 1889 to 1913]. St. Petersburg, 1914.

—— Otdel promyshlennosti. *Materialy k izucheniiu rabochago voprosa: Po ofitsial'nym dannym sostavlennym v M-ve Finansov, otdelom promyshlennosti Marta 1905* [Materials for the Study of the Social Question: According to Official Data Collected by the Ministry of Finance, Division of Industry, in March, 1905]. St. Petersburg, 1905.

—— —— *Materialy po izdaniiu zakona 2-go iunia 1897 g. ob organizatsii i raspredelenii rabochago vremeni v zavedeniiakh fabrichno-zavodskoi promyshlennosti* [Materials on the Promulgation of the Law of June 2, 1897, on the Organization and Distribution of Working Time in Industrial Establishments]. St. Petersburg, 1905.

—— —— *Svod otchetov fabrichnykh inspektorov za 1901, 1902, 1903* [The Reports of the Factory Inspectors for 1901, 1902, 1903]. St. Petersburg, 1902, 1903, 1904.

Ministerstvo Putei Soobshcheniia. Otdel statistiki i kartografii. *Statisticheskii atlas putei soobshcheniia Rossii k nachalu XX veka* [Statistical Atlas of the Means of Communication in Russia]. St. Petersburg, 1902.

Ministerstvo Vnutrennikh Del, Tsentral'nyi statisticheskii komitet. *Goroda Rossii v 1904 godu* [The Towns of Russia in 1904]. St. Petersburg, 1906.

—— *Kartogrammy i diagrammy k iubileinomu sborniku tsentral'nogo statisticheskogo komiteta M-va Vnutrennikh Del* [Charts and Diagrams for the Anniversary Collection of the Central Statistical Committee of the Ministry of the Interior]. St. Petersburg, 1913.

Ministerstvo Zemledeliia i Gosudarstvennykh Imushchestv. *Obzor kustarnykh promyslov Rossii sostavlen po porucheniiu M-va Zemledeliia i Gosudarstvennykh Imushchestv, chlenom proizvoditelem kustarnago komiteta oznachennago M-va N. V. Ponomarevym, pod redaktsiia D. A. Timiriazeva* [Survey of the Handicrafts of Russia Made, on Instruction by the Ministry of Agriculture and State Domains, by N. V. Ponomarev, Executive Secretary of the Crafts Committee of that Ministry, under the Editorship of D. A. Timiriazev]. St. Petersburg, 1902.

Mitel'man, M., B. Glebov, and A. Ulianskii, *Istoriia Putilovskogo zavoda* [The History of the Putilov Factory]. Leningrad, 1939.

Mitinskii, A. M. *Gornozavodskii Ural* [The Mining Urals]. St. Petersburg, 1909.

Moore, W. E. *Industrialization and Labor: Social Aspects of Economic Development.* Ithaca, 1951.

—— "Primitives and Peasants in Industry," *Social Research,* Vol. XV, No. 1, March, 1948.

Morley, C. *Guide to Research in Russian History.* Syracuse, 1951.

Morskoi, A. *Zubatovshchina: Stranichka iz istorii rabochago voprosa v Rossii* [The Zubatov Movement: A Page from the History of the Social Question in Russia]. Moscow, 1913.

Mossolov, A. A. *At the Court of the Last Tsar.* London, 1935.

Motylev, V. E. "Ob osobennostiakh promyshlennogo razvitiia Rossii v kontse XIX—nachale XX veka" [On the Peculiarities of Russia's Industrial Development at the End of the Nineteenth and the Beginning of the Twentieth Century], *Voprosy istorii,* No. 7, 1955.

Nagradow, W. J. *Moderne Russische Zensur and Presse.* Berlin, 1894.

Narodnoe khoziaistvo [The Economy], ed. L. V. Khodskii. St. Petersburg, January, 1900—.

Naryshkina-Witte, V. *Zapiski devochki* [A Daughter's Notes]. Leipzig, 1922.

Nasha zheleznodorozhnaia politika po dokumentam arkhiva Komiteta Ministrov [Our Railway Policy According to Documents in the Archive of the Committee of Ministers]. St. Petersburg, 1902.

Naumov, A. N. *Iz utselevshikh vospominanii, 1868–1917* [From Reminiscences Left Intact, 1868–1917]. 2 vols. New York, 1954.

Neopikhanov, A. *Russkii transport i ego planirovanie* [Russian Transport and Its Planning]. Moscow, 1924.

Nesterenko, A. A. *Ocherki istorii promyshlennosti i polozheniia proletariata Ukrainy v kontse XIX i nachale XX veka* [Essays on the History of Industry and the Condition of the Ukrainian Proletariat at the End of the Nineteenth and the Beginning of the Twentieth Century]. Moscow, 1954.

Nikolai-on. *Ocherki nashego poreformennago obshchestvennago khoziaistva* [Essays on Our Post-reform Social Economy]. St. Petersburg, 1893.

Noble, E. *Russia and the Russians.* New York, 1901.

Norman, H. *All the Russians.* New York, 1904.

Normano, J. F. *The Spirit of Russian Economics.* New York, 1949.

"Novoe o zubatovshchine" [New Information on the Zubatov Movement], *Istoriia proletariata SSSR,* Vol. II. Moscow, 1930.

"Novoe o zubatovshchine" [New Information on the Zubatov Movement], *Krasnyi arkhiv,* Vol. I, 1922.

Nurkse, R. *The Problem of Capital Formation in Underdeveloped Countries.* New York, 1933.

Obolenskii, V. *Ocherki minuvshego* [Essays on the Past]. Belgrade, 1931.

Obshchestvennoe dvizhenie v Rossii v nachale XX-go veka [The Social Movement in Russia at the Beginning of the Twentieth Century], eds. A. Potresov, L. Martov, and P. Maslov. Vol. I: *Predvestniki osnovaniia: Prichiny dvizheniia* [The Early Roots: The Causes of the Movement]. St. Petersburg, 1909. Vols. II-IV deal with the years after 1903.

Obshchestvo dlia sodeistviia Russkoi promyshlennosti i torgovli. *Trudy* [Proceedings]. St. Petersburg, 1872—.

Obshchii zvod po imperii rezultatov razrabotki dannykh po vseobshchei perepisi naseleniia, proizvedennoi 28 ianvaria 1897 goda [General Survey, for the Empire, of the Results of the Census of January 28, 1897]. Vol. I. St. Petersburg, 1906.

Obzor deiatel'nosti Ministerstva Finansov v tsarstvovanii Imperatora Aleksandra III, 1881–1894 [Survey of the Activities of the Ministry of Finance during the Reign of Alexander III, 1881–1894]. St. Petersburg, 1902.

Ocherki po istorii narodnogo khoziaistva SSSR: Sbornik statei [Essays on the History of the Economy of the USSR: A Collection of Articles]. Moscow, 1959.

Odarchenko, K. F. *Nravstvennyia i pravovyia osnovy russkago narodnago khoziaistva* [The Moral and Legal Bases of Russian Economy]. Moscow, 1897.

Ol', P. V. *Inostrannye kapitaly v khoziaistve dovoennoi Rossii* [Foreign Capital in the Economy of Prewar Russia]. Leningrad, 1925.

—— *Inostrannye kapitaly v Rossii* [Foreign Capital in Russia]. Petrograd, 1922.

Oldenburg, S. S. *Tsarstvovanie imperatora Nikolaia II* [The Reign of Emperor Nicholas II]. 2 vols. Belgrade, 1939.

Olgin, M. J. *The Soul of the Russian Revolution.* New York, 1917.

Ordinaire, J. *L'évolution industrielle Russe depuis la fin du XIX siècle.* Paris, 1927.

Ostrovskii, B. G. *Admiral Makarov.* 2d ed. Moscow, 1954.

Otchet po deloproizvodstvu gosudarstvennago soveta [The Proceedings of the State Council]. St. Petersburg, annually.

Ozerov, I. Kh. *Ekonomicheskaia Rossiia i eia finansovaia politika na izkhode XIX i v nachale XX veka* [Economic Russia and Its Financial Policy at the End of the Nineteenth and the Beginning of the Twentieth Century]. Moscow, 1905.

—— *Iz zhizni truda* [From the Life of the Workers]. Moscow, 1904.

—— *Kak raskhodiatsia v Rossii narodnyia den'gi* [How the People's Money Is Spent in Russia]. Moscow, 1907.

—— *Nash gosudarstvennyi dolg* [Our Government Debt]. Moscow, 1908.

—— *Osnovy finansovoi nauki* [Foundations of Financial Science]. Moscow, 1911–14.

—— *Politika po rabochemu voprosu za poslednie gody* [Labor Policy in Recent Years]. Moscow, 1906.

—— "The Industrial Development of Russia," *Forum,* April, 1899.

Palmer, F. H. E. *Russian Life in Town and Country.* London, 1901.

Pankratova, A. M. "Proletarizatsiia krest'ianstva i ee rol' v formirovanii promyshlennogo proletariata Rossii (60-90-e gody XIX veka)" [The Proletarianization of the Peasantry and Its Role in the Formation of an Industrial Proletariat, from the 1860s to the 1890s), *Istoricheskie zapiski,* No. 54, 1955.

—— "Rabochii klass i rabochee dvizhenie" [The Working Class and the Working Class Movement], *1905 god* [The Year 1905], Vol. I. Moscow, 1926.

Pares, B. *The Fall of the Russian Monarchy.* New York, 1939.

—— *My Russian Memoirs.* London, 1931.

—— *A Wandering Student.* Syracuse, 1948.

Pasvolsky, L., and H. G. Moulton. *Russian Debts and Russian Reconstruction: A Study of the Relations of Russia's Foreign Debts to Her Economic Recovery.* New York, 1924.

Pavlov, M. A. *Vospominaniia metallurga* [The Reminiscences of a Metallurgist]. Moscow, 1943.

Pavlovsky, G. *Agricultural Russia on the Eve of the Revolution.* London, 1930.

Pazhitnov, K. A. *Ocherki istorii tekstil'noi promyshlennosti dorevoliutsionnoi Rossii* [Essays on the History of the Textile Industry in Prerevolutionary Russia]. Moscow, 1958.

—— *Ocherki po istorii bakinskoi neftedobyvaiushchei promyshlennosti* [Essays on the History of the Baku Oil Industry]. Moscow, 1940.

—— *Polozhenie rabochego klassa v Rossii* [The Position of the Working Class in Russia]. 2d ed. St. Petersburg, 1908.

—— *Sherstianaia promyshlennost'* [The Woollen Industry]. Moscow, 1955.

—— "K voprosu o promyshlennom perevorote v Rossii" [On the Question of the Industrial Revolution in Russia], *Voprosy istorii,* No. 5, 1952.

Perepiska K. Marksa i F. Engel'sa s russkimi politicheskimi deiateliami [The Correspondence of K. Marx and F. Engels with Russian Political Figures]. 2d ed. Moscow, 1952.

Peshekhonov, A. V. *Ekonomicheskaia politika samoderzhaviia: Tsentralizatsiia ekonomicheskoi vlasti* [The Economic Policy of Autocracy: The Centralization of Economic Power]. 2d ed. St. Petersburg, 1906.

—— *Na ocherednye temy* [On Recurrent Themes]. St. Petersburg, 1907.

—— "Ekonomicheskoe polozhenie krest'ian v poreformennoe vremia" [The Economic Condition of the Peasants in the Post-reform Era], *Velikaia reforma,* Vol. VI.

Peskov, I. "Voprosy fabrichnago byta na torgovo-promyshlennykh s"ezdakh v Rossii" [The Questions of Factory Conditions at the Industrial Congresses in Russia], *Zapiski moskovskago otdela Imperatorskago Russkogo Tekhnicheskago Obshchestva,* Nos. 7–8, 1898.

Petrazhitskii, L. *Aktsionernye kompaniia* [Joint Stock Companies]. St. Petersburg, 1898.

Petrov, V. A. "Tsarskaia armiia v bor'be s massovym revoliutionnym dvizheniem v nachale XX veka" [The Tsarist Army in the Struggle with the Revolutionary Mass Movement at the Beginning of the Twentieth Century], *Istoricheskie zapiski,* Vol. XXXIV, 1950.

Pisarzhevskii, O. *D. I. Mendeleev, 1834–1907.* 2d ed. Moscow, 1952.

"Pis'mo V. K. Pleve k A. A. Kireevu" [A Letter of V. K. Plehve to A. A. Kireev], *Krasnyi arkhiv,* Vol. V (18).

Pobedonostsev, K. P. *Moskovskii sbornik* [Moscow Collection]. 3d ed. Moscow, 1896. Translated as *Reflections of a Russian Statesman,* London, 1898.

Pogozhev, A. V. *Fabrichnyi byt v Germanii i Rossii* [Factory Life in Germany and Russia]. St. Petersburg, 1882.

—— *Uchet chislennosti i sostava rabochikh v Rossii: Materialy po statistike truda* [A Calculation of the Number and Composition of Workers in Russia: Materials for Labor Statistics]. St. Petersburg, 1906.

Pogrebinskii, A. P. *Gosudarstvenno-monopoliticheskii kapitalizm v Rossii: Ocherk istorii* [State Monopoly Capitalism in Russia: A Historical Essay]. Moscow, 1959.

—— *Ocherki istorii finansov dorevoliutsionnoi Rossii* (*XIX–XX vv.*) [Essays on the History of Finance in Prerevolutionary Russia (Nineteenth and Twentieth Centuries)]. Moscow, 1954.

—— "Finansovaia politika tsarizma v 70–80-kh godakh XIX v." [The Financial Policy of Tsarism in the 1870s and 1880s], *Istoricheskii arkhiv,* No. 2, 1960.

—— "Finansovaia reforma nachala 60-kh godov XIX veka v Rossii" [The Financial Reform of the Early 1860s], *Voprosy istorii,* No. 10, 1957.

Pokrovskii, M. N. "Tsarskaia diplomatiia o zadachakh Rossii na vostoke v 1900 g." [Tsarist Diplomacy on the Tasks of Russia in the East in 1900], *Krasnyi arkhiv,* Vol. XVIII, 1926.

—— "Vitte," *Bol'shaia sovetskaia entsiklopediia,* 1st ed., Vol. II.

Polanyi, K. *The Great Transformation.* New York, 1944.

Polenov, A. D. *Issledovanie ekonomicheskago polozheniia tsentral'no-chernozemnykh guberniakh: Trudy osobago soveshchaniia 1899–1901* [Investigation of the Economic Condition of the Central Black Soil Provinces: Proceedings of the Special Commission]. Moscow, 1901.

Politicheskaia bezprintsipnost' S. Iu. Vitte: Tainye tsirkulari i doklady [Witte's Lack of Principle: Secret Circulars and Reports]. Berlin, 1903.

Polnoe sobranie zakonov Rossiiskoi Imperii, 1649–1916 [The Law Code of the Russian Empire, 1649–1916]. St. Petersburg, 1830–1916.

Polovtsev, A. A. "Dnevnik A. A. Polovtseva" [The Diary of A. A. Polovtsev], *Krasnyi arkhiv,* Vols. III, IX, XXXIII, XLVI, LXVII.

Popov, A. "Dal'nevostochnaia politika tsarizma v 1894–1906 gg." [The Far-Eastern Policy of Tsarism, 1894–1906], *Istorik Marksist,* No. 2–3, 1935.

—— "Pervye shagi russkogo imperializma na dal'nem vostoke" [The First Steps of Russian Imperialism in the Far East], *Krasnyi arkhiv,* Vol. LII.

Portal, R. *La Russie industrielle de 1881–1927.* Paris, 1956.

Posin, D. Q. *Mendeleev: The Story of a Great Scientist.* New York, 1948.

Postoiannaia komissia po delam potrebitel'nykh obshchestv, sostoiashchaia pri SPb-skom otdelenii komiteta o sel'skikh ssudosberegatel'nykh i promyshlennykh tovarishchestvakh Imperatorskogo Moskovskogo Obshchestva sel'skago khoziaistva. *Obzor polozheniia i deiatel'nosti potrebitel'nykh obshchestv v Rossii, po dannym 1897 goda* [Survey of the Condition and Activities of the Consumers Societies in Russia, According to Data of 1897]. St. Petersburg, 1899.

Preyer, W. D. *Die Russische Zuckerindustrie. Staats- und Sozialwirtschaftliche Forschungen,* No. 135, 1908.

The Progress of Underdeveloped Areas, ed. B. F. Hoselitz. Chicago, 1952.

Proizvoditel'nye sily Rossii: Kratkaia kharakteristika razlichnykh otraslei narodnago truda sootvetstvenno klassifikatsii vystavka [The Productive Forces of Russia: A Brief Characterization of the Various Branches of National Labor According to the Classification of the Exhibit], ed. V. I. Kovalevskii. St. Petersburg, 1896.

Prokopovich, S. N. *K rabochemu voprosu v Rossii* [On the Social Question in Russia]. St. Petersburg, 1905.

—— *Mestnye liudi o nuzhdakh Rossii* [The Local People on the Needs of Russia]. St. Petersburg, 1904.

—— *Über die Bedingungen der industriellen Entwicklung Russlands. Archiv für Sozialwissenschaft und Sozialpolitik,* Ergänzungsheft 10, 1913.

—— "Krest'ianstvo i poreformennaia fabrika" [The Peasantry and the Prerevolutionary Factory], *Velikaia reforma,* Vol. VI.

Promyshlennost' i zdorov'e: Vestnik professional'noi gigieny, fabrich-

nago i sanitarnago zakonodatel'stva [Industry and Health: Gazette of Professional Hygiene, Factory and Sanitary Legislation], ed. A. V. Pogozhev. St. Petersburg, 1902—.

Promyshlennyi mir [The World of Industry]. St. Petersburg, November, 1899—.

Propper, S. M. *Was nicht in die Zeitung kam: Erinnerungen der Birjewyia Wedomosti.* Frankfurt-Main, 1929.

Putevoditel' po velikoi Sibirskoi zheleznodoroge [Guide to the Great Siberian Railway], ed. A. I. Dmitriev-Mamontov and A. F. Zdziarskii. St. Petersburg, 1900.

Rabochee dvizhenie v Rossii v XIX v.: Sbornik dokumentov [The Working Class Movement in Russia in the Nineteenth Century: A Collection of Documents]. Vol. III, Part 2, 1890–94, ed. A. M. Pankratova. Moscow, 1952.

"Rabochie zavoda 'Serp i molot' (b. Guzhon) v 1905 g." [The Workers of the Factory "Hammer and Sickle" (Formerly Goujon) in 1905], *Russkie rabochie v revoliutsionnom dvizhenii.* Moscow, 1931.

Radtsig, A. A. *Finansovaia politika Rossii s 1887 goda* [The Financial Policy of Russia since 1887]. St. Petersburg, 1903.

—— *Vliianie zheleznykh dorog na sel'skoe khoziaistvo, promyshlennost' i torgovliu* [The Influence of Railroads on Agriculture, Industry, and Trade]. St. Petersburg, 1896.

Raffalovich, A. *". . . l'abominable venalité de la presse . . ." D'apres les documents des archives russes (1897–1917).* Paris, 1931.

Ragozin, E. I. *Zhelezo i ugol na Urale* [Iron and Coal in the Urals]. St. Petersburg, 1903.

Rappoport, A. S. *Home Life in Russia.* London, 1913.

Rashin, A. G. *Formirovanie promyshlennogo proletariata v Rossii: Statistiko-ekonomicheskie ocherki* [The Formation of the Industrial Proletariat in Russia: Essays in Economic Statistics]. Moscow, 1940.

—— "Dinamika chislennosti i protsess formirovaniia gorodskogo naseleniia Rossii v XIX—nachale XX vv." [The Changes in Size and the Process of the Forming of the Urban Population in Russia in the Nineteenth and Early Twentieth Centuries], *Istoricheskie zapiski,* No. 34, 1950.

—— "Gramotnost' i narodnoe obrazovanie v Rossii v XIX—nachale XX v." [Literacy and Popular Education in Russia in the Nineteenth and Early Twentieth Centuries], *Istoricheskie zapiski,* No. 37, 1951.

Raspredelenie rabochikh i prislug po gruppam zaniatii i po mestu rozhdeniia na osnovanii dannykh pervoi vseobshchei perepisi naseleniia Rossiiskoi Imperii 28 ianvaria 1897 goda [The Distribution of Workers and Servants by Occupational Groups and Their Place of Birth, According to the Data of the First General Census of the Population of the Russian Empire Held on January 28, 1897]. St. Petersburg, 1905.

Raud, V. M. *Ekonomicheskie predposylki pervoi russkoi revoliutsii, 1905–1907 gg.* [The Economic Premises of the First Russian Revolution, 1905–1907]. Leningrad, 1956.

Renouvin, P. "Les relations Franco-Russes à la fin du XIX-e et au début du XX siècle: Bilan des recherches," *Cahiers du Monde Russe et Soviétique,* Vol. I, 1959.

Rikhter, A. A. "Kak u nas raspredelen dostatok" [How Our Income Is Distributed], *Russkoe ekonomicheskoe obozrenie,* No. 2, February, 1898.

—— "Opyt razdeleniia evropeiskoi Rossii na raiony po estestvennym i ekonomicheskim priznakam" [An Attempt to Divide European Russia by Regions on the Basis of Natural and Economic Features], *Trudy Imperatorskago Vol'nago Ekonomicheskago Obshchestva,* No. 4, 1898.

Rimlinger, G. V. "Autocracy and the Factory Order in Early Russian Industrialization," *Journal of Economic History,* Vol. XX, No. 1, March, 1960.

Robinson, G. T. *Rural Russia.* New York, 1932.

Rohrbach, P. "Das Finanzsystem Witte," *Preussische Jahrbücher,* Vol. CIX, 1902.

Romanov, B. A. *Ocherki diplomaticheskoi istorii Russko-Iaponskoi voiny* [Essays on the Diplomatic History of the Russo-Japanese War]. 2d ed. Moscow, 1955.

—— *Rossiia v Mandzhurii* (*1892–1906*) [Russia in Manchuria, 1892–1906]. Leningrad, 1928; English translation, Ann Arbor, Mich., 1952.

Ronin, S. L. *Inostrannye kapitaly i russkie banki* [Foreign Capital and Russian Banks]. Moscow, 1926.

Rosen, R. R. *Forty Years of Diplomacy.* 2 vols. New York, 1922.

Rudchenko, P. "Dorozhnoe delo v nekotorykh inostrannykh gosudarstvakh i v Rossii" [Railroad Affairs in Some Foreign States and in Russia], *Russkoe ekonomicheskoe obozrenie,* No. 9, 1903.

Russen über Russland, ed. J. Melnik. Frankfurt-Main, 1906.

Russia Painted by F. de Haenen. Text by G. Dobson, H. M. Grove, and H. Stewart. London, 1913.

Russkii trud [Russian Labor], ed. S. F. Sharapov. St. Petersburg, 1897–99.

S. J. Witte, 30. August 1892–30. August 1902: Ein Gedenkblatt zum 10 jährigen Ministerjubiläum des russischen Finanzministers. Berlin, 1902.

Saenger, M. *Die Wittesche Währungsreform*. Frankfurt-Main, 1927.

Samoderzhavie i stachki: Zapiska Ministerstva Finansov o razreshenii stachek, s prilozheniem statii: "Novaia pobeda russkikh rabochikh" L. Martova [Autocracy and Strikes: A Memorandum of the Ministry of Finance on Permitting Strikes, with an Article by L. Martov: "A New Victory of the Russian Workers"]. Geneva, 1902.

Samoilov, F. *Po sledam minuvshego: Vospominaniia starogo bol'shevika* [On the Tracks of the Past: Reminiscences of an Old Bolshevik]. Moscow, 1934.

Schlesinger, M. L. *Russland im XX Jahrhundert*. Berlin, 1908.

Schulze-Gävernitz, G. von. *Volkswirtschaftliche Studien aus Russland*. Leipzig, 1899.

—— "Die Moskau-Wladimir'sche Baumwollindustrie," *Schmoller's Jahrbuch für Gesetzgebung, Verwaltung und Volkswirtschaft im Deutschen Reiche,* 1893.

—— "Der Nationalismus in Russland und seine wirtschaftlichen Träger," *Preussische Jahrbücher,* Nos. 1–3, 1894.

The Secret Letters of the Last Tsar, ed. E. J. Bing. London, 1937.

Semevskii, V. I. *Rabochie na sibirskikh zolotykh promyslakh: Istoricheskoe issledovanie* [The Workers in the Siberian Gold Crafts: A Historical Study]. 2 vols. St. Petersburg, 1898.

Seraphim, E. *Führende Deutsche im Zarenreiche*. Berlin, 1942.

—— "Zar Nikolaus II und Graf Witte (eine historisch-psychologische Studie)," *Historische Zeitschrift,* No. 161, 1940.

Sergeev, S. *Voprosy russkoi promyshlennosti* [Problems of Russian Industry]. Odessa, 1896.

Shaginian, M. *Fabrika Tornton* [The Thornton Factory]. Moscow, 1927.

Shakhovskoi, Prince N. V. *Sel'sko-khoziaistvennye otkhozhie promysli* [Agricultural Seasonal Work]. Moscow, 1896.

Sharapov, S. F. *Dve zapiski S. Sharapova o russkikh finansakh* [Two Memoranda of S. Sharapov on Russian Finances]. Berlin, 1901.

Shcherbina, F. *Krest'ianskie biudzhety* [Peasant Budgets]. Voronezh, 1900.

Shekov, G. *Sud Grafa Vitte nad samim soboiu* [Count Witte in Judgment on Himself]. Kharkov, 1908.

Shelymagin, I. I. *Fabrichno-trudovoe zakonodatel'stvo v Rossii (2-ia polovina XIX veka)* [Factory Legislation in Russia—the Second Half of the Nineteenth Century]. Moscow, 1947.

Shepelev, L. E. "Aktsionernoe uchrezhdetel'stvo v Rossii (istorichesko-statisticheskii ocherk)" [The Growth of Joint Stock Companies in Russia (Historical-statistical Essay)], in Akademiia Nauk SSSR, Trudy leningradskogo otdeleniia instituta istorii, *Iz istorii imperializma v Rossii.*

Shestakov, P. M. *Rabochie na manufakture T-va "Emil Tsindel" v Moskve* [The Workers in the Factory "Emil Zindel" in Moscow]. Moscow, 1900.

Shidlovskii, S. I. *Obshchii obzor trudov mestnykh komitetov* [General Survey of the Proceedings of the Local Committees]. St. Petersburg, 1905.

Shipov, D. N. *Vospominaniia i dumy o perezhitom* [Reminiscences and Thoughts about the Past]. Moscow, 1918.

Shlossberg, D. "Vseobshchaia stachka 1903 g. na Ukraine" [The General Strike of 1903 in the Ukraine], *Istoriia proletariata SSSR,* No. 7.

Shoemaker, M. M. *The Great Siberian Railway from St. Petersburg to Pekin.* New York, 1903.

Shpolianskii, D. I. *Monopolii ugolno-metallurgicheskoi promyshlennosti iuga Rossii v nachale XX veka* [Monopolies in the Coal and Metallurgical Industry of Southern Russia at the Beginning of the Twentieth Century]. Moscow, 1953.

Shtein, V. M. *Ocherki razvitiia russkoi obshchestvenno-ekonomicheskoi mysli XIX–XX vekov* [Essays on the Development of Russian Social-economic Thought in the Nineteenth and Twentieth Centuries]. Leningrad, 1948.

Shvanebakh, P. Kh. *Denezhnoe preobrazovanie i narodnoe khoziaistvo* [The Currency Reform and the National Economy]. St. Petersburg, 1901.

—— *Nashe podatnoe delo* [Our Tax Affairs]. St. Petersburg, 1903.

Sibir' i velikaia sibirskaia zheleznaia doroga [Siberia and the Great Siberian Railway]. 2d ed. St. Petersburg, 1896.

Sidorov, A. L. "Konversii vneshnikh zaimov Rossii v 1888–1890 gg."

[The Conversion of Russia's Foreign Loans, 1888–1890], *Istoricheskii arkhiv*, No. 3, 1959.

Sigov, S. P. *Ocherki po istorii gornozavodskoi promyshlennosti Urala* [Essays on the History of the Mining Industry in the Urals]. Sverdlovsk, 1936.

Silvin, M. A. *Kratkii ocherk istorii russkoi promyshlennosti* [A Brief Sketch of the History of Russian Industry]. St. Petersburg, 1906.

Skrobot, S. S. "Stachechnaia bor'ba peterburgskikh rabochikh v 1891–1895 gg." [The Strike Movement of St. Petersburg Workers, 1891–1895], *Istoriia SSSR*, No. 5, 1958.

Slonimskii, L. "Vitte," *Novyi entsiklopedicheskii slovar'* (Brockhaus-Efron). Vol. III.

Smirnov, A. "Fabrika i fabrichnyi rabochii" [The Factory and the Factory Worker], *Russkaia mysl'*, No. 5, 1902.

Sobolev, M. N. *Ocherki tamozhennoi politiki Rossii* [Essays on Russian Tariff Policy]. Tomsk, 1910.

—— *Tamozhennaia politika Rossii vo vtoroi polovine XIX veka* [The Tariff Policy of Russia in the Second Half of the Nineteenth Century]. Tomsk, 1911.

Solov'ev, Iu. B. "Protivorechiia v praviashchem lagere Rossii po voprosu ob inostrannykh kapitalakh v gody pervogo promyshlennogo pod"ema" [The Contradictions in the Ruling Class of Russia on the Problem of Foreign Capital in the Years of the First Industrial Boom], in Akademiia Nauk SSSR, Trudy leningradskogo otdeleniia instituta istorii, *Iz istorii imperializma v Rossii.*

Sovet s"ezda gornopromyshlennikov iuga Rossii. *Kratkii ocherk istorii s"ezdov gornopromyshlennikov iuga Rossii* [Brief Essay on the History of the Congresses of the South Russian Mine Operators]. Kharkov, 1908.

Stählin, K. *Geschichte Russlands.* 4 vols. Berlin, 1923–39.

Staley, E. *The Future of Underdeveloped Countries.* New York, 1954.

Staraia Iuzovka (1869–1905) [The Old Hughes Mill]. Moscow-Kiev, 1937.

Statisticheskii atlas goroda Moskvy [Statistical Atlas of Moscow City]. Moscow, 1911.

Statisticheskoe biuro soveta s"ezda gornopromyshlennikov iuga Rossii. *Balansy (otchet) gornozavodskikh aktsionernykh i paevykh predpriiatii iuzhnoi Rossii (1898, 1899, 1900, 1901 gg.)* [The Balance Sheets of the Mining Companies in Southern Russia]. Part I. Kharkov, 1903.

Steveni, W. B. *Petrograd Past and Present.* Philadelphia, 1916.

Stolpianskii, P. N. *Zhizn' i byt peterburgskoi fabriki, 1704–1914 gg.* [Life and Condition of a St. Petersburg Factory, 1704–1914]. Leningrad, 1925.

Strumilin, S. G. *Chernaia metallurgiia v Rossii i v SSSR* [The Ferrous Metal Industry in Russia and the USSR]. Moscow-Leningrad, 1936.

—— *Problemy ekonomii truda* [Problems of Labor Economy]. 2d ed. Moscow, 1957.

—— *Problemy truda* [Problems of Labor]. Moscow, 1926.

—— "Promyshlennye krizisy v Rossii (1873–1907 gg.)" [Industrial Crises in Russia, 1873–1907], *Problemy ekonomii,* No. 2, 1940.

Struve, P. "Graf S. Iu. Vitte: Opyt kharakteristiki" [Count S. Iu. Witte: An Attempt at a Characterization], *Russkaia mysl',* No. 3, 1915.

Sumner, B. H. "Russia in Europe," *Oxford Slavonic Papers,* No. 1.

Suvorin, A. S. *Dnevnik Suvorina* [Suvorin's Diary]. Moscow, 1923. Also in German: *Das Geheimtagebuch.* Berlin, 1925.

Sviatlovskii, V. V. *Zhilishchii vopros s ekonomicheskoi tochki zreniia* [The Housing Question from an Economic Viewpoint]. Part 4: *Zhilishchii vopros v Rossii* [The Housing Question in Russia]. St. Petersburg, 1902.

Svod vysochaishikh otmetok po vsepodanneishim otchetam za 1891 i 1892 gg. generalgubernatorov, gubernatorov, voennykh gubernatorov i gradonachal'nikov [The Emperor's Comments on the Reports Submitted in 1891 and 1892 by the Governors-General, Governors, Military Governors and Commandants]. St. Petersburg, annually, for the year following the year indicated in the title. Also available for the years 1893, 1895–1900 at the New York Public Library.

Taburno, I. P. *Eskiznyi obzor finansovo-ekonomicheskago sostoianiia Rossii za posledniia 20 let(1882–1901 gg).* [A Sketchy Survey of the Financial-economic Condition of Russia during the Past Twenty Years, 1882–1901]. St. Petersburg, 1903.

Tanera, K. *Zur Kriegszeit auf der sibirischen Bahn durch Russland.* Berlin, 1905.

Tarle, E. V. *Graf S. Iu. Vitte: Opyt kharakteristiki vneshnei politiki* [Count S. Iu. Witte: An Attempt to Characterize His Foreign Policy]. Leningrad, 1927.

—— "S. Iu. Vitte, frantsuzskaia pechat' i russkie zaimy" [S. Iu. Witte, the French Press, and Russian Loans], *Krasnyi arkhiv,* Vol. X, 1925.

Taskin, E. "K voprosu o privlechenii i uderzhanii rabochikh na kamenougolnykh kopakh donetskoi basseina" [On the Problem of Attracting and Holding Workers in the Anthracite Mines of the Donets Basin], *Gornozavodskii listok,* Nos. 1–3, 6–8, 1899.

Tidmarsh, K. "The Zubatov Idea," *American Slavic and East European Review,* Vol. XIX, No. 3, October, 1960.

Timoshenko, S. P. "The Development of Engineering Education in Russia," *The Russian Review,* Vol. XV, No. 3, July, 1956.

Tkachenko, P. S. *Moskovskii universitet v obshchestvenno-politicheskoi zhizni Rossii vtoroi poloviny XIX veka* [Moscow University in Russian Public Affairs during the Second Half of the Nineteenth Century]. Moscow, 1956.

Tompkins, S. R. "Why Witte Failed to Solve the Peasant Problem," *Journal of Modern History,* Vol. IV, No. 2, June, 1932.

—— "Witte as Minister of Finance," *Slavonic and East European Review,* Vol. XI, No. 33, April, 1933.

Toynbee, A. *The World and the West.* New York, 1953.

The Transformation of Russian Society since 1861, ed. C. E. Black. Cambridge, Mass., 1960.

Trautmann, O. P. *Die Sängerbrücke: Gedanken zur russischen Aussenpolitik, 1870–1914.* Stuttgart, 1940.

Treadgold, D. *The Great Siberian Migration.* Princeton, 1957.

Trubnikov, K. V. *Bogatstva Rossii: Issledovanie, nabliudeniia i kharakteristiki* [The Wealth of Russia: Analysis, Observations, and Characterization]. Part I. St. Petersburg, 1901.

Trudy Imperatorskago Vol'nago Ekonomicheskago Obshchestva [The Proceedings of the Imperial Free Economic Society]. St. Petersburg, 1765–1915. *Ukazatel' 1883–1903* [Index, 1883–1903] precedes No. 6, 1904, of the *Trudy.*

Trudy vysochaishe uchrezhdennago vserossiiskago torgovo-promyshlennago s"ezda 1896 g. v Nizhnem Novgorode [The Proceedings of the Imperial All-Russian Congress of Trade and Industry Held in Nizhni-Novgorod in 1896]. 3 vols. St. Petersburg, 1897.

Tsimmerman, R. E. *Kulachestvo, rostovshchichestvo: ego obshchestvenno-ekonomicheskoe znachenie* [Kulakism, Usury: Its Social-economic Significance]. St. Petersburg, 1898.

Tsion (Cyon), E. *Choses Russes.* Paris, 1893.

—— *Les finances Russes et l'épargne français.* Paris, 1895.

—— *M. Witte et ses projects de faileté devant le Conseil de l'Empire.* Paris, 1897.

——*Où la dictature de M. Witte conduit la Russie.* Paris, 1897.

Tsyperovich, G. B. *Sindikaty i tresti v Rossii* [Syndicates and Trusts in Russia]. 2d ed. Petrograd, 1919.

Tugan-Baranovskii, M. I. *Russkaia fabrika v proshlom i nastoiashchem* [The Russian Factory in the Past and the Present]. 2d ed., St. Petersburg, 1900; 3d ed., 1907. The latter, like the German translation, contains more material than earlier editions.

—— "Sovremennyi promyshlennyi krizis" [The Contemporary Industrial Crisis], *Mir bozhi,* No. 11, 1900.

Ukhtomskii, E. E. *Puteshestvie na vostok ego imperatorskago vysochestva gosudaria naslednika tsesarevicha, 1890–1891* [The Far-Eastern Journey of His Imperial Highness the Heir to the Throne]. 3 vols. St. Petersburg, 1893–97.

Ular, A. *Russia from Within.* New York, 1905.

Ulozhenie o nakazaniiakh ugolovnykh i ispravitel'nykh [The Criminal Code], ed. N. S. Tagantsev. St. Petersburg, 1903.

United Nations, Department of Economic and Social Affairs. *Processes and Problems of Industrialization in Under-developed Countries.* New York, 1955.

United States, Department of Commerce. *Russia—A Handbook on Commercial and Industrial Conditions,* ed. J. Snodgrass. Washington, 1913.

Ustav o promyshlennosti [The Industrial Code], ed. M. P. Shramchenko and K. E. Afanaser. St. Petersburg, 1909.

Vainshtein, A. L. *Narodnoe bogatstvo i narodnokhoziaistvennoe nakoplenie predrevoliutsionnoi Rossii* [The People's Wealth and the Accumulation of Wealth among Them in Prerevolutionary Russia]. Moscow, 1960.

Vanad, N. N. *Finansovyi kapital v Rossii nakanune mirovoi voiny* [Finance Capital in Russia on the Eve of the World War]. Kharkov, 1930.

Varzar, V. E. *Statisticheskiia svedeniia o stachkakh rabochikh na fabrikakh i zavodakh za 1895–1905* [Statistical Information on the Strikes of Workers in Factories and Mills for 1895 to 1904]. St. Petersburg, 1905.

Vasetskii, F. S. *D. I. Mendeleev: Filosofskie i obshchestvenno-politicheskie vzgliady* [D. I. Mendeleev: His Philosophical and Social-political Views]. Moscow, 1951.

Vasilev, B. N. "Formirovanie promyshlennogo proletariata Ivanovskoi oblasti" [The Formation of the Industrial Proletariat in the Ivanovo District], *Voprosy istorii,* No. 6, 1952.

Velikaia reforma, 1861–1911: Russkoe obshchestvo i krest'ianskii vopros v proshlom i nastoiashchem [The Great Reform, 1861–1911: Russian Society and the Peasant Question in the Past and the Present]. 6 vols. Moscow, 1911.

Verstratete, M. *La Russie industrielle: Etude sur l'exposition de N.Novgorod.* Paris, 1897.

Veselovskii, B. *Istoriia Zemstva za 40 let* [The History of the Zemstvos in the Past Forty Years]. 4 vols. St. Petersburg, 1909–11.

Ves' Peterburg, city directory for St. Petersburg.

Vlasenko, V. E. *Denezhnaia reforma v Rossii, 1895–1898* [The Currency Reform in Russia, 1895–1898]. Kiev, 1949.

Vneshniaia torgovlia Rossii v 1897 god [Russian Foreign Trade in 1897]. St. Petersburg, 1898; also annually. The volumes contain *Svedeniia o vneshnei torgovle po evropeiskoi granitse za . . .* [Information on Foreign Trade over the European Boundary for . . .] each month separately.

Vodovozov, V. V. *Graf S. Iu. Vitte i imperator Nikolai II* [Count Witte and the Emperor Nicholas II]. Petrograd, 1922.

Volfson, L. Ia., V. I. Ledovskii, and N. S. Shilnikov. *Ekonomiia transporta* [The Economics of Transport]. Moscow, 1941.

Von Laue, T. H. "A Secret Memorandum of Sergei Witte on the Industrialization of Imperial Russia," *Journal of Modern History,* Vol. XXVI, No. 1, March, 1954.

—— "Count Witte and the Russian Revolution of 1905," *American Slavic and East European Review,* Vol. XVII, No. 1, February, 1958.

—— "Die Revolution von aussen als erste Phase der russischen Revolution von 1917," *Jahrbücher für Geschichte Osteuropas,* Vol. IV, No. 2, July, 1956.

—— "Imperial Russia at the Turn of the Century: The Cultural Slope and the Revolution from Without," *Comparative Studies in Society and History,* Vol. III, No. 4, July, 1961.

—— "Of the Crises in the Russian Polity," in *Essays in Russian and Soviet History,* ed. J. S. Curtiss. New York, 1963.

—— "Problems of Modernization," in *Russian Foreign Policy,* ed. I. V. Lederer. New Haven, 1962.

—— "The State and the Economy," in *The Transformation of Russian Society since 1861,* ed. C. E. Black. Cambridge, Mass., 1960.

The following articles, closely related to the theme of this book, are listed in the order of their content:

—— "Russian Labor between Fields and Factory," *California Slavic Studies,* Vol. III (in press).

—— "Russian Peasants in the Factory," *Journal of Economic History,* Vol. XXI, No. 1, March, 1961.

—— "Factory Inspection under the 'Witte System': 1892–1903," *American Slavic and East European Review,* Vol. XIX, No. 3, October, 1960.

—— "Tsarist Labor Policy, 1895–1903," *Journal of Modern History,* Vol. XXXIV, No. 2, June, 1962.

Vonliarliarskii, V. *Moi vospominaniia 1852–1939 gg.* [My Reminiscences, 1852–1939]. Berlin, n.d.

Vsepodanneishii otchet gosudarstvennago kontrolera za . . . [The Report of the State Controller for . . .]. St. Petersburg, annually.

Vsia Rossiia: Russkaia kniga promyshlennosti, torgovli, sel'skago khoziaistva i administratsii. Adres-kalendar' rossiiskoi imperii [All Russia: The Russian Book of Industry, Trade, Agriculture, and Administration. Address Calendar of the Russian Empire]. St. Petersburg, 1895, 1899.

Walkin, J. "The Attitude of the Tsarist Government toward the Labor Problem," *American Slavic and East European Review,* Vol. XIII, No. 2, April, 1954.

Wallace, D. M. *Russia.* London, various editions, 1877–1912.

Walters, E. "Austro-Russian Relations under Goluchowski, 1895–1906," *Slavonic and East European Review,* Vol. XXXII, No. 78, December, 1953.

Warriner, D. "Some Controversial Issues in the History of Agrarian Europe," *Slavonic and East European Review,* Vol. XXXII, No. 78, December, 1953.

Wellington, A. M. *The Economic Theory of the Location of Railways.* New York, various editions, 1877–1911.

Whitman, J. "Turkestan Cotton in Imperial Russia," *American Slavic and East European Review,* Vol. XV, No. 2, April, 1956.

Wiener, L. *An Interpretation of the Russian People.* New York, 1915.

Williams, H. W. *Russia of the Russians.* London, 1915.

Witte, S. Iu. *Finanzminister Witte und der russische Reichsrat über die Finanzlage Russlands: Protokoll der Plenarsitzung des russischen Reichsrates vom 30. Dezember, 1902.* Stuttgart, 1903.

—— *Konspekt lektsii o narodnom i gosudarstvennom khoziaistve* [Lectures on the Economy and Government Finance]. 2d ed. St.

Petersburg, 1912. Translated into German under the title *Vorlesungen über Volks- und Staatswirtschaft.* 2 vols. Berlin, 1913.

—— *Konspekt lektsii o gosudarstvennom khoziaistve.* 3d ed. St. Petersburg, 1914. This is a separate edition of the second part of the *Konspekt lektsii* listed above.

—— *Po povodu natsionalizma: Natsional'naia ekonomiia i Fridrikh List* [On Nationalism: The National Economy and Friedrich List]. 2d ed. St. Petersburg, 1912.

—— *Po povodu neprelozhnosti zakonov gosudarstvennoi zhizni* [On the Immutability of the Laws of Government Life]. St. Petersburg, 1914. This is Witte's own edition of *Samoderzhavie i zemstvo* (see below).

—— *Printsip zheleznodorozhnykh tarifov po perevoske gruzov* [The Principle of Railway Freight Tariffs]. 3d ed. St. Petersburg, 1910. The second and third editions are identical.

—— *Samoderzhavie i zemstvo: Konfidentsial'naia zapiska Ministra Finansov, stats-sekretaria S. Iu. Vitte (1899 g.)* [Autocracy and Zemstvo: A Confidential Memorandum of the Minister of Finance, State-Secretary S. Iu. Witte, 1899]. 2d ed., with an introduction by P. Struve. Stuttgart, 1903.

—— *Vospominaniia: Detstvo, tsarstvovanie Aleksandra II i Aleksandra III (1849–1894)* [Reminiscences: Childhood, the Reigns of Alexander II and Alexander III, 1849–1894]. Berlin, 1923.

—— *Vospominaniia: Tsarstvovanie Nikolaia II* [Reminiscences: The Reign of Nicholas II]. 2 vols. Berlin, 1923. The three volumes of Witte's memoirs are now combined in a new Soviet set edited by A. L. Sidorov. Moscow, 1960.

—— *Vynuzhdennyia raz"iasneniia po povody otcheta General-adiutanta Kuropatkina o voine s Iaponiei* [Explanations to the Report of Adjutant-General Kuropatkin on the War with Japan]. Moscow, 1911.

—— *Zapiska po krest'ianskomu delu predsedatelia vysochaishe uchrezhdennago osobago soveshchaniia o nuzhdakh sel'sko-khoziaistvennoi promyshlennosti, stats-seketaria Vitte* [Report on Peasant Affairs by State-Secretary Witte, Chairman of the Special Commission on the Needs of Agricultural Industry]. St. Petersburg, 1904.

—— "Dokladnaia zapiska Vitte Nikolaiu II" [A Report of Witte to the Emperor], *Istorik marksist,* No. 2–3, 1935.

—— "Manufakturnoe krepostnichestvo" [Manufacturing Serfdom], *Rus',* No. 3, 1885.

—— "Perepiska Vitte i Pobedonostseva (1895–1905 gg.)" [The Correspondence between Witte and Pobedonostsev, 1895–1905], *Krasnyi arkhiv,* Vol. XXX, 1928.

—— "Pis'ma S. Iu. Vitte k D. S. Sipiaginu" [The Letters of S. Iu. Witte to D. S. Sipiagin], *Krasnyi arkhiv,* Vol. XXX, 1928.

Wittschewsky, V. *Russlands Handels-, Zoll-, and Industriepolitik von Peter dem Grossen bis auf die Gegenwart.* Berlin, 1905.

Zabriskie, E. H. *American-Russian Rivalry in the Far East: A Study in Diplomacy and Power Politics, 1895–1914.* Philadelphia, 1946.

Zagorskii, K. *Nasha zheleznodorozhnaia tarifnaia politika* [Our Railway Tariff Policy]. St. Petersburg, 1910.

Za kulisami tsarizma (*Arkhiv Badmaeva*) [Behind the Scenes of Tsarism (Badmaev's Archive)], ed. V. P. Semennikov. Leningrad, 1925.

Zenkovskii, V. V. *Istoriia Russkoi filosofii* [History of Russian Philosophy]. 2 vols. Paris, 1948–50. English translation, *A History of Russian Philosophy,* London, 1953.

Zweig, E. *Die russische Handelspolitik seit 1877. Staats- und Sozialwissenschaftliche Forschungen,* No. 123, Leipzig, 1906.

Index

Atheneum Paperbacks

HISTORY—AMERICAN

4 POWER AND DIPLOMACY *by Dean Acheson*
4 THE ROAD TO PEARL HARBOR *by Herbert Feis*
6 ROGER WILLIAMS *by Perry Miller*
7 THE REPUBLICAN ROOSEVELT *by John Morton Blum*
17 MYTHS AND REALITIES *by Carl Bridenbaugh*
32 STRANGERS IN THE LAND *by John Higham*
40 THE UNITED STATES AND MEXICO *by Howard F. Cline*
43 HOLMES-LASKI LETTERS: THE CORRESPONDENCE OF JUSTICE OLIVER
A&B WENDELL HOLMES AND HAROLD J. LASKI *1916–1935 edited by Mark De Wolfe Howe, abridged by Alger Hiss, 2 vols.*
49 THE CONCEPT OF JACKSONIAN DEMOCRACY *by Lee Benson*
51 TURMOIL AND TRADITION *by Elting E. Morison*
70 THE CHINA TANGLE *by Herbert Feis*
84 THE DIMENSIONS OF LIBERTY *by Oscar and Mary Handlin*
86 THE CORPORATION IN MODERN SOCIETY *edited by Edward S. Mason*
110 DRED SCOTT'S CASE *by Vincent C. Hopkins, S.J.*
111 THE DECLINE OF AMERICAN LIBERALISM *by Arthur A. Ekirch, Jr.*
113 HARVARD GUIDE TO AMERICAN HISTORY *edited by Oscar Handlin, Arthur Meier Schlesinger, Samuel Eliot Morison, Frederick Merk, Arthur Meier Schlesinger, Jr., Paul Herman Buck*
115 THE ROOTS OF AMERICAN LOYALTY *by Merle Curti*
116 THE POLITICS OF PREJUDICE *by Roger Daniels*
117 CENTURY OF STRUGGLE *by Eleanor Flexner*
118 BOSTON'S IMMIGRANTS *by Oscar Handlin*
123 THE AMERICAN APPROACH TO FOREIGN POLICY *by Dexter Perkins*
125 THE EIGHTEENTH-CENTURY COMMONWEALTHMAN *by Caroline Robbins*
126 THE AMERICAN AS REFORMER *by Arthur M. Schlesinger*
129 THE LEGEND OF HENRY FORD *by Keith Sward*
132 ASA GRAY *by A. Hunter Dupree*
134 THE COLONIAL MERCHANTS AND THE AMERICAN REVOLUTION— *1763–1776 by Arthur M. Schlesinger*
136 THE ROAD TO APPOMATTOX *by Bell Irvin Wiley*
137 FREE SPEECH IN THE UNITED STATES *by Zechariah Chafee, Jr.*
139 CONSERVATION AND THE GOSPEL OF EFFICIENCY *by Samuel P. Hays*
140 MASSACHUSETTS PEOPLE AND POLITICS, 1919–1933 *by J. Joseph Huthmacher*
142 THE PROFESSIONAL ALTRUIST *by Roy Lubove*
144 POVERTY AND PROGRESS *by Stephan Thernstrom*
145 STREETCAR SUBURBS *by Sam B. Warner*
TAP THE ADAMS PAPERS: DIARY AND AUTOBIOGRAPHY OF JOHN ADAMS
1,2,3,4 *edited by L. H. Butterfield, 4 vols.*
TAP THE ADAMS PAPERS: ADAMS FAMILY CORRESPONDENCE *edited by*
5,6 *L. H. Butterfield, 2 vols.*
TAP THE ADAMS PAPERS: DIARY OF CHARLES FRANCIS ADAMS *edited by*
7,8 *L. H. Butterfield, 2 vols.*
TAP THE ADAMS PAPERS: LEGAL PAPERS OF JOHN ADAMS *edited by*
9,10,11 *L. H. Butterfield, 3 vols.*

Atheneum Paperbacks

HISTORY

3 SIX MEDIEVAL MEN AND WOMEN *by H. S. Bennett*
10 TRAVEL AND DISCOVERY IN THE RENAISSANCE *by Boies Penrose*
30 GHANA IN TRANSITION *by David E. Apter*
58 TROTSKY'S DIARY IN EXILE—1935 *translated by Elena Zarudnaya*
63 THE SINO-SOVIET CONFLICT 1956–1961 *by Donald S. Zagoria*
65 LORD AND PEASANT IN RUSSIA FROM THE NINTH TO THE NINETEENTH CENTURY *by Jerome Blum*
68 TWELVE WHO RULED *by Robert R. Palmer*
83 KARAMZIN'S MEMOIR ON ANCIENT AND MODERN RUSSIA *by Richard Pipes*
97 THE EIGHTEENTH CENTURY CONFRONTS THE GODS *by Frank E. Manuel*
103 JACOBEAN PAGEANT *by G. P. V. Akrigg*
104 THE MAKING OF VICTORIAN ENGLAND *by G. Kitson Clark*
107 RUSSIA LEAVES THE WAR *by George F. Kennan*
108 THE DECISION TO INTERVENE *by George F. Kennan*
121 DRIVING FORCES IN HISTORY *by Halvdan Koht*
124 THE FORMATION OF THE SOVIET UNION *by Richard Pipes*
127 THE THREE LIVES OF CHARLES DE GAULLE *by David Schoenbrun*
128 AS FRANCE GOES *by David Schoenbrun*
141 SERGEI WITTE AND THE INDUSTRIALIZATION OF RUSSIA *by Theodore Von Laue*

HISTORY–ASIA

44 CHINA'S RESPONSE TO THE WEST *by Ssu-Yü Teng and John K. Fairbank*
63 THE SINO-SOVIET CONFLICT 1956–1961 *by Donald S. Zagoria*
64 CONFUCIANISM AND CHINESE CIVILIZATION *edited by Arthur F. Wright*
70 THE CHINA TANGLE *by Herbert Feis*
77 BUDDHISM IN CHINESE HISTORY *by Arthur F. Wright*
87 A DOCUMENTARY HISTORY OF CHINESE COMMUNISM *by Conrad Brandt, Benjamin Schwartz and John K. Fairbank*
92 THE LAST STAND OF CHINESE CONSERVATISM *by Mary Clabaugh Wright*
93 THE TRAGEDY OF THE CHINESE REVOLUTION *by Harold R. Isaacs*
94 THE AGRARIAN ORIGINS OF MODERN JAPAN *by Thomas C. Smith*

THE NEW YORK TIMES BYLINE BOOKS

CHINA *by Harry Schwartz*
RUSSIA *by Harrison E. Salisbury*
THE MIDDLE EAST *by Jay Walz*
AFRICA *by Waldemar A. Nielsen*
LATIN AMERICA *by Tad Szulc*
SOUTHEAST ASIA *by Tillman Durdin*

Atheneum Paperbacks

STUDIES IN AMERICAN NEGRO LIFE

NL1 THE NEGRO IN COLONIAL NEW ENGLAND *by Lorenzo Johnston Greene*
NL2 SEPARATE AND UNEQUAL *by Louis R. Harlan*
NL3 AFTER FREEDOM *by Hortense Powdermaker*
NL4 FREDERICK DOUGLASS *by Benjamin Quarles*
NL5 PREFACE TO PEASANTRY *by Arthur F. Raper*
NL6 W.E.B. DU BOIS: PROPAGANDIST OF THE NEGRO PROTEST *by Elliott Rudwick*
NL7 THE BLACK WORKER *by Sterling D. Spero and Abram L. Harris*
NL8 A&B THE MAKING OF BLACK AMERICA *edited by August Meier and Elliott Rudwick, 2 vols.*
NL9 BLACK MANHATTAN *by James Weldon Johnson*
NL10 THE NEW NEGRO *edited by Alain Locke*
NL11 THE NEGRO'S GOD AS REFLECTED IN HIS LITERATURE *by Benjamin Mays*
NL12 NEGRO POETRY AND DRAMA AND THE NEGRO IN AMERICAN FICTION *by Sterling Brown*
NL13 WHEN NEGROES MARCH *by Herbert Garfinkel*
NL14 PHILOSOPHY AND OPINIONS OF MARCUS GARVEY *by Marcus Garvey, edited by Amy Jacques-Garvey*
NL15 FREE NEGRO LABOR AND PROPERTY IN ANTE-BELLUM VIRGINIA *by Luther Jackson*
NL17 SEA ISLAND TO CITY *by Clyde Vernon Kiser*
NL18 NEGRO EDUCATION IN ALABAMA *by Horace Mann Bond*

LAW AND GOVERNMENT

20 A&B DOCUMENTS ON FUNDAMENTAL HUMAN RIGHTS *edited by Zechariah Chafee, Jr., 2 vols.*
23 THE CONSTITUTION AND WHAT IT MEANS TODAY *by Edward S. Corwin*
27 COURTS ON TRIAL *by Jerome Frank*
30 GHANA IN TRANSITION *by David E. Apter*
46 THE FUTURE OF FEDERALISM *by Nelson A. Rockefeller*
53 THE BILL OF RIGHTS *by Learned Hand*
72 MR. JUSTICE HOLMES AND THE SUPREME COURT *by Felix Frankfurter*
73 THE STRUCTURE OF FREEDOM *by Christian Bay*
84 THE DIMENSIONS OF LIBERTY *by Oscar and Mary Handlin*
89 MAKERS OF MODERN STRATEGY *edited by Edward M. Earle*
105 DILEMMAS OF URBAN AMERICA *by Robert C. Weaver*
110 DRED SCOTT'S CASE *by Vincent C. Hopkins, S.J.*
130 THE REVOLUTION OF THE SAINTS *by Michael Walzer*
138 OF LAW AND LIFE AND OTHER THINGS THAT MATTER *by Felix Frankfurter, edited by Philip B. Kurland*

Atheneum Paperbacks

DIPLOMACY AND INTERNATIONAL RELATIONS

2 POWER AND DIPLOMACY *by Dean Acheson*
4 THE ROAD TO PEARL HARBOR *by Herbert Feis*
15 CALL TO GREATNESS *by Adlai E. Stevenson*
34 THE DIPLOMACY OF ECONOMIC DEVELOPMENT *by Eugene B. Black*
40 THE UNITED STATES AND MEXICO *by Howard F. Cline*
41 THE DIPLOMATS 1919–1939 *by Gordon A. Craig and*
A&B *Felix Gilbert*
44 CHINA'S RESPONSE TO THE WEST *by Ssu-Yü Teng and John K. Fairbank*
54 STRATEGIC SURRENDER *by Paul Kecskemeti*
63 THE SINO-SOVIET CONFLICT 1956–1961 *by Donald S. Zagoria*
70 THE CHINA TANGLE *by Herbert Feis*
74 STALIN'S FOREIGN POLICY REAPPRAISED *by Marshall Shulman*
89 MAKERS OF MODERN STRATEGY *edited by Edward M. Earle*
107 RUSSIA LEAVES THE WAR *by George F. Kennan*
108 THE DECISION TO INTERVENE *by George F. Kennan*

ECONOMICS AND BUSINESS

21 BIG BUSINESS LEADERS IN AMERICA *by W. Lloyd Warner and James Abegglen*
24 PROSPERITY AND DEPRESSION *by Gottfried Haberler*
34 THE DIPLOMACY OF ECONOMIC DEVELOPMENT *by Eugene R. Black*
47 ECONOMIC CONCENTRATION AND THE MONOPOLY PROBLEM *by Edward S. Mason*
78 THE ECONOMICS OF DEFENSE IN THE NUCLEAR AGE *by Charles J. Hitch and Roland N. McKean*
80 FOUNDATIONS OF ECONOMIC ANALYSIS *by Paul Anthony Samuelson*
86 THE CORPORATION IN MODERN SOCIETY *edited by Edward S. Mason*

PSYCHOLOGY AND SOCIOLOGY

21 BIG BUSINESS LEADERS IN AMERICA *by W. Lloyd Warner and James Abegglen*
67 ON KNOWING *by Jerome S. Bruner*
79 THE SOCIETY OF CAPTIVES *by Gresham M. Sykes*
109 AFRICAN HOMICIDE AND SUICIDE *edited by Paul Bohannan*
119 THE LAW OF PRIMITIVE MAN *by E. Adamson Hoebel*
120 THE SOVIET CITIZEN *by Alex Inkeles and Raymond Bauer*
133 THE FAMILY REVOLUTION IN MODERN CHINA *by Marion J. Levy, Jr.*

Atheneum Paperbacks

LIFE SCIENCES AND ANTHROPOLOGY

9 MATTER, MIND AND MAN *by Edmund W. Sinnott*
16 THE HORMONES IN HUMAN REPRODUCTION *by George W. Corner*
26 THE OLD STONE AGE *by Miles C. Burkitt*
28 MORPHOGENESIS *by John Tyler Bonner*
33 LOST CITY OF THE INCAS *by Hiram Bingham*
35 GENETICS, PALEONTOLOGY, AND EVOLUTION *edited by Glenn L. Jepsen, Ernst Mayr and George Gaylord Simpson*
45 THE SEA SHORE *by C. M. Yonge*
48 TRISTES TROPIQUES *by Claude Lévi-Strauss*
62 TERRITORY IN BIRD LIFE *by Eliot Howard*
71 HEREDITY AND EVOLUTION IN HUMAN POPULATIONS *by L. C. Dunn*
85 THE INTEGRITY OF THE BODY *by F. M. Burnet, F.R.S.*
88 SPEECH AND BRAIN-MECHANISMS *by Wilder Penfield and Lamar Roberts*
91 CELLS AND SOCIETIES *by John Tyler Bonner*
95 THE FIRMAMENT OF TIME *by Loren Eiseley*
98 IDEAS ON HUMAN EVOLUTION *edited by William Howells*
101 COMMUNICATION AMONG SOCIAL BEES *by Martin Lindauer*
106 ON THE ORIGIN OF SPECIES *by Charles Darwin, a Facsimile of the First Edition, edited by Ernst Mayr*
109 AFRICAN HOMICIDE AND SUICIDE *edited by Paul Bohannon*

PHYSICAL SCIENCES AND MATHEMATICS

13 THE AIM AND STRUCTURE OF PHYSICAL THEORY *by Pierre Duhem*
31 PHILOSOPHY OF MATHEMATICS AND NATURAL SCIENCE *by Hermann Weyl*
56 THE EARTH BENEATH THE SEA *by Francis P. Shepard*
57 SATELLITE OF THE SUN *by Athelstan Spilhaus*
59 PLAYING WITH INFINITY *by Rózsa Péter*
100 GALAXIES *by Harlow Shapley*

PHILOSOPHY AND RELIGION

6 ROGER WILLIAMS *by Perry Miller*
9 MATTER, MIND AND MAN *by Edmund W. Sinnott*
19 BUDDHISM IN TRANSLATIONS *by Henry Clarke Warren*
31 PHILOSOPHY OF MATHEMATICS AND NATURAL SCIENCE *by Hermann Weyl*
38 TOWARD REUNION IN PHILOSOPHY *by Morton White*
52 RELIGION IN TWENTIETH CENTURY AMERICA *by Herbert W. Schneider*
60 HERACLITUS *by Philip Wheelwright*
64 CONFUCIANISM AND CHINESE CIVILIZATION *edited by Arthur F. Wright*
69 ON THE USE OF PHILOSOPHY *by Jacques Maritain*
75 RELIGIOUS PHILOSOPHY *by Harry Austryn Wolfson*
77 BUDDHISM IN CHINESE HISTORY *by Arthur F. Wright*
97 THE EIGHTEENTH CENTURY CONFRONTS THE GODS *by Frank E. Manuel*

Atheneum Paperbacks

THE WORLDS OF NATURE AND MAN

5 OF MEN AND MOUNTAINS *by William O. Douglas*
18 THE SUDDEN VIEW *by Sybille Bedford*
22 SPRING IN WASHINGTON *by Louis J. Halle*
33 LOST CITY OF THE INCAS *by Hiram Bingham*
45 THE SEA SHORE *by C. M. Yonge*
61 THE NEW YORK TIMES GUIDE TO DINING OUT IN NEW YORK *edited by Craig Claiborne*
81 THE NEW YORK TIMES GUIDE TO HOME FURNISHING *edited by Barbara Plumb and Elizabeth Sverbeyeff*
82 BIRDS AND MEN *by Robert H. Welker*
95 THE FIRMAMENT OF TIME *by Loren Eiseley*

LITERATURE AND THE ARTS

1 ROME AND A VILLA *by Eleanor Clark*
8 THE MUSICAL EXPERIENCE OF COMPOSER, PERFORMER, LISTENER *by Roger Sessions*
11 THE GRANDMOTHERS *by Glenway Wescott*
12 i: SIX NONLECTURES *by e. e. cummings*
14 THE PRESENCE OF GRACE *by J. F. Powers*
18 THE SUDDEN VIEW *by Sybille Bedford*
25 THE ROBBER BRIDEGROOM *by Eudora Welty*
29 CONTEXTS OF CRITICISM *by Harry Levin*
36 GEORGE BERNARD SHAW *by Hesketh Pearson*
37 THE TERRITORY AHEAD *by Wright Morris*
39 THE LETTERS OF VINCENT VAN GOGH *edited by Mark Roskill*
42 THE GREEN MARE *by Marcel Aymé*
50 AMERICAN ARCHITECTURE AND OTHER WRITINGS *by Montgomery Schuyer, edited by William H. Jordy and Ralph Coe; abridged by William H. Jordy*
55 PNIN *by Vladimir Nabokov*
66 SELECTED POEMS INCLUDING THE WOMAN AT THE WASHINGTON ZOO *by Randall Jarrell*
76 THE SINGER OF TALES *by Albert B. Lord*
90 ANATOMY OF CRITICISM *by Northrop Frye*
96 CONRAD THE NOVELIST *by Albert J. Guerard*
99 MARK TWAIN *by Henry Nash Smith*
102 EMILY DICKINSON *by Thomas H. Johnson*
112 THE LIFE OF THE DRAMA *by Eric Bentley*
114 SELECTED MARK TWAIN-HOWELLS LETTERS *edited by Frederick Anderson, William Gibson, and Henry Nash Smith*
122 REPORTING THE NEWS *edited by Louis M. Lyons*
131 WHAT IS THEATRE? (*incorporating* THE DRAMATIC EVENT) *by Eric Bentley*
135 THE HERO OF THE WAVERLY NOVELS *by Alexander Welsh*
143 POETS OF REALITY *by J. Hillis Miller*